JEWISH AND CHRISTIAN TEXTS IN CONTEXTS AND RELATED STUDIES

30

Executive Editor
James H. Charlesworth

Editorial Board of Advisors
Motti Aviam, Michael Davis, Casey Elledge, Craig Evans,
Loren Johns, Amy-Jill Levine, Lee McDonald, Lidia Novakovic,
Gerbern Oegema, Henry Rietz, Brent Strawn

AFTERLIFE AND RESURRECTION BELIEFS IN THE PSEUDEPIGRAPHA

Jan A. Sigvartsen

LONDON • NEW YORK • OXFORD • NEW DELHI • SYDNEY

T&T CLARK
Bloomsbury Publishing Plc
50 Bedford Square, London, WC1B 3DP, UK
1385 Broadway, New York, NY 10018, USA
29 Earlsfort Terrace, Dublin 2, Ireland

BLOOMSBURY, T&T CLARK and the T&T Clark logo are trademarks of
Bloomsbury Publishing Plc

First published in Great Britain 2019
This paperback edition published in 2021

Copyright © Jan A. Sigvartsen, 2019

Jan A. Sigvartsen has asserted his right under the Copyright, Designs and Patents
Act, 1988, to be identified as the Author of this work.

All rights reserved. No part of this publication may be reproduced or transmitted
in any form or by any means, electronic or mechanical, including photocopying,
recording, or any information storage or retrieval system, without prior permission in
writing from the publishers.

Bloomsbury Publishing Plc does not have any control over, or responsibility for, any
third-party websites referred to or in this book. All internet addresses given in this
book were correct at the time of going to press. The author and publisher regret any
inconvenience caused if addresses have changed or sites have ceased to exist, but
can accept no responsibility for any such changes.

Scripture quotations from the Apocrypha are from the Revised Standard Version of
the Bible, copyright © 1946, 1952, and 1971; and from the New Revised Standard
Version Bible, copyright © 1989 National Council of the Churches of Christ in the
United States of America. Used by permission. All rights reserved.

A catalogue record for this book is available from the British Library.

Library of Congress Cataloging-in-Publication Data
Names: Sigvartsen, Jan Age, author.
Title: Afterlife and resurrection beliefs in the Pseudepigrapha / by Jan A. Sigvartsen.
Description: 1 [edition]. | New York: T&T Clark, 2019. |
Series: Jewish and Christian texts; 31 | Includes bibliographical references and index.
Identifiers: LCCN 2019009766 | ISBN 9780567685544 (hardback) |
ISBN 9780567685551 (epdf)
Subjects: LCSH: Apocryphal books (Old Testament)–Criticism, interpretation, etc. |
Future life–Biblical teaching. | Resurrection–Biblical teaching.
Classification: LCC BS1700 .S55 2019 | DDC 229/.906–dc23
LC record available at https://lccn.loc.gov/2019009766

ISBN: HB: 978-0-5676-8554-4
PB: 978-0-5677-0059-9
ePDF: 978-0-5676-8555-1

Series: Jewish and Christian Texts, volume 30

Typeset by Forthcoming Publications (www.forthpub.com)

To find out more about our authors and books visit
www.bloomsbury.com and sign up for our newsletters.

For
Jack and Nancy Krogstad
my American parents

Contents

Acknowledgments — ix
List of Abbreviations — xi
Figures — xvi
Tables — xvii

OUR PERENNIAL YEARNING FOR POSTMORTEM EXISTENCE
OR RESURRECTION
James Hamilton Charlesworth — xix

FOREWORD
C. E. Elledge — xxiii

Chapter 1
INTRODUCTION — 1

Chapter 2
TESTAMENTS
(OFTEN WITH APOCALYPTIC SECTIONS) — 10

Chapter 3
EXPANSIONS OF STORIES AND LEGENDS — 50

Chapter 4
WISDOM AND PHILOSOPHICAL LITERATURE — 104

Chapter 5
PRAYERS, *PSALMS*, AND *ODES* — 160

Chapter 6
THE POSTHUMOUS BODY AND THE SOUL — 178

Chapter 7
SUMMARY AND CONCLUSION — 209

APPENDIX A:
CLASSIFICATION AND ANTHOLOGY OF RESURRECTION TEXTS   228

APPENDIX B:
RESURRECTION PASSAGES IN QUMRAN, JOSEPHUS, NEW TESTAMENT,
AND EARLY RABBINIC JUDAISM   279

Bibliography   301
Index of References   307
Index of Authors   330

ACKNOWLEDGMENTS

My interest and study into the Apocrypha and Pseudepigrapha was initially motivated by P. Richard Choi, Professor of New Testament and Chair of the New Testament Department at Andrews University, Michigan. I would like to take this opportunity to thank him for launching me on this rewarding journey.

I also wish to thank Michael E. Stone (now Emeritus), who was my professor when I was a visiting research fellow at Hebrew University of Jerusalem, Israel, who encouraged me and set me firmly on the track of making this area of study my specialization.

I would also like to thank Casey C. Elledge, Associate Professor at Gustavus Adolphus College, Minnesota, for his invaluable review, feedback, and encouragement of this work.

Thanks also goes to my long-time professor and mentor, Jacques B. Doukhan, Professor of Hebrew and Old Testament Exegesis and Director of the Institute of Jewish-Christian Studies at Andrews University, Michigan. Enjoy your retirement – although now you will probably be busier than ever.

I also wish to convey my sincere gratitude to the administrators of Theologische Hochschule, Friedensau, Germany, where I currently work, for their support and special funding that brought this publication to fruition. Special thanks to Dekon Stefan Höschele, Rektor Roland Fisher, and Kanzler Tobias Koch.

Thank you also to Duncan Burns for all his work in preparing this manuscript for publication and for undertaking the indexing.

Thanks also to Yale University Press for allowing me to license a substantial amount of material from their translation of the Pseudepigrapha, edited by James H. Charlesworth, Executive Editor of this series. I would also like to thank Michael More from Fortress Press for allowing me to licence material from their translation of *1 Enoch* and *2 Baruch* and for waiving the licensing fee; Nicole Tilford from the Society of Biblical Literature Press and John Reeves, Blumenthal Professor of Judaic Studies, University of North Carolina, for allowing me to licence material from his translation of *Sefer Elijah* and for waiving the licensing fee; and the

National Council of the Churches of Christ, USA, for their generous free use policy and for use of their translation of the Apocrypha. The support of scholarship by these organizations and individuals is much appreciated.

Finally, but most importantly, I would like to thank my wife, Leanne M. Sigvartsen, for listening to me talk endlessly about this topic, reading my manuscripts, for providing feedback, and encouraging me to complete this work.

Abbreviations

AB	Anchor Bible
ABD	*Anchor Bible Dictionary*
ABRL	Anchor Bible Reference Library
AnBib	Analecta biblica
ANEM	Ancient Near East Monographs/Monografías sobre el Antiquo Cercano
ANF	Ante-Nicene Fathers
AUSDDS	Andrews University Seminary Doctoral Dissertation Series
AUSS	*Andrews University Seminary Studies*
BAR	Biblical Archaeology Review
BCE	Before the Common Era = BC
BETL	Bibliotheca ephemeridum theologicarum lovaniensium
CANE	Civilizations of the Ancient Near East
CBQ	*Catholic Biblical Quarterly*
CBQMS	Catholic Biblical Quarterly Monograph Series
CE	Common Era = AD
CEJL	Commentaries on Early Jewish Literature
ConBNT	Coniectanea neotestamentica or Coniectanea biblica: New Testament Series
COQG	Christian Origins and the Question of God
CSB	Holman Christian Standard Bible
DCLS	Deuterocanonical and Cognate Literature Studies
DEJ	*Dictionary of Early Judaism*
DNTB	Dictionary of New Testament Background
DSS	Dead Sea Scrolls
Ebib	*Etudes bibliques*
EncJud	*Encyclopaedia Judaica*
EncJud²	Encyclopaedia Judaica 2nd Edition
ET	English Text
FB	Forschung zur Bibel
GHMSSTL	GlossaHouse Monograph Series: Studies in Texts & Language
Hen	*Henoch: Studies on Judaism and Christianity from Second Temple to Late Antiquity*
HSS	Harvard Semitic Studies
HTR	*Harvard Theological Review*

HUCA	Hebrew Union College Annual
IDB	The Interpreter's Dictionary of the Bible
JATS	Journal of the Adventist Theological Society
JBL	Journal of Biblical Literature
JBQ	Jewish Bible Quarterly
JCTS	Jewish and Christian Texts Series
JE	Jewish Encyclopedia
JETS	Journal of the Evangelical Theological Society
JNES	Journal of Near Eastern Studies
JSJ	Journal for the Study of Judaism
JSJSup	Supplements to the Journal for the Study of Judaism
JSOT	Journal for the Study of the Old Testament
JSOTSup	Journal for the Study of the Old Testament: Supplement Series
JSP	Journal for the Study of the Pseudepigrapha
JTS	Journal of Theological Studies
JWSTP	Jewish Writings of the Second Temple Period: Apocrypha, Pseudepigrapha, Qumran Sectarian Writings, Philo, Josephus
KJA	King James Version Apocrypha
LXT/LXX	Septuagint – Ancient Greek translation of the Hebrew Bible
MGWJ	Die Seele als Vogel: Ein Beitrag zu den Anschauungen der Agada
MJT	Melanesian Journal of Theology
MT	Masoretic Text
NICNT	New International Commentary on the New Testament
NIDNTT	New International Dictionary of New Testament Theology
NIDOTTE	New International Dictionary of Old Testament Theology and Exegesis
NovTSup	Novum Testamentum: Supplements
NRSV	New Revised Standard Version
OTL	Old Testament Library
OTP	Old Testament Pseudepigrapha
RBS	Resources for Biblical Studies
SBLDS	Society of Biblical Literature Dissertation Series
SBT	Studies in Biblical Theology
Sem	Semitica
SVTP	Studia in Veteris Testamenti Pseudepigrapha
TaNaKh	Hebrew based acronym = Torah – Prophet – Writings = Jewish Bible
TBM	Themes in Biblical Narrative: Jewish and Christian Traditions
Tg. Onq.	Targum Onqelos
Tg. Ps.-J.	Targum Pseudo-Jonathan
TMP	The Minor Prophets – An Exegetical & Expository Commentary
TNTC	Tyndale New Testament Commentary
TRENT	Traditions of the Rabbis from the Era of the New Testament
TWOT	Theological Wordbook of the Old Testament
VC	Vigiliae Christianae
VT	Vetus Testamentum

WBC	Word Biblical Commentary
WGRW	Writings from the Greco-Roman World
WUNT	Wissenschaftliche Untersuchungen zum Neuen Testament
ZAW	*Zeitschrift für die alttestamentliche Wissenschaft*

Second Temple Period Literature

Apocrypha/Pseudepigrapha

Apoc. Elij. (C)	*Coptic Apocalypse of Elijah*
Apoc. Elij. (H)	*Hebrew Apocalypse of Elijah*
Apoc. Ezek.	*Apocryphon of Ezekiel*
Apoc. Mos.	*Apocalypse of Moses*
2 *Bar.*	2 *Baruch*
4 *Bar.*	4 *Baruch*
1 En.	*1 Enoch (Ethiopic Apocalypse)*
2 En.	*2 Enoch (Slavonic Apocalypse)*
3 En.	*3 Enoch (Hebrew Apocalypse)*
2 Esd	2 Esdras
Gk. Apoc. Ezra	*Greek Apocalypse of Ezra*
Hel. Syn. Pr.	*Hellenistic Synagogal Prayers*
Hist. Rech.	*History of the Rechabites*
Jos. Asen.	*Joseph and Aseneth*
Jub.	*Jubilees*
L.A.B.	*Liber antiquitatum biblicarum*
Lad. Jac.	*Ladder of Jacob*
L.A.E.	*Life of Adam and Eve*
Liv. Proph.	*Lives of the Prophets*
2 Macc.	2 Maccabees
4 Macc.	*4 Maccabees*
Mart. Ascen. Isa.	*Martyrdom and Ascension of Isaiah*
Odes	*Odes of Solomon*
Ps.-Philo	*Pseudo-Philo*
Ps.-Phoc.	*Pseudo-Phocylides*
Pss. Sol.	*Psalms of Solomon*
Ques. Ezra	*Questions of Ezra*
Sib. Or.	*Sibylline Oracles*
Sir.	Sirach/Ecclesiasticus
T12P	*Testament of the Twelve Prophets*
T. Ab.	*Testament of Abraham*
T. Adam	*Testament of Adam*
T. Ash.	*Testament of Asher*
T. Benj.	*Testament of Benjamin*
T. Dan	*Testament of Dan*
T. Gad	*Testament of Gad*
T. Iss.	*Testament of Issachar*
T. Job	*Testament of Job*

T. Jos.	*Testament of Joseph*
T. Jud.	*Testament of Judah*
T. Levi	*Testament of Levi*
T. Mos.	*Testament (Assumption) of Moses*
T. 12 Patr.	*Testament of the Twelve Patriarchs*
T. Sim.	*Testament of Simeon*
T. Zeb.	*Testament of Zebulun*
Vita	*Vita Adae et Evae*
Wis.	Wisdom of Solomon

Dead Sea Scrolls

4Q386	4QPseudo-Ezekiel^b
4Q388	4QPseudo-Ezekiel^d
4Q416	4QInstruction^b
4Q418	4QInstruction^d
4Q504	4QWords of the Luminaries^a
4Q521	4QMessianic Apocalypse
4Q548	4QVisions of Amramf? ar

Josephus

Ant.	*Jewish Antiquities*
J.W.	*Jewish War*

New Testament

Mt.	Matthew
Mk	Mark
Lk.	Luke
Jn	John
Acts	Acts
Rom.	Romans
1 Cor.	1 Corinthians
2 Cor.	2 Corinthians
Gal.	Galatians
Eph.	Ephesians
Phil.	Philippians
Col.	Colossians
1 Thess.	1 Thessalonians
2 Thess.	2 Thessalonians
1 Tim.	1 Timothy
2 Tim.	2 Timothy
Heb.	Hebrews
Jas	James

1 Pet.	1 Peter
2 Pet.	2 Peter
Jude	Jude
Rev.	Revelation

Rabbinic Works

'Abod. Zar.	*Avodah Zarah*
b.	Babylonian Talmud
B. Bat.	*Baba Bathra*
Ber.	*Berakhot*
Chag.	*Chagigah*
Chul.	*Chullin*
Deut. Rab.	*Rabbah Deuteronomy*
Eccl. Rab.	*Rabbah Ecclesiastes*
Esth. Rab.	*Rabbah Esther*
Exod. Rab.	*Rabbah Exodus*
Gen. Rab.	*Rabbah Genesis*
Ketub	*Ketubbot*
Lam. Rab.	*Rabbah Lamentation*
Lev. Rab.	*Rabbah Leviticus*
m.	Mishnah
Meg.	*Megillah*
Nid.	*Niddah*
Num. Rab.	*Rabbah Numbers*
Pesach	*Pesachim*
Qidd.	*Kiddushin*
Rab.	*Rabbah*
Roš Haš.	*Rosh HaShana*
Šabb.	*Shabat*
San.	*Sanhedrin*
Song. Rab.	*Rabbah Song of Songs*
Sot	*Sotah*
t.	Tosefta
Ta'an.	*Ta'anith*

FIGURES

1.	Death and Resurrection in the *Testament of Abraham*	40
2.	Death and Resurrection in the *Martyrdom and Ascension of Isaiah*	67
3.	Death and Resurrection in *Pseudo-Philo*	93
4.	Death and Resurrection in *4 Maccabees*	147
5.	Death and Resurrection in *Pseudo-Phocylides*	158
6.	Death and Resurrection in the *Psalms of Solomon*	166
7.	Human Anthropology – The Apocrypha and Pseudepigrapha	211
8.	Human Anthropology – The Souls of the Wicked	216
9.	Harmonized Resurrection View	223

TABLES

1.	Literary genre of the Pseudepigrapha	6
2.	Resurrection texts in the *Testaments*	13
3.	Structural overview of the *Testaments of the Twelve Patriarchs*	18
4.	Resurrection texts in expansions on stories and legends	52
5.	The Eden Narrative and the *Books of the Life of Adam and Eve*	73
6.	Death and resurrection view derived from the *Apocalypse of Moses*	84
7.	Resurrection statement and allusions in *Pseudo-Philo*	86
8.	Resurrection texts in wisdom and philosophical literature	105
9.	Outline of 2 Maccabees 7 and *4 Maccabees* 8–18	110
10.	The final destiny of the righteous and the wicked in 2 Maccabees 7 and *4 Maccabees* 8–18	133
11.	Helpful examples to remember (*4 Macc.* 18:11-13)	140
12.	Resurrection Texts in *Prayers*, *Psalms*, and *Odes*	160
13.	Description of the disembodied soul – pre-resurrected and resurrected	180
14.	The bodily forms of the soul	188
15.	Description of the eschatological resurrected body	193
16.	The nature of the eschatological resurrected body in 1 Corinthians 15	208
17.	The disembodied souls	213
18.	Number of judgments presented in the 18 unique resurrection views of the Apocrypha and the Pseudepigrapha	218
19.	Final destiny of the righteous and the wicked	221
20.	List of the TaNaKh passages referred or alluded to in the Context of the resurrection statements surveyed from the Apocrypha and the Pseudepigrapha	226
21.	The 18 distinct afterlife views and the TaNaKh	227
22.	Resurrection texts in the *Testaments*	231

23.	Resurrection texts in expansions on stories and legends	242
24.	Resurrection texts in wisdom and philosophical literature	260
25.	Resurrection texts in *Prayers*, *Psalms*, and *Odes*	265
26.	List of categories used in the five resurrection texts tables	281
27.	List of resurrection texts: Dead Sea Scrolls	282
28.	List of resurrection texts: Josephus	283
29.	List of resurrection texts: New Testament	284
30.	List of resurrection texts: Jewish Liturgy	294
31.	List of resurrection texts: Rabbinic Literature	295

Our Perennial Yearning for Postmortem Existence or Resurrection

James Hamilton Charlesworth
Princeton

For millennia, as *homo sapiens*, we have universally yearned for a continuation of life. Death is horrifically too final. About 9000 BCE in Jericho, human skulls with clay as "skin" seem to reflect ancestor worship. These "revived skulls" perhaps harbor the dream that loved ones had not disappeared and may be experienced again. About 2400 BCE, and even earlier, in Egypt, the pyramids and the pyramid texts preserve imaginations that some life continued after death, perhaps only for those who seem to be divine, at least partly.

Humans knew that death was certain and everywhere they created beliefs that some existence continued after mortality. In the early first millennium BCE in India, sometimes the concept was a return to an ocean of being, as in Hinduism. A little later and also in India, the authors of the *Upanishads* believed the human is defined by the elements in all living things, including trees. According to one memorable text, crushing a seed a father told a son: "That art Thou." What continued after life was not the person but the elements once collected into a finite human. In a similar fashion, Greek philosophers contemplated something survived the death of a human. Sometimes it was a return to the originating and immortal "atoms," the primordial fundamental element of being.

In Mesopotamia, about the middle of the fifth century BCE (perhaps) thinkers concluded that "resurrection" was promised, for all or for only those who had lived exemplary lives. Resurrection beliefs preserved the hope that not elements but the person, in an immortal form, survived death and decay. Perhaps resurrection beliefs can be located in some later compositions in the Davidic Psalter, but the clearest evidence is in Daniel, which can be dated to the middle of the second century BCE. Daniel may have early portions from Mesopotamia but the final form appeared in ancient Palestine.

Resurrection beliefs are evident within the Dead Sea Scrolls (the Qumran Scrolls) and *On Resurrection* (or *Messianic Apocalypse*; 4Q521) is a document found in Qumran Cave IV. Within the Apocrypha and Pseudepigrapha of the Old Testament, resurrection beliefs appear more and more frequently and can be dated from the second century BCE to the second century CE.

Not everyone in Early Judaism believed in the resurrection of the body after death. Beginning in about the middle of the second century BCE, the Sadducees, who controlled the cult in the Jerusalem Temple, rejected a resurrection belief because they claimed it could not be found in the Pentateuch, which to them was the only *sacra scriptura*. Most of the authors of books collected into the Old Testament (TANAKH) reflect a belief in a lifeless abode of the dead in Sheol and offer no resurrection beliefs.

In contrast to the Sadducees, most Jews did not have a limited or closed canon. For them some of the so-called apocryphal works were also full of God's revelation and were revelatory "sacred scripture." In these compositions, now on the fringes of our canon, are found many passages in which beliefs in a resurrection "of the body" are articulated.

Daniel and the Apocalypse of John are the two apocalypses in the Christian canon. Each of them affirms belief in the resurrection of believers. In the Old Testament Pseudepigrapha and the Qumran Scrolls are many apocalypses. They are attributed to many biblical saints, including Adam, Enoch, Abraham, David, Solomon, Elijah, Isaiah, Jeremiah, and Ezra. Jews placed the abode of the dead who await resurrection in many places on earth or in one of the heavens. Some Jews believed that resurrection occurred only at the Endtime, others harbored the belief that resurrection occurred immediately or soon after death. Many Jews and Christians held to the belief that bones in graves or ossuaries (or in the bellies of beasts or the depths of the sea) did not prove the person had not been resurrected. The Creator had created *ex nihilo*, so to revive life where it had once been was not impossible for the Supernatural One.

Philosophers debate if "resurrection beliefs" are merely the wish becoming the father of the thought. Surely, virtually all humans wish that life does not end so tragically in the ebbing of energy and then life. They would add growing old is a part of dying. How can God be a loving Father if the latter years are the lesser years?

Many Jews today believe that they will be resurrected. In fact, the belief is immortalized in the *Eighteen Benedictions* recited with religious fervor in synagogues. Christians are united by the belief that God raised Jesus from the dead, and confess this common belief liturgically in churches.[1] As one of my closest friends, a surgeon, stated: "Believing in the resurrection is the best insurance policy going."

On the one hand, if there is no resurrection, I would believe in it since it enriches my life and memories of my loved ones, especially my father and mother. On the other hand, living the Jewish-Christian faith creates an existential insight that moves me from believing in Jesus' resurrection to knowing it.

Jan A. Sigvartsen reviews and offers insight into the major passages focused on resurrection in the Apocrypha and Pseudepigrapha, Qumran, Josephus, the New Testament, and Rabbinics. The appendices provide clear avenues to texts and passages. The "tables" provide clarification and point to the major texts. The "figures" provide symbolic images to explore the minds of the ancients and our own rich reflections. Sigvartsen wisely sees the influence of Zoroastrianism in the development of Jewish creative thinking on resurrection and that it is to be distinguished from the Hellenistic belief in the immortality of the soul. The book brings forward the major texts in translation with judicious use of Hebrew and Greek. The book is ideal for classes and private study.

James H. Charlesworth
Princeton
Spring, 2019

---

1. Some ecclesiastical authorities in the USA judge resurrection belief to be a relic of ancient mythology.

FOREWORD

Resurrection of the dead was in antiquity – and in contemporary theological studies – a celebrated, yet also controverted topic. In historical retrospect, one can appreciate how this insurgent hope that took shape in postexilic Judaism gradually emerged as a landmark eschatological doctrine within Rabbinic Judaism and Early Christianity. Much remains in darkness, however, regarding the formation, conceptual diversity, and social settings of resurrection within earlier Judaism. Monumental tomes have treated vast bodies of evidence; yet there also remains the need for more selective studies of particular features of resurrection.

It is all the more commendable that Jan A. Sigvartsen has concentrated his energies upon one select feature of the problem: the presence of scriptural language and imagery throughout a range of early Jewish and Christian expressions for resurrection. Jon Levenson, in fact, laments the lack of scholarly attention to this problem, calling for a deeper appreciation of the intertextual features of early Jewish discourse of resurrection (Levenson, *Resurrection and the Restoration of Israel*, 185). This unfulfilled desideratum is even surprising, since it has long been recognized that both Daniel 12 and 1 Corinthians 15, two of the most significant canonical expressions of resurrection, both rely heavily upon particular interpretive assumptions about underlying scriptural prophecies. Yet there has been no comprehensive study of this phenomenon among expressions of the afterlife in the broader literature of the Apocrypha, Pseudepigrapha, and other early Jewish/nascent Christian writings.

Sigvartsen's timely volume addresses this pressing need in a thorough exploration of the Pseudepigrapha, which preserve some of the most significant writings for understanding early expressions of resurrection. His study leads the reader on an enlightening journey into the rich interpretive culture that stood behind early references to resurrection. As a result, one may more fully appreciate the possibility that resurrection was not merely directed to the fate of human remains or to retribution *per se*, important as these conceptual problems were within select literary texts. Indeed, expressions for resurrection remained conceptually diverse, and the hope could offer redress to a variety of religious problems. Yet, as Sigvartsen carefully documents, one of the more unifying strands amid the often bewildering evidence is the conviction that resurrection affirmed the integrity of the divine promises to Israel, so fragile and so repeatedly endangered by the historical contexts in which resurrection originally flourished. In so doing, his focused volume presents a reservoir for more fully understanding the interrelationships between scriptural traditions, eschatological hopes, and ancient theodicies that flourish from within the writings of the Pseudepigrapha.

C. D. Elledge
Gustavus Adolphus College

Chapter 1

INTRODUCTION

The Hebrew Scriptures reflect little regarding the destiny of the individual after their death. The overall impression from a study of TaNaKh[1] passages relating to the afterlife is that death was not considered the start of the next life, but the end of the present one.[2] The biblical writers focused on the present life and emphasized the covenant relationship between humans and God. Matthew Suriano suggests that "with the exception of Dan 12:1-3, which dates to a late stage in the Hebrew Bible's history, there is no vetting of the dead. Instead the afterlife ideal is presented as reunion with dead kind" as illustrated in Gen. 15:15-16.[3] He observes "that the concept of death was centered specifically on the treatment of the dead rather than their destiny. Death, in the world of

---

1. The reader should be aware that the acronym TaNaKh is used anachronistically as it is difficult to determine what constituted "scripture" or which literary composition was considered authoritative or canonical by differing religious communities during the Second Temple period. Even in the case of the Qumran community and the Dead Sea Scrolls, it is difficult to identify whether the community considered all these scrolls sacred and authoritative, or whether the number of copies of specific scrolls reveals something regarding their authoritative standing. The Dead Sea Scrolls could even have been a part of a library collection and, as such, a certain scroll may not necessarily reflect the ethos of the community nor provide reliable insight into its authoritative nature within that community. It was only when sacred texts were collected into a codex that the canon became rigid as it became necessary to decide which texts should be included and which texts should be left out.

The canon was rather fluid during this period, at least in the earlier part thereof. Therefore, this study uses the acronym TaNaKh out of convenience as it is the most neutral term for the body of literature recognized as sacred by both present-day Jewish and Christian communities.

2. See, e.g., Philip S. Johnston, *Shades of Sheol: Death and Afterlife in the Old Testament* (Downers Grove, IL: InterVarsity, 2002), 65, and N. T. Wright, *The Resurrection of the Son of God*, COQG 3 (Minneapolis: Fortress, 2003), 97.

3. Matthew J. Suriano, *A History of Death in the Hebrew Bible* (Oxford: Oxford University Press, 2018), 1.

the Old Testament writers, was a dynamic process…rather than a static event." Thus, he argues "death as transition and the relational nature of the dead" are interconnected aspects. He writes: "In ancient Israel, early Judaism, and the Hebrew Bible, the transition of the dead did not involve the migration of an immortal soul to some otherworldly destination. It was not a question of place – heaven or hell – but of status. The biblical ideal was the status of *ancestor*, which provided the dead with a certain form of immortality. But his status was conditioned upon how the living interacted with the dead; hence, death was relational."[4] Suriano considers the introductory statement (Sir. 44:7-15) to the list of biblical heroes (Sir. 44:1–49:16) written by Yeshua ben Sira (second century BCE), a scribe from Jerusalem, to summarize this biblical ideal.[5] It describes those who are forgotten, those who do not have a name which lives on past their death, those who seem to have "perished as though they have never existed" (Sir. 44:10), noting that they are still a part of the greater collective, thereby receiving a sense of immortality in the same manner as those who received the deity's reward of "offspring and the blessedness of future generations."[6] Sirach 44:7-15 (NRS) reads:

> [7]All these were honored in their generations, and were the pride of their times. [8]Some of them have left behind a name, so that others declare their praise. [9]But of others there is no memory; they have perished as though they had never existed; they have become as though they had never been born, they and their children after them. [10]But these also were godly men, whose righteous deeds have not been forgotten; [11]their wealth will remain with their descendants, and their inheritance with their children's children. [12]Their descendants stand by the covenants; their children also, for their sake. [13]Their offspring will continue forever, and their glory will never be blotted out. [14]Their bodies are buried in peace, but their name lives on generation after generation. [15]The assembly declares their wisdom, and the congregation proclaims their praise.

---

4. Ibid., 2.

5. Ibid., 256–7. For a discussion on the afterlife and resurrection views appearing in Sirach (Ecclesiasticus), specifically in the Greek translation by Ben Sira's grandson, see the companion monograph: Jan A. Sigvartsen, *Afterlife and Resurrection Beliefs in the Apocrypha and the Apocalyptic Literature*, JCT 30 (London: Bloomsbury T&T Clark, 2019).

6. C. D. Elledge, *Resurrection of the Dead in Early Judaism: 200 BCE–CE 200* (Oxford: Oxford University Press, 2017), 104. For a discussion by Elledge on the denial of the afterlife in early Judaism and how this view could still satisfy the problem of theodicy for those who adhered to this belief, see the chapter titled "Denial," 87–106.

The close of the First Temple period and the return of the Jews from Babylonian exile heralded much more exploration of the issues of the afterlife among the Jews during the Second Temple period. Scholars argue that increased interest in angels, the battle between good and evil, and the interest in a future bodily resurrection and judgment as seen in these Jewish writings, could be due to the influence of the Zoroastrian religion of the Persians. The belief in an immortal soul, which exists separately from the physical body after the moment of death, could be viewed as a part of the Hellenization of Judaism. It was also during this period that the problem of theodicy became more apparent for the Jews. The traditional belief that God would reward the righteous, Torah-observant Jews with a long and prosperous life while cutting short the life of the wicked needed adjustment. This was a period of foreign occupation and oppression; oppression of the righteous poor, religious persecution, and martyrdom. For the Torah-observant Jews, justice had been perverted: the righteous were receiving the curses of the wicked, while the wicked enjoyed the blessings promised the righteous. Only a belief in an afterlife could solve this acute problem. If there was an afterlife, it was argued, God could set things straight and give the righteous and the wicked their proper due.

The Jews of the Second Temple period borrowed religious and philosophical concepts from Persia and Greece and synthesized and amalgamated these views into their own religious framework. Thus, multiple afterlife beliefs developed and appeared in their literature, in an attempt to solve the problem of theodicy. By the end of this period, a belief in a bodily resurrection had become the mainstream belief in both surviving strands of Second Temple Judaism: Rabbinic Judaism and the early Christian Church. It was a central tenet for both communities. For the Christians, questioning this doctrine was equated with questioning the historicity of Jesus' resurrection, which was the guarantor for the Christians' salvation hope (e.g. Rom. 6:3-6; 1 Cor. 15; 1 Pet. 1:3-4). For Rabbinic Judaism, questioning this faith would disqualify the person from any share in the world to come: "All Israelites have a share in the world to come… And these are the ones who have no portion in the world to come: (1) He who says, the resurrection of the dead is a teaching which does not derive from the Torah, (2) and the Torah does not come from Heaven; and (3) an Epicurean" (*m. Sanh.* 10:1).

This monograph is a continuation of the companion volume, *Afterlife and Resurrection Beliefs in the Apocrypha and Apocalyptic Literature*. Both volumes will demonstrate beliefs in resurrection were indeed abundant and, in turn, address Levenson's *desideratum* regarding their abundance, ensuring scholars do not "underestimate the verbal particularity and the textual character of its appearance – points of great significance to the ancient Jewish culture itself."[7] This monograph attempts to provide a better understanding of how the TaNaKh was read by Jewish sects during this important period and the role the TaNaKh played in the overall development of the resurrection belief that became a central article of faith in both Christianity and Rabbinic Judaism.

This monograph has a companion monograph which systematically outlines the numerous afterlife beliefs in the Apocrypha and Apocalyptic literature, and identifies and analyzes the texts from the TaNaKh that support a resurrection belief within Jewish extra-biblical passages, from the Second Temple period, the Apocrypha and the Pseudepigrapha, which imply or state a belief in resurrection. The companion monograph identifies twelve distinct and complete views. The afterlife beliefs appearing in the non-apocalyptic literature of the Pseudepigrapha are presented in this monograph.

Pseudepigrapha

The Pseudepigrapha is a catch-all category which includes all the books of the Second Temple period apart from the Apocrypha, Dead Sea Scrolls, Philo, Josephus, New Testament, and Rabbinic material. This monograph follows the broad description suggested by James H. Charlesworth:

> Those writings 1) that, with the exception of Ahiqar, are Jewish or Christian; 2) that are often attributed to ideal figures in Israel's past; 3) that customarily claim to contain God's word or message; 4) that frequently build upon ideas and narratives present in the Old Testament; 5) and that almost always were composed either during the period 200 B.C. to A.D. 200 or, though late, apparently preserve, albeit in an edited form, Jewish traditions that date from that period.[8]

The term *Pseudepigrapha* comes from the Greek words ψευδής, "false," and ἐπιγραφή, "inscription," referring to books bearing a false inscription. David A. deSilva notes that this term "highlights primarily a literary characteristic of many writings from the Hellenistic and Greco-Roman periods, that is, writings under the assumed name of a great figure from the distant past," however, he adds that Roman Catholic and Orthodox writers use the term Apocrypha when referring to this body

---

7. Jon Douglas Levenson, *Resurrection and the Restoration of Israel: The Ultimate Victory of the God of Life* (New Haven: Yale University Press, 2006), 185.

8. James H. Charlesworth, "Introduction for the General Reader," *OTP* 1:xxv.

of literature while many scholars and Jewish writers often use the term "outside books."⁹

Like the term Apocrypha discussed in the companion monograph, *Afterlife and Resurrection Beliefs in the Apocrypha and Apocalyptic Literature*, this term also has its limitations – the first term "derives from canonical debates and usage; the other from a peculiar literary characteristic."[10] Nickelsburg notes that this term "ignores the pseudonymous nature of some of the Apocrypha (e.g. Tobit and the Wisdom of Solomon) and some canonical (e.g. Job and Ruth) writings"[11] and C. T. Fritsch observes that some of the Pseudepigraphical books are better described as anonymous than pseudonymous. Fritsch also states that these books were never included into the Greek and Latin manuscripts of the Bible, so their canonicity was never an issue in mainstream Christianity. However, "many of these works were preserved in the various branches of the oriental churches, and so they came down to us in such languages as Syriac, Ethiopic, Coptic, Georgian, Armenian, Slavonic, etc."[12]

The Old Testament Pseudepigrapha represent several literary genres which fall into the following six categories:

1. Apocalypses;
2. Testaments;
3. Expansion of TaNaKh narratives;
4. Wisdom and philosophical literature;
5. Prayers, psalms and odes; and
6. Fragments of now-lost Judeo-Hellenistic works.

This monograph considers the last five categories, the first category, *Apocalyptic* literature, is considered in the companion monograph. Table 1 shows the literary genre of the Pseudepigrapha, the date of composition,[13] and the books containing a resurrection belief, either stated or implied (bolded and highlighted) based on the analysis in Appendix A of this monograph and Appendix A in the companion monograph. This will help

---

9. D. A. deSilva, "Apocrypha and Pseudepigrapha," *DNTB* 58–9.

10. Ibid., 60.

11. George W. E. Nickelsburg, *Jewish Literature between the Bible and the Mishnah* (Philadelphia: Fortress, 1981), 6.

12. C. T. Fritsch, "Pseudepigrapha," *IDB* 3:963.

13. The suggested dates are primarily based on Charlesworth's *OTP* and to a lesser degree on Craig A. Evans, *Ancient Texts for New Testament Studies: A Guide to the Background Literature* (Peabody, MA: Hendrickson, 2005).

the reader to easily see the extent of this belief in the pseudepigraphical books.

Chapters 2–5 of this monograph considers the passages from the last five categories of Charlesworth's two-volume collection of pseudepigraphical writings that imply or state a resurrection belief which also refers or alludes to the TaNaKh for the foundation of this belief. Chapter 6 considers briefly the nature of the posthumous body and the soul appearing in the Apocrypha and the Pseudepigrapha and compares it with relevant afterlife and resurrection passages from the New Testament. The final chapter provides a summary and conclusion based on all the afterlife and resurrection passages appearing in the Apocrypha and the Pseudepigrapha, thus, functioning as the conclusion not only to this monograph but also to the companion volume.

Table 1. Literary genre of the Pseudepigrapha

Literary Genre	Pseudepigraphical Texts	Date
Apocalyptic Literature and Related Works	**1 Enoch**	3rd cent. BCE–50 CE
	2 Enoch	Late 1st cent. CE
	3 Enoch	5th–6th Century CE
	Sibylline Oracles	2nd cent. BCE–7th cent. CE
	Treatise of Shem	1st cent. BCE
	Apocryphon of Ezekiel	50 BCE–50 CE
	Apocalypse of Zephaniah	100 BCE–70 CE
	Fourth book of Ezra [= 2 Esdras 3–14] (see OT Apocrypha)	Late 1st cent. CE
	Greek Apocalypse of Ezra	2nd–9th cent. CE
	Vision of Ezra	4th–7th cent. CE
	Questions of Ezra	?
	Revelation of Ezra	2nd–9th cent. CE
	Apocalypse of Sedrach	2nd–5th cent. CE
	2 Baruch	Early 2nd cent. CE
	3 Baruch	1st–3rd cent. CE
	Apocalypse of Abraham	1st–2nd cent. CE
	Apocalypse of Adam	1st–4th cent. CE
	Apocalypse of Elijah	1st–4th cent. CE
	Apocalypse of Daniel	9th cent. CE

Literary Genre	Pseudepigraphical Texts	Date
Testaments (Often with Apocalyptic Sections)	*Testament of the 12 Patriarchs*	2nd cent. BCE
	Testament of Reuben	
	Testament of Simeon	
	Testament of Levi	
	Testament of Judah	
	Testament of Issachar	
	Testament of Zebulun	
	Testament of Dan	
	Testament of Naphtali	
	Testament of Gad	
	Testament of Asher	
	Testament of Joseph	
	Testament of Benjamin	
	Testament of Job	Early 1st cent. BCE
	Testament of the Three Patriarchs	1st cent. CE
	Testament of Abraham	1st–2nd cent. CE
	Testament of Isaac	1st–2nd cent. CE
	Testament of Jacob	2nd–3rd cent. CE ?
	Testament (Assumption) of Moses	1st cent. CE
	Testament of Solomon	1st–3rd cent. CE
	Testament of Adam	2nd–5th cent. CE
Expansions of the "Old Testament" and Legends	*Letter of Aristeas*	130–70 BCE
	Jubilees	135–105 BCE
	Martyrdom and Ascension of Isaiah [3:13-4:22 = *Testament of Hezekiah*]	2nd cent. BCE
	Joseph and Aseneth	1st cent. BCE–2nd cent. CE
	Life of Adam and Eve	1st cent. BCE–1st cent. CE
	Pseudo-Philo [= *Biblical Antiquities*]	2nd cent. BCE–late 1st cent. CE
	Lives of the Prophets	1st cent. CE
	Ladder of Jacob	1st cent. CE
	4 Baruch [= *Omissions of Jeremiah*]	Late 1st–early 2nd cent. CE
	Jannes and Jambres	1st–2nd cent. CE
	History of the Rechabites	1st–4th cent. CE
	Eldad and Modad	> 2nd cent. CE
	History of Joseph	> 400 CE

Literary Genre	Pseudepigraphical Texts	Date
Wisdom and Philosophical Literature	Ahiqar	6th–7th cent. CE
	3 Maccabees	1st cent. CE
	4 Maccabees	1st cent. CE
	Pseudo-Phocylides	1st cent. BCE
	The Sentences of the Syriac Menander	3rd cent. CE
Prayers, Psalms, and Odes	More Psalms of David *Psalm 151* (see OT Apocrypha) *Psalm 152* *Psalm 153* *Psalm 154* *Psalm 155*	3rd cent. BCE–1st cent. CE
	Prayer of Manasseh (see OT Apocrypha)	2nd–1st cent. BCE
	Psalms of Solomon	c. 50 BCE
	Hellenistic Synagogal Prayers	2nd–3rd cent. CE
	Prayer of Joseph	1st cent. CE
	Prayer of Jacob	1st–4th cent. CE
	Odes of Solomon	Late 1st–early 2nd cent. CE
Fragments of Lost Judeo-Hellenistic Work	Philo the Epic Poet	3rd–2nd cent. BCE
	Theodotus	2nd–1st cent. BCE
	Orphica	1st cent. BCE/CE
	Ezekiel the Tragedian	2nd cent. BCE
	Fragments of Pseudo-Greek Poets Pseudo-Hesiod Pseudo-Pythagoras Pseudo-Aeschylus Pseudo-Sophocles Pseudo-Euripides Pseudo-Philemon Pseudo-Diphilus Pseudo-Menander	3rd–2nd cent. BCE
Fragments of Lost Judeo-Hellenistic Work	Aristobulus	2nd cent. BCE
	Demetrius the Chronographer	3rd cent. BCE
	Aristeas the Exegete	Late 2nd–early 1st cent. BCE
	Eupolemus	Late 2nd–early 1st cent. BCE
	Pseudo-Eupolemus	> 1st cent. BCE
	Cleodemus Malchus	> 1st cent. BCE
	Artapanus	3rd–2nd cent. BCE
	Pseudo-Hecataeus	c. 300 BCE

Appendix A forms the foundation of this study as it provides a comprehensive list of resurrection passages from Second Temple period Jewish literature, compiled from the last five categories of the Pseudepigrapha. These passages are divided into appropriate tables in which they are categorized and analyzed, noting when a specific resurrection text is referring or alluding to the TaNaKh. Additionally, each table is followed by an anthology of the listed passages to show the larger context of each resurrection statement and provide the reader easy access to these resurrection texts. These anthologies are highlighted and annotated. The "Reference to the TaNaKh" category includes both "citation" (the author quotes the TaNaKh passage verbatim and includes the textual reference) and "quotation" (the author quotes a TaNaKh passage verbatim without including the textual reference) and is the most objective category. The "Allusion-to-the-TaNaKh" category is rather broad and more subjective as the original author does not quote the TaNaKh passage verbatim, but similarly rephrases, reshapes, or re-purposes the passage. It is apparent, and therefore assumed, that both the original author and the original target audience were aware of the primary source of the allusion.

Appendix B provides similar tables for the resurrection passages found in the Dead Sea Scrolls, Josephus, New Testament, Jewish Liturgy, and Rabbinic Literature. However, these passages will not be considered in this study (nor in the companion volume), although references to them will be made throughout this work and the companion volume, when deemed relevant. These passages are considered in a separate study currently being concluded by the author.

Chapter 2

TESTAMENTS
(OFTEN WITH APOCALYPTIC SECTIONS)

The second genre category of pseudepigraphical books, *Testaments*, follows the pattern of last words or blessings of Jacob to his sons in Genesis 49, and Moses' final words to the people of Israel in Deuteronomy 32–33. In these two passages, Jacob and Moses use poetic language, reflecting on key events in the past which are relevant to each of the sons/tribes before turning their attention to the future. Both of these "proto-testaments" are introduced by the technical term, בְּאַחֲרִית הַיָּמִים, "*in the last days*" (Gen. 49:1; Deut. 31:29), suggesting that these two poetic texts will also reveal something about the distant future, thus also including apocalyptic material.[1] This understanding of the term becomes apparent from Targum Pseudo-Jonathan's expansion upon the introductory words of Jacob's blessings of his sons:

וַיִּקְרָא יַעֲקֹב אֶל־בָּנָיו וַיֹּאמֶר   וקרא יעקב לבנוי ואמר להום
 אידכו מסואבותא
 ואיחוי לכון רזייא סתימיא קיציא גניזיא
 ומתן אגרהון דצדיקייא
 ופורענותהון דרשיעייא
 ושלויתא דעדן מה הוא

---

1. This technical term is also used in Num. 24:14, in Balaam's blessing of the people of Israel, revealing aspects of their distant future, hinting at the Messianic age (Num. 24:17-19), and the future destruction of Israel's enemies. However, George Buchanan cautions the reader not to automatically assume that this expression should be understood eschatologically. He writes: "Modern Bible students should not be misled by the word ἔσχατος [the LXX translation for אחרית] in this expression and should not read eschatological meanings into contexts which do not anticipate any kind of an end, but only future time" (George Wesley Buchanan, "Eschatology and the 'End of Days,'" *JNES* 20 [1961]: 191).

2. Testaments (Often with Apocalyptic Sections)

הֵאָסְפוּ וְאַגִּידָה לָכֶם אֵת אֲשֶׁר־יִקְרָא אֶתְכֶם בְּאַחֲרִית הַיָּמִים:	כחדא מתכנשין תריסר שבטי ישראל מקפין דרגשא דדהבא דרביע עלה ומן דאיתגלי איקר שכינתא דייי קיצא דעתיד מלכא משיחא למיתי איתכסי מיניה ובכין אמר איתו ואיתני לכון מה דיארע יתכון בסוף יומיא:
⁴⁹·¹ Then Jacob called his sons and said, "Gather around, and I will tell you what will happen to you **in the days to come.**" (CSB)	⁴⁹·¹ And Jakob called his sons and said to them, Purify yourselves from uncleanness, and **I will show you the hidden mysteries, the ends concealed, the recompense of reward for the righteous, the retribution of the wicked, and the bower of Eden, what it is**. And the twelve tribes of Israel gathered themselves together around the golden bed whereon he reclined, and where was revealed to him the Shekina of the Lord, **(though) the end for which the king Meshiha is to come had been concealed from him**. Then said he, Come, and **I will declare to you what shall befall you at the end of the days**. (PJE)

In the expansion found in the Targum, several new elements are introduced regarding "the days to come." This apocalyptic time will include the reward of the righteous and the retribution of the wicked, and the bower of Eden, a possible allusion to the eschatological universal resurrection followed by the judgment of all. This future time will also see the arrival of the king Meshiha, and, it could be assumed, the Messianic age.[2]

---

2. The Messianic aspect of Jacob's blessings is most clearly seen in the blessing given to his son Judah (Gen. 49:8-12), a theme greatly expanded upon by Targum Pseudo-Jonathan. However, this ancient poem also uses Messianic language in the blessing given to Jacob's favorite son, Joseph. The Joseph oracle is the earliest biblical hint of the suffering Messiah, later referred to as Messiah ben Joseph/Ephraim (e.g. *b. Sanh.* 98b; *b. Suk.* 52a, b; *y. Suk.* 5.2; *Tg. Jer.* Zech. 12.1; *Tg. Onq.* Exod. 40.9-11), which becomes a key element of Isaiah's Suffering Servant songs and comes to a climax in Isa. 52:13–53:12. For an analysis of the Messianic aspect of the Joseph oracle (Gen. 49:22-26), see Jan A. Sigvartsen, *Messiah ben Joseph: A Type both in Jewish and Christian Traditions*, GHMSSTL 1 (Wilmore, KY: GlossaHouse, 2018). The Priestly Messiah, Messiah ben Levi, who appears in the Dead Sea scrolls (e.g.

John Sailhamer observes regarding the Pentateuch's use of this technical term:

> The author shows throughout his work an interest in past events. His repeated and strategic return to the notion of "the last days" in giving his work its final shape reveals that his interest is in the future as well... Because of the terminology he uses (viz., "the end of days"), we could call it an eschatological reading of his historical narratives. The narrative texts of past events are presented as pointers to future events. Past events foreshadow the future.[3]

Thus, these "proto-testaments" include material from the preceding narratives, give ethical evaluations of these key events, may add new elements from the past which has not been revealed in the preceding narratives and concludes with remarks pertaining to the near and distant future. It is little wonder then that Charlesworth states the pseudepigraphical Testament genre is not well defined as it includes material which falls into several different genre categories like "apocalyptic, ethical, and Midrashic types of literature."[4] During Second Temple period Judaism, several literary pieces were written containing the "last words" or testament of an important Patriarch or character from the TaNaKh. The apocalyptic section of these testaments often contains the resurrection hope. Table 2 provides a list of resurrection passages appearing in the *Testaments*:

4Q175; 4QD^a 7.18-21; 12.23–13.1; 14.18-19; 19.9-11; 1QS), who will rule together (1Q28a 2.11-21) with the Royal Messiah, Messiah ben David, derives from an interpretation of Balaam's blessing in Num. 24:14. Jewish tradition also mentions the Messiah to be a prophet (1QS 9.9b-11) or one having prophetic attributes, possibly an interpretation of Deut. 18:15-18 and Deut. 34:10, which mention that there will come a future prophet who will be greater than Moses. New Testament writers attempt to make a case that Jesus is the fulfillment of this prophecy – that Jesus is the new Moses or the new Lawgiver.

3. John H. Sailhamer, *The Pentateuch as Narrative: A Biblical-Theological Commentary*, Library of Biblical Interpretation (Grand Rapids: Zondervan, 1992), 37.

4. Charlesworth, *OTP* 1:773. He also notes these texts seem to have the following loose format in common: "The ideal figure faces death and causes his relatives and intimate friends to circle around his bed. He occasionally informs them of his fatal flaw and exhorts them to avoid certain temptations; he typically instructs them regarding the way of righteousness and utters blessings and curses. Often he illustrates his words – as the apocalyptic seer in the apocalypses – with descriptions of the future as it has been revealed to him in a dream or vision" (ibid.).

2. Testaments (Often with Apocalyptic Sections)

Table 2. Resurrection texts in the *Testaments*

				Resurrection			Classification		
	Passage		Notes	Implied	Stated	Ref.	Allude	Phil.	Assum.
Testament of the Twelve Patriarchs	Simeon	6	Arise in joy		×		×		×
		8:1	Sleep ‖ Death	×					
	Levi	18:14	Patriarchs share in the eschatological blessings	×					
	Judah	25	Resurrection of Patriarchs		×		×		
		26:4	Sleep = Death	×					×
	Issachar	7:9	Sleep ‖ Death	×					×
	Zebulun	10:1-7	Righteous/Wicked		×				×
	Dan	5:7-13	The work of the dual Messiah		×				×
	Gad	7:1	Sleep ‖ Death	×					×
		8:1	Sleep ‖ Death	×					×
	Asher	8:1	Sleep ‖ Death	×					×
	Joseph	20:4	Sleep ‖ Death			×			×
	Benjamin	10:4-10	Resurrection of patriarchs/transformation/Judgment		×				×

Table 2. Resurrection texts in the *Testaments* (cont.)

	Passage		Notes	Resurrection			Classification		
				Implied	Stated	Ref.	Allude	Phil.	Assum.
Testament of Job	4:9		Regarding the impending calamities		×	×			×
	33; 41:4		Job's throne in Heaven	×					×
	39:12		The children have been taken up to heaven	×					×
	43		The two ways	×					×
	47:11; 52; 53		Coming for the immortal Soul Death ‖ Sleep	×					×
Testament of the Three Patriarchs	Testament of Abraham	B7:16	Resurrection after 7000 ages are fulfilled		×				×
Testament of Moses	1:15		Death = Sleep	×					×
	10:9		The End-time	×			×		×
	10:14		Death = Sleep	×					×
Testament of Adam	3:2		Created in God's image	×				×	×
	3:4		Resurrection/ 2nd Adam		×		×		×

1. *Testament of the Twelve Patriarchs*

The *Testament of the Twelve Patriarchs* records the deathbed exhortation of each of the twelve patriarchs to their descendants inspired and modeled after Jacob's last words to his sons in Genesis 49 and Moses' words to the tribes of Israel in Deuteronomy 31–32. James L. Kugel states "the *Testaments* have a complicated, and much disputed, history of composition," and suggests the genre's "history probably begins in the Hasmonean period, sometimes in the last half of the 2nd century BCE."[5] Kugel argues that the exalted position given to Levi and the importance of showing obedience towards him in these testaments would seem unwarranted following "the Roman conquest of Judah by Pompey (63 BCE)."[6] Evans believes this composition was "written between 109 and 106 BCE by a Pharisee who greatly admired John Hyrcanus at the zenith of the Maccabean (or Hasmonean) dynasty."[7]

In contrast, Harm W. Hollander and Marinus deJonge argue that the *Testaments of the Twelve Patriarchs*, in its present form, is a Christian composition which was completed late in the second century CE. Although they would acknowledge that parts of this composition probably developed in pre-Christian Jewish circles, in light of the Dead Sea Scrolls (1QapGen; 4QPBless; 11QMelch; 4QPRNab ar.; 4QFlor; 4QTLevi ar^a; TNap), they believe that it would be impossible to reconstruct the Jewish version of this Testament.[8] They conclude: "A fortiori, it is practically impossible to answer the question whether there ever existed Jewish Testaments in some form. If they existed, we shall never be able to reconstruct them with any degree of certainty."[9] Robert Kugler writes in his survey of the various scholarly views held on the compositional history of the *Testaments*, that this latter view is the view he finds the most judicious but notes that "converts to deJonge's view are remarkably slow in coming." Kugler still believes that deJonge's "insistence that we cannot achieve sufficient consensus on a pre-Christian form of the *Testaments*

---

5. James L. Kugel, "Testament of the Twelve Patriarchs," in *Outside the Bible: Ancient Jewish Writings Related to Scripture*, ed. Louis H. Feldman, James L. Kugel, and Lawrence H. Schiffman, 3 vols. (Philadelphia: Jewish Publication Society of America, 2013), 2:1697. Robert A. Kugler provides an extensive survey of the various scholarly views held regarding the composition history in *The Testaments of the Twelve Patriarchs* (Sheffield: Sheffield Academic, 2001), 31–8.

6. Kugel, "The Testament of the Twelve Patriarchs," 1699.

7. Evans, *Ancient Texts for New Testament Studies*, 40.

8. Harm W. Hollander and Marinus De Jonge, *The Testaments of the Twelve Patriarchs: A Commentary*, SVTP 8 (Leiden: Brill, 1985), 82–5.

9. Ibid., 85.

to make the pursuit of one worthwhile seems destined to win the day."[10] Be that as it may, the majority view is that the *Testaments of the Twelve Patriarchs* is a Jewish composition with Christian interpolations.[11] Kugel states:

> The most reasonable conclusion appears to be that the *Testaments*: 1) Started off as a Jewish text in Hasmonean times; a text that 2) was later slightly revised while still in Hebrew, with specific insertions critical of the priesthood (as well as perhaps other material); 3) was still later freely translated into Greek with a number of a [*sic*] new passages added; and then finally 4) was supplemented by a relatively small and easily identifiable set of Christian interpolations.

Howard C. Kee suggests that each of the twelve Testaments contains six key elements, elements that have been utilized for the creation of Table 3. They are: (1) an introduction to the testament, typically laying the setting; (2) a narrative of the life of the patriarch;[12] (3) an ethical

---

10. Kugler, *Testaments of the Twelve Patriarchs*, 38. See also Robert A. Kugler, "Testaments," *DEJ* 1296–7.

11. The following sections from the *Testaments of the Twelve Patriarchs* have been suggested as Christian interpolations and have been compiled from the Kugel commentary on the "Testaments of the Twelve Patriarchs," in Feldman, Kugel, and Schiffman, eds., *Outside the Bible*, 2:1697–855 and Evans, *Ancient Texts for New Testament Studies*, 40. They are: *T. Reu.* 6:8; *T. Sim.* 6:5, 7; 7:1, 2; *T. Levi* 2:11; 4:1, 4, 5; 5:2; 8:5, 12-15; 10:2, 3; 14:1, 2; 16:3, 5; 17:2; 18:3, 7, 9-12, 14; *T. Jud.* 22:2; 24:2, 4; *T. Iss.* 7:7; *T. Zeb.* 9:8-9; *T. Dan* 5:10, 12-13; 6:6-7, 9; *T. Naph.* 4:5; 8:2, 3; *T. Gad* 8:2; *T. Ash.* 7:3-5; *T. Jos.* 19:3-6, 7, 8, 11; *T. Benj.* 3:8; 9:2-3, 3-5; 10:6-10; 11:2-5. It should be noted that the process of determining whether a given section in a piece of literature is a Christian interpolation is not completely objective; thus, some scholars have a more extensive list of interpolations than others. It is important to keep in mind that just because a statement sounds "Christian" does not necessarily mean that it could not be pre-Christian and have been written by a Jewish writer. Many Jewish concepts, theological positions, ethical standards, eschatological expectations, and apocalyptic elements were adopted by the early Christian Church, given that the first Christians were all "Messianic Jews."

12. The narrative element is missing in the *Testament of Asher*. Several of the narrative sections in these testaments allude to and comment/expand upon the Genesis narrative in addition to the Jacob's blessing itself: the *Testament of Reuben* expands on his affair with his father's concubine Bilhah (*T. Reu.* 3:11-15 || Gen. 35:32); the *Testament of Simeon* uses the account in Gen. 42:18-25 (*T. Sim.* 4:1-3) which have the brothers choose Simon to remain behind in Egypt as a springboard for the ethical discussion on anger and jealousy (*T. Sim.* 2:5-13, also a reference to Gen. 37:25-28) and also expands on the extent of Joseph's forgiveness (*T. Sim.* 4:4, 6 || Gen. 47:11);

exhortation;[13] (4) a prediction regarding the future, an apocalyptic section, followed by (5) a second exhortation; a conclusion detailing (6) the death and burial of said patriarch.[14]

In the following table, the resurrection statements and allusions in the *Testaments of the Twelve Patriarchs* have been highlighted in gray. The table shows that all but one of these statements appear in the apocalyptic section of the Testaments (*T. Sim.* 6:7; *T. Levi* 18:14; *T. Jud.* 25:4; *T. Zeb.* 10:1-3; *T. Dan* 5:7-13). The remaining resurrection statements appear in the second exhortation of the *Testament of Benjamin* (*T. Benj.* 10:6-10).

The use of "sleep" as an analogy, metaphor, or euphemism for death, implying a resurrection, will be discussed and has not been highlighted in Table 3. Table 3 also shows that most of the Christian interpolations and textual references, given in parentheses,[15] appear in the apocalyptic sections of the Testaments with the exception of the Testaments of

Testament of Levi justifies Levi's slaughter of the people of Shechem in Gen. 34:25-31 (*T. Levi* 2:2; 6:3–7:4); the *Testament of Judah* expands on the Tamar narrative in Gen. 38 and places Judah's actions in a better light (*T. Jud.* 8–12); the *Testament of Issachar* comments on the mandrakes incident in Gen. 30:1-24 (*T. Iss.* 1:2–2:5); the *Testament of Zebulun* provides more details regarding the brother's conspiracy against Joseph (*T. Zeb.* 1:5–4:13 || Gen. 37); the *Testament of Dan* also provides additional details to the brother's conspiracy (*T. Dan* 1:4-9 || Gen. 37); the *Testament of Naphtali* expands on Naphtali's birth narrative and Bilhah's background (*T. Naph.* 1:6-12 || Gen. 30:8); the *Testament of Gad* expands on the report Joseph gave to his father regarding his brother's bad deeds (*T. Gad* 1:3–9 || Gen. 37:2); the *Testament of Joseph* expands on the brothers' plot against Joseph in Genesis 37 (*T. Jos.* 10–16) and Joseph's sexual temptation in Gen. 39 (*T. Jos.* 2–9); and the *Testament of Benjamin* adds some additional details to Benjamin's birth (*T. Benj.* 1:3-6 || Gen. 35:16-20) and to the brother's conspiracy (*T. Benj.* 2:1-5 || Gen. 37).

13. Each of the *Testaments* seems to address a main ethical concern, the *Testament of Reuben* deals with the theme of lust; the *Testament of Simeon* with envy; the *Testament of Levi* with pride and arrogance; the *Testament of Judah* with courage, greed, and fornication; the *Testament of Issachar* with asceticism; the *Testament of Zebulun* with piety and compassion; the *Testament of Dan* with anger and falsehood; the *Testament of Naphtali* with sexual relations and natural goodness; the *Testament of Gad* with hatred, and hate versus love; the *Testament of Asher* with vice and virtue; the *Testament of Joseph* with chastity; and finally in the *Testament of Benjamin* with the importance of having a pure heart.

14. Howard C. Kee, "*Testaments of the Twelve Patriarchs*," *DNTB* 1201.

15. These texts are compiled from Robert H. Charles, *The Greek Versions of the Testaments of the Twelve Patriarchs* (Oxford: Oxford University Press, 1960), xlviii–li; Marc Philonenko and Howard Kee, *Les interpolations chrétiennes des Testaments des douze patriarches et les manuscrits de Qumrân*, CRHPR 35 (Paris: Presses Universitaires de France, 1960).

Reuben, Issachar, and Naphtali. It should also be noted that the narrative of the life of Levi section in the *Testament of Levi* alternates between events from his life and visions from God:

Narrative section regarding Levi's life (2:1-2) → First Vision (2:3–5:7)

Narrative section regarding Levi's life (6:1–7:4) → Second Vision (8:1-19)

Narrative section regarding Levi's life (9:1-14) → Third Vision (10:1-5)

Narrative section regarding Levi's life (11:1–12:5)

Table 3. Structural overview of the *Testament of the Twelve Patriarchs*

SON	Introduction	Narrative of the Life	Ethical Exhortation	Prediction Regarding Future	Second Exhortation	Death and Burial
Reuben	1:1-5	1:6–3:15	4:1–6:4	6:5-7	6:8-12	7:1-2
Simeon	1:1-2	2:1-13	3:1–5:3	5:4–6:7 (6:5, 7)	7:1-3	7:4–9:2
Levi	1:1-2	2:1–12:5 (2:11; 4:1, 4; 10:2-3)	13:1-9	14:1–18:14 (14:1, 2; 16:3; 17:2; 18:7, 9)	19:1-4a	19:4b-5
Judah	1:1-6	2:1–12:12	13:1–20:5	21:1–25:5 (24:4)	26:1	26:2-4
Issachar	1:1	1:2–3:8	4:1–5:8	6:1-4	7:1-7 (7:7)	7:8-9
Zebulun	1:1-2	1:3–4:13	5:1–8:1	8:2–10:3 (9:8)	10:4-5	10:6
Dan	1:1-2	1:3-9	2:1–5:5	5:6-13 (5:10, 13)	6:1-11 (6:7, 9)	7:1-3
Naphtali	1:1-4	1:5–2:8	2:9–3:5	4:1–8:1	8:2-10 (8:2, 3)	9:1-2
Gad	1:1-2	1:3–2:5	3:1–7:7	8:1-2 (8:2)	8:3a	8:3b-4
Asher	1:1-2	–	1:3–6:5	7:1-3 (7:3)	7:4-7	8:1-2
Joseph	1:1	1:2–16:5	17:1–18:4	19:1-10 (19:8)	19:11-12 (19:11)	20:1-6
Benjamin	1:1-6	2:1-5	3:1–8:3 (3:8)	9:1-3 (9:3-5)	10:1–11:5 (10:7, 8, 9)	12:1-4

a. Sleep as a Metaphor for Death

In the Testaments of the Twelve Patriarchs, most of the "death and burial" elements of the individual Testaments use "sleep" as a metaphor for death (*T. Sim.* 8:1; *T. Jud.* 26:4; *T. Iss.* 7:9; *T. Zeb.* 10:6; *T. Dan* 7:1; *T. Gad* 8:1; *T. Ash.* 8:1; *T. Jos.* 20:4). Two Greek terms for sleep appear in these passages, which are in the following list: κοιμάω (underlined text) and ὑπνόω/ὕπνος (bolded text). Based on the context, these two terms could be understood literally as a reference to natural sleep – or metaphorically as a reference to death. In these cases, they have all been used metaphorically.

Reference	Death and Burial using sleep as a metaphor for death
T. Sim. 8:1-2	He fell asleep (κοιμωμένην) with his fathers at the age of one hundred and twenty years. They placed him in a wooden coffin in order to carry his bones up to Hebron.
T. Jud. 26:4	Judah fell asleep (ἐκοιμήθη Ἰούδας) and his sons did everything as he had instructed them, and they buried him in Hebron with his fathers.
T. Iss. 7:9	And he stretched his legs and died at a good old age – the fifth son, with all his members sound and still strong; he slept the eternal sleep (ὕπνωσεν ὕπνον αἰώνιον).
T. Zeb. 10:6	When he had said this, he fell into a beautiful sleep (ἐκοιμήθη ὕπνῳ καλῷ), and his sons placed him in a coffin. Later they carried him up to Hebron and buried him with his fathers.
T. Dan 7:1	When he had said this, he kissed them and slept an eternal sleep (ὕπνωσεν ὕπνον αἰώνιον). And his sons buried him and later they carried his bones to be near Abraham, Isaac, and Jacob.
T. Gad 8:1	He drew up his feet and fell asleep in peace (ἐκοιμήθη ἐν εἰρήνῃ). And after five years they took him up and buried him in Hebron with his fathers.
T. Ash. 8:1	After he had said these things he gave instructions, saying, "Bury me in Hebron." And he died, having fallen into a beautiful sleep (ὕπνῳ καλῷ κοιμηθείς).
T. Jos. 20:4	And after he had said this he stretched out his feet and fell into a beautiful sleep (ἐκοιμήθη ὕπνον αἰώνιον). And all Israel and all Egypt mourned with great lamentation.

It should be noted that the term κοιμάω appears only in one other passage in the Testaments, and in that context it is used twice in its literal meaning, referring to Bilhah's drunken sleep which prevented her from waking up when Reuben raped her (*T. Reu.* 3:12, 13). The second term, ὑπνόω/ὕπνος, is defined by the author of *Testament of Reuben* as: "In addition to all these is an eighth spirit, [that] of sleep, through which is created the trance-like state [that occurs in] nature, as well as a likeness of death" (*T. Reu.* 3:1) and is "joined to deceit and imagination."[16] This is also the term used for Reuben's inability to sleep until he had performed the act of raping Bilhah (*T. Reu.* 3:12). Apart from these three passages in the *Testament of Reuben*, ὑπνόω/ὕπνος is used in five additional passages in its literal sense (*T. Sim.* 4:9 ×2; *T. Levi* 2:5 [trance-like state?]; *T. Jud.* 18:4; *T. Iss.* 3:5). It could be argued that, based on the usage of these two terms in the rape narrative, ὑπνόω/ὕπνος seems to also carry an "unconscious" aspect to this literal sleep, since Bilhah was unaware of what Reuben did to her, perhaps alluding to the unconscious state of death.

These two words allude to a resurrection hope since "sleep" suggests that death is not permanent – if a person sleeps it is assumed that he/she will wake up from said sleep at some point in the future. This figurative language is also used in Dan. 12:2 when describing death (καθεύδω)[17] and resurrection (ἀνίστημι), and is well attested in the New Testament, where the word κοιμάω is mostly used in its metaphorical sense for death.[18] It is interesting that the term ὑπνόω/ὕπνος is never used when referring to death in the New Testament[19] and only carries this meaning in three out of 21 passages in the LXX (Pss. 13:4; 76:5; Jer. 28:39). The allusion to the resurrection hope when using the metaphor of sleep becomes clear in the resurrection passage found in *T. Jud.* 25:4, which describes resurrection as waking up to life: "And those who died in sorrow shall be raised in joy; and those who died in poverty for the Lord's sake shall be made rich; those who died on account of the Lord shall be wakened to life" (καὶ οἱ διὰ Κύριον ἀποθανόντες ἐξυπνισθήσονται ἐν ζωῇ).[20]

---

16. Kugel, "*Testament of the Twelve Patriarchs*," 1709.

17. The New Testament also uses the word "sleep" literally (as a reference to regular sleep) and metaphorically (as a reference to death). It is used literally in: Mt. 8:24; 13:25; 25:5; 26:40, 43, 45; Mk 4:27, 38; 13:36; 14:37 (×2), 40, 41; Lk. 22:46; 1 Thess. 5:6, 7 (×2); and as a reference to death in: Mt. 9:24; Mk 5:39; Lk. 8:52; Eph. 5:14; 1 Thess. 5:10.

18. It is used for describing death in Mt. 27:52; Jn 11:11; Acts 7:60; 13:36; 1 Cor. 7:39; 11:30; 15:6, 18, 20, 51; 1 Thess. 4:13, 14, 15; 2 Pet. 3:4. The word has only been used in its literal sense in Mt. 28:13; Lk. 22:45; Jn 11:12; Acts 12:6.

19. It is used in four passages to describe natural sleep (Mt. 1:24; Lk. 9:32; Jn 11:13; Acts 20:9). A fifth passage uses the word metaphorically as waking up from "sleep" so they can be prepared for the Second Coming (Rom. 13:11).

20. The Greek text of the *Testaments of the Twelve Patriarchs* is from Ken Penner and Michael S. Heiser, *Old Testament Greek Pseudepigrapha with Morphology*

b. Clear Resurrection Hope

There are six clear resurrection passages in the Testaments of the Twelve Patriarchs (*T. Sim.* 6:7; *T. Levi* 18:14; *T. Jud.* 25; *T. Zeb.* 10:1-3; *T. Dan* 5:7-13; *T. Benj.* 10:4-10). However, unlike the apocalyptic books discussed in the companion volume, *Afterlife and Resurrection Beliefs in the Apocrypha and Apocalyptic Literature*, they reveal little with regard to what happens upon death or give a lot of details surrounding the eschatological resurrection.[21] These clear resurrection passages all appear in Testaments referring to the writings of Enoch as a source of eschatological knowledge (*T. Sim.* 5:4; *T. Levi* 10:5; 14:1; *T. Jud.* 18:1; *T. Zeb.* 3:4; *T. Dan* 3:4; *T. Benj.* 9:1), and all but two (*T. Levi* 18:14; *T. Dan* 5:7-13) use the Greek word ἀνίστημι, "cause to stand up," in the context of this resurrection hope (*T. Sim.* 6:7; *T. Jud.* 25:1; *T. Zeb.* 10:2; *T. Benj.* 10:6). As mentioned previously, all but one (*T. Benj.* 10:6-8, 11) of these resurrection passages appear in the apocalyptic section of the book (see Table 3). Only two of these resurrection passages do not contain any Christian interpolation (*T. Jud.* 25; *T. Zeb.* 10:1-7), although the extent of the Christian interpolations in the other passages (*T. Sim.* 6:7; *T. Levi* 10:14; *T. Dan* 5:11; *T. Benj.* 10:6-8, 11) are still being discussed by scholars. It should also be noted that all but one (*T. Dan* 5:7-13) of these resurrection passages emphasizes the resurrection of the patriarch (*T. Sim.* 6:7; *T. Zeb.* 10:2) or the patriarchs in general (*T. Levi* 18:13-14; *T. Jud.* 25; *T. Benj.* 10:6). These six resurrection passages can also be divided into two groups, the first describing a limited resurrection of only the patriarch and the righteous (*T. Sim.* 6:7; *T. Levi* 18:14; *T. Jud.* 25; *T. Zeb.* 10:1-3; *T. Dan* 5:7-13) while the second describes a universal resurrection of both the righteous and the wicked (*T. Benj.* 10:5-10).

(Bellingham, WA: Lexham, 2008). The word ἐξυπνίζω, "to cause to wake up," as the counterpoint to a natural sleep, or a vision, is used in *T. Levi* 8:18 and *T. Naph.* 1:3; and ἔξυπνος, "awaken," in *T. Levi* 5:7, again in the context of a vision.

21. The *Testament of Levi* reveals some details regarding the eschatological judgment, noting that when Levi was shown the three (or the seven in some textual traditions) heavens, he saw the lowest (or second) heaven which contains "the fire, snow, and ice, ready for the day determined by God's righteous judgment. In it are all the spirits of those dispatched to achieve the punishment of mankind" (*T. Levi* 3:1-2), implying an eschatological resurrection of the wicked souls who will be punished. The *Testament of Dan* reveals that Beliar keeps the souls of the Saints captive, but during the messianic age, they will be liberated, thus implying a resurrection of these righteous souls (*T. Dan* 5:11).

1. Limited Resurrection

The "limited resurrection" passages focus on the eschatological resurrection of the patriarch and the saints, while the destiny of the wicked is mostly ignored.

a. *Testament of Simeon* 6:7. In *Testament of Simeon*, the resurrection hope concludes the apocalyptic section (*T. Sim.* 5:4–6:7) which is based on what Simeon has "seen in a copy of the book of Enoch" (5:4). The resurrection follows a period of sexual promiscuity which will destroy the tribe (6:7), a rebellion against the leadership of the tribe of Levi and Judah which will not succeed (5:4-6), the glorification of Shem, the manifestation of God upon the earth [as a man][22] who will save Adam (6:5), and final destruction of the evil spirits (6:6). Simeon concludes his apocalyptic statement by affirming his strong conviction that he will resurrect in gladness after these tumultuous events and bless God for his marvelous work. A second Christian interpolation expands on this work by adding "because God has taken a body, eats with human beings, and saves human beings" (6:7c). It should be noted that the resurrection statement in the *Testament of Simeon* is limited to him personally and, as such, does not reveal the extent of it – if it will include other righteous dead or if it would also include the wicked dead.

b. *Testament of Levi* 18:14. In the *Testament of Levi*, Levi reveals to his sons what he has learned from the writings of Enoch regarding the end of time (14:1), more specifically what will take place during the seventy weeks (17:1), and the priesthood belonging to each of the jubilees during this time period.[23] He concludes his apocalyptic statement revealing the

---

22. This is most likely a Christian interpolation referring to Jesus' incarnation and death, which would bring salvation and undo the curse which entered this world through Adam's rebellion.

23. This might be an interpretation of the 70-week prophecy in Dan. 9:24-27. Based on the interpretation of this time period provided to Daniel by the angel, it becomes apparent that these 70 weeks describes a much longer time-period than a mere 1260 days or 3½ years, and that this 490-day period should rather be understood as a 490-year period (1 week = 7 years → 70 weeks × 7 years = 490 years). It is interesting that the *Testament of Levi* combines this 70-week period with the jubilee cycle, a different way of calculating time (one jubilee cycle is 49 years long). Thus, if understanding the 70-week period as 70 weeks of years (490 years), this time period would contain exactly ten jubilee cycles (10 cycles × 49 years = 490 years). The 70 weeks could also be a parallel to the 70 generations of *1 En.* 10:11-15 which also ends with the eschatological judgment and resurrection.

events that will take place during the messianic age, when "the Lord will raise up a new priest" (18:1) who will rule "from generation to generation forever" (18:8). During the reign of the Priestly Messiah, there will be peace on earth (18:4); "the knowledge of the Lord will be poured out on the earth like the water of the seas" (18:5); sin will cease (18:9); Messiah ben Levi will open the gates of Paradise and provide the people full access to the tree of life (18:10); Beliar will be bound (18:12a), while the wicked spirits will lose their powers (18:12b); and there will be an eschatological resurrection of the saints. Levi declares: "Then Abraham, Isaac, and Jacob will rejoice, and I shall be glad, and all the saints shall be clothed in righteousness" (18:14).

Compared with the resurrection statement in the *Testament of Simeon* 6:8, this passage includes Abraham, Isaac, and Jacob, together with all the saints, in the eschatological resurrection. This passage, however, does not discuss the final destiny of the wicked dead, suggesting a limited resurrection which would only include the righteous dead. If this passage is read in conjunction with *T. Levi* 3:1-2, this eschatological resurrection could also include the wicked souls who will be punished, thus describing a more universal resurrection.

c. *Testament of Judah* 25. In the apocalyptic section of *Testament of Judah* (*T. Jud.* 21–25), Judah reveals to his children that the kingship has been given to him but would be subjugated to the priesthood which was given to Levi (21:2-5). Judah also notes that in the book of Enoch, there will be a great apostasy which will bring an end to his rulership (18:1; 22:2). However, his descendants will repent and turn back to God, who will bring them back from captivity (23:5). Only after this will the eschatological king, the "Star from Jacob," the "Sun of Righteousness," the sinless king, "the Shoot of God," be established from Judah's posterity (24:1-2). This messianic king will "judge and save all that call on the Lord" (24:6). It is after this eschatological king has been firmly established by God that the resurrection will take place (25:1).

The resurrection described in this passage is also limited in its scope since it does not reveal the destiny of the wicked dead. In addition to Abraham, Isaac, Jacob, and the twelve patriarchs who will once more be chiefs among the people (*T. Jud.* 25:1), the resurrection will also include all those who died in sorrow, poverty, and "who died on account of the Lord shall be wakened to life," with joy and riches (25:4). The righteous will once more be one people and speak one language (25:3), a reversal of what took place at the Tower of Babel (Gen. 11:6-9) and a restoration of the pre-fallen condition of humanity. Beliar will be thrown into the eternal fire (*T. Jud.* 25:3), which will put an end to the spirit of error and "the impious shall mourn and sinners shall weep" (25:5). This eschatological resurrection brings in the great reversal: curses are undone, sorrow is turned into joy, poverty into riches, death into life, while the impious shall mourn and sinners shall weep.

d. *Testament of Zebulun* 10:1-3. The *Testament of Zebulun* also expresses a strong personal resurrection hope. The author of the testament concludes his apocalyptic statement (*T. Zeb.* 8:2–10:3) by alluding to the Messianic hope in Mal. 4:2 [MT 3:20], that the son of righteousness will rise with healing in his wings (*T. Zeb.* 9:8), following their repentance (9:7) after their great apostasy (9:5-6). However, Zebulun predicts a second apostasy which will last until "the time of the end" (9:9), when the eschatological resurrection will take place (10:2-3). He tells his children not to view his death as the end, since he will resurrect, and once more be a leader of his tribe – of those who "keep the Law of the Lord and the commandments of Zebulun" (10:2). The ungodly, according to Zebulun, will be destroyed by eternal fire for all generations (πῦρ αἰώνιον, καὶ ἀπολέσει αὐτοὺς ἕως γενεῶν, 10:3).

It is not clear from this passage if this eschatological resurrection will be universal. Zebulun believes strongly that he will resurrect, but does this resurrection include all the righteous dead? He also mentions the punishment of the wicked, but will this punishment include the wicked dead?

e. *Testament of Dan* 5:7-13. The apocalyptic section of the *Testament of Dan* also describes the future apostasy, captivity, and return to the Lord (*T. Dan* 5:5-9), which preceded the arrival of the Lord's salvation from the tribe of Judah and the tribe of Levi (5:10), who "will make war against Beliar" and win, thus liberating the souls of the saints which Beliar had held captive (5:11a), implying their resurrection. This messianic figure will also turn the hearts of the disobedient people towards the Lord (5:11b) and "grant eternal peace to those who call upon the Lord (5:11c). During this messianic era, the righteous will "refresh themselves in Eden" and "rejoice in the New Jerusalem" for all eternity (5:12), and the Lord will protect them by living among them (5:13c). This promised savior "will rule over them in humility and poverty" (5:13d), while those who trust him "shall reign in truth in heaven" (5:13e).

The eschatological resurrection mentioned in this text seems only to concern itself with the destiny of the righteous souls, mentioning that they will be liberated from Beliar's captivity. The destiny of the wicked dead, on the other hand, seems to be of no interest to the writer. Thus, the eschatological resurrection described in this passage seems to be limited to the righteous who will receive their everlasting reward, to dwell in the presence of the Lord.

2. *A Universal Resurrection*

The only universal resurrection passage appearing in the *Testaments of the Twelve Patriarchs* is *T. Benj.* 10:5-10. This passage is also unique as it does not appear in the apocalyptic section of the Testament, but rather in the second exhortation (*T. Benj.* 10:1–11:5).

a. *Testament of Benjamin* 10:4-10. The apocalyptic section of the *Testament of Benjamin* (*T. Benj.* 9) also reveals, based on the words of Enoch (9:1), that there will be a great period of apostasy (9:1-2), but God will bring the twelve tribes back from their exile to the rebuilt temple of God, where they will remain until God "sends forth his salvation through the ministration of the unique prophet" (9:2).[24]

In Benjamin's second exhortation to his children, he urges them to "keep God's commandments until the Lord reveals his salvation to all the nations" (*T. Benj.* 10:5) so they will be a part of the eschatological resurrection of the righteous: "And then you will see Enoch and Seth and Abraham and Isaac and Jacob being raised up at the right hand in great joy" (10:6) and "then shall we also be raised, each of us over our tribe, and we shall prostrate ourselves before the heavenly king" (10:6). Following this resurrection, everyone will be changed, "some destined for glory, others for dishonor" (10:8) as a result of the eschatological judgment (10:10).

This resurrection statement borrows the phraseology of Dan. 12:2 (highlighted below in gray) while making an interpretative change regarding the scope of this resurrection. In Dan. 12:2, "many" (πολλοί) will resurrect on that day, suggesting a limited resurrection. However, in the *Testament of Benjamin* "all" (πάντες) will resurrect, suggesting a universal resurrection. It should also be noted that the reward for the righteous

---

24. The coming of an eschatological prophet who will bring salvation to the people, is a unique element in Benjamin's apocalyptic speech. It is interesting to note that there are four central savior figures appearing in this Testament, they are: Messiah ben Joseph (*T. Benj.* 3:8); Messiah the prophet (9:2); Messiah ben Judah (11:2); and Messiah ben Levi (11:2). Each of these figures plays a significant role in God's plan. Messiah ben Joseph will suffer and die in order to bring salvation to the Gentiles and the people of Israel and bring destruction to Beliar and his servants (3:8). Messiah the Prophet will also bring salvation to the people. According to the Christian interpolation (9:3), Jesus will die, resurrect from Hades, and return to Heaven where he will be glorified. Lastly, the Testament also mentions Messiah ben Judah and Messiah ben Levi, who God will raise up "in later times" and who will also work towards the salvation of God's people (11:2-5).

has been changed from eternal life (ζωὴν αἰώνιον) to glory (δόξαν), while the punishment in store for the wicked has been shortened from shame (ὀνειδισμόν), dispersion (διασπορὰν), and everlasting contempt (αἰσχύνην αἰώνιον) to only shame/dishonor (ἀτιμίαν). The resurrection event in the *Testament of Benjamin* is clearly set in the context of the eschatological judgment (*T. Benj.* 10:8b-10), which is only implied in Dan. 12:1, when those who are written in the heavenly book will be saved (καὶ ἐν ἐκείνῃ τῇ ἡμέρᾳ ὑψωθήσεται πᾶς ὁ λαός ὃς ἂν εὑρεθῇ ἐγγεγραμμένος ἐν τῷ βιβλίῳ). Furthermore, both these resurrection statements follow a period of great tribulation (*T. Benj.* 9:1-2 || Dan. 12:1).

Testament of Benjamin 10:8	Daniel 12:2 (BGT and NETS)
τότε καὶ **πάντες** ἀναστήσονται,	καὶ **πολλοὶ** τῶν καθευδόντων ἐν τῷ πλάτει τῆς γῆς ἀναστήσονται
οἱ μὲν εἰς δόξαν,	οἱ μὲν εἰς ζωὴν αἰώνιον
οἱ δὲ εἰς ἀτιμίαν.	οἱ δὲ εἰς ὀνειδισμόν
	οἱ δὲ εἰς διασπορὰν καὶ αἰσχύνην αἰώνιον.
Καὶ κρινεῖ Κύριος ἐν πρώτοις τὸν Ἰσραήλ, [*περὶ τῆς εἰς αὐτὸν ἀδικίας, ὅτι παραγενόμενον Θεὸν ἐν σαρκὶ ἐλευθερωτὴν οὐκ ἐπίστευσαν*].[25]	
Then also **all men** will rise,	And **many of those** who sleep in the flat of the earth will arise,
some unto glory	some to everlasting life
and some unto shame.	but others to shame [reproach] and others to dispersion [and contempt] everlasting.
And the Lord will judge Israel first [*for the unrighteousness done to him, because they did not believe that God appeared in the flesh as a deliverer*].[26]	

The text in italics is a Christian interpolation stating that the people of Israel will be held responsible for their unrighteous acts toward God incarnated. Be that as it may, the eschatological judgment seems to have three phases: first, God will judge the people of Israel (*T. Benj.* 10:8b); second, God will judge the other nations (10:9); and third, God will "judge Israel

---

25. The Greek text is taken from Penner and Heiser, *Old Testament Greek Pseudepigrapha*, Logos edition, *T. Benj.* 10:8.
26. This translation is taken from, Hollander and De Jonge, *Testaments of the Twelve Patriarchs*, 437.

by the chosen gentiles as he tested Esau by the Midianites who loved their brothers" (10:10).

Benjamin concludes his eschatological resurrection and judgment statement with the wish that all his children will be counted among the righteous on that day as those who fear the Lord. He exhorts his children to "live in holiness, in accord with the Lord's commands." If they do, they will "again dwell with me [Benjamin] in hope; all Israel will be gathered to the Lord" (*T. Benj.* 10:10-11). This exhortation does not only summarize the message of the *Testament of Benjamin*, but it also summarizes the message of the whole *Testaments of the Twelve Patriarchs*.

3. Concluding Remarks

The *Testament of the Twelve Patriarchs* reveals little about the period between death and the resurrection, apart from the souls of the righteous being imprisoned by Belial (*T. Dan* 5:11) until the messianic age and that "the spirits of those dispatched to achieve the punishment of mankind" are kept in the lowest heaven (*T. Levi* 3:1-2), both passages implying an eschatological resurrection. These testaments also contain several allusions to the eschatological resurrection in eight of the "death and burial" sections of the book (*T. Sim.* 8:1-2; *T. Jud.* 26:4; *T. Iss.* 7:9; *T. Zeb.* 10:6; *T. Dan* 7:1; *T. Gad* 8:1; *T. Ash.* 8:1; *T. Jos.* 20:4). In these passages, the word "sleep" is used as a metaphor for death which implies that at one point in the future, they will be woken up from their sleep and regain life.

There are six clear resurrection passages in these testaments (*T. Sim.* 6:7; *T. Levi* 18:14; *T. Jud.* 25; *T. Zeb.* 10:1-3; *T. Dan* 5:7-13; *T. Benj.* 10:4-10), but only one, *T. Benj.* 10:4-10, describes an eschatological resurrection which will also be universal, borrowing phraseology from Dan. 12:2. The other five describe a limited resurrection of only the patriarch and the righteous.

2. Testament of Job

The *Testament of Job* was most likely written in Greek during the first century BCE, or perhaps as late as the second century CE, by a Hellenistic Jew living in Egypt.[27] Like the *Testament of the Twelve Patriarchs*,

27. Harold W. Attridge headings in his commentary on "Testament of Job," in Feldman, Kugel, and Schiffman, eds., *Outside the Bible*, 2:1872–3; Thomas S. Cason, "The Rhetoric of Disablement and Repair in the Testament of Job" (PhD diss., Florida State University, 2007), 9–17; John J. Collins, "Testament," in *Jewish Writings of the Second Temple Period: Apocrypha, Pseudepigrapha, Qumran Sectarian Writings, Philo, Josephus*, ed. Michael Stone, CRINT 2 (Assen: Van Gorcum; Philadelphia:

discussed in the previous section, the author uses the words of a dying biblical character as a vehicle for his/her ethical instructions, with some added apocalyptic and eschatological material.

Most scholars would note that the *Testament of Job* is a re-writing of the Masoretic version of the book of Job adding several elements from the Septuagint version of the book[28] and elements which parallel Rabbinic Midrash and Jewish legends (i.e., Dinah, Jacob's daughter is named as Job's second wife; Abraham's conversion journey and iconoclastic fervor).[29] It also contains a highly developed view of Satan (*T. Job* 6:1–27:7), shows a special interest in the female characters associated with Job (his two wives and three daughters), and contains apocalyptic and mystic elements (chs. 46–53).

Perhaps the two most important elements taken from the Septuagint are the resurrection belief and the persevering theme. The resurrection belief appears in several passages throughout the Testament, the clearest and most crucial statement being found in *T. Job* 4:9. If it is also implied in *T. Job* 33; 39:12; 41:4; 43; 47:11; 52–53. The following outline shows the literary structure of the *Testament of Job* and is based on Harold W. Attridge's commentary on this Testament.[30] The sections where the resurrection passages appear are bolded and highlighted in gray. The fourth literary division of the main body and the conclusion of the Testament have been shaded in gray to indicate that these last few chapters may be a later addition to the composition. If this is the case, then *T. Job* 45:1-4 may have served as the original conclusion of the Testament.[31]

Fortress, 1984), 353–4; Evans, *Ancient Texts for New Testament Studies*, 42; Russell P. Spittler, "Testament of Job," *OTP* 1:833–4; idem, "Testament of Job," *DNTB* 1190–1.

28. Some of these include: a further expansion of the speech of Job's wife which started in the LXX version of Job 2:9 (see *T. Job* 24:1-10 and 25:9-10); Job's name change from Jobab to Job; and revealing that both Job and his friends were kings. Spittler writes: "The Testament of Job draws mainly from the narrative framework of the Septuagint Book of Job, which appears at Job 1–2; 42:7-17. But in addition, Job 29–31 (LXX) furnished Testament of Job 9–16 with numerous concepts and phrases by which to amplify Job's wealth, piety, and generosity. At times, merely a phrase of the Septuagint language is worked into the Testament (seven thousand sheep: Job 1:3 LXX; *T. Job* 9:3). In a few instances, more complete Septuagint quotations appear" ("Testament of Job," 1:831).

29. Joel S. Allen, "Job 3: History of Interpretation," *DNTB* 363–4.

30. Attridge, "Testament of Job," 1874–98.

31. For the textual evidence for viewing *T. Job* 46–53 as a later addition and the function of this addition, see R. A. Kraft, *The Testament of Job According to the SV Text*, Pseudepigrapha Series 4 (Missoula, MT: Scholars Press, 1974), 58–69, and Spittler, "Testament of Job," *OTP* 1:834.

2. Testaments (Often with Apocalyptic Sections) 29

I. Prologue (1:1-7)
   - Title (1:1)
   - Setting (1:2-7)
II. Four Literary Divisions (2:1–50:3)
   1. Job and the Revealing Angel (2:1–5:3)
      - Job's perplexity over idolatry (2:1–3:7)
      - **The angel's discourse of impending calamities (4:1-11)**
      - Job's destruction of the idol's shrine (5:1-3)
   2. Job and Satan (6:1–27:7)
      - Satan's attack and Job's tragedy (6:1–8:3)
         - Satan disguised as a beggar (6:1-13)
         - Satan implores the Lord for power over Job (8:1-3)
      - Job's generosity and piety (9:1–15:9)
         - His philanthropy (9:1-8)
         - His hospitality (10:1-6)
         - His underwritten charities (11:1–12:3)
         - His fabulous wealth in cattle; the buttered mountains (13:1-6)
         - His musical prowess (14:1–15:9)
      - Job's losses (16:1–26:6)
         - His cattle (16:1-7)
         - His children (17:1–19:2)
         - His wife (21:1–26:6)
            - Sitis enslavement (21:1–22:2)
            - Sitis sells her hair to Satan (22:3–23:11)
            - The speech of Sitis: Begun (24:1-10)
            - A lament for Sitis (25:1-8)
            - The speech of Sitis: Concluded (25:9-10)
            - Job's response (26:1-6)
      - Job's triumph and Satan's defeat (27:1-7)
   3. Job and the Three Kings (28:1–45:4)
      - Job recognized and the kings astonished (28:1–30:3)
      - Eliphas: Laments Job's losses (31:1–34:5)
         - Eliphas confirms Job's identity (31:1-6)
         - A lament for Eliphas (31:7–32:12)
         - **Job's psalm of affirmation (33:1-9)**
         - Eliphas's rejoinder (34:1-5)
      - Baldad test Job's sanity (35:1–38:5)
      - Sophar: Offers the royal physicians (38:6-8)
      - **Sitis: Laments her children, dies, and is buried (39:1–40:14)**
      - Job's recovery and vindication (41:1–45:4)
         - **Elihu's insult (41:1-6)**
         - The kings forgiven through Job's intercession (42:1-8)
         - **A hymn against Elihu (43:1-17)**
         - Job's restoration (44:1-5)
         - Job's final counsels and division of the inheritance (45:1-4)

> 4. Job and His Three Daughters (46:1–50:3)
>   - The daughters' inheritance: Their father's phylactery (46:1–47:11)
>   - The charismatic sashes (48:1–50:3)
> III. Epilogue (51:1–53:8)
>   - Nereus's Literary Activity (51:1-4)
>   - Job's Death, Soul Ascent, and Burial (52:1–53:8)

This new resurrection element reframes the entire book of Job. The Hebrew version of the canonical book of Job explores the problem of theodicy, a concern barely voiced in the Testament,[32] placing God on trial in the proverbial courtroom. In this context, John Walton sees God as the accused and notes that it is his policies that are questioned by הַשָּׂטָן, *haSatan*, the accuser.[33] Job, however, just happens to serve as "exhibit-A" for the defense team.[34] In the *Testament of Job*, the resurrection belief solves the problem of theodicy, thus the focus has shifted to Job's perseverance and victory against Satan's revenge attack after Job destroyed one of his shrines (*T. Job* 4:4; 5:1-3). Job had been forewarned about the coming suffering if he proceeded with his plans (*T. Job* 4:1-11) and the ultimate reward if he persevered, turning the Hebrew Job from a passive sufferer into a Job who, in Collins words, "understands and accepts his suffering," a Job who willingly enters into a conflict with Satan.[35]

---

32. The problem of theodicy is only briefly mentioned in Job's response to his friend Baldad (*T. Job* 37:5-7), when Baldad is attempting to test Job's sanity (*T. Job* 35:1–38:5).

33. It is important to note that הַשָּׂטָן, *haSatan*, is not a proper noun since it has a definite article, instead it describes the function of the person or the office of the accuser or persecutor. Over time, this title became a proper noun/name for a specific individual, Satan, the archenemy of God.

34. John H. Walton, "Job 1: Book of," *DNTB* 340–2. Walton notes that there are three positions held in this court drama: (1) God is just – argued by Elihu; (2) Job is righteous – stated in the prologue and claimed by Job himself; and (3) the retribution principle (God rewards the righteous and punishes the wicked) – defended by Job's three friends. These three positions are mutually exclusive. The two questions under consideration are: (1) Is a person righteous because of the blessings God bestows on them or are they righteous regardless of their lot in life? – the question raised by the accuser and answered by Job's loyalty to God; and (2) Why do righteous people suffer? – the question Job asks God but is never answered in the book. However, God asks Job to trust his wisdom, since he is the only person who sees the full picture, and thus, knows the best way to rule.

35. Collins, "Testaments," 349.

The perseverance theme was already introduced in the LXX version of the book of Job, as Allen writes: "In the opinion of the majority of scholars the Greek translator of Job rendered the text into a Greek version [LXX] that transformed the Job of the poetic sections [in the Hebrew version] from bombastic doubter into pious and persevering sufferer."[36] However, in this Testament, it is explored even further.

a. *Testament of Job* 4:4-11

The clearest resurrection statement in the *Testament of Job* appears in the angel's discourse of impending calamities (*T. Job* 4:1-11) before Job's destruction of the idol's shrine (5:1-3). In this discourse, Job is warned about the consequences of his planned actions – that Satan will be enraged and take his vengeance upon Job by sending many plagues, in addition to depriving Job of his wealth and children (4:4a-5). However, he is also told that if he is patient and perseveres against Satan's attack, he will receive a great reward in the end. If Job is victorious, his name will be renowned throughout the world until "the consummation of the ages," his wealth will be doubled, and he will be raised up in the eschatological resurrection (4:6-9).

In this key passage, Job is compared to an athlete who will have to suffer great pain to become victorious and win the crown (*T. Job* 4:10). This is the same imagery used or alluded to in the New Testament (1 Cor. 9:24-26; Gal. 2:2; 5:7; Phil. 2:16; 2 Tim. 2:5; 4:7; Heb. 12:1) when encouraging the followers of Christ to walk on the straight path in order to gain the ultimate reward, which will never fade. Thus, Job is told that there is a reward in store for him both in the near (after 48 years on the dung heap [*T. Job* 21:1] he was healed and had his possessions doubled) and in the distant future (resurrection and heavenly kingship [*T. Job* 31]), as long as he would persevere in his suffering. This promised reward, when Job "wins the crown" of victory at the end of "the race," will demonstrate that the Lord is indeed just, true, and strong, helping his elect to persevere and that he is impartial since he renders "good things to each one who obeys" (*T. Job* 4:7-8, 11).

---

36. Allen, "Job 3," 362. The perseverance theme is also the focus of the only reference to Job in the New Testament: "You have heard of Job's endurance and have seen the outcome from the Lord. The Lord is very compassionate and merciful" (Jas 5:11, CSB).

Testament of Job 4:4-11

⁴Ἐὰν ἐπιχειρήσεις καθαρίσαι τὸν τόπον τοῦ Σατανᾶ, ἐπαναστήσεταί σοι μετὰ ὀργῆς εἰς πόλεμον· μόνον ὅτι τὸν θάνατόν σοι οὐ δυνήσεται ἐπενεγκεῖν· ἐπιφέρει δέ σοι πληγὰς πολλάς· ⁵ἀφαιρεῖται σου τὰ ὑπάρχοντα· τὰ παιδία σου ἀναιρήσει. ⁶ἀλλ' ἐὰν ὑπομείνῃς, ποιήσω σου τὸ ὄνομα ὀνομαστὸν ἐν πάσαις ταῖς γενεαῖς τῆς γῆς ἄχρι τῆς συντελείας τοῦ αἰῶνος· ⁷<u>καὶ πάλιν ἀνακάμψω σε ἐπὶ τὰ ὑπάρχοντά σου, καὶ ἀποδοθήσεταί σοι διπλάσιον</u>· ⁸<u>ἵνα γνῶς ὅτι ἀπροσωπόληπτός ἐστιν, ἀποδιδοὺς ἑκάστῳ τῷ ὑπακούοντι ἀγαθά</u>· ⁹**καὶ ἐγερθήσῃ ἐν τῇ ἀναστάσει**. ¹⁰ἔσῃ γὰρ ὡς ἀθλητὴς πυκτεύων καὶ καρτερῶν πόνους καὶ ἐκδεχόμενος τὸν στέφανον· ¹¹<u>τότε γνώσει ὅτι δίκαιος καὶ ἀληθινὸς καὶ ἰσχυρὸς ὁ κύριος, ἐνισχύων τοὺς ἐκλεκτοὺς αὐτοῦ</u>.[37]

Job 42:17 (BGT/LXE)

καὶ ἐτελεύτησεν Ιωβ πρεσβύτερος καὶ πλήρης ἡμερῶν [1] **γέγραπται δὲ αὐτὸν πάλιν ἀναστήσεσθαι μεθ' ὧν ὁ κύριος ἀνίστησιν** [2] οὗτος ἑρμηνεύεται ἐκ τῆς Συριακῆς βίβλου ἐν μὲν γῇ κατοικῶν τῇ Αυσίτιδι ἐπὶ τοῖς ὁρίοις τῆς Ιδουμαίας καὶ 'Αραβίας προϋπῆρχεν δὲ αὐτῷ ὄνομα **Ιωβαβ** [3] λαβὼν δὲ <u>γυναῖκα 'Αράβισσαν</u> γεννᾷ υἱόν ᾧ ὄνομα Εννων ἦν δὲ αὐτὸς πατρὸς μὲν Ζαρε **τῶν Ησαυ** υἱῶν υἱός μητρὸς δὲ Βοσορρας ὥστε εἶναι αὐτὸν πέμπτον ἀπὸ Αβρααμ [4] καὶ οὗτοι οἱ βασιλεῖς **οἱ βασιλεύσαντες ἐν Εδωμ** ἧς καὶ αὐτὸς ἦρξεν χώρας πρῶτος Βαλακ ὁ τοῦ Βεωρ καὶ ὄνομα τῇ πόλει αὐτοῦ Δενναβα μετὰ δὲ Βαλακ Ιωβαβ ὁ καλούμενος Ιωβ μετὰ δὲ τοῦτον Ασομ ὁ ὑπάρχων ἡγεμὼν ἐκ τῆς Θαιμανίτιδος χώρας μετὰ δὲ τοῦτον Αδαδ υἱὸς Βαραδ ὁ ἐκκόψας Μαδιαμ ἐν τῷ πεδίῳ Μωαβ καὶ ὄνομα τῇ πόλει αὐτοῦ Γεθθαιμ [5] οἱ δὲ ἐλθόντες πρὸς αὐτὸν φίλοι Ελιφας τῶν Ησαυ υἱῶν Θαιμανων **βασιλεύς** Βαλδαδ ὁ Σαυχαίων τύραννος, Σωφαρ ὁ Μιναίων **βασιλεύς**.

⁴If you attempt to purge the place of Satan, death upon you. He will bring on you many plagues, ⁵he will take away for himself your goods, he will carry off your children. ⁶But if you are patient, I will make your name renowned in all generations of the earth till the consummation of the age. ⁷<u>And I will return you again to your goods. It will be repaid to you doubly,</u> ⁸<u>so you may know that the LORD is impartial – rendering good things to each on who obeys.</u>

¹⁷And Job died, an old man and full of days: [1] **and it is written that he will rise again with those whom the Lord raises up.** [2] This man is described in the Syriac book *as* living in the land of Ausis, on the borders of Idumea and Arabia: and his name before was **Jobab**; [3] and having taken an <u>Arabian wife</u>, he begot a son whose name was Ennon. And he himself was the son of his father Zare, **one of the sons of Esau**, and of his mother Bosorrha, so that he was the fifth from Abraam.

---

37. Penner and Heiser, *Old Testament Greek Pseudepigrapha with Morphology*, Logos edition, *T. Job* 4:4-11.

⁹**And you shall be raised up in the resurrection**. ¹⁰For you will be like a sparring athlete, both enduring pains and winning the crown. ¹¹<u>Then will you know that the LORD is just, true, and strong, giving strength to his elect ones</u>."³⁸	[4] And these were **the kings who reigned in Edom**, which country he also ruled over: first, Balac, the son of Beor, and the name of his city was Dennaba: but after Balac, Jobab, who is called Job, and after him Asom, who was governor out of the country of Thaeman: and after him Adad, the son of Barad, who destroyed Madiam in the plain of Moab; and the name of his city was Gethaim. [5] And *his* friends who came to him were Eliphaz, of the children of Esau, **king** of the Thaemanites, Baldad son of the Sauchaeans, Sophar **king** of the Minaeans.

In the Septuagint, the resurrection promise is mentioned almost as an afterthought as a part of the conclusion (Job 42:17 [1]), which also states Job's original name, Jobab (Job 42:17 [2]), biographical material (Job 42:17 [3]-[4]), and additional information regarding his friends (Job 42:17 [5]), all these elements are integrated into the *Testament of Job* (*T. Job* 4:4-11). In contrast, the promise appears in the framing of the story in the *Testament of Job*, and the promise is alluded to in key places throughout the narrative. Although *T. Job* 4:9 reveals little regarding the nature of this resurrection, it is clear from the context that it is a part of the promised reward held in store for Job and the use of the definite article, ἐν τῇ ἀναστάσει, "in the resurrection," suggests that this resurrection is a specific event still in the future.

b. Allusions to the Resurrection

The first allusion to the resurrection appears in "Job's psalm of affirmation" (*T. Job* 33:1-9), following Eliphas' lament over Job's great losses (31:7–32:12). In Job's response, he tells his friends not to judge him based on his earthly situation. Although he has lost his earthly wealth and power, Job claims his throne is in heaven, in the upper world (33:3a), among the holy ones (33:2), receiving its "splendor and majesty" from the right hand of the father (33:3b).³⁹ According to Job, his throne and kingdom

---

38. Translation is taken from Attridge, "*Testament of* Job," 1876.

39. Job's words are similar to the response Jesus gave to Pilate when Pilate asked him if he was the King of the Jews: "'*My kingdom is not of this world*,' said Jesus.

will last forever since it is in "the world of the changeless one" (33:5-9).[40] These words regarding Job's heavenly throne demonstrates his strong resurrection hope, and that his focus had shifted from earthly matters toward the heavenly reward, to the upper world, a world which will have no end.[41]

The second allusion to the resurrection follows Sitis' lament over her dead children, in which she begs Job's royal friends to give her ten dead children a proper burial since they are still buried in the ruins after all these years (*T. Job* 39:4-11). Job's friends are more than happy to oblige, but Job forbade them, telling them that they would not be able to find the bodies of his children since "they were taken up into heaven by the Creator their King" (39:11), suggesting a bodily resurrection, although not an eschatological one.[42] Not unexpectedly, Job's friends did not believe him, and one could also wonder how his wife Sitis reacted to Job's words, if this was the first time he had revealed their children's destiny to her or if she had not believed him earlier. Be that as it may, after Job had prayed to the heavenly Father, he asked them to "look up with your eyes to the east and see my children crowned with the splendor of the heavenly one" (40:1). When his wife saw her resurrected children she worshiped God and said, "Now I know that I have a memorial with the Lord. So I shall

---

'If My kingdom were of this world, My servants would fight, so that I wouldn't be handed over to the Jews. As it is, *My kingdom does not have its origin here*'" (Jn 18:36, CSB – my emphasis).

40. Eliphas found Job's words enraging (*T. Job* 34:1) and later, Elihu, "inspired by Satan' (41:5), took issue with these words, which he viewed as "boastful grandeur" (41:4). Elihu's insulting words against Job, not recorded in the Testament, were deemed unforgivable. As a consequence, Elihu would suffer the destiny kept in store for the wicked (42:1-2; 43:4-13).

41. This change of focus is also seen in Job's response to Baldad, when his friend is testing his sanity by asking Job if his heart was untroubled: "My heart is not fixed on earthly concerns, since the earth and those who dwell in it are unstable. But my heart is fixed on heavenly concerns, for there is not upset in heaven" (*T. Job* 36:3).

42. There are a few biblical characters who were taken to heaven at the end of their earthly life or following closely after their death. Genesis 5:24 records that Enoch did not die but was taken by God, suggesting that he was brought to heaven (an interpretation suggested by Heb. 11:5 and later by *3 En.* 6:2). According to ancient traditions, Moses was taken to heaven following his death (alluded to in Jude 1:9 and suggested by Josephus in *Ant.* 4.326), based on an interpretation of the comment that Moses' burial place was unknown (Deut. 34:5-6). 2 Kings 2:1 records Elijah's heavenly journey with a horse of fire, at the end of his life (2 Kgs 2:1, 11). It is interesting that the latter two characters, Elijah and Moses, appear with Jesus on the Mountain of Transfiguration (Mt. 17:3-4), lending further support to this tradition.

arise and return to the city and nap awhile and then refresh myself before the duties of my servitude" (40:4). With this newfound resurrection hope, Job's wife died in good spirit that very night (40:6).

The third allusion to the resurrection belief appears in the hymn against Elihu (*T. Job* 43:1-17), which concerns the destiny of the righteous and the wicked. God is righteous, and his judgment is true, and he will judge everyone together (κρινεῖ ἡμᾶς ὁμοθυμαδόν) without showing favoritism (43:13), a possible allusion to the eschatological judgment which would require an eschatological resurrection. The first half of the hymn concerns those, like Elihu, whose sins are not forgiven by God. They will have "no memorial among the living" (43:5) – instead, "the honor of his tent lies in Hades" (43:7). He will be forgotten by the Lord and abandoned by the holy ones (43:10), "wrath and anger shall be his tent," and he will have no hope or peace (43:11). The righteous, on the other hand, represented by Job's three friends, Eliphas, Baldad, and Sophar, will receive the splendor they awaited (43:16) since their sins are gone and their lawlessness cleansed (43:17).

The last allusion to the resurrection belief is found in the conclusion of the Testament (*T. Job* 46:1–53:8), which has a strong emphasis on the better world, the future life in heaven (47:2; 48:2; 49:1; 50:2). In this final section of the Testament, Job reveals to his three daughters that "the creatures [angels?] of God" are about to come for his soul (47:11), which takes place three days later when a gleaming chariot arrives and then, journeying east, takes his soul back to heaven (52:6).[43] Job's body, however, was left behind and was prepared for proper burial in a tomb (52:11; 53:5). Three days later, "they laid him in the tomb in a beautiful sleep (53:7).

c. Concluding Remarks

The separation of body and soul upon Job's death (*T. Job* 52:10) is different from the view presented earlier in the Testament, where Job stated the bodies of his dead children would not be found among the ruins since they had already been taken to heaven by their Creator (*T. Job* 39:11). There could be two explanations for this important difference; first, the concluding chapters could be a later addition to the Testament (see the outline of the book) and the author of this addition held a different

---

43. Like Enoch and Elijah, Job was also taken to heaven in a chariot when he was about to die. However, unlike Enoch and Elijah, the heavenly rider only came for Job's soul, leaving his body for an earthly burial, where it would rest, perhaps in wait for the day of resurrection when the soul and body may once more be unified.

death and resurrection view than the author of the preceding chapters; second, these two views could be harmonized in the sense that the death of Job and the death of his children represent two different death scenarios. Job's case could be the type of death most people would experience, where there will be an eschatological resurrection, while the death of his children represents more of a unique situation in which a person is resurrected not long after their death and are brought to heaven, similar to the case of Moses.

Based on the clear resurrection statement which seems to derive from the concluding remarks from the Septuagint version of the book of Job (Job 42:17 [1]), and the several allusions to this hope found in the *Testament of Job*, it is still not clear whether there will be a universal eschatological resurrection of both the righteous and the wicked dead, although there are hints in the text to support such a view. However, there is little doubt that the righteous can rest in the hope of a coming resurrection which would bring them great heavenly reward while the wicked will dwell in Hades. On the other hand, whether the soul will be separated from the body until the day of the resurrection (as with Job), or whether body and soul go directly to heaven upon death (like in the case of Job's children), is still open for scholarly discussion, as is the question of whether these two views could be harmonized.

3. *Testament of Abraham*

The *Testament of Abraham* was most likely written during the first or the second century CE by a Hellenistic Jewish author in Egypt.[44] Ed P. Sanders notes that this testament was probably a part of a larger work which together with the *Testament of Isaac* and the *Testament of Jacob*, would have formed the *Testament of the Three Patriarchs*.[45] Even so, the *Testament of Abraham* exists in two manuscript traditions, the longer manuscript tradition being referred to as Recension A and the shorter as Recension B. Both traditions probably derive from a common source which is believed to have been closer to the longer manuscript tradition.[46] Although the title of this literary work suggests that it falls within the testament genre, it is very different from the *Testament of the Twelve Patriarchs* and the *Testament of Job*, as discussed earlier. John Collins writes: "it is now well-known that the *Testament of Abraham* is not a

---

44. Annette Yoshiko Reed, "Testament of Abraham," in Feldman, Kugel, and Schiffman, eds., *Outside the Bible*, 1:1671.
45. Ed P. Sanders, "Testament of the Three Patriarchs," *OTP* 1:869.
46. Jonathan M. Knight, "Testament of Abraham," *DNTB* 1188.

testament at all, since it contains no farewell discourse by Abraham"; instead, he argues that the testament could be "viewed either as a narrative or as an apocalypse, but it is clearly not a testament."[47]

In the *Testament of Abraham*, the archangel Michael is sent by God to inform Abraham that he is "about to leave this vain world and depart from the body," and Abraham's soul will come to dwell with God (*T. Abr.* A1:7). However, before Abraham is willing to give up his soul and leave this world, he requests to see "all the inhabited world and all the created things" which God had established (*T. Abr.* A9:6; cf. B7:8). Upon seeing the evil on earth, Abraham demands the destruction of the sinners (A10:6, 9, 11; cf. B12:3, 7, 10), which causes God to put an end to Abraham's tour since God fears that if Abraham "were to see all those who pass their lives in sin, he would destroy everything that exists" (A10:13; cf. B12:12). This lack of mercy on sinners by Abraham causes God so much concern that Abraham is brought to the first gate of heaven, "so that he may see the judgments and the recompenses and repent over the souls of the sinners which he destroyed" (A10:15).[48]

Michael reveals to Abraham that each person will experience three tribunals (*T. Abr.* A13:8). The first judgment (A11:1–13:5) is an individual judgment which takes place upon a person's death, when the soul parts the body and is brought to the first gate of heaven. Abel determines, based on the record, which gate they should enter – the Strait Gate is for the righteous and leads to life in Paradise (A11:10) while the Broad Gate is intended for the wicked and "leads to the destruction and eternal punishment (A11:11). The second judgment is the universal

---

47. Collins, "Testament," 326. For further reading, see Anitra Bingham Kolenkow, "The Genre Testament and the *Testament of Abraham*," in *Studies on the Testament of Abraham*, ed. George W. E. Nickelsburg (Missoula, MT: Scholars Press, 1976), 139–62.

48. Although both recensions of this Testament (A and B) have the same overarching narrative structure (a bipartite structure), the earthly journey and the journey to the place of judgment have been reversed in Recension B, which affects the role and purpose of these two narrative elements. In Recension B, the judgment scene no longer functions as a corrective element to change Abraham's attitude towards sinners and make him into a more compassionate person, more like God, who "delay the death of the sinners until he should convert and live" (*T. Abr.* A10:14; cf. B12:13). Instead, the Abraham of Recension B seems to be unchanged by witnessing the judgment; thus, upon seeing sinful behavior on the preceding earthly journey, he demands the destruction of the wicked (*T. Abr.* B 12:1-12). For the structure of the *Testament of Abraham*, see George W. E. Nickelsburg, "Structure and Message in the Testament of Abraham," in Nickelsburg, ed., *Studies on the Testament of Abraham*, 85–93.

eschatological judgment in which everyone will be "judged by the twelve tribes of Israel" (A13:6). The third and final judgment is given by God himself (A13:7).[49] These three judgments will ensure that the matter of God's justice is ultimately settled, following the directions of Deut. 19:15, which requires three witnesses to give a sentence in a criminal matter. The Targum adds that the Word of the Lord is also required since only he knows the crimes committed in secrecy.

T. Abr. A13:8	Deut. 19:15 - BGT/LXT	Deut. 19:15 - PJT/PJE
καὶ διὰ τοῦτο ἐπὶ ἑνὸς ἢ δύο μαρτύρων οὐκ ἀσφαλίζεται λόγος εἰς τέλος· ἀλλ' ἐπὶ <u>τριῶν μαρτύρων σταθήσεται πᾶν ῥῆμα</u>.	οὐκ ἐμμενεῖ μάρτυς εἷς μαρτυρῆσαι κατὰ ἀνθρώπου κατὰ πᾶσαν ἀδικίαν καὶ κατὰ πᾶν ἁμάρτημα καὶ κατὰ πᾶσαν ἁμαρτίαν ἣν ἂν ἁμάρτῃ ἐπὶ στόματος δύο μαρτύρων καὶ ἐπὶ στόματος <u>τριῶν μαρτύρων σταθήσεται πᾶν ῥῆμα</u>	לא יתקיים סהדן דחד בגבר לכל סורחן נפש ולכל חוב ממון ולכל חטא דיחפי **ברם על מימרא דייי הוא למתפרפא על טומריא** על מימר סהיד חד יומי למיכפור ית מה דמסהיד עלוי ועל מימר תרין סהדין או תלתא סהדין יתקיים פיתגמא:
And therefore a matter is not ultimately established by one or two witnesses, but every matter <u>shall be established by three witnesses</u>.	One witness shall not stand to testify against a man for any iniquity, or for any fault, or for any sin which he may commit; by the mouth of two witnesses, or by the mouth of <u>three witnesses, shall every word be established</u>.	The testimony of one (witness) shall not be valid against a man for any crime (regarding the taking) of life, or guilt concerning money, or any sin with which one may be charged with sinning; ***but, by the Word of the Lord, (to ensure) retribution upon secret crimes***, (while) one witness may swear to deny what hath been attested against him, the sentence shall be confirmed upon the mouth of two witnesses, or of three.

---

49. For further reading regarding the judgment scene in the *Testament of Abraham*, see George W. E. Nickelsburg, "Eschatology in the Testament of Abraham: A Study of the Judgment Scene in the Two Recensions," in Nickelsburg, ed., *Studies on the Testament of Abraham*, 23–64.

Abraham also learns that there are some souls who are found neither righteous nor wicked and would have needed one more righteous deed than sin to have been saved (*T. Abr.* A14:4; cf. SrB9:8). These souls will be kept in limbo until the second coming, unless someone does supplications and offers prayers on their behalf (A14:6). The Testament ends with the death of Abraham, when he is tricked by death to give up his soul (A20:9), and Michael and the other angels "bore his precious soul in their hands in divinely woven linen" (A20:10), while his body was prepared for funeral and was buried three days later (A20:11).

There are only two clear resurrection passages in this testament. The first case is a temporary resurrection (*T. Abr.* A18:9-11; B14:6), which regards the resurrection of Abraham's servants who died from the shock of seeing the true nature of death (A18:3, 6; B14:5). The second case only appears in Recension B and describes the universal resurrection which will take place in the eschatological future:

Testament of Abraham B7:15b-16

¹⁵ᵇ καὶ <u>ἀναλαμβανέσαι εἰς τοὺς οὐρανοὺς</u>,¹⁶ τὸ δὲ <u>σῶμά σου μένει ἐπὶ τῆς γῆς</u> ἕως ἂν πληρωθῶσιν ἑπτακισχίλιοι αἰῶνες· **τότε γὰρ ἐγερθήσεται π σα σάρξ.**	¹⁵ᵇ and <u>you will be taken up into the heaven</u>. ¹⁶ while <u>your body remains on the earth</u> until seven thousand ages are fulfilled. **For then all flesh will be raised.**

According to this text, the soul gets separated from the body upon death. From the chapters that follow, Abraham learns that the soul will then proceed directly to the place of judgment where it will be led through one of two gates, either for punishment or reward, paralleling the first judgment in Recension A (*T. Abr.* A11:1–13:5). However, unlike Recension A, this textual tradition does not mention the additional two judgments which are both eschatological and universal. The body, on the other hand, remains on the earth (μένει ἐπὶ τῆς γῆς), in the grave, until it will be resurrected at the end of the seven thousand ages in a universal judgment of both the righteous and the wicked. At this point, it could be assumed that the soul will once more unite with the body, in order to reverse the process of dying, when the soul left the body. Although Recension B does not mention the two eschatological and universal judgments, and this could be a point of divergence between these two traditions, it would not be difficult to speculate that the second and third judgment, which are both universal, would take place following this universal resurrection. However tempting it is to harmonize the recensions, one element they do have in common is the ambiguity regarding what happens to the soul between the first judgment and the eschatological events, the two universal judgments (Recensions A), the bodily resurrection (Recension B), or a combination of the two (harmonized view). Do the souls receive the described reward or punishment upon the completion of the first judgment or are the souls only shown the reward or punishment held in store for them in the eschatological time? If the former, will the souls receive additional reward or punishment in the eschatological time? If the latter, what will be the condition of the righteous and the wicked souls while waiting for that eschatological time? From this, it seems the main concern of the *Testament of Abraham* is the importance of the judgment scene, that the judgment follows a set procedure, that everyone will be judged by the same standard, whether the person is a Jew or Gentile, and that God is full of mercy but at the same time he is also ultimately just. This justice is beyond reproach. This message is in line with the canonical wisdom literature. Figure 1 illustrates the resurrection concept in the *Testament of Abraham*.

Figure 1. Death and Resurrection in the *Testament of Abraham*

		Life	Death T. Abr. A11:1-13:5		Second Coming (Resurrection)[c] Judgment 2:[d] Universal by 12 Tribes of Israel T. Abr. A13:6	Judgment 3:[e] Universal by God T. Abr. A13:7	Eternity T. Abr. A11:10-12
			Phase 1: Judgment 1[a] Individual by Abel	Phase 2:[b] Waiting Area			
Paradise (Straight Gate)				Righteous Soul			T. Abr. A11:10
Limbo			T. Abr. A11:10	Neutral Soul	T. Abr. A14:16		
Destruction (Broad Gate)				Wicked Soul			T. Abr. A11:11-12 B11:9-10
1st Gate of Heaven			Soul	T. Abr. A11:11			
World		Body Soul	T. Abr. B7:15-16		Body Soul	Body Soul	
Grave			Body		T. Abr. B7:15-16		

ᵃ The first of three judgments (*T. Abr.* A13:8) is an individual judgment which takes place upon a person's death, when the soul parts from the body and is brought to the first gate of heaven. Based on the records of a person's life, Abel determines which gate the soul should enter. The body, on the other hand, is buried in the grave.

ᵇ Based on the first judgment, the righteous are led to the straight gate to a life in Paradise. The wicked are led to the broad gate which "leads to the destruction and eternal punishment" (*T. Abr.* A11:11). However, there are some souls who are found neither righteous nor wicked and would have needed one more righteous deed than sin to have received their reward (*T. Abr.* A14:4). These souls will be kept in limbo until the second coming, unless someone offers supplications and prayers on their behalf (*T. Abr.* A14:6), thus enabling them to move to the place of the righteous. It is not clear from this testament if the described reward or punishment for the soul will be experienced immediately following the judgment or if it should be understood as the soul's future fate which will become a reality following the third judgment in the eschatological age.

ᶜ A bodily resurrection is only specifically mentioned in Recension B of the testament, although it is implied in Recension A. This resurrection will take place at the end of the seven thousand ages, when the soul will once more unite with the body (*T. Abr.* B7:15b-16). Although the resurrection of Recension B would easily be harmonized with Recension A as it would fit between Judgment 1 and the following two judgments. If this eschatological resurrection is indeed a unique element in Recension B, there seems to be little reason for the soul to be reunified with the body prior to the eschatological and universal second judgment which will be presided over by the twelve tribes of Israel.

ᵈ The third and final judgment is given by God himself (*T. Abr.* A13:7). This will ensure that the matter of God's justice is ultimately settled, as the three-part judgment process follows the direction of Deut. 19:15, which requires three witnesses to give a sentence in a criminal matter. Based on these three judgments, a person receives access to Paradise or their punishment (*T. Abr.* A11:9-12).

~ ~ ~

4. *Testament of Moses*

The *Testament of Moses*, also known as the *Assumption of Moses*, was most likely written by a Jewish author living in Levant "during the 1ˢᵗ century BCE and later updated or composed during the 1ˢᵗ century CE."[50] While

---

50. Kenneth Atkinson, "*Testament of Moses*," in Feldman, Kugel, and Schiffman, eds., *Outside the Bible*, 2:1856. For a concise discussion on the dating and setting of this testament, see David A. deSilva, "Testament of Moses," *DNTB* 1193–5. See also Nickelsburg's discussion, "Excursus A: The Date and Provenance of the Testament of Moses," in his *Resurrection, Immortality, and Eternal Life in Intertestamental Judaism and Early Christianity*, HTS 56 (Cambridge, MA: Harvard University Press, 2006), 61–4.

it was probably composed in Hebrew or Aramaic, it has only survived in a badly damaged manuscript in Latin, dated to the sixth century CE. It is estimated that only half or two-thirds of the composition has survived to the present day. Thus, the concluding section of the Testament is missing.[51]

Nickelsburg notes this testament is a "rewriting of Deuteronomy 31–34," and follows closely the historical scheme outlined in Moses' final words to the twelve tribes as demonstrated by the following outline:[52]

Theme	*Deuteronomy*	*Testament of Moses*	
Sin	28:15	2:1-9	5:1-6
Punishment	28:16-68	3:1-4	8:1-5
Repentance	30:2	3:5–4:4	9:1-7
Salvation	30:3-10	4:5-8	10:1-15

Moses' prophetic deathbed words to Joshua is a great example of *ex eventu* prophecy. John Priest observes: "Deuteronomy 31–34 is clearly the author's model, though he has recast his own work in light of the history of the people from the conquest to his own day and through the prism of his own apocalyptic outlook."[53] Interestingly, the author of the testament, in the process of recasting Moses' prophecy, gave Deuteronomy 32–33 an eschatological reading by providing his own speculation of the events which will take place leading up to the eschatological judgment (*T. Mos.* 10), when God will finally "avenge the blood of His servants, and render vengeance to His adversaries" and "provide atonement for His land and His people" (Deut. 32:43, NKJV). This is due to the great covenant loyalty demonstrated by Taxo, the Levite, and his seven sons' suggested martyrdom (*T. Mos.* 9:6-7).[54] This eschatological reading of Moses' final words, however, should not come as a surprise since his words are

---

51. deSilva, "Testament of Moses," 1192. He also notes that it has been specuelated that Jude may have been aware of this Testament when referring to Michael and the devil's battle over Moses' body (Jude 9), assuming the assumption of Moses was a part of the now-lost conclusion of the testament (see the discussion under the subheading "Echoes in the New Testament and Other Early Christian Literature," in "Testament of Moses," 1198; see also, John Priest, "Testament of Moses," *OTP* 1:924–5).

52. Nickelsburg, *Resurrection, Immortality, and Eternal Life*, 43–4.

53. Priest, *"Testament of Moses,"* 1:923.

54. Covenant loyalty plays a similar function in 2 Macc. 7; see the discussion in the companion volume, *Afterlife and Resurrection Beliefs in the Apocrypha and Apocalyptic Literature*. Like the suggested martyrdom of Taxo and his seven sons provoked God into action, so too did the martyrdom of the mother and her seven

introduced by the technical term, בְּאַחֲרִית הַיָּמִים, "in the last days" (Deut. 31:29), referring to the eschatological time.

There are three allusions to the resurrection belief in the *Testament of Moses*. In two texts, sleep is used as a metaphor for death (*T. Mos.* 1:15; 10:14), similar to the usage in the *Testament of the Twelve Patriarchs* (*T. Sim.* 8:1-2; *T. Jud.* 26:4; *T. Iss.* 7:9; *T. Zeb.* 10:6; *T. Dan* 7:1; *T. Gad* 8:1; *T. Ash.* 8:1; *T. Jos.* 20:4) and the *Testament of Job* (*T. Job* 53:7), suggesting a future resurrection. The second sleep-death metaphor (*T. Mos.* 10:14) and the third resurrection allusion (10:9) both appear in the eschatological salvation-judgment section at the end of Moses' prophetic revelation, in which God will defeat the devil and put an end to sorrow (10:1). At that moment, God's appointed messenger will avenge the enemies of the righteous (10:2) and God will appear to "work vengeance on the nations" and destroy their idols (10:3-7). This judgment scene borrows language from several eschatological judgment texts in the TaNaKh, in which it is associated with earthquakes, the sun losing its light, the moon turning into blood, and the stars being thrown into disarray (Isa. 13:10; 24:23; 34:4; Ezek. 32:7; Joel 2–3; Amos 5:20; 8:9; Mic. 1:3-4; Hab. 3; Zeph. 1; Eccl. 12:2). The drying up of the waters or rivers is also viewed as a part of God's act of judgment (Isa. 11:15; 19:5-8).

Following the judgment upon the nations, the prophecy turns to the destiny of Israel (*T. Mos.* 10:8-10), who will be exalted "above the necks and the wings of an eagle" (*T. Mos.* 10:8b), a possible allusion to God's work of salvation and loving care for his people in the past and promised blessing in store for those who show loyalty towards the covenant (Exod. 19:4; Deut. 32:11-13; Isa. 40:31). The testament also notes that God "will fix you [Israel] firmly in the heaven of the stars, in the place of their habitations" (*T. Mos.* 10:9) – a very similar language used in Dan. 12:3 when describing the reward of the resurrected righteous: "Those who are wise will shine like the bright expanse of the heavens, and those who lead many to righteousness, like the stars forever and ever" (Dan. 12:3, CSB). The final phase of the exaltation process is to see the destiny of their enemies, who are still living on earth or, as suggested by Robert Charles, in Gehenna[55] (*T. Mos.* 10:10b). Recognizing the destiny of their former enemies, they will rejoice and give praise to God and confess their creator

---

sons atone for the sins of the people of Israel and mended the covenant relationship with God. Thus, it brought to an end the Antiochian persecution and heralding the Maccabean revolt.

55. Robert Henry Charles, ed., *Commentary on the Pseudepigrapha of the Old Testament*, 2 vols. (Oxford: Clarendon, 1913), 2:422.

(*T. Mos* 10:10c-d). If Charles' translation of the Latin phrase *in terram* as "Gehenna" is accepted, the described punishment seems to be individual in nature, describing the final destiny of the wicked. This suggests the described exaltation of Israel could also be understood as individual in nature, describing the final destiny of the righteous as being in heaven or receiving astral immortality.

In addition to the similar image used when describing the reward of Israel or the righteous (*T. Mos.* 10:9 || Dan. 12:3), the overall structure of this eschatological salvation-judgment scene parallels the prophetic vision of Daniel 11–12. Both visions describe a prophetic vision starting with the key character, Daniel or Moses. Both visions end with the eschatological judgment. Both prophecies reveal the final destiny of the righteous and the wicked before they conclude with a statement that Daniel and Moses will fall asleep as a metaphor for death. In Dan. 12:13, Daniel is asked to rest until the day of resurrection when he will receive his reward, while Moses states that he will sleep with his fathers (*T. Mos.* 10:14), noting that 250 times will pass between his burial until his coming (*T. Mos.* 10:12) and the beginning of the judgment. It should also be noted that, in both accounts, instructions were given to keep the prophetic visions in a book for future generations (Dan. 12:4 [Daniel] || *T. Mos.* 10:11 [Joshua]).

However, in contrast to Dan. 12:2-3, the surviving part of the *Testament of Moses* does not explicitly state a resurrection hope. It is not even clear from the context if the judgment scene described in the Testament will be individual – referring to the righteous and the wicked person, or corporate – referring to the nation of Israel and her enemy nations. Even if we assume this eschatological judgment will be individual in scope, there is still a question of whether this judgment will be limited or universal in nature. Will God judge all the righteous and wicked who are alive during the eschatological judgment or only some, or will he also include the righteous and wicked dead? The latter option would require a limited or universal resurrection. Since a large part of the testament is missing, any attempt to answer these questions would involve speculation.

5. *Testament of Adam*

The *Testament of Adam* was most likely written by a Jewish author in Syriac, though it contains Christian interpolations in the prophetic section of the Testament. Stephen Robinson notes the three sections of the Testament, the Horarium (*T. Adam* 1:1–2:12), the Prophecy (3:1-6), and the Hierarchy (4:1-8), "were not written at the same time, but the final Christian redaction, in which the testament took on its present form, probably occurred in the middle or late third century A.D."⁵⁶ However, he adds that "the Jewish portions of the testament are likely older than the Christian additions, the Horarium and perhaps some of the Prophecy may date from considerably before the third century A.D."⁵⁷ The resurrection hope appears in two statements in Adam's prophecy to his son Seth, alluded to in *T. Adam* 3:2 and explicitly stated in 3:4 in a Christian interpolation.

Adam's prophecy reveals key events, with an emphasis on God's act of salvation. It begins with the incarnation of God and summarizes His miraculous work while dwelling among the people (*T. Adam* 3:1), noting that God had revealed this to him, Adam, in Paradise "after I [Adam] picked some of the fruit in which death was hiding" (*T. Adam* 3:2). This was probably an explanation of the cryptic words to the Serpent in Gen. 3:15 in which a future seed of the woman would crush the head of the Serpent, but in the process would have his heel struck by the Serpent, prophesying death for both parties. The prophecy also reveals the reason for Adam eating the fruit, noting that Adam wanted to become a god (*T. Adam* 3:2, 4), an allusion to the promised effect of the fruit (Gen. 3:5) and God's described consequence following the act of eating it (Gen. 3:22). Interestingly, Adam's motivation to be a god becomes a central part of the two resurrection promises in the Testament.

Following Adam's failed attempt to become a god, God reveals to him that He will grant him the wish and will make him a god. However, Adam must first be handed over to death, and he and his descendant's bodies will be eaten by maggots and worms since he had listened to the Serpent (*T. Adam* 3:2b-3b). However, Adam will be shown mercy since he was created in God's image, and as such, will not be left in Sheol to waste away forever (*T. Adam* 3:3c-f),⁵⁸ hinting at a future resurrection.

---

56. Stephen E. Robinson, "Testament of Adam," *OTP* 1:990.
57. Ibid.
58. This part of the prophecy seems to expand on the two attributes of the forbidden fruit and the meaning of being created in the image of God. God warned the humans against the death aspect of the fruit, when He stated that the day they eat from it, they will certainly die (Gen. 2:17; cf. Gen. 3:3). However, the Serpent suggests a different aspect, a "divinity" aspect, when stating that they would not die but would instead become like God if they ate the fruit (Gen. 3:5).

Depending on how God's evaluation of the new reality following Adam and Eve's act of eating of the fruit is understood, the words, הָאָדָם הָיָה כְּאַחַד מִמֶּנּוּ could either affirm the Serpent's promise, if the verb הָיָה (qal perf. 3rd m.sg) is understood as "has become" (man has become like one of us), suggesting humans were not like

At this point in the prophecy, there is clear Christian interpolation which adds to God's act of salvation mentioned at the beginning of the prophecy (*T. Adam* 3:1). It reveals how the promise of restoration given to Adam will be realized (3:3-5), and the time frame (3:5). In the following extract the resurrection statement is highlighted in gray, while the time reference is highlighted in italic. It should also be noted that this part of the prophecy places the blame for the creation of sin squarely on Eve.[59] It provides a rationale for Cain's murderous act of Abel as being due to a great passion for his sister Lebuda who was intended as a wife for Abel,[60]

God before they ate the fruit, or emphasizing their pre-fall divine nature if the verb is understood as a simple past "was" (man was like one of us), suggesting humans used to be like God, but after eating the fruit, they are not.

This section of the prophecy also notes that humans were created in God's image and likeness (Gen. 1:26-27), suggesting godlike attributes from the beginning, and explains why Adam's body needed saving, when Adam would once more be elevated, be made a god, and be seated at the right hand of "my divinity" (*T. Adam* 3:4). The word צֶלֶם, "image," used in the Creation narrative, is the same word as used for idols, an image representing a deity; thus, humans are an idol of God. In the *Books of Adam and Eve*, it is this association between humans and an idol of God that causes Satan to rebel. Satan and the other angels were commanded to bow down and worship Adam, the image of God (*Vita* 13:2–15:3), something Satan refused since he argued that he was created first and therefore should be ranked higher than Adam (14:3). As a consequence of this rebellion, he and his followers were expelled from Heaven (16:1).

59. It should be noted that the Eden Narrative (Gen. 2–3) does not place the blame for the fall solely on Eve, as is evidenced in the *T. Adam* 3:5; instead, the emphasis is both the woman and the man ate the fruit, they both rebelled, and they both had to suffer the consequences for this act: expulsion from the Garden, pain, and suffering. However, the process of placing the responsibility for the rebellion on Eve alone took place during Second Temple Period Judaism; see Jan A. Sigvartsen, "The Creation Order – Hierarchical or Egalitarian?" *AUSS* 53 (2015): 127–42.

60. Genesis 4:8 does not reveal what Cain said to Abel before he killed him, it merely states: וַיֹּאמֶר קַיִן אֶל־הֶבֶל אָחִיו, "and Cain said to his brother Abel…," leaving ample room for gap filling by a later interpreter. The Septuagint, Syriac, and the Vulgate translation of this text complete the sentence by adding "let us go out into the field." However, Jewish Midrash suggests several more elaborate topics of conversation between Cain and Abel, which ended with Cain killing Abel. *Genesis Rabbah* 22:7 suggests four possible topics of dispute between Cain and Abel. First, a dispute over Land and property: Cain claimed the land and demanded that Abel should "fly" so as to get literally right off the ground, leaving Abel nowhere to go. Second, a dispute regarding a religious matter, where the Temple should be built. Cain claimed it should be built in his area. Third, a dispute regarding the first Eve (a possible reference to the mythological figure Lilith, who did not "submit herself" to Adam (*Sepher Ben Sira* 23 A-B). And fourth, a dispute over a woman: each brother was

and suggests that the daughters of men in Gen. 6:2, 4 are the daughters of Cain (*T. Adam* 3:5).⁶¹

Testament of Adam 3:3-5 (*OTP* 1:994)

For your sake I will be born of the Virgin Mary.
For your sake I will taste death and enter the house of the dead.
For your sake *I will make a new heaven*,
   and I will be established over your posterity.

And after *three days*, while I am in the tomb,
   I will raise up the body I received from you.
And I will set you at the right hand of my divinity,
and I will make you a god just like you wanted.
And I will receive favor from God,
and I will restore to you and to your posterity that which is the justice of heaven.

born with their own twin sister who was intended to become their spouse; however, Cain wanted Abel's twin sister since she was the most beautiful of the two sisters (*Pirke De-Rabbi Eliezer*, 22). This tradition seems to be reflected in the *T. Adam* 3:5. A fifth possible topic of dispute is suggested by *Targum Pseudo-Jonathan* on Gen. 4:8. In this expansion to the text, Cain and Abel have a heated theological discussion involving the theodicy of God, eschatological judgment and the world to come, which would imply a resurrection belief. The targum states: "I perceive that the world was created in goodness, but it is not governed (or conducted) according to the fruit of good works, for there is respect to persons in judgment; therefore it is that thy offering was accepted, and mine not accepted with good will. Habel answered and said to Kain, In goodness was the world created, and according to the fruit of good works is it governed; and there is no respect of persons in judgment; but because the fruits of my works were better than thine, my oblation, before thine, hath been accepted with good will. Kain answered and said to Habel, There is neither judgment nor Judge, nor another world; nor will good reward be given to the righteous, nor vengeance be taken of the wicked. And Habel answered and said to Kain, There is a judgment, and there is a Judge; and there is another world, and a good reward given to the righteous, and vengeance taken of the wicked. And because of these words they had contention upon the face of the field; and Kain arose against Habel his brother, and drove a stone into his forehead, and killed him."

61. The *Testament of Adam*, however, does not reveal the identity of the "sons of God," whether they are the fallen angels (cf. Job 1:6; 2:1; 38:7) or humans. If humans, the phrase could refer to the noble class, or the male descendants of Seth marrying the female descendants of Cain, or the "sons of God" could represent the righteous who adhere to God's way; as such, the "daughters of men" would represent the wicked, who rebel against God, as did Cain. For further discussion, see Shubert Spero, "Sons of God, Daughters of Men?" *JBQ* 40, no. 1 (2012): 15–18.

You have heard, my son Seth, that **a Flood is coming and will wash the whole earth** <u>because</u> of the daughters of Cain, your brother, who killed your brother Abel out of passion for your sister Lebuda, <u>since sins had been created through your mother, Eve</u>.

And **after the Flood** there will be *<u>six thousand years (left) to the form of the world</u>*, and *then its end will come*.

God makes it clear to Adam that it was for his sake that he would come to the earth and die, make a new heaven, receive favor from God, and become a ruler over Adam's posterity – all this in order to bring salvation to him and his posterity. God will die; however, he will resurrect from the tomb after three days and bring Adam's body with him. Upon Adam's resurrection, Adam will be established on the right hand of God's divinity and have his wish of becoming a god granted. The final phase of God's salvation work is perhaps the most important detail in this prophecy since it expands God's saving work from just restoring Adam to also include Adam's posterity, according to the justice of heaven. This added detail would suggest a future universal resurrection for the righteous dead, probably at the end of the six thousand years[62] after the flood, when it is suggested the end will come.[63]

The prophecy in the *Testament of Adam* concludes with Adam's death and funeral (*T. Adam* 3:6), in which Adam was borne to his grave by the angels since Adam had been created in God's image, and the sun and the moon were darkened for seven days following his death. It is important to note that this death scene, unlike the *Testament of Job* 52–53 and *Testament of Abraham* A20/B14, does not mention Adam's soul parting his body upon dying, suggesting that the soul is not immortal or can be separated from the body. As far as this prophecy is concerned, Adam's body (and that of his posterity) will be buried in the grave, be consumed by maggots and worms (*T. Adam* 3:2), and become food for the serpent (3:3). However, God will not let Adam (and his posterity) be left to "waste away in Sheol" forever (3:3), but in his grace, he will resurrect Adam's

---

62. This is a similar time frame to *2 En.* 33:1-2; the *T. Moses* A19:7; and *Ps.-Philo* 28:8 where the world's history is stated as being seven thousand years long, or six thousand years following the flood.

63. Several elements appearing in this prophecy regarding God's act of saving Adam and his posterity are also found in two of the death and resurrection passages from the New Testament, 1 Cor. 15:20-28 (regarding the work of the New Adam) and 1 Pet. 3:18-22 (regarding Jesus work while dead and his exaltation following his resurrection), and in the *Nicene Creed*.

body when he comes into this world (3:3-4) and, it could be assumed, the bodies of his posterity at the end of the world (3:5). God will make Adam into a god, placing him at "the right hand of my divinity" and restore to Adam and his posterity "that which is the justice of heaven" (3:4).

Chapter 3

EXPANSIONS OF STORIES AND LEGENDS

Due to the very economic writing style of the authors of the biblical books, the narratives of the TaNaKh emphasize the verbs, the doing, and often lack details regarding the feelings, thoughts, and emotions of the character that is the subject of the doing. There are also narrative gaps, which raises the question of what took place in those gaps. In some narratives, God is surprisingly absent (e.g. the book of Esther), which sets the stage for later writers to make additions to show God's place in the narrative and celebrate his guidance and covenant loyalty towards his faithful (e.g. the LXX version of the book of Esther). Sometimes names are mentioned in the plot-line without a proper introduction, as if they were known to the original audience, but this common knowledge has been lost to later generations of readers. Alternatively, other characters are mentioned briefly, and then just disappear from the scene. There are also unresolved ambiguities in the narrative, which raises several questions when it comes to interpretation. These are some of the reasons why biblical narratives lent themselves to narrative expansions during Second Temple period literature, and the reason legends developed around certain characters, such as Adam, Enoch, Abraham, Melchizedek, Joseph, and Moses. James Charlesworth notes "the biblical narratives were clarified, enriched, expanded, and sometimes retold from a different perspective,"[1] and some of these traditions were written down and became a part of the extensive literature from the Second Temple period.

Some of the books belonging to this category of pseudepigraphal literature are apocalyptic in nature (*Jubilees*, *Martyrdom and Ascension of Isaiah*, [*Ladder of Jacob*], and *4 Baruch*); others are apologetic, showing the superiority of Judaism, possibly to draw converts to the faith (e.g. *Joseph and Aseneth*); some are legends and expansions on stories

---

1. James H. Charlesworth, "Introduction," *OTP* 2:5.

(*Letter of Aristeas, Life of Adam and Eve, Lives of the Prophets, Jannes and Jambres, History of the Rechabites, Eldad and Modad, History of Joseph*); and yet others are retelling of the sacred history of Israel from a different perspective and agenda (*Jubilees* and *Pseudo-Philo*). These books are interesting since, as noted by George Nickelsburg, "works that interpreted biblical stories by retelling and paraphrasing them, often adding new material,"[2] shed some light on how these narratives were understood, and provide some indicators regarding what elements of a narrative these pseudepigraphal writers found troublesome, problematic, interesting, and/or important to warrant said expansion. Rewritten Bible, according to Bruce Fisk, "open[s] a window on early Jewish exegesis around the turn of the era and demonstrates the deeply held conviction that the ancient stories bore a message for the present day."[3] Table 4 provides a list of allusions and explicit resurrection passages appearing in the books categorized as "Expansions on Stories and Legends," with the main emphasis being placed on clear resurrection statements. The discussion for some of these passages will be brief since the details given in the book regarding the resurrection belief is scant.

---

2. George W. E. Nickelsburg, "The Bible Rewritten and Expanded," in Stone, ed., *Jewish Writings of the Second Temple Period*, 130.

3. Bruce N. Fisk, "Rewritten Bible in Pseudepigrapha and Qumran," *DNTB* 947. In his article, Fisk gives some of the basic characteristics of the rewritten Bible. First, it is a retelling of the biblical narrative often following the chronological order. Second, it integrates extra biblical traditions into the narrative account. Third, "narrative additions function as implicit biblical exegesis, by filling gaps, solving problems and explaining connections in the biblical text" (948). Fourth, the rewritten account, although consistent, presupposes the reader's awareness of the biblical account. Fisk also identifies various techniques or interpretative methods used by the author of the rewritten Bible, like (1) solving ambiguities in the biblical text; (2) paying close attention to the larger narrative context, assuming "that adjacent scriptural episodes were meaningfully related and thus mutually illuminating" (951); (3) one scriptural passage could be used to interpret another since scripture was considered "a single, unified story" (952); and (4) the idealization of biblical characters.

Table 4. Resurrection texts in the expansions on stories and legends

Passage		Notes	Resurrection			Classification		
			Implied	Stated	Ref.	Allude	Phil.	Assum.
Jubilees	4:24; 5:10; 10:17; 23:11; 30:23; 36:10-11; 37:19; 39:6	Judgment Texts (Implied Resurrection)	x				x	x
	10:15; 23:1; 36:18; 45:15	Sleep ‖ Death	x					x
	23:27-31	Bones rest in the earth, Spirits will increase joy	x					x
Martyrdom and Ascension of Isaiah	1:3-5	Hezekiah's vision	x					x
	3:18	Faith → salvation	x					
	4:14-22	Second Coming		x				x
	7:4; 8:14, 23, 27; 11:35	Rope of Flesh Rope of Angels	x					x
	9:7-11	Saints in Heaven	x					x
	9:16-18	Resurrection of Jesus and the Saints	x					x

3. Expansions of Stories and Legends

Passage		Notes	Resurrection			Classification		
			Implied	Stated	Ref.	Allude	Phil.	Assum.
Joseph and Aseneth	8:(10)–(11)	Joseph's blessing of Aseneth	×			×		
	12:(12)	God's gift	×					×
	15:3-6, (7), 12×, 16:(8)	The Book of Life	×					×
	16:21-23	Resurrection of bees		×				×
	20:7	God is the life giver		×				×
	22:(9)	Aseneth's place of rest	×					×
	27:10	The immortality of the Soul	×					×
Apocalypse of Moses (Life of Adam and Eve)	10:2	Eve's woe		×				×
	13:2-6	Michael's words to Seth		×		×		×
	28:4	If you are righteous → resurrection → immortality		×			?	×
	37:5	Adam taken to Paradise	×					×
	39:2-3	Promise given to Adam	×					×
	41	Promised resurrection		×	×			×
	43:2-3	Burial practice Body → earth Soul → after 7 days back to heaven		×				×
Vita (Life of Adam and Eve)	47:2-3	Resurrection/judgment	×	×				×
	51:2	The Sabbath is a sign of the resurrection		×	×			×

Passage		Notes	Resurrection			Classification		
			Implied	Stated	Ref.	Allude	Phil.	Assum.
Pseudo-Philo	3:10	Resurrection/Judgment		x				x
	16:3	Rebellion of Korah	x					x
	19:2, 6	Death = sleep	x					x
	19:12-13	Resurrection of Moses		x				x
	23:13	The righteous		x	x			x
	25:7	Repentance → resurrection		x				x
	28:10	Death = sleep	x					x
	29:4	Death = sleep	x					x
	33:2-3	No repentance after death		x				x
	33:6	Death = Sleep	x					x
	35:3	Death = sleep	x					x
	48:1	Ascension of Phinehas	x					x
	62:9	The souls will know each other	x					x
	64:6-9	Samuel's resurrection caused by Saul		x	x			x
Lives of the Prophets	2:11-19	The ark will appear at the resurrection		x				x
	3:10-12	Hope for Israel		x				x
Ladder of Jacob	7:21	Resurrection of Eve		x				x
4 Baruch	6:6-10	Promise to Abimelech	x					x
	7:18	Resurrection of the dead man		x				x
	9:12-14	Jesus the resurrector		x				x
History of the Rechabites	14-16	Soul		x				x
		Body						

1. *Jubilees*

The book of *Jubilees* belongs to the genre of "rewritten Bible" and retells the biblical account starting with the Creation (Gen. 1) and ending with God establishing his covenant with the people of Israel at Mt. Sinai (Exod. 19–24).[4] The introduction to the book provides the setting and the purpose of God's revelation recorded in the book of *Jubilees*:

> This is *The Account of the Division of Days of the Law and the Testimony for Annual Observance according to their Weeks and their Jubilees throughout all the Years of the World* just as the LORD told it to Moses on Mount Sinai when he went up to receive the tablets of the Law and the commandment by the word of the LORD, as he said to him, "Come up to the top of the mountain." [Exod. 24:12]

Thus, the content of this book, according to the title and the first chapter, was revealed to Moses during the forty days and forty nights he was on the mountain (*Jub.* 1:4a || Exod. 24:18), when God "revealed to him both what (was) in the beginning and what will occur (in the future), the account of the division of all of the days of the Law and the testimony" (*Jub.* 1:4b). There are only two sections of this book which describe the distant future from the standpoint of Moses – the introduction chapter of this literary work and *Jub.* 23:9-32, an excursus following the death of Abraham. The only "resurrection" passage in this book appears in the latter section (*Jub.* 23:29b-31).[5] Wintermute provides the following brief outline of the book of *Jubilees*,[6] showing the chapters and narrative sections. James L. Kugel's list of passages and labels, attributed to a later interpolator, have been added to this outline:[7]

---

4. In the process of retelling the biblical narratives, O. S. Wintermute notes that the author of *Jubilees* condensed, omitted, expurgated, explained, supplemented, and sometimes significantly recast these narratives (O. S. Wintermute, "Jubilees: A New Translation and Introduction," *OTP* 2:35).

5. There are several allusions to the resurrection or a future afterlife in *Jubilees*. Sleep is used as an analogy for death in several passages (*Jub.* 10:15; 23:1; 36:18; 45:15), which presumes a temporary nature for death as it alludes to a future time when the person will awaken (not be dead). There are also several judgment texts in *Jubilees* (*Jub.* 4:24; 5:10; 10:17; 23:11; 30:23; 36:10-11; 37:19; 39:6), which would imply some form of resurrection and/or afterlife since each person will be held responsible for their actions in the present life.

6. Wintermute, "Jubilees," 35.

7. James L. Kugel, "Jubilees," in Feldman, Kugel, and Schiffman, eds., *Outside the Bible*, 1:281.

Chapter	Narrative section		Attributed to the interpolator
1	Introduction		
2–4	Creation and Adam stories	2:24-33	The laws of the Sabbath
		3:9-14	Impurity after childbirth
		3:29-31	Nudity forbidden
		4:5-6	Cain's curse anticipates Deut. 27:24
		4:31-32	Death of Cain and Lev. 24:19-20
5–10	Noah stories	5:13-19	Strict justice after the Flood and the Day of Atonement
		6:10-14	Blood not to be eaten, but instead used for *Tamid* sacrifices (connection to Exod. 29:38-42 and Num. 28:3-8)
		6:17-22	The Festival of Shavuot
		6:23-38	The 364-Day Calendar
11:1– 23:8	Abraham stories	13:25-27	Law of the Tithe
		14:20b	Abraham kept Shavuot (connected to "The Festival of Shavuot" in *Jub.* 6:17-22)
		15:25-34	Addition to the Laws of Circumcision
		16:3-4	Isaac's name was already written in Heavenly Tablets
		16:9	Lot condemned
		16:28-31	Supplement to Festival of Booths Laws
		18:18-19	The binding of Isaac took place on Passover
23:9-32	Digression on Abraham's death	23:32	Moses's predictions recapitulate the Heavenly Tablets
24–45	Jacob and his family	24:33	Isaac's curse of Philistines recapitulates the Heavenly Tablets
		28:6b-7	Wrong to marry the younger daughter first
		30:8-17	Prohibition of intermarriage operates in both directions
		30:18-23	God's friends and enemies
		31:31-32	Isaac's blessing written on the Heavenly Tablets
		32:9c-15	Law of the Second Tithe
		33:10-20	The Eighth Day of Assembly
		41:23-26	Why Reuben and Bilhah were not killed
46–50	Moses stories	49:2-17	Laws of Passover Sacrifice
		49:22-23	Law of Unleavened Bread

Regarding the dating and provenance of the book of *Jubilees*, we can say that this literary work was originally written in Hebrew[8] by a Jew who lived in Palestine, more specifically "in or near Jerusalem."[9] Due to his special interest in such religious matters as the origin of festivals, sacred times, cults and rituals, a strict interpretation of the Law, and the focus on the tribe of Levi, the author probably belonged to a priestly family.[10] VanderKam argues the most likely date for *Jubilees* is between the late 160s BCE and 100 BCE based on: (1) the oldest fragment of the book of *Jubilees* found among the Dead Sea Scrolls (4Q216) is dated to 125–100 BCE; (2) the Damascus Document (CD 16.2-4) quotes *Jubilees* as an authority in the mid-first century BCE; and (3) that the author of the *Jubilees* does not seem to be aware of the Enochic Animal Apocalypse (*1 En.* 85–90) which is dated to the late 160s BCE.[11] He concludes: "it seems best to say, in view of all the evidence, that the author composed *Jubilees* in the period between 160–150 BCE. One cannot exclude a slightly earlier date, but it was probably not written at a later time."[12] The listed interpolations in the outline of the book of *Jubilees* are of a later date.[13] However, the "resurrection" passage, which will be considered in the following section, is not among these texts, but is instead a part of the oldest strata of the book.

a. *Jubilees* 23:29b-31

The resurrection passage, *Jub.* 23:29b-31, is a part of a larger apocalypse (23:16-31) which describes the "events of Israelite history that lead up to and constitute the eschaton."[14] The conclusion of this apocalypse (23:29b-31), as noted by Nickelsburg, describes the eschatological judgment (vv. 30f and 31c, underlined in the following texts) in which the righteous will

---

8. Several fragments of the book of *Jubilees* have been identified among the Dead Sea Scrolls, which attests to its Hebrew origin. At one point, someone translated the Hebrew version of the book into Greek and perhaps Syriac. Still later, the Greek version was translated into Latin and into Ethiopic. Only the Ethiopic version has survived more or less intact into the present time. For an overview of textual history of the book, see Kugel, "Jubilees," 272–3; James C. VanderKam, *The Book of Jubilees* (Sheffield: Sheffield Academic, 2001), 13–17; idem, "Jubilees," *DNTB* 600–601; Wintermute, "Jubilees," 43.
9. Kugel, "Jubilees," 272; see also Wintermute, "Jubilees," 45.
10. Wintermute, "Jubilees," 45.
11. VanderKam, "Jubilees," 600; see also idem, *The Book of Jubilees*, 17–21; Wintermute, "Jubilees," 43–4.
12. VanderKam, *The Book of Jubilees*, 21.
13. Kugel, "Jubilees," 278–81.
14. Nickelsburg, *Resurrection, Immortality, and Eternal Life*, 47.

receive mercy and their reward and the wicked their punishment (v. 30f, highlighted in bold font), emphasizing the vindication of the righteous (v. 31c, highlighted in italic font).[15] The text is as follows (the "resurrection" statement has been highlighted in grey, v. 31a-b):

Jubilees 23:29b-31 (*OTP* 2:102)

29b) and there will be no Satan and no evil (one) who will destroy,
 c) because all of their days will be days of blessing and healing.
30a) And then the LORD will heal his servants,
 b) and they will rise up and see great peace.
 c) And they will drive out their enemies,
 d) and the righteous ones will see and give praise,
 e) and rejoice forever and ever with joy;
 f) <u>and they will see all of their judgments and all of **their curses among their enemies**</u>.
31a) And their bones will rest in the earth,
 b) and their spirits will increase joy,
 c) <u>and they will know that *the LORD is an executor of judgment*</u>;
 d) but he will show mercy to hundreds and thousands, to all who love him.

The key element of this passage is the reward given to the righteous. In addition to seeing the punishment of their enemies (v. 30f), which will be an important part of their vindication by God (v. 31c), their bones will rest in the earth while their spirits will increase joy (v. 31a-b), suggesting an eternal afterlife filled with joy for the righteous (v. 30e). In the contrast between the bones and spirit, Nickelsburg presumes the spirit will experience much joy in heaven. Thus, the contrast is between the bones in the earth and the spirits in heaven. However, he notes "the passage does not say whether the spirits pass directly into heaven at the time of death or whether they are resurrected at some specific time in the future, viz., at the judgment."[16] Nickelsburg argues that it all comes down to the relationship between the "servants" mentioned in v. 30a-b and the "righteous ones" in vv. 30d-31. If they are the same, it would support a resurrection of the souls of the righteous. If, on the other hand, the "servants" and the "righteous ones" refer to two different groups, the "servants" would describe those who are still alive at the time of God's intervention describing how they "rise from their humility and their subjugation to their enemies, or how they are taken up to join the spirits of the righteous, who are already in heaven."[17]

15. Ibid.
16. Ibid., 47–8.
17. Ibid., 48.

2. *Martyrdom and Ascension of Isaiah*

The *Martyrdom and Ascension of Isaiah* is the Ethiopic title[18] of a composite work. It consists of two distinct literary works which probably existed independently from each other.[19] The first half of this work, chs. 1–5, is the oldest and is often titled the *Martyrdom of Isaiah*. M. Knibb notes this section is also a composite – a Jewish part (1:1–3:12; 5:1-16) and a Christian part (3:13–4:22). He remarks that the Jewish section, *Martyrdom of Isaiah*, contains the tradition regarding Isaiah's martyrdom and probably dates to the second century BCE, to the period of the persecution by Antiochus Epiphanes. It was most likely written in Hebrew by a Jewish author living in Palestine. However, he adds the Christian apocalypse (3:13–4:22), also known by the title *Testament of Hezekiah*, which is embedded in the Jewish section, may also have existed as an independent work, and probably dates to the end of the first century CE, most likely written in Greek. This Christian addition explains Satan's anger towards Isaiah, which ultimately caused his death by the hand of Manasseh.[20]

The second half of this work, chs. 6–11, is also known as the *Ascension of Isaiah* or *Vision of Isaiah* and records Isaiah's journey through the seven heavens which took place in the "twentieth year of the reign of Hezekiah" (6:1), six years prior to Isaiah's martyrdom (1:1). This is a Christian apocalypse, originating in Greek probably at the end of the first or beginning of the second century CE.

A final Christian redactor probably combined these three sections into the present work by the third or the fourth century CE which, as noted by Knibb, is "confirmed by the fact that Jerome seems to have known the complete book," although "it is possible that there were two stages in this process, first the combination of 3:13–4:22 with the Martyrdom, and second the combination of the enlarged Martyrdom with the Vision."[21] He also notes that this final Christian redactor is probably responsible for the Christian interpolation appearing in the introduction of the *Martyrdom of Isaiah* (1:2b-6a).

---

18. The most complete version of this literary work is the Ethiopic translation, although parts of this work is also attested in Greek, Latin, Coptic, and Slavonic.
19. M. A. Knibb, "Martyrdom and Ascension of Isaiah: A New Translation and Introduction," *OTP* 2:143.
20. Ibid., 143, 146–50.
21. Ibid., 150.

Following is an outline of the book[22] and the five resurrection passages: 1:3-5; 3:15b-20; 4:14-22; 9:6-11; and 9:16-18 (highlighted in gray), in the larger context of the book. From this, it becomes clear that all five of the passages appear in the Christian material of the book, the first passage in the final redactor's Christian interpolation (*Mar. Ascen. Isa.* 1:2b-6a, appearing in brackets in the outline).

Outline of the book	Chapters	Resurrection
I. Martyrdom of Isaiah	1–5	
Martyrdom - Part 1		
Hezekiah summons Manasseh	1:1-13	1:3-5
	(1:2b-6a)	
Manasseh's wicked reign	2:1-6	
Isaiah withdraws from Jerusalem	2:7-16	
Isaiah is accused	3:1-12	
Testament of Hezekiah		
A prophecy about the beloved and the Church	**3:13-20** 3:21-31	3:15b-20
The Corruption of the Church	4:1-13	
The reign of Beliar	**4:14-22**	4:14-22
The second coming of the Lord		
Martyrdom - Part 2	5:1-16	
The Execution of Isaiah		
II. The Ascension of Isaiah	6–11	
Visits Hezekiah and has a vision	6:1-17	
Journey through the seven heavens	7:1-8	
The Firmament	7:9-12	
First Heaven	7:13-17	
Second Heaven	7:18-23	
Third Heaven	7:24-27	
Fourth Heaven	7:28-31	
Fifth Heaven	7:32-37	
Air of the Sixth Heaven	8:1-15	
Sixth Heaven	8:16-28	
Air of the Seventh Heaven	9:1-5	
Seventh Heaven	**9:6-18**	9:6-11, 16-18
Record of men's deeds	9:19-23	
Robes/thrones/crowns	9:24-26	
Worship of the Lord	9:27-32	
Worship of the angel of the Holy spirit	9:33-36	
Worship of God	9:37-42	

22. This outline utilizes the section headings used in Knibb's translation of *Martyrdom and Ascension of Isaiah*, ibid., 156–76.

Worship of the Father by the six lower Heavens	10:1-6
Lord Christ is commissioned by the Father	10:7-16
Descent of the Lord through the seven Heavens	10:17-31
Miraculous birth of the Lord	11:1-16
Infancy and life of the Lord	11:17-21
Ascension of the Lord through the seven Heavens	11:22-33
Conclusion of the vision	11:34-35
Instructions to Hezekiah	11:36-43

a. *Martyrdom and Ascension of Isaiah* 1:3-5

The first resurrection passage appears in a Christian interpolation (*Mar. Ascen. Isa.* 1:2b-6a) by the final redactor of this literary work, in which King Hezekiah summons his son Manasseh "in order to hand over to him the words of righteousness" which Hezekiah himself had seen (1:2). This passage provides a whole list of topics Hezekiah brought up with his son:

a. the eternal judgment;
b. the torments of Gehenna;
c. the prince of this world, his angels, and his powers;
d. the words concerning faith in the Beloved [Christ];
e. the judgment of the angels;
f. the destruction of this world;
g. the robes of the saints;
h. the going out and the transformation, the persecution, and the ascension of the Beloved.

It should be noted that no details are provided in this passage regarding these topics, although most of them are expanded upon at a later point in this literary work. Regardless, this list shows that these issues were a part of the final redactor's worldview. The resurrection is only implied in this list, which mentions the eternal judgment, the destiny of the wicked (torments of Gehenna), and the reward of the righteous (robes of the saints). Most of these themes are discussed at a later point in this literary work.

b. *Martyrdom and Ascension of Isaiah* 3:15b-20

The second resurrection passage appears at the beginning of the *Testament of Hezekiah*, the Christian apocalypse imbedded in *Martyrdom of Isaiah* (see Table 7), in a passage which summarizes the key elements of Christ's first coming and the spread of the gospel following his ascension to Heaven (*Mar. Ascen. Isa.* 3:13-20). The resurrection statement itself regards the resurrection of the Beloved (Jesus Christ), who will rise from his grave on the third day (3:16), and who will "send out his twelve disciples, and they will teach all nations and every tongue the resurrection of the Beloved, and those who believe in his cross will be saved" (3:17-18). In light of the reference to "the angel of the church which is in Heaven, whom he will summon in the last day" (3:15), this passage seems to hint at a future eschatological event. The nature of this event, however, is not revealed in this passage.

c. *Martyrdom and Ascension of Isaiah* 4:14-18

The third resurrection passage appears at the end of the *Testament of Hezekiah*, at the climax of the vision, which summarizes the key events that will take place following the second coming of Christ (*Mar. Ascen. Isa.* 4:14-18). According to this apocalypse, the second coming of the Lord and the establishment of his temporary Messianic kingdom will take place following the 1,332-day reign of Beliar (4:12, 14),[23] during which the saints had to flee "from desert to desert" for safety while awaiting his coming (4:13).[24] This Apocalypse also states that following the Lord's

23. This time period is reminiscent to the 1,335 days of Dan. 12:12. Knibb notes the 1,332 days (*Mar. Ascen. Isa.* 4:14) or the three years, seven months, and twenty-seven-day period (4:12) are the same and, according to the Julian calendar, adds up to 1,335 days (Knibb, "Martyrdom and Ascension of Isaiah," 162 n. j). Jonathan Knight observes that the 1,332 days is most likely an error for 1,335, thus bringing the two references to the reign of Belial into agreement (Jonathan Knight, *The Ascension of Isaiah*, Guides to Apocrypha and Pseudepigrapha [Sheffield: Sheffield Academic, 1995], 62). There is a precedence from the book of Revelation, a contemporary work, which refers to the same time-period in three different ways, as three and a half years (Dan. 7:25; 12:7; Rev. 12:14), 1,260 days (Rev. 11:3; 12:6), and also as 42 months (Rev. 13:5).

If the time-period in this text is indeed 1,335 days, it is a clear link to the resurrection passage of Dan. 12, which describes a resurrection of the righteous and the wicked. It would also shed some light on how the author of this apocalypse understood the 1,335-day-period of Dan. 12:12, understanding that the end of this period would see the second coming and the establishment of an earthly Messianic kingdom, possibly an interpretation of the following passages from the book of Dan. 2:34-35, 44-45; 7:13-14, 18, 22, 26-27; 12:1-13.

24. This is a similar image to the one given in Rev. 12:6, where the woman has to flee to the wilderness for protection during the 1,260-day period, to a place God had prepared for her.

3. *Expansions of Stories and Legends* 63

arrival from the seventh heaven accompanied by his angels and the hosts of the saints,[25] his first act in establishing his kingdom is to drag Beliar and his hosts[26] into Gehenna[27] (4:14). This act will bring "rest" to the righteous, who were persecuted by Beliar and his hosts. In doing so, this would effectively bring an end to evil, thus establishing the supreme authority of the Lord (4:15).

The hosts of saints returning from the seventh heaven to earth at the beginning of the Messianic kingdom is the resurrection of the righteous. Upon dying, the righteous leave their "robes of the flesh" and ascend to the seventh heaven where they receive their "robes of above."[28] The righteous will once more be clothed in the "robes of the flesh" when

---

25. Although this passage does not mention who these saints are, the fourth resurrection passage notes that all the righteous, upon death, go to dwell with God in the seventh heaven, leaving the "robes of the flesh" behind to receive "the robes of above" (*Mar. Ascen. Isa.* 9:7-9). This might be an interpretation of Zech. 14:5, which states: "You will flee by My mountain valley, for the valley of the mountains will extend to Azal. You will flee as you fled from the earthquake in the days of Uzziah king of Judah. Then the LORD my God will come and *all the holy ones with Him* (כָּל־קְדֹשִׁים עִמָּךְ/καὶ πάντες οἱ ἅγιοι μετ᾽ αὐτοῦ)" (CSB, my emphasis). This image is also present in the New Testament writings, where either angels (Mt. 16:27; 24:29-31; 25:31; Mk 8:38; 13:24-27; Lk. 9:26; 2 Thess. 1:7; Rev. 19:14) or the saints (1 Thess. 3:13 [μετὰ πάντων τῶν ἁγίων αὐτου]; Jude 1:14 [ἐν ἁγίαις μυριάσιν αὐτου]) are depicted as coming with Jesus Christ at the Second Coming. The third resurrection passage mentions both the angels and the saints accompanying the Lord.

26. From the immediate context, the hosts of Beliar seems to parallel the hosts of saints coming with the Lord. It is not clear whether Beliar's hosts would also include Beliar's loyal angels since, in the parallel, the angels of the Lord were mentioned in addition to the saints.

27. It is not clear what the nature of this "Gehenna" is in this passage, whether it is a place of eternal torment as suggested by the final Christian redactor in *Mar. Ascen. Isa.* 1:3. However, *Mar. Ascen. Isa.* 10:8 makes a distinction between Sheol and Haguel, an Ethiopian word which means, "perdition." Knibb adds that "'destruction' is probably intended here as the name of the final place of punishment for the wicked" (Knibb, "Martyrdom and Ascension of Isaiah," 137 n. l). Even though it may be tempting to assume Gehenna carries the same meaning as in Jewish apocalyptic literature, as a place of eternal punishment (*4 Ezra* 7:36; *1 En.* 90:26; *Sib. Or.* 4:186; *2 Bar.* 59:10), there is no indication in this Christian apocalypse that the wicked have an immortal soul; rather, the emphasis is on their complete destruction (*Mar. Ascen. Isa.* 4:18).

28. The "robe of above," which will be given to the righteous upon their ascension to the seventh heaven, is also mentioned in: *Mar. Ascen. Isa.* 1:5; 3:25; 7:22; 8:14, 26; 9:2, 9, 17-18, 24-26; 11:40. This robe symbolizes the necessary transformation which needs to take place in order to enable a person to dwell in the seventh heaven with God.

returning to the earth (*Mar. Ascen. Isa.* 4:16), and they will become members of the temporary earthly Messianic kingdom, which will only include the "resurrected saints" (those who arrived with the Lord) and the righteous remnant who were still alive at the second coming. Although there are no indications in this resurrection passage, nor in this apocalypse as a whole, regarding the duration of this Messianic kingdom, it does reveal that there will be a second resurrection at the end of this period. This second resurrection is of the wicked dead who will be judged[29] and sentenced to eternal destruction by an all-consuming fire caused by the Beloved: "it will consume all the impious, and they will become as if they had not been created" (4:18).[30] The righteous, on the other hand, will leave this earth, leaving their "robes of flesh" (bodies) behind and ascend to the seventh heaven where they will dwell for all eternity in their "robes of above" (4:17), bringing to an end the earthly Messianic kingdom. The end of this world, as noted by Knight, "would involve a full-scale destruction in which the Beloved's voice would angrily reprove"[31] the whole creation (4:18), thus returning it to the state of pre-creation. There will be no need for a recreation, a new heaven, or a new earth since all the righteous are gathered in the seventh heaven, their eternal home.

It seems the author of this Christian apocalypse has expanded upon the resurrection view appearing in Dan. 12:2, which suggests there will be a resurrection of the righteous and a resurrection of the wicked, although the reader is left with the impression that these two resurrections will take place at the same time. However, as already discussed, these two resurrections bookend the earthly Messianic kingdom, although no time interval is mentioned. The book of Revelation, on the other hand, follows a similar scenario to this apocalypse, but there are also several fundamental differences. For instance, the description of the second coming in *Mar. Ascen.*

---

29. It can be assumed there is a preliminary judgment taking place upon death in which the righteous are brought to the seventh heaven while the wicked will remain in their graves or Sheol until the second resurrection and judgment of the wicked.

30. It should be noted that this apocalypse is not clear if Beliar and his hosts, who were dragged to Gehenna at the beginning of the era of the Messianic kingdom, are the ones who are resurrected in the resurrection of the wicked, judged, and completely destroyed at the end of this era. If Beliar is not included in this destruction, he would remain in Gehenna, or on the primeval earth, much like John describes Satan's destiny during the thousand years between the resurrection of the righteous and the resurrection of the wicked (Rev. 20:1-3; the Greek word ἀβύσσου, "abyss," used to describe the place in which Satan would be bound, is the same word used in the Gen. 1:2 [LXX] when describing the condition of the earth prior to the creation).

31. Knight, *The Ascension of Isaiah*, 63.

Isa. 4:14-18, the resurrection of the righteous (Rev. 20:6) and the neutralization of Satan (Rev. 20:1-3) are the starting point of the Messianic era (Rev. 20:6), and the resurrection of the wicked will take place at the end of this special period (Rev. 20:5). However, the book of Revelation reckons the time interval between the first and second resurrection to be 1,000 years (Rev. 20:4, 6). While the apocalypse in *Martyrdom and Ascension of Isaiah* seems to suggest that the Messianic kingdom will be an earthly kingdom as opposed to a heavenly one (*Mar. Ascen. Isa.* 4:16), Rev. 20:4-6 does not provide the specific location of the millennium kingdom.[32] Both apocalypses have the wicked resurrected, judged, and then destroyed by fire; however, the book of Revelation mentions specifically that Satan will be included in this destruction (Rev. 20:9-10, 15; 21:8). There is a major structural difference between these two second-coming accounts. First, the book of Revelation does not mention the saints[33] ascending from heaven at the second coming. Instead, the righteous dead will be

---

32. Joel Badina makes a case for the millennium kingdom being located in heaven based on a word-study of the word θρόνους, "throne," used in Rev. 20:4. This word appears 47 times throughout the apocalypse and the throne's location is always in heaven when associated with God or Jesus (three of the 47 cases refer to the throne of Satan [Rev. 2:13], dragon [Rev. 13:2] or the beast [Rev. 16:10], all of which are located on earth as opposed to heaven). Thus, he states: "it is reasonable to conclude that the thrones of 20:4 are in heaven, too, since they are thrones of people who will '[reign]' with Christ a thousand years' (20:4, 6)." Badina also finds support for his conclusion by linking the "conquerors" in Rev. 20:4 with the "conquerors" seen in Rev. 15:2 and 3:21, who are located in heaven (see Joel Badina, "The Millennium," in *Symposium on Revelation – Book II*, ed. Frank B. Holbrook, DARCOM 7 [Silver Springs, MD: Biblical Research Institute and General Conference of Seventh-day Adventists, 1992], 239–41). These two arguments assume the location of God's/Jesus' throne is stagnant and does not move from heaven to earth at the second coming event. A case could be made that, if the messianic kingdom was established on earth, his throne would also be based on earth.

William Shea adds a third argument for locating the millennium kingdom in heaven based on the parallel literary structure of Rev. 12 and 20. Based on his analysis, he sees a similar shift – "earth–heaven–earth" – in both chapters, thus considering Rev. 20:1-3 and 20:7-15 as describing events taking place on earth while the middle section (Rev. 20:4-6) takes place in heaven, thereby viewing the millennium kingdom as a heavenly kingdom (William Shea, "The Parallel Literary Structure of Revelation 12 and 20," *AUSS* 23 [1985]: 47).

33. Revelation 19:14 mentions the armies of heaven accompanying the Messiah; however, this may be an allusion to one of God's titles used frequently (245×) in the TaNaKh, יְהוָה צְבָאוֹת, "the Lord of Hosts or armies," is most likely a reference to His angels.

resurrected from the earth (20:4, 6). Moreover, following the 1,000 years, John the Revelator states that God will create a new heaven and a new earth (21:1), where the New Jerusalem will be located (21:2), and all the saints will dwell in this city with God forever (Rev. 21–22). According to the third resurrection passage, the righteous ascend to the seventh heaven where they will receive "robes of above" while leaving their "robes of flesh" behind on earth. They will dwell in Heaven until the second-coming when they will descend to the earth together with the Lord and take on their "robes of flesh," which is the resurrection of the righteous, and dwell with Him on earth and be a part of His Messianic kingdom. At the end of the Messianic era, there will be a resurrection of the wicked, who will be destroyed by fire, and the righteous will ascend to the seventh heaven, leaving their "robes of flesh" to receive the "robes of above." The earth will be uninhabitable, but the saints will dwell in the seventh heaven for all eternity. In the book of Revelation scenario, upon death, the righteous dwell in the ground until the resurrection of the righteous at the beginning of the millennium kingdom which also seems to be located on earth. At the end of the 1,000 years, the resurrection of the wicked and their judgment will take place before they are destroyed by the lake of fire. God will create a new heaven and a new earth on which the righteous will live together with God for all eternity.

Figure 2 illustrates the resurrection concept in the *Martyrdom and Ascension of Isaiah* 4:14-18. The final two resurrection texts in this composite work add a few more details and appear in Isaiah's description of the seventh heaven (see the outline of the book).

d. *Martyrdom and Ascension of Isaiah* 9:6-11

The fourth resurrection passage appears in Isaiah's description of the seventh heaven, where he "saw all the righteous from the time of Adam onwards," including "Abel and all the righteous" and "Enoch and all who (were) with him" (*Mar. Ascen. Isa.* 9:7-9), therefore indicating that all the righteous are brought to the seventh heaven upon their death. This passage also notes that, following death, the righteous are stripped of their "robes of flesh" and are instead given their "robes of above," thus becoming like angels in appearance (9:9).

e. *Martyrdom and Ascension of Isaiah* 9:16-18

The final resurrection passage appears in the author's description of Christ's first coming, when he descends from the seventh heaven, dies on the cross, and plunders the angel of death (*Mar. Ascen. Isa.* 9:12-16). When Jesus resurrects on the third day, Isaiah states that "many of the righteous will ascend with him to the seventh heaven (9:17-18). This raises the question of who these righteous people liberated from the angel of death were and why these righteous people had not ascended directly to the seventh heaven upon their death. The *Martyrdom and Ascension of Isaiah* does not provide these answers, and instead leaves these questions open for speculation.

f. Concluding Remarks

All of the aforementioned five resurrection passages are considered to be of Christian origin. The most important of these texts is *Mar. Ascen. Isa.* 4:14-18, which is also the basis for Figure 2 which illustrates the resurrection concept in *Martyrdom and Ascension of Isaiah*.

Figure 2. Death and Resurrection in *Martyrdom and Ascension of Isaiah*

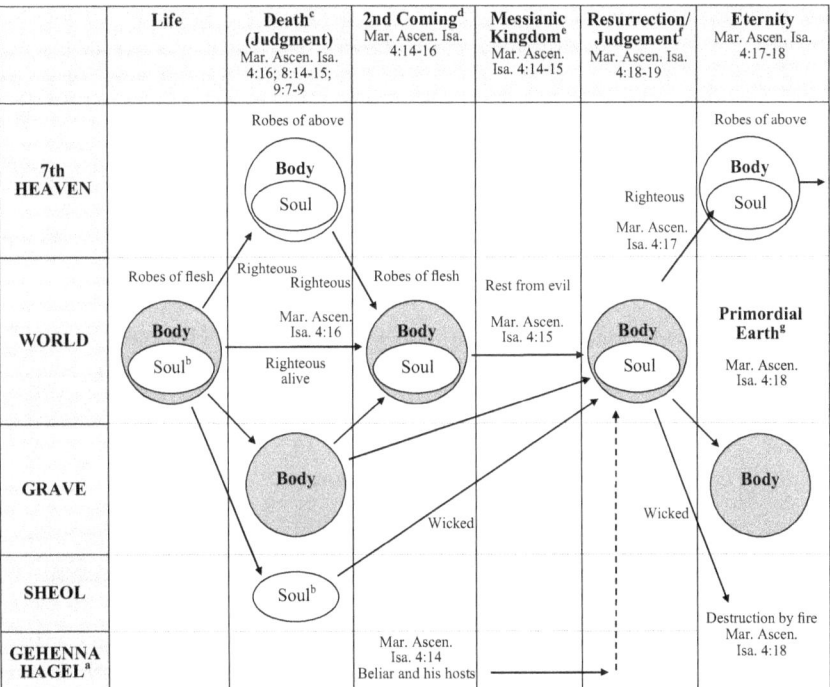

[a] *Martyrdom and Ascension of Isaiah* 1:2 mentions the torments of Gehenna. However, the text makes a clear distinction between Gehenna and Sheol (10:8). It is not mentioned in the text how long the torment will last, but *Mar. Ascen. Isa.* 4:18 states fire "will consume all the impious, and they will become as if they had not been created."

ᵇ This apocalypse does not mention the soul specifically, while it does mention the "robes of flesh" and the "robes of above," indicating that something lives on that is separate from the "robes" or "body." The type of "robes" the wicked will have after death is not revealed in the text.

ᶜ At the point of death, it could be assumed a judgment of the soul takes place as the righteous soul leaves the "robes of flesh" behind and is brought to the seventh heaven to receive the "robes of above" and be with the saints (*Mar. Ascen. Isa.* 4:16; 8:14-15; 9:7-9). Although not specifically stated, it could be assumed the wicked are brought to Sheol (or perhaps Gehenna) where they will be kept until the resurrection of the wicked.

ᵈ The Second Coming follows the 1,335-day-long reign of Beliar (*Mar. Ascen. Isa.* 4:12, 14), based on an interpretation of Dan. 12:12. The host of saints who accompany God and his angels (alluding to Zech. 14:15) when descending from the seventh heaven is the resurrection of the righteous, as they will once more be clothed in the "robes of flesh" and become a part of the earthly messianic kingdom. As a part of the Second Coming, Beliar and his hosts will be dragged to Gehenna, where, it could be assumed, they will remain until the day of resurrection and judgment of the wicked.

ᵉ The messianic kingdom will be a temporary earthly kingdom bookended by the resurrection of the righteous and the resurrection and judgment of the wicked. As Beliar and his hosts reside in Gehenna, this unspecified time period will be without wickedness (*Mar. Ascen. Isa.* 4:14-15).

ᶠ The period of the earthly messianic kingdom concludes with the resurrection and the judgment of the wicked. The wicked will be destroyed by fire while the righteous will return to the seventh heaven, leaving their "robes of flesh" behind and receiving their "robes of above" (*Mar. Ascen. Isa.* 4:18-19).

ᵍ The whole of creation will return to the state of pre-creation (*Mar. Ascen. Isa.* 4:18) while the seventh heaven will become the eternal home for the righteous (4:17). The wicked are destroyed permanently by fire (4:18).

~ ~ ~

3. *Joseph and Aseneth*

Joseph and Aseneth is an ancient Greek novel[34] which most likely originated in Egypt between 100 BCE and 115 CE.[35] This novel is a rewrite of

---

34. Patricia Ahearne-Kroll categorizes this Jewish composition as an ancient Greek novel and notes the particular plot lines it shares with other works falling into this genre classification. However, as a Jewish composition, she also notes several distinct features, the most notable is Aseneth's embrace of Judaism, the encounter with angels, and various instructions regarding Jewish ethical standards and customs. See Patricia Ahearne-Kroll, "*Joseph and Aseneth*," in Feldman, Kugel, and Schiffman, eds., *Outside the Bible*, 3:2525–6.

35. For further reading regarding dating and providence of this book, see ibid., 2526; C. Burchard, "Joseph and Aseneth: A New Translation and Introduction," *OTP* 2:187–8; W. Klassen, "Joseph and Aseneth," *DNTB* 588.

the Joseph narrative (Gen. 37–50) and begins "in the first year of the seven years of plenty" (*Jos. Asen.* 1:1), just following Joseph's interpretation of Pharaoh's dream (Gen. 41:1-36) and Pharaoh's act of making Joseph second in Egypt, only Pharaoh himself outranking him (Gen. 41:39-44).

This novel consists of two main sections. The first section (*Jos. Asen.* 1–21) significantly expands on Gen. 41:50 concerning Joseph's marriage to Aseneth (*Jos. Asen.* 1–17), the daughter of Potiphera, the priest at On. This section concludes with the birth of Manasseh and Ephraim (*Jos. Asen.* 18–21), paralleling Gen. 41:50-52. The primary concern being, as stated by Klassen, "How can this famous Jewish patriarch have married a non-Jewish woman and how does this apply to the men in our community who are also tempted to marry outside the Jewish community?"[36] To solve this apparent problem, the author of the novel provides Aseneth's conversion story. The second half of the novel (*Jos. Asen.* 22–29) takes place after the family reunification (Gen. 46–47) and is filled with intrigues regarding the plot to have Joseph and Aseneth killed. This plot was masterminded by the son of Pharaoh, who had wanted to marry Aseneth, and involved Joseph's brothers birthed by the concubines Bilhah and Zilpah. It concludes with Joseph and Aseneth being made the king and queen of Egypt (*Jos. Asen.* 29:8b-9).

Although there are no clear eschatological bodily resurrection passages in this novel, there are several allusions to the resurrection and a future life following death (see Table 23). In Joseph's intercessory prayer on behalf of Aseneth, which refers to God as the source of all life and who calls from death to life, Joseph petitions God to restore Aseneth to "life with your life" (reviving her from the state of distress [*Jos. Asen.* 8:8(10)]), "let her enter your resting place, which you prepared for your chosen one," and "let her live in your eternal life forever" (8:9[11]). Allusions to eternal life also appear in Aseneth's confession of sin and prayer for acceptance, when she compares worldly possessions with divine gifts: "For behold, all the gifts of my father Pentephres, which he gave me as an inheritance, are transient and obscure; but the gifts of your inheritance, Lord, are incorruptible and eternal" (12:[12]). Aseneth also expresses a belief in the immortality of her soul when she was about to be killed by the sons of Bilhah and Zilpah. She addresses God, asking him to deliver her and reminded him of his promise that: "your soul shall live forever" (27:10). Levi also notes Aseneth's future and saw "her place of rest in the highest, and her walls like adamantine eternal walls, and her foundations founded upon a rock of the seventh heaven" (22:[9]).

---

36. Klassen, "Joseph and Aseneth," 588.

There is also a reference to the "Book of the Living"[37] in this novel, and Aseneth is told that her name is written in it: "for behold, your name was written in the book of the living in heaven; in the beginning of the book, as the very first of all, your name was written by my finger, and it will not be erased forever" (*Jos. Asen.* 15:4[3]). This "heavenly register" or "book of life" is not a foreign biblical concept. However, it appears more frequently in Second Temple period Jewish literature.[38] It suggests Aseneth is a citizen of the heavenly kingdom, following her conversion which made her into a new being: "Behold, from today, you will be renewed and formed anew and made alive again, and you will eat blessed bread of life, and drink a blessed cup of immortality, and anoint yourself with the blessed ointment of incorruptibility" (15:5[4]). A similar point is made a few verses later when the author notes that "for all who repent she [Repentance] prepared a place of rest in the heavens. And she will renew all who repent, and wait on them herself forever (and) ever" (15:[7]).

Allusions to the resurrection and life after death also appear in the narrative section concerning the heavenly bees (*Jos. Asen.* 15:13–17:4). The angel reveals to Aseneth that all those who repent and "attach themselves to the Lord God" will eat from the comb of the heavenly bees – an angelic food. This comb is described as "big and white as snow and full of honey" (*Jos. Asen.* 16:8) and full of the spirit of life (*Jos. Asen.* 16:14). Its honey "was like dew from heaven and its exaltation like breath of life" (*Jos. Asen.* 16:8). As such, the comb is a "comb of life, and everyone who eats of it will not die forever (and) ever" (*Jos. Asen.* 16:13-14), alluding to the life-sustaining Manna given to God's people in the wilderness (Exod. 16:31, 35; Deut. 8:3), whereas the "breath of life" alludes to God's life-giving breath/spirit as a part of the creation process of humans recorded in the Eden narrative (Gen. 2:7).

The novel also describes the subservient bees who did not wish to return to heaven at the angel's request (*Jos. Asen.* 16:20-21) but instead

---

37. *Joseph and Aseneth* 15:1 (×2) suggests God also has a heavenly book containing the unspoken names of the righteous angels, those who remained loyal to Him.

38. See the following references from the TaNaKh: Exod. 32:32-33 (Moses asks God to be removed from the book he has written, if he is not willing to forgive the people); Ps. 69:28 (asks God to remove his enemies from the book of life and not be counted among the righteous); Dan. 7:10 (books were open at the beginning of the judgment); 12:1 (those who are written in the book will escape); from the Pseudepigrapha: *Jub.* 30:20-22 (mentioning the "Book of life" and the "Book of death"); 36:10 (referring to the two books in the context of the judgment); *1 En.* 47:3; 81:4; 89:61-77; 90:17-20; 98:76; 104:1, 7; 108:3; *2 Bar.* 24:1; *Ascen. Isa.* 9:20; and from the New Testament: Lk. 10:8; Phil. 4:3; and Rev. 3:5; 13:8; 17:8; 20:12-15.

tried to attack Aseneth. Due to their disobedience, they all died. However, the angel resurrected them and bade them to dwell in Aseneth's courtyard and settle in the fruit-trees (16:22-23). Although the only clear resurrection statement in the book regards these bees, this passage does reveal a familiarity with the resurrection concept and, more specifically, with the bodily resurrection concept. The closest this novel comes to a clear human resurrection statement is the reaction of Aseneth's family upon seeing her transformation as a result of her conversion: "they were amazed at her beauty and rejoiced and gave glory to God who gives life to the dead," and they sat down and celebrated with her (20:7-8). Burchard notes the phrase "He who gives life to the death" became "all but a definition of God in Judaism,"[39] which emphasizes God's powers and sovereignty, even over death. Therefore, although this novel does not specifically mention an eschatological resurrection, due to the many references to eternal life and life after death, a resurrection is not excluded as a possible element within this afterlife framework.

4. Books of the *Life of Adam and Eve*

It was traditionally believed that the *Life of Adam and Eve* was written by a Palestinian Jew around the Common Era (100 BCE–200 CE). However, among present-day scholars, there is no consensus regarding the dating and provenance of this book.[40] Highly valued by the Christian communities who safeguarded this book, Christian interpolations were added over time. Although the original language of this composition may have been Hebrew or possibly Greek, it only survived through its two textual traditions reflected in the various translations. The longer tradition is represented in Latin (by the name, "*Vita*"), Armenian, Georgian, and Slavonic, while the shorter tradition in the current Greek form (by the name, "*Apocalypse of Moses*"). These five textual traditions in their different languages are labeled the *Books of Adam and Eve*,[41] and with them, many textual variations reflect how the Adam and Eve tradition

---

39. Burchard, "Joseph and Aseneth," 234 n. p.
40. For a discussion on the providence and dating of the book, see Gary A. Anderson, "*Life of Adam and Eve*," in Feldman, Kugel, and Schiffman, eds., *Outside the Bible*, 2:1332–3; Evans, *Ancient Texts for New Testament Studies*, 49; M. D. Johnson, "Life of Adam and Eve: A New Translation and Introduction," *OTP* 252; J. Levison, "Adam and Eve, Literature Concerning," *DNTB* 4–5.
41. For a synopsis of these books, see Gary A. Anderson and Michael E. Stone, eds., *A Synopsis of the Books of Adam and Eve*, 2nd ed., SBLEJL 17 (Atlanta: Scholars Press, 1999).

developed independently in the various Christian communities.[42] The following outline by Gary Anderson shows the main content difference between the shorter (Greek) and the longer (Latin) version of the book, also known as the *Apocalypse of Moses* and the *Vita*. It shows the Latin version has two additional sections, "Adam's penitence" and "Adam's vision," while missing one section that is found in the Greek version alone, "Eve's story of the fall." The resurrection passages have been added to the narrative units in brackets in this outline and are highlighted in gray. The Greek ch. 43 and Latin chs. 49–51 have been added to the last narrative unit.

Narrative Unit	Greek	Latin
Adam's penitence	–	1–21
Cain and Abel	1–4	22–24
Adam's vision	–	25–29
Adam's story of the fall	5–14 (**10:2; 13:3-5**)	30–44
Eve's Story of the fall	15–30 (**28:4**)	–
Death and burial of Adam and Eve	31–43 (**37:5; 39:2; 41:3; 43:2**)	45–51 (**42:1-5; 47:3; 51:2**)

The Eden narrative is the focus of this book and the "blessings" and "curses" mentioned in Genesis 3 are expanded upon and explained in more detail. The narrative gap between Gen. 3:24 and Genesis 4 has been addressed by the author of this book, who inserted a lengthy narrative section which, when read with the Eden Narrative, adds several new elements to the story.[43] This composition follows closely and expands upon the Eden Narrative. Table 5 shows the topic expanded upon, including the biblical reference with the corresponding reference to the *Life of Adam and Eve*.[44] (The resurrection passages are added in brackets and highlighted in gray.)

Table 5 also shows that only one resurrection passage (*Apoc. Mos.* 28:4) appears in the narrative section which describes Adam and Eve's time in the Garden of Eden, although at this point in the narrative they have already eaten the forbidden fruit and God is in the process of expelling them from the Garden. The remaining six resurrection passages appear after the expulsion (*Apoc. Mos.* 10:2; 13:3-5||*Vita* 42:1-5; *Apoc. Mos.* 37:5||*Vita* 47:3; *Apoc. Mos.* 39:2-3; 41:3; 43:2||*Vita* 51:2). Therefore, for those who guard themselves "from all evil, preferring death to it"

---

42. Sigvartsen, "The Creation Order," 135.
43. Ibid., 136.
44. Ibid., 137.

(*Apoc. Mos.* 28:4a), the resurrection hope is a crucial element in God's plan of undoing the consequences of their rebellion – death and lack of access to the Garden.

Table 5. The Eden Narrative and the Books of the *Life of Adam and Eve*

Topic	Genesis 3	Life of Adam and Eve	Pericope
Satan's explanation for why he tempted humans		*Vita* 11:1–17:2 also in Ar./Ge.	4-5
Temptation of the serpent	3:1	*Apoc. Mos.* 15:1–16:4b Ar./Ge. [44](15):1-[44](16):4b Sl. 18-20.1–18-20.6	17-18
Temptation of Eve	3:1-6a	*Apoc. Mos.* 17:1–20:5 Ar./Ge. [44](17):1-[44](20):5 Sl. 18-20.7–21-22.4a	19-22
Temptation of Adam	3:6b-7	*Apoc. Mos.* 21:1-6 Ar./Ge. [44](21):1-[44](21):6 Sl. 21-22.4b–21-22.8	23
God's investigation	3:8	*Apoc. Mos.* 22:1-4 Ar./Ge. [44](22):1-[44](22):4 Sl. 23-24.1–23-24.5	24
God questions Adam	3:9-11	*Apoc. Mos.* 23:1-3 Ar./Ge. [44](23):1-[44](23):5 Sl. 23-24.6–23-24.9	
Adam blames Eve	3:12	*Apoc. Mos.* 23:4a Ar./Ge. [44](23):4a	
Eve blames Serpent	3:13	*Apoc. Mos.* 23:4b-5 Ar./Ge. [44](23):4b-[44](23):5	
God gives sentence to Adam	3:17-19	*Apoc. Mos.* 24:1-4 Ar./Ge. [44](24):1-[44](24):4	25
God gives sentence to Eve	3:16	*Apoc. Mos.* 25:1-4 Ar./Ge. [44](25):1-[44](25):4	
God gives sentence to Serpent	3:14-15	*Apoc. Mos.* 26:1-4 Ar./Ge. [44](26):1-[44](26):4	
Adam and Eve expelled from Garden	3:22-24	*Apoc. Mos.* 27:1–29:6 (**28:4**) Ar./Ge. [44](27):1-[44](29):6 Sl. 25-27.1–25-27.12	26-27
Life outside the Garden	4:1–5:5	Remaining sections (***Apoc. Mos.* 10:2;** ***Apoc. Mos.* 13:3-5∥*Vita* 42:1-5;** ***Apoc. Mos.* 37:5∥*Vita* 47:3;** ***Apoc. Mos.* 39:2-3; 41:3;** ***Apoc. Mos.* 43:2∥*Vita* 51:2)**	1-16 28-35

a. *Apocalypse of Moses* 10:2

The first reference to the resurrection in the Books of Adam and Eve appears in *Apoc. Mos.* 10:2 in a narrative section entitled "Encounter with Beast" (Pericope 12). It reveals little about the resurrection itself apart from Eve acknowledging her blame in bringing evil into this world and her sorrow that all those who have sinned will curse her on the day of resurrection, alluding to a resurrection of both the righteous and the wicked. The Armenian and Georgian tradition places Eve's fear in the context of the Day of Judgment, while the Slavonic tradition has it in the context of the second coming (see the highlighted sections in the following parallel texts). This textual variation between these traditions, however, could easily be harmonized by considering the day of resurrection, the Day of Judgment, and the second coming as a reference to the same eschatological event. The Armenian tradition notes that all sins will be blamed on Eve, the Georgian tradition states that all the sins will burn her, and the Slavonic tradition notes that Eve introduced sin into this world (see the underlined sections in the following parallel texts). The Slavonic tradition is unique in its emphasis on the perpetual blame of Eve, in contrast to the other three which consider blame in the context of the day of Judgment (Ar./Ge.) or the resurrection (Gr.).

Gr. 10:2	Ar. 37(10):2	Ge. 37(10):2	Sl. 11-15.6a
And Eve wept, saying, "Woe is me! For when I come to **the day of resurrection**, all who have sinned will curse me, saying that Eve did not keep the command of God."	Eve began to weep and she said, "[When] **the day of Judgment** comes; all sins will be blamed upon me and (men) will say, 'Our mother did not hearken to the commandment of the Lord God!'"	Then Eve began to weep and said, "Woe is me, for when I arrive at **the day of Judgment**, all my sins will burn me and (people) will tell me, 'In the first instance, it was you who did not observe God's orders.'"	Eve began to cry bitterly and said, "Woe is me, my sweet child, from now on until the end and until **the second coming** all will ruse me, because it is on my account all sorts of evil have multiplied.

b. *Apocalypse of Moses* 13:3-5 || *Vita* 42:1-5

The second resurrection passage appears in Michael's reply to Seth (Pericope 14)[45] when he was requesting oil of mercy from the Garden so

---

45. Michael is one of the archangels (*Apoc. Mos.* 13:2a). In the Armenian and the Georgian traditions, he is in charge of souls ([41](13):2a), while in the *Vita* he has been given power over the human body (41:1).

3. *Expansions of Stories and Legends*

he could anoint his dying father, to soothe his pain. From this passage, a few more details emerge regarding the eschatological event. According to the *Vita* and the Georgian tradition, this event will take place 5,500 years into the future (underlined in the text).

Gr. 13:3-5	*Vita* 42:1-5	Ar. 42(13):3a-4	Ge. 42(13):3a-4
³For it shall not be yours now, [but <u>at the end of the times</u>. Then shall all flesh be raised up from Adam till that great day, – all that shall be of the holy people.	¹[For in no wise can you receive any until the last days, <u>after 5,500 years have passed.</u>	³ᵃThis cannot be now: but then, at that time <u>when the years of the end are filled and complete,</u>	³ᵃThis is not to be right now but in the future times, <u>when five thousand years have been completed. Then, at the 5,500th year</u>
⁴Then shall the delights of the Garden be given to them and God shall be in their midst ⁵And they shall no longer sin before his face, for the evil heart shall be taken from them and there shall be given them a heart understanding the good and to serve God only.]	²Then the most loving king of God will come upon the earth to resurrect the body of Adam and, with him, the bodies of the dead.	³ᵇthen the beloved Christ will come to resurrect Adam's body, because of his sins which took place.	³ᵇthe beloved Son of God, Christ, will come upon the earth to re[[surrect]] Adam's body from his fall, because of the transgression of the commands.
	³The very Son of God, when he comes, will be baptized in the river Jordan, and when he comes forth from the water of Jordan, he will then anoint all who believe in him with the oil of mercy.	³ᶜHe will come to the Jordan and be baptized [by] him, and when he will come forth from the water, then Michael will come and anoint the new Adam with the oil of joy.	³ᶜHe will come and he will be baptized in the river Jordan. And as soon as he will have come forth from the water, with the (anointing) of oil, he will anoint him.

> | | | |
> |---|---|---|
> | ⁴This oil of mercy will be from generation to generation on those who are reborn of water and the Holy Spirit into eternal life.

⁵Then, the most loving Son of God will descend into the earth and lead your father, Adam, back into the Garden to the tree of mercy.] | ⁴Then after that, it shall happen in the same fashion to all the wild beasts of the earth, who will arise in resurrection and be worthy of entering the Garden. I shall anoint them with that oil. | ⁴and all his descendants, so that they will rise at the time of the resurrection. The Lord said, "I will admit them into the Garden and I will anoint them with that function." |

From this resurrection passage, Michael reveals that everyone from the time of Adam until the "great day," will be a part of the resurrection. The Armenian tradition even includes the wild beasts of the earth in this resurrection and suggests that they will be worthy to enter the Garden. No distinction is mentioned between the righteous and the wicked in the Apocalypse, although the *Vita* seems to make a distinction by focusing on those "who are reborn of water and the Holy Spirit [baptism] into eternal life" (*Vita* 42:4b). In the Apocalypse, all the resurrected will be made into a holy people through the process of removing the evil heart and replacing it with "a heart that understands the good and worships God alone" (*Apoc. Mos.* 13:5). This is an allusion to the prophecy of Jeremiah and Ezekiel that God will give his people a new heart and write his law in their hearts (Jer. 31:33; Ezek. 18:31; 36:26). This procedure guarantees there will be no more sinners, they will "be given every joy of Paradise and God shall be in their midst" (*Apoc. Mos.* 13:4). According to the textual tradition recorded in the *Vita*, Armenian, and the Georgian version, it is Christ who will resurrect Adam and all his descendants (*Vita* 42:2; Ge. [42](13):4). The *Vita* also alludes to Christ's journey to Hades: "Son of God will descend into the earth and lead your father, Adam, back into the Garden" (*Vita* 42:5). The subject of the oil of mercy or the tree of mercy (*Apoc. Mos.* 13:1-2; *Vita* 42:5; Ar. [42](13):4; Ge. [42](13):4) refers to the healing property of the oil – a lack of access to this tree means a loss of immortal life. However, access will be regained through the resurrection and, with it, a renewed access to the Garden.

c. *Apocalypse of Moses* 28:4

The third resurrection passage appearing in Eve's tale regarding Adam's plea (Pericope 26) provides a hope for a future life even though Adam and Eve had broken God's command and eaten the fruit, an act which would lead to certain death (Gen. 2:17; 3:3, 19b). They are told that if they keep themselves from all evil after their expulsion, they will be a part of the eschatological resurrection, suggesting a different destiny for the righteous and the wicked (see the underlined sections in the following texts). Thus, there is hope for the righteous since they will be part of a future resurrection and regain access to the Tree of Life, which will make them immortal forever (highlighted in gray). The wicked, on the other hand, will not be a part of the resurrection and will not receive fruit from the Tree of Life. As such, they will not have eternal life, but instead, death. Interestingly, the general statement that they should keep themselves from all evil is expanded upon in the Armenian tradition as: "slander, harlotry, adultery, sorcery, love of money, avarice, from all sin" (Ar. [44](28):4).

Gr. 28:4	Ar. [44](28):4	Ge. [44](28):4
"Yet when you have gone out of the Garden, if you keep yourself from all evil, as one wishing to die, when again the Resurrection has come to pass, I will raise you up and then there shall be given to you from the Tree of Life and you will be without death forever."	"Rather, when you go out of the Garden, guard yourself from slander, from harlotry, from adultery, from sorcery, from the love of money, from avarice and from all sins. Then, you shall arise from death (in the) resurrection which is going to take place. At that time, I will give you of the Tree of Life and you will be eternally undying."	"If you go out of the Garden and guard yourself from every evil, [you will die and after death you will arise in the future resurrection. Then, indeed,] I will give you of the Tree of Life and you will be undying forever."

d. *Apocalypse of Moses* 37:5 || *Vita* 47:3

The fourth passage appears in the "assumption of Adam to Paradise" section (Pericope 31) and strongly alludes to the resurrection in most textual traditions. After the whole of nature prayed on Adam's behalf, God pardoned him (*Apoc. Mos.* 37:2) for his rebellious deed. Upon his pardon, a Seraph came to retrieve his body and brought it to the Acherusian Lake to wash him before he was led before God. God then hands Adam over to the archangel Michael, who is in charge of souls or of dead bodies. He leads him to the third heaven where Adam will remain until God's resurrection (Sl. 45:46.2b), the day of God's judgment (*Apoc. Mos.* 37:5; *Vita* 47:3), or the day of "oikonomia" (Ge. [47](37):5), highlighted in gray in the following texts. The eschatological judgment suggests there will be a day of reckoning when everyone will be held responsible for their evil deeds, which implies there are righteous and wicked who will meet different destinies in the judgment.

Gr. 37:5	Vita 47:3	Ge. [47](37):5	Sl. 45-46.2b
"Lift him up into the Garden unto the third Heaven, and leave him there until that fearful day of my reckoning, which I will make in the world."	"Let him be in your care until the day of retribution, in supplication until the last year when I shall change his mourning into joy. Then he will sit on the throne of him who beguiled him."	"Take him to the third heaven, to the Garden, and leave him before the altar until the day of the "oikonomia" which I contemplate concerning all the fleshly (beings) with my well beloved Son."	"Carry his corpse into Paradise; his spirit shall tarry in the third Heaven, but his corpse shall remain here until my resurrection."

e. *Apocalypse of Moses* 39:2-3

The fifth resurrection passage is also only an allusion. It is a part of Adam and Abel's funerary rites (Pericope 32), in which God takes an active part in coming to the Garden the same way he came to the Garden when pronouncing his judgment after the rebellion (*Apoc. Mos.* 38:3; Ar./Ge. [47](38):3 || *Apoc. Mos.* 22:1-4; Ar./Ge. [44](22):1-4 and Sl. 23-24.1-4). The passage states that God grieved greatly over Adam's death, revealing God's feelings and emotions (*Apoc. Mos.* 39:1; Ar./Ge. [47](39):1). It is not clear from the text if the Garden or third Heaven is a different place than the earth. The enemy referred to in this text is clearly Satan, but the text is also referring to "those who borne you down to this place" without revealing who "those" are. It could be a reference to the angels who joined Satan in his rebellion. Regardless, this resurrection passage concerns the great reversal that will take place as a result of the eschatological resurrection. Those who show joy over Adam's downfall and death will see Adam reinstated following the resurrection, and Adam will be seated on the throne of his deceiver. Following Adam's future glorification, Satan and those who obeyed him "shall grieve when he see [*sic*] you [Adam] sitting upon his throne" (*Apoc. Mos.* 39:3) or be cast "into a place of darkness and death" (Ar. [47](39):3) (see the underlined section in the following texts).

Gr. 39:2-3	Ar. [47](39):2-3	Ge. [47](39):2-3
²Yet, I tell you that I will turn their joy to grief and your grief to joy, and I will return you to your rule, and seat you on the throne of your deceiver.	²But I will turn their rejoicing into sorrow, and I will turn your sorrow into rejoicing. I shall make you the beginning of rejoicing and I shall set you on the throne of him who deceived you,	²But I will change his joy into sorrow and I will lead you back towards this realm and I will set you upon your enemy's throne, where he was seated, close (by the place) where his rebellion was discovered.
³But that one [the one who sat on it prior to his becoming arrogant] shall be cast into this place that he may see you seated upon it. <u>Then he himself shall be condemned along with those who obeyed him and he shall grieve when he see [*sic*] you sitting upon his throne</u>.	³and <u>I shall cast them into a place of darkness and death</u>."	³<u>He will fall in the place (where) you (are) and he will see you in that (other) place sitting upon a throne</u>."

f. *Apocalypse of Moses* 41:1-3

The sixth resurrection passage appears in the dialogue between God and Adam's dead body (Pericope 32) and is based on an interpretation of Gen. 3:19. In the Eden Narrative, God reveals to Adam that he will have to work hard for a living until the day he dies, when his body will once more return to the earth from which it was once taken. The author of the Apocalypse expands on this statement and has God calling out to Adam's body, who answers Him from the earth (underlined in the following texts). The Armenian tradition makes an even stronger link by emphasizing the dust, having God call to Adam's body through the dust, and Adam's body telling the dust to answer God.

The dialogue in the Apocalypse begins with God calling out to Adam's body. It continues with Adam's body answering God and concludes with God repeating the words from Gen. 3:19b (bolded in the following text), that death is inevitable and that the body will return to dust.

Genesis 3:19	Apoc. Mos. 41:1b-2
¹⁹ᵃ ἐν ἱδρῶτι τοῦ προσώπου σου φάγῃ τὸν ἄρτον σου ἕως τοῦ ἀποστρέψαι σε εἰς τὴν γῆν, ἐξ ἧς ἐλήμφθης ¹⁹ᵇ **ὅτι γῆ εἶ καὶ εἰς γῆν ἀπελεύσῃ**	¹ᵇ καὶ <u>ἀποκριθὲν τὸ σῶμα ἐκ τῆς γῆς</u> εἶπεν· ἰδοὺ ἐγώ, κύριε. ² καὶ λέγει αὐτῷ ὁ κύριος· εἶπόν σοι **ὅτι γῆ, καὶ εἰς γῆν ἀπελεύσει.**
¹⁹ᵃ In the sweat of your face you will eat bread <u>until you return to the earth out of which you were taken,</u> ¹⁹ᵇ **For dust you are and unto dust you will return**	¹ᵇ And <u>the body answered from the earth</u> and said: "Here am I, Lord." ² And the Lord said to him, "I told you **dust you are and unto dust you will return**.

However, God adds that this death is not final since there will be a universal eschatological resurrection (highlighted in gray in the following texts). The resurrection addition is similar to the interpretation discussed in the "Apocalyptic Literature" chapter in the companion volume, *Afterlife and Resurrection Beliefs in the Apocrypha and Apocalyptic Literature*, in relation to *2 Enoch* J32 and *Sib. Or.* 8.96-99. This resurrection interpretation is also evident in the *Hel. Syn. Pr.* 3:25-26 and 12:49-50 as discussed in the section "*Prayers, Psalms*, and *Odes*."

Gr. 41:1-3	Ar. [48](41):1-3	Ge. [48](41):1-3	Sl. 49-50.1-3
¹And God called and said, "Adam, Adam." And <u>the body answered from the earth</u> and said: "Here am I, Lord."	¹God called to <u>Adam's body through the dust</u> and said, "Adam, Adam." Adam's body said to the dust, "Answer and say, 'Here (I am), Lord.'"	¹Then God turned and called Adam. <u>Adam's body answered him from the soil</u> and said, "Here I am, [[Lord]]."	¹And the Lord called Adam to himself and said, "Adam, Adam, where are you?" ²And <u>his body answered</u>, "I am here, O Lord,"
²And God said to him: "I told you (that) **earth you are and to earth shall you return**. ³Again I promise to you the Resurrection: I will raise you up in the Resurrection with every man, who is of your seed."	²The Lord said to him, "Behold, just as I said to you, 'Adam, **you are dust and you return to dust**'; ³but I will raise you in the resurrection which [I] promised you."	²And the Lord told him, "Behold, as I told you, **you are soil and you have returned to the soil**, ³but I will raise you up in the resurrection which I have promised you, at the time of resurrection.	³ᵃThe Lord said, "So I told you, '**You are earth and to the same earth you will return again.**' ³ᵇAnd at the resurrection, you will rise with all of mankind."

It should be noted that this apocalypse does not mention the eschatological judgment of *Targ. Ps.-J.* Gen. 3:19 in which everyone will be held responsible for their actions; instead, it only emphasizes the universal nature of the eschatological resurrection.

g. *Apocalypse of Moses* 43:2-3 || *Vita* 51:2

The seventh and last resurrection passage in the books of the *Life of Adam and Eve* appears in a narrative section which concerns Eve's funeral (Pericope 35). In this part of the narrative, Michael instructs Seth how to prepare Eve for burial before the angels came for her body to bury her with Adam and Abel. Michael then instructs Seth that this should be the burial practice until the day of the resurrection (highlighted in gray in the following texts). Both the Apocalypse and the Slavonic traditions mention the souls of the righteous as a separate entity from the body, an aspect also appearing in the *Vita*, which mentions that following the resurrection, the soul and the body of the holy will be joined together for all eternity, never to be separated again by death (see the boxed sections in the following parallel texts).

Gr. 43:2-3	*Vita* 51:2	Ar. [51] (43):2-3	Ge. [51] (43):2-3	Sl. 49-50.3-4
²And afterwards Michael spoke to Seth saying: "Lay out in this manner every man that dies until the day of the Resurrection."		²After this, Michael spoke with Seth and said, "Thus shall you **dress every human being** who dies, until the day of the end, through the resurrection."	²And after that, the angel Michael told him, "Thus **dress every dead person** who dies, until the death of all human beings."	³And the archangel said to Seth, "So shall you bury every person who dies until the resurrection."

³And after giving him this rule he said: "**Mourn not beyond six days, but on the seventh day, rest and rejoice on it,** because on that very day, God and we the angels rejoice with the righteous soul, who has passed away from the earth."	² "**Man of God, mourn no longer than six days,** for the seventh day is the sign of the resurrection, the repose of the coming age, and *on the seventh day the Lord rested from all his works*. [III+ all his work. Indeed the eighth day is (the sign) of the future and eternal blessedness, in which all the holy will reign throughout endless ages with the Creator and Savior himself, in both soul and body, never again to die Amen.]III	³When the angels had said this to Seth, he ascended to heaven, praising the Father and the Son and the Holy Spirit, now and forever.	³When he had taught Seth all that, he ascended to the uppermost heaven, far from Seth, and told him, "**Do not mourn for the dead more than five days** and *on the seventh day rejoice* for *on that day God rested from all his (works) which the Lord had made.*"	⁴Again he said to him, "**Arrange a memorial ceremony on the third day and on the ninth and on the twentieth and on the fortieth,** and arrange everything in proper order, so that we angels might take joy in it along with the souls of the righteous."

The variations between the burial practices in these five traditions may reflect the local practice in the region represented by each tradition. The Armenian and Georgian traditions emphasize the importance of dressing the dead before burial. The Apocalypse, *Vita*, and the Georgian traditions mention the maximum length of mourning. In the case of the Apocalypse and the *Vita*, mourning should be limited to six days, while the Georgian version limits it to five days (see the bolded text). The Slavonic tradition does not mention a mourning time but instead focuses on the need of arranging several memorial ceremonies to celebrate the dead person. The first ceremony takes place on the third day, the second on the ninth day, the third on the twentieth day, and the final ceremony on the fortieth (see the bolded text). The rationale for this mourning practice is also given in this passage (introduced by the underlined words). Both the *Vita* and the Georgian traditions associate the end of the grieving period with the

Sabbath rest (text in italics), with the *Vita* adding that "the seventh day is the sign of the resurrection, the repose of the coming age." In some of the manuscripts of the *Vita*, the Christian interpolation considers the eighth day as an additional sign to the seventh day, which is the sign of the resurrection. The eighth day is a sign of "the future and eternal blessedness, in which all the holy will reign throughout endless ages with the Creator and Savior himself."[46] The Apocalypse also associates the end of mourning with rest, but unlike the *Vita* and the Georgian traditions, the rest is associated with the joy God and his angels have on that very day for "the righteous soul, who has passed away from the earth" (*Apoc. Mos.* 43:3). The Slavonic memorial ceremonies are "arranged in proper order, so that the angels might take joy in it along with the souls of the righteous" (Sl. 49-50.4).

g. Concluding Remarks

All the resurrection passages appear in the Apocalypse and in a combination of the Armenian, Georgian, and Slavonic textual traditions, while only three of them are recorded in the *Vita*. From the Apocalypse, the reader learns there will be both a universal eschatological resurrection and judgment. Those who have kept themselves from evil will be given access to the Tree of Life, thus gaining immortality while the unrighteous will be condemned. Upon death, a person will be mourned for no more than six days. On the seventh, "God will rejoice with the righteous soul, who has passed away from the earth." However, at the resurrection, the soul will once more join the body. One of the resurrection passages seems to suggest everyone will be made into holy people through the process of removing the evil heart and replacing it with a heart that understands the good and worships God alone. Thus, they will not sin anymore. It is also suggested that, following the resurrection, they will have full access to the Garden and God will be in their midst. Table 6 summarizes the death and resurrection view found in the *Apocalypse of Moses*. However, the reader should keep in mind that most of the description in this table relates specifically to Adam, Eve, and the Satan; as such, the author of the Apocalypse may not have intended all the details to have a universal application.

---

46. The importance of the eighth day in Christian circles is attested in the Epistle of Barnabas, which states: "Your present Sabbaths are not acceptable to Me, but that is which I have made, [namely this,] when, giving rest to all things, I shall make a beginning of the eighth day, that is, a beginning of another world. Wherefore, also, we keep the eighth day with joyfulness, the day also on which Jesus rose again from the dead. And when He had manifested Himself, He ascended into the heavens" (*Barn.* 25).

Table 6. Death and resurrection view derived from the *Apocalypse of Moses*

Life *Ap. Mos.* 28:4; 39:1	Death *Ap. Mos.* 13	Day of Resurrection *Ap. Mos.* 10:2; 13:3-5; 28:4	Judgment *Ap. Mos.* 37:5	Reward/ Punishment *Ap. Mos.* 39:2-3
- "If you keep yourself from all evil, as one wishing to die, when again the Resurrection has come to pass, I will raise you up" (28:4). - If you had kept my commandments (39:1).	- Adam's soul departs with an awesome ascent (13:6). - Adam's body in the ground until the day of resurrection (41:1-3). - Eve's body buried in the ground (43:1). - Seventh day, the soul of the righteous leaves the earth (43:3) - Adam soul brought to the Third Heaven (37:5). → not a state of non-existence	- All who have sinned will curse me, Eve (10:2). - All the righteous to be given to Paradise, and God shall be in their midst, no more sinners before God, be given ever joy of Paradise, the evil heart shall be given a heart that understands the good and worship God alone (13:3). - Given the three of life → become immortal forever (13:4). - Their joy shall be turned into sorrow, but your sorrow shall be turned into joy (39:2). - Establish Adam on the Throne of Satan (39:2).	"Fearful day of my reckoning, which I will make in the world" (37:5).	Reward for Adam/the righteous (39:2) - Grief turned into joy. - Adam will regain his rule, and be seated on the throne of his deceiver. - Access to the three of life → immortality (13:4; 28:4) Punishment of the Satan/ wicked (39:3) - Be cased down. - Be condemned. - Shall greatly mourn and weep when they see Adam sitting on the glorious throne.

5. *Pseudo-Philo*

Pseudo-Philo refers to the unknown author of the *Biblical Antiquities*, also known as *Liber antiquitatum biblicarum* in Latin, and covers biblical history from Adam to David (Genesis–1 Samuel). This work belongs to the genre of Rewritten Bible and was most likely composed in Hebrew by a Palestinian Jew and later translated into Greek and Latin. Evans notes this work "may have been written as early as the first or even second century BCE, but most scholars favor a date toward the end of the first century."[47] Harrington considers this work "as a reflection of how Palestinian Jews in the first century A.D. interpreted the Jewish Scriptures, as a source for popular biblical theology of the period and as a repository for motifs and legends that are paralleled or even unique in ancient Jewish literature."[48]

Eschatological material appears throughout the book rather than being gathered into one section. This material focuses on what takes place after death, the events related to God's eschatological visitation, and what comes after. Following is a list of details regarding the "afterlife" and the eschatological elements found in the book.

Afterlife and Eschatological Elements	Textual Reference (*Pseudo-Philo*)
Present World/World to Come	3:10; 16:3; 19:7, 13; 32:17; 62:9
Death ‖ Sleep	19:2, 6; 28:10; 29:4; 33:6; 35:3
Judgment I - the deeds done while living in the present world determine a person's placement while waiting for the resurrection	44:10
Cannot repent after death	33:2-5
Souls of the just → experience peace until the eschatological resurrection	23:13; 28:10; 51:5
Souls of the wicked → experience punishment for their sins until the eschatological resurrection	16:3; 23:6; 31:7; 36:4; 38:4; 44:10; 51:5; 63:4
God will visit the world, which will introduce the age of the world-to-come	3:9; 16:3; 19:12-13, 15; 23:13; 26:12; 48:1
Resurrection/judgment II	3:9-10; 19:12-13; 25:7
The just will dwell in happiness with God	19:12-13; 23:13
The wicked like Korah and his band will be annihilated	16:3

---

47. Evans, *Ancient Texts for New Testament Studies*, 49. See also D. J. Harrington, "Pseudo-Philo," *DNTB* 865; idem, "Pseudo-Philo," *OTP* 2:299; Howard Jacobson, "*Pseudo-Philo*, Book of Biblical Antiquities," in Feldman, Kugel, and Schiffman, eds., *Outside the Bible*, 1:470.

48. Harrington, "Pseudo-Philo," *DNTB* 864.

The most crucial element is the two separate ages, this present world and the world-to-come, which will be introduced by God recreating heaven and the earth. The author of the *Biblical Antiquities* makes it clear that a person's prospects in the world-to-come are based on his/her decisions in the present world. Thus, there will be no opportunity for repentance following death, nor is it possible to intercede on their behalf. Instead, upon death, the soul parts from the body. Based on this judgment, the soul will either join the souls of the righteous to experience peace, or the souls of the wicked to be punished until God's visitation, the time of the universal resurrection and judgment. Table 7 shows narrative sections, the textual references to the TaNaKh and *Pseudo-Philo*, and the eschatological resurrection passages in the *Biblical Antiquities* (as listed in Table 4). The passages alluding to the resurrection are placed in brackets, most of these use sleep as an analogy for death (*Ps.-Philo* 19:2, 6; 28:10; 29:4; 33:6; 35:3), suggesting death was regarded as a temporary condition like sleep.[49]

Table 7. Resurrection statement and allusions in *Pseudo-Philo*

Subject matter	TaNaKh	*Ps.-Philo*	Resurrection passages (allusions) in *Pseudo-Philo*
Adam → Joseph	Genesis	1–8	3:9-10
Moses	Exodus	9–12	
	Leviticus	13	
	Numbers	14–18	(16:3)
	Deuteronomy	19	19:(2, 6-7), 12-13
Joshua	Joshua	20–24	23:(6), 13
Kenaz		25–29	25:7; (28:10; 29:4)
Deborah	Judges	30–33	(31:7); 33:2-5, (6)
Aod → Phinehas		34–48	(35:3; 36:4; 38:4; 44:10; 48:1)
Samuel → David	1 Samuel	49–65	(51:5; 62:9; 63:4); 64:6-9

The following five clear resurrection passages, *Ps.-Philo* 3:10; 19:12-13; 25:7; 33:1-3; 64:6-9, will be considered briefly in the following sections.

a. *Pseudo-Philo* 3:10

The first clear resurrection statement appears in God's promise to Noah following the flood. God promises that he will never again destroy

---

49. This figurative language is also used in Dan. 12:2 when describing death and resurrection and is well attested in the New Testament (Mt. 27:52; Jn 11:11; Acts 7:60; 13:36; 1 Cor. 7:39; 11:30; 15:6, 18, 20, 51; 1 Thess. 4:13–15; 2 Pet. 3:4).

all living creatures together as he had just done with the worldwide flood, "until time is fulfilled" (*Ps.-Philo* 3:9). However, at the end of the present world, there will be a universal resurrection including both the righteous and the wicked, who will both be judged. God will judge between soul and flesh, a possible allusion to the tradition appearing in the *Apocryphon of Ezekiel* (see the discussion in the "Apocalyptic Literature" chapter in the companion volume, *Afterlife and Resurrection Beliefs in the Apocrypha and the Pseudepigrapha*), that for a person to be judged, both his body and soul has to be unified and judged as a whole since it was this united entity that committed both good and evil deeds during the present age. Those who are pardoned in the judgment will not be tainted. God concludes by declaring "there will be another earth and another heaven, an everlasting dwelling place" for those who were pardoned in the judgment (*Ps.-Philo* 3:10), using similar language as Isa. 65:17 and 66:22. Thus, this resurrection statement also alludes to a future destruction of the present world, though this passage does not reveal how it will be destroyed. It should also be noted that this passage does not reveal the final destination of those who were deemed wicked in the eschatological judgment, nor does it present a clear view on the immortality of the soul question.

This passage uses sleep as an analogy for death and describes the resurrection of the dead as raising "up the sleeping from the earth," the same concept used in Dan. 12:2. However, unlike Daniel, *Biblical Antiquities* describes a universal event. Resurrection is not a reward for the righteous, but rather the precursor for the eschatological judgment in which everyone will be judged and receive their due. In the resurrection process, "the underworld will pay back its debt, and the place of perdition will return its deposit" (note the commercial terminology). Following the judgment, the author adds: "death will be extinguished, and the underworld will close its mouth," describing death as a devouring beast, which will no longer serve a purpose since the righteous will become immortal.

b. *Pseudo-Philo* 19:12-13

The second resurrection passage appears in Moses' farewell speech, where God promises Moses that his death is not the end – rather, he will be resurrected. Moses resurrection is mentioned in both the New Testament (Moses and Elijah came to Jesus on the Mount of Transfiguration [Mt. 17:3-4; Mk 9:4-5; Lk. 9:30-33] and Michael and the devil disputed over Moses' dead body [Jude 1:9]) and in Rabbinic Literature (*b. Sanh.* 90b). More details regarding this eschatological event are provided in the current text. It suggests God himself will visit the world to raise Moses and his fathers from the earth. Like the previous passage, this passage also uses the metaphor of sleep for death, emphasizing the temporary condition of death. Moses will be awoken from his unknown grave and join his fathers to "dwell in the immortal dwelling place that is not subject to time."

c. *Pseudo-Philo* 25:7

The third clear resurrection statement is a part of Kenaz's[50] speech to the people in which he encourages sinners to confess, referring to the story of how Achan confessed his sins when confronted by Joshua when he had been singled out by God (Josh. 7). However, unlike the story of Achan, which ended with him and his entire family being stoned to death by the people of Israel and their remains being burnt (Josh. 7:25-26), Kenaz suggests that their confession may have an impact on their prospects in the eschatological judgment. He encourages their confession because "And who knows that if you tell the truth to us, even if you die now, nevertheless God will have mercy on you when he will resurrect the dead?" (*Ps.-Philo* 25:7). Since the death of Achan and his family turned God's wrath away from the people of Israel, *Pseudo-Philo* may have speculated that Achan's confession, although not saving him from an untimely death in the present world, may have functioned as an atonement, like in Achan's case. Otherwise what purpose did his confession serve? The possible mercy mentioned by Kenaz may most likely refer to the judgment taking place after the universal resurrection, suggesting that God would accept their confessions and forgive their sins, thereby counting them among the righteous who will receive their reward in the world-to-come.

d. *Pseudo-Philo* 33:1-5

The fourth clear resurrection passage appears in Deborah's farewell speech to the people of Israel, mirroring Joshua's exhortation to the people before he died (Josh. 23–24). She states everyone will die, using the words of Joshua (Josh. 23:14), and emphasizes the importance of directing their hearts to the Lord in the present world since there will be

---

50. Kenaz is presented by *Pseudo-Philo* as the first judge of Israel and a major figure. However, in the book of Judges he is only mentioned briefly as Caleb's youngest brother and the father of Othniel, who, according to the TaNaKh, was the first judge of Israel (Judg. 3:9-10).

no chance of repentance following death (*Ps.-Philo* 33:2). To underscore the latter point, she notes that in the underworld, even if they wanted to commit sins, which is far easier than doing righteous deeds, her listeners would not be able to since "the desire for sinning will cease and the evil impulse will lose its power" (*Ps.-Philo* 33:3). In other words, when God demands the souls back from the underworld at the time of the eschatological resurrection, they will be in the same state as when he deposited them. A righteous person deposited in the underworld upon death will still be righteous when resurrected to stand in the eschatological judgment. The same would be true for the wicked. This being the case, Deborah implores the people to obey her voice and amend their ways and put their relationship with God in order while they are still living and there is time.

Upon hearing Deborah's exhortation, according to *Pseudo-Philo*, the people implored her to pray for them and requested that her soul should be mindful of them forever after she had passed away (*Ps.-Philo* 33:4). However, Deborah once more reminds them that when a person dies and enters the underworld, they cease to have an impact on others' destinies as they will no longer be able to pray or be mindful of anyone. She concludes by reiterating that the only way the righteous dead can profit, is by making them examples to follow. Her dying words to the people end with the promise that if they live righteous lives, they "will be like the stars of the heaven" (*Ps.-Philo* 33:5), a possible allusion to Dan. 12:3. Howard Jacobson notes in the *Sifre* (Deut. 10) "that in the future world the faces of the righteous will shine like seven things, and included are the sun, the heaven, and the stars."[51] This view may be based on Exod. 34:29-35, which describes Moses' face radiating light when returning from God's presence.

e. *Pseudo-Philo* 64:6-9

The last clear resurrection passage appears at the end of the *Biblical Antiquities*, in *Pseudo-Philo*'s retelling of the narrative concerning Saul's visit to the Witch of Endor, recorded in 1 Sam. 28:7-20. Following are the two parallel accounts. The highlighted texts will be discussed in the following section.

---

51. Jacobson, "Pseudo-Philo, Book of Biblical Antiquities," 554.

Ps.-Philo 64:5-8	1 Samuel 28:12-19
⁵ And when the woman saw Samuel rising up and she saw Saul with him, she shouted out and said, "Behold you are Saul, and why have you deceived me?" And he said to her, "Do not be afraid, but tell what you have seen." She said, "Behold forty years have passed since I began raising up the dead for the Philistines, but such a sight as this has never been seen before nor will it be seen afterward." ⁶And Saul said to her, "What is his appearance?" She said, "You are asking me about divine beings. For behold his appearance is not the appearance of a man. <u>For he is clothed in a white robe with a mantle placed over it</u>, and two angels are leading him." And Saul remembered the mantle that Samuel tore when he was alive, and he struck his hand on the ground and pounded it. ⁷And [Samuel] said to him, "<u>Why have you disturbed me by raising me up?</u> I thought that the time for being rendered the rewards of my deeds had arrived. And so do not boast, King, nor you, woman; for you have not brought me forth, but that order that **God spoke to me while I was still alive, that I should come and tell you** that you have sinned now a second time in neglecting God. Therefore after rendering up my soul my bones have been disturbed so that **I who am dead should tell you what I heard while I was alive**.	¹² When the woman saw Samuel, she screamed, and then she asked Saul, "Why did you deceive me? You are Saul!" ¹³ But the king said to her, "Don't be afraid. What do you see?" "I see a spirit form coming up out of the earth," the woman answered. ¹⁴ Then Saul asked her, "What does he look like?" "An old man is coming up," she replied. "<u>He's wearing a robe.</u>" Then Saul knew that it was Samuel, and he bowed his face to the ground and paid homage. ¹⁵ "<u>Why have you disturbed me by bringing me up?</u>" [Samuel] asked [Saul]. "I'm in serious trouble," replied [Saul]. "The Philistines are fighting against me and God has turned away from me. He doesn't answer me anymore, either through the prophets or in dreams. So I've called on you to tell me what I should do."

	¹⁶Samuel answered, "Since the LORD has turned away from you and has become your enemy, why are you asking me? ¹⁷The LORD has done exactly what He said through me: The LORD has torn the kingship out of your hand and given it to your neighbor David. ¹⁸You did not obey the LORD and did not carry out His burning anger against Amalek; therefore the LORD has done this to you today.
⁸Now therefore tomorrow you and your sons will be with me when the people have been delivered into the hands of the Philistines; and because your insides were eaten up with jealousy, what is yours will be taken from you."	¹⁹The LORD will also hand Israel over to the Philistines along with you. Tomorrow you and your sons will be with me, and the LORD will hand Israel's army over to the Philistines."

When viewing these two accounts side by side it is easy to see the additions and the narrative sections left out by *Pseudo-Philo*. Both of these accounts concern the temporary resurrection of the prophet Samuel. Both accounts also state the message Samuel gave to King Saul. However, the concern of *Pseudo-Philo* is how Samuel could have known what to say to Saul since he was dead and supposedly did not communicate with God while dead. To solve this problem, *Pseudo-Philo* suggests that God had already revealed to Samuel what to tell Saul while he was still alive. Therefore, when resurrected, he could give Saul that very message (see the bolded text).

Samuel is also presented as looking different from the dead Philistines that the witch had resurrected during her 40-year-long career, stating that she had never seen such as sight nor will she see it again. She describes Samuel as a divine being clothed in a white robe with a mantle placed over it, escorted by two angels. The witch of Endor's description suggests that the righteous dead, when brought back to life, look different from those who are wicked.

The most significant difference between the two accounts are the words spoken by Samuel following the question: "Why have you disturbed me by raising me up?" (*Ps.-Philo* 64:7 ‖ 1 Sam. 28:15). While in the biblical account this question opens a dialogue between Samuel and Saul, in the *Biblical Antiquities* it functions more as a rhetorical question, introducing a long monologue by Samuel. In this monologue,

Samuel says it was not due to the powers of Saul nor the witch who had called him back from death; rather, it was solely on God's order that he had come back to life. Additionally, Samuel states that when he died he had rendered up his soul. As such he seems a little surprised at being resurrected. His expectation was that he was being brought to life in the eschatological resurrection to receive his reward in the eschatological judgment, but instead, his bones had just been disturbed (*Ps.-Philo* 64:7, see the text highlighted in gray).

At the conclusion of the parallel temporary resurrection passage, Samuel reveals to King Saul that he will die together with his sons the following day. Saul's reaction in these two accounts is quite different. In the biblical account, Saul becomes terrified by the prospect of his imminent death and was not able to eat nor drink. In the *Biblical Antiquities*, Saul is also described as growing faint upon hearing Samuel's words, yet eventually, he embraces his fate stating: "perhaps my destruction will be an atonement for my wickedness," a possible hint that Saul hoped for a favorable outcome in the eschatological judgment.

e. Concluding Remarks

The clear resurrection passage in the *Biblical Antiquities* presents a universal eschatological resurrection and judgment. Upon death, the soul leaves the body and enters the first judgment, whereupon a decision is taken regarding with the soul will be placed with the righteous or the wicked souls. The righteous souls will experience peace, while the wicked souls will be punished as they wait for God's eschatological visitation. At that time, God will resurrect all the dead in order to bring them to the judgment. Those who are deemed righteous will gain eternal life in the world-to-come, while those deemed wicked will be annihilated. Figure 3 illustrates the resurrection concept in *Pseudo-Philo*.

Figure 3. Death and Resurrection in *Pseudo-Philo*

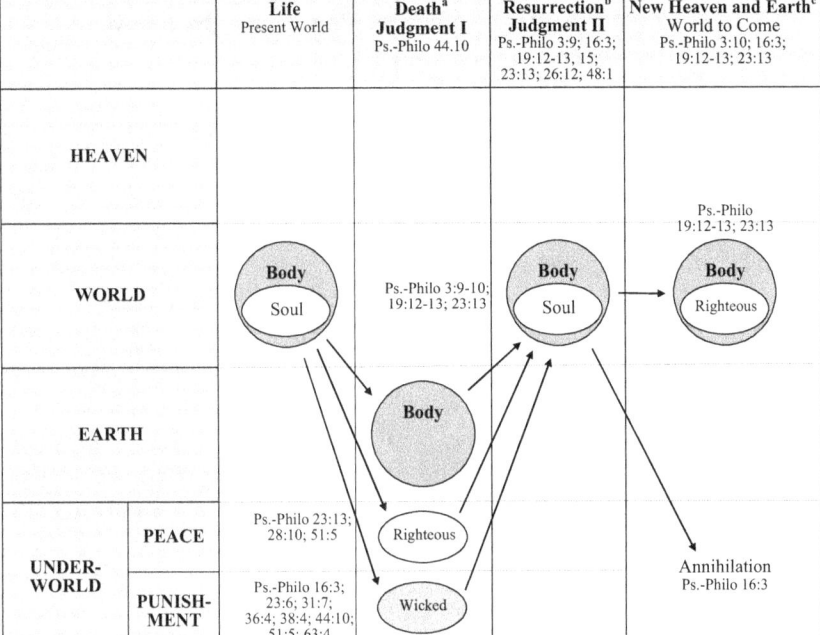

ᵃ Upon death, the soul parts from the body and the soul is judged based on the person's decisions in this life (*Ps.-Philo* 44:10). Based on this judgment, the soul will either join the souls of the righteous or the souls of the wicked in the underworld. The souls of the righteous will experience peace (23:13; 28:10; 51:5) and the souls of the wicked will be punished for their sins (16:3; 23:6; 31:7; 36:4; 38:4; 44:10; 51:5; 63:4) until God's eschatological visitation (3:9; 16:3; 19:12-13, 15; 23:13; 26:12; 48:1), the time of the universal resurrection and judgment. While the souls are in the underworld, there will be no opportunity for repentance (33:2-5), nor can they intercede on the behalf of the living (33:4). In other words, when God demands the souls back from the underworld at the time of the eschatological resurrection, they will be in the same state as when he deposited them.

ᵇ At the time of God's eschatological visitation (*Ps.-Philo* 19:12-13), God will resurrect all the dead in order to bring them to the second judgment. The souls will once more be unified with their bodies and they will be judged as a unit (3:9-10; 19:12-13; 25:7). Those who are deemed righteous will gain eternal life and dwell in happiness with God in the world-to-come (19:12-13; 23:13) while those deemed wicked will be annihilated (16:3).

ᶜ At the conclusion of the eschatological judgment, God will create a new heaven and a new earth (*Ps.-Philo* 3:10), suggesting the destruction of the present world. Since the wicked will be annihilated (16:3) and the righteous will become immortal (19:12-13; 23:13), "death will be extinguished, and the underworld will close its mouth" (3:10), thus, no longer serving a purpose.

~ ~ ~

6. *Lives of the Prophets*

The *Lives of the Prophets* is a Jewish composition most likely written in Greek during the first half of the first century CE, perhaps even predating Jesus' public ministry. Based on the content, the author probably lived in Jerusalem or in the surrounding area due to the great familiarity shown of its geography. This literary work provides insight into the popular religion of the first century. As such, the sparse theological views presented could be considered a part of mainstream Judaism.[52] The purpose of the *Lives of the Prophets* is clearly expressed in the opening statement: "The names of the prophets, and where they are from, and where they died and how, and where they lie."[53] The book mentions twenty-three prophets from the TaNaKh – all the literary prophets[54] and seven of the nonliterary prophets.[55] George Nickelsburg notes that in addition to the geographical framework, which in some cases also provides the prophet's tribal affiliation, "the bulk of the composition is given over to narratives of a decidedly legendary character. Some of these tales are purely extra-biblical and otherwise unattested."[56] Several statements in the *Lives of the Prophets* reveal a belief in some form of life after death (*Liv. Proph.* 1:8; 2:4, 19) and allude to a future judgment (13:2; 15:5; 21:3); however, there are only two clear eschatological[57] resurrection passages in this work (2:11-19; 3:10-12).

---

52. Douglas R. A. Hare, "Lives of the Prophets," *DNTB* 653.
53. Douglas R. A. Hare, "The Lives of the Prophets: A New Translation and Introduction," *OTP* 2:385.
54. The four major prophets: Isaiah (*Liv. Proph.* 1:1-13), Jeremiah (2:1-19), Ezekiel (3:1-19), and Daniel (4:1-21), and the twelve minor prophets: Hosea (5:1-2), Joel (8:1-2), Amos (7:1-3), Obadiah (9:1-5), Jonah (10:1-11), Micah (6:1-3), Nahum (11:1-4), Habakkuk (12:1-13), Zephaniah (13:1-3), Haggai (14:1-2), Zechariah (15:1-6), and Malachi (16:1-4).
55. The seven nonliterary prophets mentioned are: Nathan (*Liv. Proph.* 17:1-4), Ahijah (18:1-5), Joad (19:1-2), Azariah (20:1-2), Elijah (21:1-15), Elisha (22:1-17), and Zechariah son of Jehoiada (23:1-2).
56. George W. E. Nickelsburg, "Stories of Biblical and Early Post-Biblical Times," in Stone, ed., *Jewish Writings of the Second Temple Period*, 57.
57. There are several references to a temporary bodily resurrection in which a person is resurrected to continue the present life, and will experience death a second time at some point in the future (*Liv. Proph.* 10:5-6; 21:7 || 1 Kgs 17:17-24; *Liv. Proph.* 22:9-10 || 2 Kgs 4:8-37; *Liv. Proph.* 22:17 || 2 Kgs 13:20-21).

a. *Lives of the Prophets* 2:15

The first resurrection statement is a part of the Jewish tradition that Jeremiah hid the ark of the covenant before the Babylonian army captured the city of Jerusalem and its Temple. In this passage (*Liv. Proph.* 2:11-19; cf. 2 Macc. 2:4-8) it is suggested that the work was swallowed up in a rock. The parallel tradition in *4 Baruch* reveals the ark and the vessels were delivered to the earth by Jeremiah with the aid of his scribe, Baruch (*4 Bar.* 3:8-20). An earlier version of this tradition has Jeremiah hiding the ark, the tabernacle, and the altar of incense in a cave at Mount Nebo where God had previously shown Moses the Promised Land before he passed away (2 Macc. 2:1-8). According to the *Lives of the Prophets*, the ark will be hidden until the eschatological resurrection: "And in the resurrection the ark will be the first to be resurrected and will come out of the rock and be placed on Mount Sinai, and all the saints will be gathered to it there as they await the Lord and flee from the enemy who wishes to destroy them" (*Liv. Proph.* 2:15). Apart from a belief in an eschatological resurrection and that all the Saints will gather around it on Mount Sinai waiting for the Lord fleeing from their persecutors, this text does not reveal much regarding the nature of this resurrection and what will come after.

b. *Lives of the Prophets* 3:12

The second resurrection statement appears in a terrifying warning Ezekiel gave the enemy leaders who wished to destroy the people of Israel. His warning is based on the vision of the Valley of the Bones (Ezek. 37:1-14): "'Are we lost? Has our hope perished?' And in the wonder of the dead bones he persuaded them that there is hope for Israel both here and in the coming (age)" (*Liv. Proph.* 3:12). This passage shows a dual understanding of Ezekiel's vision, giving it both a personal and a corporate interpretation. Thus, it seems Ezekiel would argue that both the nation of Israel and the individual person will have a future. The enemy may think they will be able to defeat or destroy the nation of Israel, yet this will only be a temporary defeat since the nation will have a future in the present age and will be restored. The same is true on a personal level. Individuals are killed, yet through their resurrection they will have a future in the age to come.

c. Concluding Remarks

Not much is revealed regarding the eschatological resurrection in the *Life of the Prophets*, but the scant details show that the resurrection hope was a part of mainstream Judaism during the early part of the first century CE, especially due to the non-polemic nature of the resurrection statement which simply takes the resurrection belief for granted. It also becomes evident that during this period, Ezek. 37:1–14 was understood both as a reference to a personal eschatological resurrection and to the restoration of the nation of Israel following the Babylonian captivity.

7. *Ladder of Jacob*

The *Ladder of Jacob* has a complex compositional history. Although it is possible that the original was written in Hebrew, Greek seems to be more likely.[58] However, it has only survived into the present in Old Church Slavonic as a part of the *Tolkovaja paleja*, which contains stories from the TaNaKh with commentaries. H. Lunt notes that "the date and provenance of the Ladder are unknown," and "the time, place, and shape of the original compilation are controversial."[59] It was probably authored by a first-century CE Jew[60] who wanted to emphasize God's sovereignty, although ch. 7 contains Christian interpolations "concerning the birth of Jesus and also the crucifixion."[61]

Christfried Böttrich suggests the author of this literary work gave Jacob's dream, recorded in Gen. 28:11-22, an apocalyptic interpretation, adding "that is why it seems plausible to attribute the *Ladder of Jacob* first of all to the genre of apocalypse."[62] The ladder of Jacob's dream is considered a representation of the history of the world stretching from the time of Jacob to the end of time, when his descendants will finally possess the promised land and see God's promises spoken to Abraham in Gen. 12:1-3 fulfilled (*Lad. Jac.* 1:9-11).

Ladder of Jacob 7:21 is the only reference to the resurrection in this composition, in a section with extensive Christian interpolation – or, as noted by Lunt, a chapter which should probably "be regarded as an

---

58. Evans, *Ancient Texts for New Testament Studies*, 51; H. G. Lunt, "Ladder of Jacob: A New Translation and Introduction," *OTP* 2:403; Andrei A. Orlov, "The Face as the Heavenly Counterpart of the Visionary in the Slavonic *Ladder of Jacob*," in *Of Scribes and Sages*, ed. Craig A. Evans (London: T&T Clark/Continuum, 2004), 60-61.

59. Lunt, "Ladder of Jacob," 2:404.

60. For a discussion on the Jewish or Christian provenance of this work and dating, see Christfried Böttrich, "Apocalyptic Tradition and Mystical Prayer in the *Ladder of Jacob*," *JSP* 23 (2004): 304–5; Orlov, "The Face as the Heavenly Counterpart of the Visionary in the Slavonic *Ladder of Jacob*," 60–61.

61. Lunt, "Ladder of Jacob," 2:402.

62. Böttrich, "Apocalyptic Tradition and Mystical Prayer," 294.

independent work, juxtaposed to the *Ladder of Jacob* by a Slavic editor of the Palaia."⁶³ This resurrection passage concerns the resurrection of Eve: "And he [Christ] will revive Eve, who died by the fruit of the tree" (*Lad. Jac.* 7:21). However, this passage does not clearly state when this event will take place, nor the extent of this resurrection, if the resurrection will happen at Christ's first coming, or in a future eschatological event. Also, it does not clearly state whether Eve will be resurrected in a unique event, whether she will be a part of a universal resurrection, or whether this resurrection comes within the context of a judgment. Despite its brevity, the *Ladder of Jacob* still bears witness to a resurrection belief.

8. *4 Baruch*

4 Baruch, according to its Greek title, ΤΑ ΠΑΡΑΛΕΙΠΟΜΕΝΑ ΙΕΡΕΜΙΟΥ ΤΟΥ ΠΡΟΦΗΤΟΥ, contains "things omitted from the Prophet Jeremiah," or, as the Ethiopic title states, "the rest of the words of Baruch."⁶⁴ Unlike *2 Baruch* and *3 Baruch*, which are also attributed to Jeremiah's scribe,⁶⁵ this book, although dependent on *2 Baruch*, falls into the "rewritten Bible" genre instead of *Apocalyptic Literature* since it does not contain a heavenly ascension element.

Stephen Robinson notes there seem to be three redaction levels in this literary work, two of which are Jewish,⁶⁶ and a third by a Christian redactor,⁶⁷ who interpolated the concluding section of the book, *4 Bar.* 8:12–9:32, and possibly *4 Bar.* 6:7, 13, 25,⁶⁸ into this work following the failed Bar Kokhba revolt (132–136 CE), when "Judaism repudiated much of its apocalyptic tradition and the literature it produced, including

---

63. Lunt, "Ladder of Jacob," 2:402.

64. Penner and Heiser, *Old Testament Greek Pseudepigrapha with Morphology*, from the section "*4 Baruch* – Title, Summary, Genre"; and Stephen E. Robinson, "4 Baruch: A Translation and Introduction," *OTP* 2:415.

65. That four books are attributed to Baruch – the *Book of Baruch* (*1 Baruch*) is a part of the apocrypha and appears in the Septuagint, while the other three (*2 Baruch*, *3 Baruch*, and *4 Baruch*) are a part of the Pseudepigrapha. *2 Baruch* is discussed in the Apocalyptic Literature chapter in the companion volume, *Afterlife and Resurrection Beliefs in the Apocrypha and Apocalyptic Literature*, since it contains a complex resurrection belief. The *Book of Baruch* and *3 Baruch*, however, do not contain any resurrection material.

66. This could explain the shift in main characters of this book from Jeremiah (*4 Bar.* 1–4) to his scribe, Baruch (*4 Bar.* 7–8).

67. Stephen E. Robinson, "Baruch, Book of 4," *ABD* 1:622.

68. Evans, *Ancient Texts for New Testament Studies*, 51.

4 Baruch," and left it to the various Christian communities to preserve it.[69] Thus, although *4 Baruch* was probably composed in Hebrew, it only survived into the present time in several non-Semitic versions: Greek, Ethiopic, Armenian, Old Church Slavonic, and Romanian.[70]

4 Baruch was probably authored by a Jew living in the Jerusalem region, given the writer's familiarity with the geographical places mentioned.[71] The reference to the vineyard or farm of Herod Agrippa I (*4 Bar.* 3:14, 21; 5:22) would rule out any compositional date prior to 41 CE, when Agrippa took possession of Judea and Samaria. Hence, the topic of the Chaldean destruction of Jerusalem in *4 Baruch* 1–4 is best understood as a comment on the cataclysmic events relating to Titus' destruction of the Jewish Temple in Jerusalem in 70 CE.[72] *4 Baruch*, as noted by Jens Herzer, "picks up on certain feelings that were important among the Jewish people in the period 117–132 C.E." and the author seems "aware of the seething messianic atmosphere" which inevitably led to the second Jewish revolt.[73] The Christian redaction probably took place soon after the failure of the revolt, and *4 Baruch* may have reached its current form by the middle of second century CE, serving as a "vehicle for validating Christian claims."[74]

Herzer considers the theology of *4 Baruch*, with its de-emphasis on the role of an earthly temple, as being in line with the Pharisaic wing of Judaism, which succeeded following the destruction of the Temple, and the spiritual-religious reorientation that took place under the leadership of Rabbi Johanan ben Zakkai and his successors in Yavneh, which secured the survival of Judaism.[75] *4 Baruch* emphasizes the importance of God's law as the path to salvation, the eschatological resurrection hope associated with said salvation, and the focus on the Heavenly Jerusalem as the future home of the saved (5:34), thus stressing this salvation can only come on God's initiative (6:20-21; 8:1-2).[76] This eschatological perspective also

---

69. Robinson, "Baruch, Book of 4," 1:622.
70. Robinson, "4 Baruch," 2:413–14.
71. Jens Herzer, *4 Baruch (Paraleipomena Jeremiou)*, WGRW 22 (Atlanta, GA: Society of Biblical Literature, 2005), xxxiv; Robinson, "4 Baruch," 2:415.
72. Robinson, "4 Baruch," 2:414.
73. Herzer, *4 Baruch*, xxxiv. For further reading regarding the dating of this book, see the section titled "Author, Location, and Date," in Herzer, *4 Baruch*, xxx–xxxvi; Robinson, "4 Baruch," 2:414; idem, "Baruch, Book of 4," 1:622; and the section regarding "Language, Texts, Date, and Authorship" of *4 Baruch*, in Penner and Heiser, *Old Testament Greek Pseudepigrapha with Morphology*.
74. Robinson, "4 Baruch," 2:416.
75. Herzer, *4 Baruch*, xxxi–xxxii.
76. Ibid., xxxiv.

fits well with the perspective presented by the early Christian Church. The three resurrection passages in this composition are, 6:6-10, 7:18, and 9:12-14. The third passage is in the Christian addition of the book.

a. *4 Baruch* 6:6-10

The first resurrection passage appears at the conclusion of the story regarding Abimelech the Ethiopian, who pulled Jeremiah out of the muddy cistern (*4 Bar.* 3:12 ‖ Jer. 38:4-13). Upon learning of the impending destruction of Jerusalem (*4 Bar.* 1–3), Jeremiah asks God to show Abimelech mercy and protect him from seeing the destruction of the city and its desolation (*4 Bar.* 3:13). God promises Jeremiah that he will shelter Abimelech until God returns the people from exile, provided Jeremiah sends him to the vineyard of Agrippa the following morning (3:14). He follows God's request and sends Abimelech to the farm to "get a few figs to give to the sick among the people" (3:21). While picking figs on the farm, Abimelech decided to have a rest and fell into a sixty-six-year long sleep (5:1-2). When he woke up, he thought he had only slept for a short time and his figs were still dripping milk, but he could not recognize the city of Jerusalem nor find any of his neighbors (5:4, 7). When Abimelech finally found Baruch and showed him his basket of still "newly picked" 66-year-old figs, Baruch considered the miraculous preservation of the figs and Abimelech's awakening as proof of resurrection, representing the "Jewish belief in both personal and corporate resurrection."[77] Baruch states that God rewards those who love him, and he will raise them in their tabernacles. According to Baruch, they shall believe that they once more will live again (*4 Bar.* 6:6). He adds:

> [8]Look at this basket of figs; for behold, they are sixty-six years old and they have not withered nor do they stink, but they are dripping with milk. [9]Thus will it be for you, my flesh, if you do the things commanded you by the angel of righteousness. [10]He who preserved the basket of figs, the same one again will preserve you by his power. (*4 Bar.* 6:8-10)

Robinson comments that the fig is an appropriate symbol for life since it "drips of" milk and is filled with seeds. Interestingly, according to some Jewish traditions, like the *Apoc. Mos.* 20:4-5, the fig was the forbidden fruit of the Garden of Eden.[78]

---

77. Penner and Heiser, *Old Testament Greek Pseudepigrapha with Morphology*, in the section titled "*4 Baruch*: Relevance for Exegesis in Canonical Material."

78. In the Apocalypse, following Eve eating from the forbidden fruit, all the leaves fell from the trees except from the forbidden tree itself, thus, the reason

b. *4 Baruch* 7:18

The second resurrection passage appears in the context of a funeral, officiated by Jeremiah, outside the city with the permission of King Nebuchadnezzar. The party was interrupted by an eagle, which carried a letter from Baruch and Abimelech. Jeremiah gathered together all the people and returned to the eagle to hear the message. At that moment the eagle resurrects the person who was about to be buried as a sign that the nation would be resurrected and they would return from their exile and once more live in Jerusalem. Thus, the second resurrection passage also links a personal and corporate resurrection, although the resurrection taking place in this passage was of a temporary nature, functioning as a type of the eschatological resurrection.

c. *4 Baruch* 9:12-14

The third resurrection passage appears in the last chapter, the Christianized ending of the book (*4 Bar.* 8:12–9:32), "where Jeremiah's ecstatic faint is described in terms reminiscent of the resurrection of Christ."[79] Jeremiah's faint is described by the author as making him become "as one of those who have given up their soul" (9:7). Both Baruch and Abimelech thought he was dead and started weeping and crying: "woe to us, because our father Jeremiah has left us; the priest of God has departed" (9:8). However, God told them not to bury him since he was still alive and that his soul would return to his body again (9:12). Three days later, Jeremiah's soul returned to his body and his ecstatic faint ended. Before he started to describe to Baruch and Abimelech what he had seen, Jeremiah praised God saying: "Glorify God with one voice! All (of you) glorify God, and the Son of God who awakens us, Jesus Christ the light of all the aeons, the inextinguishable lamp, the life of faith!" (9:14).

Jeremiah's ecstatic faint foreshadows the death and the eschatological resurrection experience. In the same way as Jeremiah's soul left his tabernacle or body at the beginning of his ecstatic faint, so does the soul of a person leave the body upon death. The Christian redactor mentions that it is Michael, "the archangel of righteousness who opens the gates for the righteous" (*4 Bar.* 9:5), although it is not clear if this is with regard to the

---

Eve covered herself with fig leaves (see also, *b. Ber.* 40a; *b. Sanh.* 70b). The other potential candidates for the forbidden fruit are: wheat (*b. Ber.* 40a; *b. Sanh.* 70b; *Gen. Rab.* 15:7); grapes or wine (*b. Ber.* 40a; *b. Sanh.* 70b; *Gen. Rab.* 15:7; *Zohar* 1:73a); etrog/citron (*Gen. Rab.* 15:7), or a unique fruit which was a combination of these fruits (*b. Ber.* 40a).

79. Robinson, "4 Baruch," 2:416.

soul of the righteous dead, or the resurrected righteous in the eschatological time. Be that as it may, in the eschatological resurrection, which will be orchestrated by the Son of God (9:14), the soul will return and will dwell once more in its tabernacle, in a way similar to how Jeremiah's soul returned to his body after the three-day long ecstatic faint, and the person will return to life.

d. Concluding Remarks

4 Baruch presents a clear resurrection hope, both on a personal (bodily) and corporate level (the nation of Israel), based on the following three piece of evidence, none of which are based on a biblical argument: the first is Abimelech's 66-year-long sleep and the preservation of the harvested figs (*4 Bar.* 3–6); the second, the resurrection, which took place at the funeral service led by Jeremiah (*4 Bar.* 7); and the final piece of evidence of Jeremiah's ecstatic faint (*4 Bar.* 9). However, *4 Baruch* does not show any concern for the period between death and resurrection, nor for what will happen to the wicked. Instead, *4 Baruch* reveals that the soul parts from its tabernacle (body) following death, to be reunified at the time of the eschatological resurrection. The resurrection is presented as the reward for those who love God, who will be brought to the Heavenly Jerusalem (*4 Bar.* 5:34).

9. *History of the Rechabites*

James Charlesworth proposes that it would be "unwise to state the probable original language, date, or provenance of this document until critical editions of the Greek, Syriac, and Ethiopic texts are available,"[80] for the *History of the Rechabites*. However, he notes the title found in MS D (fols. 209r-201v) supports the hypothesis of a Hebrew/Aramaic original, which was later translated into Greek since it states:

> The History of the Blessed Ones, the Sons of the Rechabites, Whose Record Is Recorded by Jeremiah the Prophet When He Said That They Are the Sons of Jonadab, the Son of Rechab, Who Are Inhabitants of the City Jerusalem. It Was Translated from Hebrew into Greek and from Greek into Syriac by the Hands of the Reverend Mar Jacob of Edessa.[81]

---

80. J. H. Charlesworth, "*History of the Rechabites*: A New Translation and Introduction," 2:444.
81. Ibid., 2:450 n. b.

If the original language was indeed Hebrew, the earliest strata of this document was probably authored by a Jew residing in Palestine, while the Christian sections were interpolated into this Jewish document at a later date. Charlesworth suggests that, based on the Greek document, the main body of the book (chs. 3–15) seems to have a Jewish provenance probably dated to the first or second century CE, while the introduction (chs. 1–2), ch. 16, and the conclusion (chs. 19–23) are of a clearly Christian origin and may have been added in the third to fourth century.[82] However, Chris Knights argues for a Christian provenance for the whole document,[83] even the self-contained document *Abode of the Blessed* (chs. 11–16) containing the "resurrection" expectation,[84] which concludes that this work "should no longer be classified among the Pseudepigrapha of the Old Testament."[85]

The *History of the Rechabites* records the journey of Zosimus to the island of the Blessed Ones (*Hist. Rech.* 1:1-3), where he meets the Rechabites who left Jerusalem in the time of Jeremiah (*Hist. Rech.* 8:1a–10:8 || Jer. 35), who live in an Eden-like condition (*Hist. Rech.* 14:1). Through his conversation with the Rechabites, he gains significant insight regarding death and the afterlife, and the ascent of the soul (*Hist. Rech.* 14:1a–16:8g).

a. *History of the Rechabites* 14:1a–16:8g

In this resurrection passage, it is revealed to Zosimus by the Blessed Ones that "(the soul) discerns and knows the day of its departure through a revelation from holy angels" (*Hist. Rech.* 15:4), when the angels of God come for the Rechabite's pure soul (14:2-5). Upon death, the soul parts the body (14:2), in full view of the other members of the community (15:10) and ascends in joy (15:9a), guided by the angels to the highest heaven and brought before God to worship him (16:1, 4). The soul, when leaving the body, is described as appearing in "the likeness of a glorious light, and formed and imprinted in the likeness and type of the body" (15:10). When God raises the soul from its worship he "sends that soul to a stately mansion (to await) the day of resurrection for (the rest of our) community" (16:7). Meanwhile, the body the soul left behind, when it ascended to Heaven, is buried by the angels in a sepulcher (15:7, 8).

---

82. Ibid., 2:444–5.
83. Chris H. Knights, "The Rechabites Revisited: The *History of the Rechabites* Twenty-Five Years Later," *JSP* 23 (2014): 307–20.
84. Ibid., 309.
85. Ibid., 318.

b. Concluding Remarks

This resurrection passage only concerns itself with the final destiny of the Rechabites and not the righteous in general, although it could be expected they would have a similar fate – the soul awaiting resurrection in a stately mansion. Thus, no interest is shown toward the final destiny of the wicked or what will happen to the wicked souls when it parts from the body. The nature of the resurrection is not revealed either, whether it will be limited to the Rechabites, or if it would be universal, including all the righteous and the wicked. This passage does not address what will take place following the resurrection, whether the soul will once more unify with the body, where the righteous and the wicked souls will go, and finally, whether there will be an eschatological judgment. No scriptural references or allusions are used in support of the resurrection belief in the *History of the Rechabites*; rather, this belief seems to be taken for granted.

Chapter 4

WISDOM AND PHILOSOPHICAL LITERATURE

There is a strong wisdom tradition in Judaism which originated in the TaNaKh with Proverbs, Ecclesiastes, Job, Song of Songs, and some Psalms. Unlike the biblical wisdom books, which are primarily associated with Solomon (Proverbs, Ecclesiastes, and Song of Songs), the wisdom literature of the Pseudepigrapha, with the exception of the *Testament of Solomon*, are not. The books belonging to this category endeavor to present the best way of life and the ideal to follow, often using Greek philosophical terms and concepts. They also attempt to demonstrate the superiority of the Jewish religion, showing that the teaching of the Greek philosophers is biblical. James Charlesworth notes the generic character and the lack of God's presence in the pseudepigraphal work as a complicating factor when demarcating unique Jewish aspects in the literature belonging to this category of Second Temple literature.[1] However, two of the books in this category, *4 Maccabees* and *Pseudo-Phocylides*, contain references to God and a strong belief in a life after death. Table 8 lists all the "resurrection" and "life-after-death" passages in these two books. These will be addressed in the following pages. *4 Maccabees* emphasizes the immortality of the soul with little interest in a bodily resurrection, while *Pseudo-Phocylides* presents a tripartite view of human anthropology, body–spirit–soul, with a clear bodily resurrection expectation.

---

1. James H. Charlesworth, "Wisdom and Philosophical Literature: Introduction," *OTP* 2:476.

Table 8. Resurrection texts in wisdom and philosophical literature

Passage		Notes	Resurrection		Classification			
			Imp.	Stat.	Ref.	Allude	Phil.	Assum.
4 Maccabees	7:18-19	Conquer the passion of the flesh → resurrection	×				?	×
	9:8-9, 22	The reward for virtue	×					×
	10:2-4	"Cannot touch my soul"	×					×
	13:9-18	"Our forefathers will receive us"	×					×
	14:4-6	Righteous' death → immortality	×					×
	15:3-4, 27	Righteous' death → immortality	×					×
	16:12-13, 25	Righteous' death → immortality	×					×
	17:4-5	Hope of endurance	×			×		×
	17:11-12, 17-21	Prizes for victory	×					×
	18:3	Martyrs → worthy of the divine portion	×					×
	18:10-23	The Father's teaching		×	×			×
Pseudo-Phocylides	91-115	Death and afterlife; Immortality of the soul		×		×		×

1. *4 Maccabees*

4 Maccabees is a theological-philosophical treaty which appears in the appendix to the Greek Bible. It is not, however, counted among the Apocryphal writings.[2] It was originally composed in Greek by a devout Hellenized Jew, most likely from Asia Minor, between 18 and 72 CE.[3] David deSilva suggests it is difficult to be more specific than this since the composition "is attached to no known author, connected with no known location, tied to no particular occasion, and devoid of references to contemporary events."[4] Although in early Church history both Eusebius (*Hist. eccl.* 3.10.6) and Jerome (*De vir. ill.* 13; *Dial. ad. Pelag.* 2.6) attributed this treaty to Flavius Josephus, deSilva states most scholars have rejected this provenance due to "historical inaccuracies, different styles and radically different stances towards accommodation to Gentile culture" than what is found in the writings of Josephus.[5]

Scholars have noted that the name *4 Maccabees* is a misleading title since this composition neither dates to the Maccabean period nor gives an account of the events which took place during this crucial period in Jewish history, with the exception of the historical setting (*4 Macc.* 3:19–4:26), martyrdom of Eleazar (2 Macc. 6 || *4 Macc.* 5:1–6:30), and the seven sons (2 Macc. 7:1-40 || *4 Macc.* 8:1–12:19), which concludes with the death of the mother of these sons (2 Macc. 7:41 || *4 Macc.* 14:11–17:1). Both Eusebius (*Hist. eccl.* 3.10.6) and Jerome (*De vir. ill.* 13) gave this work the more fitting title, Περὶ αὐτοκράτορος λογισμοῦ, "On the Absolute Power of Reason," which is more in line with the purpose and context stated in the exordium of the book: "(1) Since I am about to demonstrate a most philosophical statement – that pious reason (ὁ εὐσεβὴς λογισμός) is absolute master of the passion (τῶν παθῶ[ν]) – I would rightly counsel you that you should pay close attention to this philosophical inquiry."[6]

The final example used in this theological-philosophical treaty to how the superior nature of Judaism and the teaching provided by the Torah in achieving a virtuous life, to become fully in control of one's passion, "a goal almost universally admired by Greek and Roman ethicist,"[7] is the

---

2. See Table 2 in the companion volume, *Afterlife and Resurrection in the Apocrypha and Apocalyptic Literature.*

3. David A. deSilva, "*4 Maccabees*," in Feldman, Kugel, and Schiffman, eds., *Outside the Bible*, 2363.

4. David A. deSilva, *4 Maccabees*, Septuagint Commentary Series (Leiden: Brill, 2006), xiv.

5. David A. deSilva, "3 and 4 Maccabees," *DNTB* 664.

6. Translation from deSilva, *4 Maccabees*, 3.

7. deSilva, "3 and 4 Maccabees," 665.

4. Wisdom and Philosophical Literature

martyrdom of the seven brothers and their mother (*4 Macc.* 8–18). Their loyalty to God and their Torah-trained reason have given these heroes full control of their passion – so much so that they would rather die than comply with Antiochus' (representative of the Hellenistic culture) demands to eat defiling food, which would have been a transgression of the ancestral commands (*4 Macc.* 9:1-2). Apart from the "resurrection" hope stated in the author's reflection following the martyrdom of Eleazar the priest (*4 Macc.* 7:16-23), all the "resurrection" passages in *4 Maccabees* appear in this section (*4 Macc.* 8–18), see Table 11.

a. *4 Maccabees* 7:18-19 || *4 Maccabees* 13:17

The first "resurrection" statement in *4 Maccabees* appears in the author's concluding remarks regarding the account of Eleazar's torture and death (*4 Macc.* 7:18-19). A similar statement appears in the author's reflection following the martyrdom of the seven brothers (*4 Macc.* 13:17; 16:25). The parallel words in these three passages have been indicated and the relevant dying-living aspect has been underlined.

4 Maccabees 7:18-19	*4 Maccabees* 13:17	*4 Maccabees* 16:25
¹⁸ ἀλλ' ὅσοι τῆς εὐσεβείας προνοοῦσιν ἐξ ὅλης καρδίας, ο?τοι μόνοι δύνανται κρατεῖν τῶν τῆς σαρκὸς παθῶν. ¹⁹ πιστεύοντες ὅτι θεῷ οὐκ ἀποθνῄσκουσιν, ὥσπερ οὐδὲ οἱ πατριάρχαι ἡμῶν Ἀβρααμ καὶ Ἰσαακ καὶ Ἰακωβ, ἀλλὰ ζῶσιν τῷ θεῷ.	¹⁷ οὕτω γὰρ θανόντας ἡμᾶς Ἀβρααμ καὶ Ἰσαακ καὶ Ἰακωβ ὑποδέξονται καὶ πάντες οἱ πατέρες ἐπαινέσουσιν.	²⁵ ἔτι δὲ καὶ ταῦτα εἰδότες ὅτι οἱ διὰ τὸν θεὸν ἀποθνῄσκοντες ζῶσιν τῷ θεῷ ὥσπερ Ἀβρααμ καὶ Ἰσαακ καὶ Ἰακωβ καὶ πάντες οἱ πατριάρχαι
¹⁸ But as many as have a care for piety from the whole heart – these alone are able to restrain the passions of the flesh, ¹⁹ trusting that they do not die to God, just as neither our **patriarchs** Abraham and Isaac and Jacob did, but **live to God**.	¹⁷ For Abraham and Isaac and Jacob will welcome us, and all the father praise us, for dying in this way.	²⁵ but also, moreover, with them knowing these things – that those dying on account of God continue **to live to God**, just as Abraham and Isaac and Jacob and all **the patriarchs**.

In these three texts the author suggests that the patriarchs, Abraham, Isaac, and Jacob, are not dead but alive, extrapolating that Eleazar and the seven brothers (and the mother [*4 Macc.* 17:5]) did not die to God (θεῷ οὐκ ἀποθνήσκουσιν) but instead live to God (ζῶσιν τῷ θεῷ). Thus, these heroes will be welcomed (ὑποδέξονται) by the patriarchs and all the fathers will praise them (ἐπαινέσουσιν). The author's reference to the patriarchs in support of a future after death is not unique. The same argument was used by Jesus when making the case for a bodily resurrection in his discussion with the Sadducees (Mt. 22:31-32; Mk 12:26-27; Lk. 20:37-38), basing it on a grammatical observation in Exod. 3:6. The parallels between *4 Macc.* 7:18-19, Mt. 22:31-32, and Exod. 3:6 have been highlighted to better see the link between these passages. The words highlighted in gray appear in all three passages, while the words in italics only appear in Matthew and Exodus. Jesus' and the author of *4 Maccabees* "resurrection" application of Exod. 3:6 is underlined.

4 Maccabees 7:18-19	Matthew 22:31-32 (BGT)	Exodus 3:6 (WTT/BGT)
¹⁸ ἀλλ' ὅσοι τῆς εὐσεβείας προνοοῦσιν ἐξ ὅλης καρδίας, οὗτοι μόνοι δύνανται κρατεῖν τῶν τῆς σαρκὸς παθῶν. ¹⁹ πιστεύοντες ὅτι θεῷ οὐκ ἀποθνήσκουσιν, ὥσπερ οὐδὲ οἱ πατριάρχαι ἡμῶν Αβρααμ καὶ Ισαακ καὶ Ιακωβ, ἀλλὰ ζῶσιν τῷ θεῷ.	³¹ περὶ δὲ τῆς ἀναστάσεως τῶν νεκρῶν οὐκ ἀνέγνωτε τὸ ῥηθὲν ὑμῖν ὑπὸ τοῦ θεοῦ λέγοντος ³² *ἐγώ εἰμι* ὁ *θεὸς* Ἀβραὰμ καὶ ὁ *θεὸς* Ἰσαὰκ καὶ ὁ *θεὸς* Ἰακώβ; οὐκ ἔστιν [ὁ] θεὸς νεκρῶν ἀλλὰ ζώντων.	וַיֹּאמֶר אָנֹכִי אֱלֹהֵי אָבִיךָ אֱלֹהֵי אַבְרָהָם אֱלֹהֵי יִצְחָק וֵאלֹהֵי יַעֲקֹב וַיַּסְתֵּר מֹשֶׁה פָּנָיו כִּי יָרֵא מֵהַבִּיט אֶל־הָאֱלֹהִים׃ καὶ εἶπεν αὐτῷ *ἐγώ εἰμι* ὁ θεὸς τοῦ πατρός σου *θεὸς* Αβρααμ καὶ *θεὸς* Ισαακ καὶ θεὸς Ιακωβ ἀπέστρεψεν δὲ Μωυσῆς τὸ πρόσωπον αὐτοῦ εὐλαβεῖτο γὰρ κατεμβλέψαι ἐνώπιον τοῦ θεοῦ
¹⁸ But as many as have a care for piety from the whole heart – these alone are able to restrain the passions of the flesh, ¹⁹ trusting that they do not die to God, just as neither our patriarchs Abraham and Isaac and Jacob did, **but live to God**.	³¹ Now concerning the resurrection of the dead, haven't you read what was spoken to you by God: ³² *I am* the God of Abraham and *the God of* Isaac and *the God of* Jacob? He is not the God of the dead, **but of the living**."	And he said, *I am* the God of thy father, *the God of* Abraam, and *the God of* Isaac, and *the God of* Jacob; and Moses turned away his face, for he was afraid to gaze at God.

The "resurrection" application hinges on the word tense used in Exod. 3:6 (boxed phrases). The "I am" statement is in a present form in the Septuagint (εἰμι – first person singular, present active indicative) and is a nominal clause in Hebrew (אָנֹכִי אֱלֹהֵי אָבִיךָ, *I am the God of your fathers*), thus suggesting the patriarchs must still be alive, since God is still their God, nor was nor will become their God sometime in the future.[8]

The last phrase ζῶσιν τῷ θεῷ, *live to God* (*4 Macc.* 7:19) and its parallel, ζῶσιν τῷ θεῷ, *[God] of the living* (Mt. 22:32), is a key term used by Paul when describing the new reality experienced by those who have died to their self and have instead embraced a life in Christ (Rom. 6:10-11; 14:8; Gal. 2:19), who has conquered death (Rom. 6:9; 14:9). This is an interesting similarity to the core message of *4 Maccabees*, in the same way as Paul emphasizes the importance of dying to self in order to be living to God in Christ (Rom. 6:11). The author of *4 Maccabees* argues that a person who has gained control over his passion, through God's Torah, can rely on God to ensure they will not die.[9]

Comparing the application of Exod. 3:6 by *4 Macc.* 7:18-19 and Mt. 22:31-32, it becomes clear that although the author of *4 Maccabees* and Jesus alludes to and uses this passage in support of their "resurrection" hope, the resurrection hope itself is different. While Jesus argues for a bodily resurrection, the author of *4 Maccabees* presents a very different view, in which a person is judged and receives his/her eternal destiny at the point of death, leaving no need for an eschatological resurrection and judgment. The remaining "resurrection" passages appear in *4 Maccabees* 8–18 (see Table 8).

b. *4 Maccabees 8–18*

The dialogues and the author's comments and exhortations in the martyr account of the seven sons and their mother have been greatly expanded

---

8. A similar grammatical "proof-text" argument in support of a resurrection belief is used by Rabbi Simai: "Whence do we learn resurrection from the Torah? – From the verse, And I also have established my covenant with them, [sc. the Patriarchs] to give them the land of Canaan [Exod. 6:4]: '[to give] you' is not said, but 'to give them' [personally]; thus, resurrection is proved from the Torah" (*b. Sanh.* 90b). The only way for this promise to be literally fulfilled is through the Patriarchs' bodily resurrection.

9. This is very similar to the theological perspective voiced by Sirach and in rabbinic literature that each person is born with two inclinations, a good and an evil, with the necessity of the latter to be controlled by the former, and where the Torah functions as the "antidote" against uncontrolled passion, and will help a person gain full control over his/her evil desire. For further reading, see Joseph Jacobs, "Yezer ha-ra," *JE* 12:601–2.

from the much older account in 2 Maccabees 7,[10] from one chapter in 2 Maccabees to eleven chapters in *4 Maccabees*. Table 9 shows the nature and the extent of this expansion. It should be noted that the mother's two speeches between the death of her sixth and seventh son in 2 Maccabees (2 Macc. 7:20-23, 27-29) are missing in *4 Maccabees*. However, the mother plays an important part in the five-chapter-long philosophical dialogue (*4 Macc.* 14:11–15:32 and 18:6-9) towards the end of *4 Maccabees* (*4 Macc.* 13:1–18:19). This additional theological-philosophical element in *4 Maccabees* provides not only the "moral" of the martyrdom story but it also serves as the climax and the ultimate example in support of the thesis put forth in the introduction of the book.

To get a better impression of the differences between these two accounts of the martyrdom of the seven sons and their mother, the following parallel texts show these two accounts. The core issue of eating defiled food has been underlined in the text, while the references to the ancestral laws are in italics. The dialogues given by the brothers and the mother are bolded, while references to the future hope are highlighted in gray. Relevant references are placed within square brackets.

Table 9. Outline of 2 Maccabees 7 and *4 Maccabees* 8–18

	2 Maccabees 7	***4 Maccabees* 8–18**
Introduction	7:1-2	8:1–9:10
First Brother	7:3-6	9:11-25
Second Brother	7:7-9	9:26-32
Third Brother	7:10-12	10:1-11
Fourth Brother	7:13-14	10:12-21
Fifth Brother	7:15-17	11:1-12
Sixth Brother	7:18-19	11:13-27
Mother's Speech I	7:20-23	–
Seventh Brother	7:24-26	12:1-19
Mother's Speech II	7:27-29	
Seventh Brother	7:30-40	
Theological-philosophical Remark		13:1–14:10
Example of Mother		14:11–15:32
Philosophical Remark	–	16:1–18:5
Mother's words to her sons		18:6-9
Their Father's teaching		18:10-19
Conclusion	7:41-42	18:20-24

---

10. 2 Maccabees 7 is discussed in the companion volume, *Afterlife and Resurrection Beliefs in the Apocrypha and Apocalyptic Literature*.

4. *Wisdom and Philosophical Literature* 111

2 Maccabees 7 (NRS)

¹It happened also that seven brothers and their mother were arrested and were being compelled by the king, under torture with whips and thongs, to partake of unlawful swine's flesh. ²One of them, acting as their spokesman, said, **"What do you intend to ask and learn from us? For we are ready to die rather than transgress** *the laws of our ancestors.*"

4 Maccabees 8–18 (NRS)

⁸⁻¹For this is why even the very young, by following a philosophy in accordance with devout reason, have prevailed over the most painful instruments of torture. ²For when the tyrant was conspicuously defeated in his first attempt, being unable to compel an aged man to eat defiling foods [2 Macc. 6:20-21], then in violent rage he commanded that others of the Hebrew captives be brought, and that any who ate defiling food would be freed after eating, but if any were to refuse, they would be tortured even more cruelly. ³When the tyrant had given these orders, seven brothers – handsome, modest, noble, and accomplished in every way – were brought before him along with their aged mother. ⁴When the tyrant saw them, grouped about their mother as though a chorus, he was pleased with them. And struck by their appearance and nobility, he smiled at them, and summoned them nearer and said, ⁵"Young men, with favorable feelings I admire each and every one of you, and greatly respect the beauty and the number of such brothers. Not only do I advise you not to display the same madness as that of the old man who has just been tortured, but I also exhort you to yield to me and enjoy my friendship. ⁶Just as I am able to punish those who disobey my orders, so I can be a benefactor to those who obey me. ⁷Trust me, then, and you will have positions of authority in my government if you will renounce the ancestral tradition of your national life. ⁸Enjoy your youth by adopting the Greek way of life and by changing your manner of living. ⁹But if by disobedience you rouse my anger, you will compel me to destroy each and every one of you with dreadful punishments through tortures.

¹⁰Therefore take pity on yourselves. Even I, your enemy, have compassion for your youth and handsome appearance. ¹¹Will you not consider this, that if you disobey, nothing remains for you but to die on the rack?" ¹²When he had said these things, he ordered the instruments of torture to be brought forward so as to persuade them out of fear to eat the defiling food. ¹³When the guards had placed before them wheels and joint-dislocators, rack and hooks and catapults and caldrons, braziers and thumbscrews and iron claws and wedges and bellows, the tyrant resumed speaking: ¹⁴"Be afraid, young fellows; whatever justice you revere will be merciful to you when you transgress under compulsion." ¹⁵But when they had heard the inducements and saw the dreadful devices, not only were they not afraid, but they also opposed the tyrant with their own philosophy, and by their right reasoning nullified his tyranny. ¹⁶Let us consider, on the other hand, what arguments might have been used if some of them had been cowardly and unmanly. Would they not have been the following? ¹⁷"O wretches that we are and so senseless! Since the king has summoned and exhorted us to accept kind treatment if we obey him, ¹⁸why do we take pleasure in vain resolves and venture upon a disobedience that brings death? ¹⁹O men and brothers, should we not fear the instruments of torture and consider the threats of torments, and give up this vain opinion and this arrogance that threatens to destroy us? ²⁰Let us take pity on our youth and have compassion on our mother's age; ²¹and let us seriously consider that if we disobey we are dead! ²²Also, divine justice will excuse us for fearing the king when we are under compulsion ²³Why do we banish ourselves from this most pleasant life and deprive ourselves of this delightful world?

²⁴Let us not struggle against compulsion or take hollow pride in being put to the rack. ²⁵Not even the law itself would arbitrarily put us to death for fearing the instruments of torture. ²⁶Why does such contentiousness excite us and such a fatal stubbornness please us, when we can live in peace if we obey the king?" ²⁷But the youths, though about to be tortured, neither said any of these things nor even seriously considered them. ²⁸For they were contemptuous of the emotions and sovereign over agonies, ²⁹so that as soon as the tyrant had ceased counseling them <u>to eat defiling food</u>, all with one voice together, as from one mind, said: **⁹:¹"Why do you delay, O tyrant? For we are ready to die rather than transgress our ancestral commandments; ²we are obviously putting our forebears to shame unless we should practice ready** *obedience to the law and to Moses our counselor.* **³Tyrant and counselor of lawlessness, in your hatred for us do not pity us more than we pity ourselves. ⁴For we consider this pity of yours, which ensures our safety through transgression of the law, to be more grievous than death itself. ⁵You are trying to terrify us by threatening us with death by torture, as though a short time ago you learned nothing from Eleazar. ⁶And if the aged men of the Hebrews because of their religion lived piously while enduring torture, it would be even more fitting that we young men should die despising your coercive tortures, which our aged instructor also overcame.**

³The king fell into a rage, and gave orders to have pans and caldrons heated. ⁴These were heated immediately, and he commanded that the tongue of their spokesman be cut out and that they scalp him and cut off his hands and feet, while the rest of the brothers and the mother looked on.

⁵When he was utterly helpless, the king ordered them to take him to the fire, still breathing, and to fry him in a pan. The smoke from the pan spread widely, but the brothers and their mother encouraged one another to die nobly, saying, ⁶**"The Lord God is watching over us and in truth has compassion on us, as Moses declared in his song that bore witness against the people to their faces, when he said, 'And he will have compassion on his servants'** [Deut. 32:36]."

⁷**Therefore, tyrant, put us to the test; and** if you take our lives because of our religion, do not suppose that you can injure us by torturing us. ⁸For we, through this severe suffering and endurance, shall have the prize of virtue and shall be with God, on whose account we suffer; ⁹but you, because of your bloodthirstiness toward us will deservedly undergo from the divine justice eternal torment by fire." ¹⁰When they had said these things, the tyrant was not only indignant, as at those who are disobedient, but also infuriated, as at those who are ungrateful.

¹¹Then at his command the guards brought forward the eldest, and having torn off his tunic, they bound his hands and arms with thongs on each side. ¹²When they had worn themselves out beating him with scourges, without accomplishing anything, they placed him upon the wheel. ¹³When the noble youth was stretched out around this, his limbs were dislocated, ¹⁴and with every member disjointed he denounced the tyrant, saying,

¹⁵**"Most abominable tyrant, enemy of heavenly justice, savage of mind, you are mangling me in this manner, not because I am a murderer, or as one who acts impiously, but because I protect the divine law."** ¹⁶And when the guards said, "Agree to eat so that you may be released from the tortures," ¹⁷he replied, **"You abominable lackeys, your wheel is not so powerful as to strangle my reason. Cut my limbs, burn my flesh, and twist my joints; ¹⁸through all these tortures I will convince you that children of the Hebrews alone are invincible where virtue is concerned."**

4. *Wisdom and Philosophical Literature* 115

⁷After the first brother had died in this way, they brought forward the second for their sport. They tore off the skin of his head with the hair, and asked him, "Will you eat rather than have your body punished limb by limb?"

¹⁹While he was saying these things, they spread fire under him, and while fanning the flames they tightened the wheel further. ²⁰The wheel was completely smeared with blood, and the heap of coals was being quenched by the drippings of gore, and pieces of flesh were falling off the axles of the machine. ²¹Although the ligaments joining his bones were already severed, the courageous youth, worthy of Abraham, did not groan, ²²but as though transformed by fire [Mal. 3:2-3] into immortality, he nobly endured the rackings. ²³**"Imitate me, brothers,"** he said. **"Do not leave your post in my struggle or renounce our courageous family ties. ²⁴Fight the sacred and noble battle for religion. Thereby the just Providence of our ancestors may become merciful to our nation and take vengeance on the accursed tyrant."** ²⁵When he had said this, the saintly youth broke the thread of life.

²⁶While all were marveling at his courageous spirit, the guards brought in the next eldest, and after fitting themselves with iron gauntlets having sharp hooks, they bound him to the torture machine and catapult. ²⁷Before torturing him, they inquired *if he were willing to eat*, and they heard his noble decision.

⁸He replied in the language of his ancestors and said to them, **"No."** Therefore he in turn underwent tortures as the first brother had done. ⁹And when he was at his last breath, he said, **"You accursed wretch, you dismiss us from this present life, but the King of the universe will raise us up to an everlasting renewal of life, because we have died for his laws."**

¹⁰After him, the third was the victim of their sport. When it was demanded, he quickly put out his tongue and courageously stretched forth his hands, ¹¹and said nobly, **"I got these from Heaven, and because of his laws I disdain them,** and from him I hope to get them back again." ¹²As a result the king himself and those with him were astonished at the young man's spirit, for he regarded his sufferings as nothing.

²⁸These leopard-like beasts tore out his sinews with the iron hands, flayed all his flesh up to his chin, and tore away his scalp. But he steadfastly endured this agony and said, ²⁹ **"How sweet is any kind of death for the religion of our ancestors!"** ³⁰To the tyrant he said, **"Do you not think, you most savage tyrant, that you are being tortured more than I, as you see the arrogant design of your tyranny being defeated by our endurance for the sake of religion? ³¹I lighten my pain by the joys that come from virtue, ³²but you suffer torture by the threats that come from impiety. You will not escape, you most abominable tyrant, the judgments of the divine wrath."**

¹⁰˙¹When he too had endured a glorious death, the third was led in, and many repeatedly urged him to save himself by tasting the meat. ²But he shouted, **"Do you not know that the same father begot me as well as those who died, and the same mother bore me, and that** I was brought up on the same teachings? ³**I do not renounce the noble kinship that binds me to my brothers."** ⁴ ⁵Enraged by the man's boldness, they disjointed his hands and feet with their instruments, dismembering him by prying his limbs from their sockets, ⁶and breaking his fingers and arms and legs and elbows. ⁷Since they were not able in any way to break his spirit, they abandoned the instruments and scalped him with their fingernails in a Scythian fashion. ⁸They immediately brought him to the wheel, and while his vertebrae were being dislocated by this, he saw his own flesh torn all around and drops of blood flowing from his entrails. ⁹When he was about to die, he said, ¹⁰**"We, most abominable tyrant, are suffering because of our godly training and virtue, ¹¹but you, because of your impiety and bloodthirstiness, will undergo unceasing torments."**

¹³After he too had died, they maltreated and tortured the fourth in the same way. ¹⁴When he was near death, he said, **"One cannot but choose to die at the hands of mortals and** to cherish the hope God gives of being raised again by him. But for you there will be no resurrection to life!"

¹⁵Next they brought forward the fifth and maltreated him. ¹⁶But he looked at the king, and said, **"Because you have authority among mortals, though you also are mortal, you do what you please. But do not think that God has** forsaken our people. ¹⁷Keep on, and see how his mighty power will torture you and your descendants!"

¹²When he too had died in a manner worthy of his brothers, they dragged in the fourth, saying, ¹³"As for you, do not give way to the same insanity as your brothers, but obey the king and save yourself." ¹⁴But he said to them, **"You do not have a fire hot enough to make me play the coward. ¹⁵No – by the blessed death of my brothers, by** the eternal destruction of the tyrant, and by the everlasting life of the pious, **I will not renounce our noble family ties. ¹⁶Contrive tortures, tyrant, so that you may learn from them that I am a brother to those who have just now been tortured."** ¹⁷When he heard this, the bloodthirsty, murderous, and utterly abominable Antiochus gave orders to cut out his tongue. ¹⁸But he said, **"Even if you remove my organ of speech, God hears also those who are mute. ¹⁹See, here is my tongue; cut it off, for in spite of this you will not make our reason speechless. ²⁰Gladly, for the sake of God, we let our bodily members be mutilated. ²¹God will visit you swiftly, for you are cutting out a tongue that has been melodious with divine hymns."**

¹¹:¹When he too died, after being cruelly tortured, the fifth leaped up, saying, ²**"I will not refuse, tyrant, to be tortured for the sake of virtue. ³I have come of my own accord,** so that by murdering me you will incur punishment from the heavenly justice for even more crimes. ⁴**Hater of virtue, hater of humankind, for what act of ours are you destroying us in this way? ⁵Is it because we revere the Creator of all things and live according to his virtuous law? ⁶But these deeds deserve honors, not tortures."**

⁷ ⁸ ⁹While he was saying these things, the guards bound him and dragged him to the catapult; ¹⁰they tied him to it on his knees, and fitting iron clamps on them, they twisted his back around the wedge on the wheel, so that he was completely curled back like a scorpion, and all his members were disjointed. ¹¹In this condition, gasping for breath and in anguish of body, ¹²he said, **"Tyrant, they are splendid favors that you grant us against your will, because through these noble sufferings you give us an opportunity to show our endurance for the law."**

¹³When he too had died, the sixth, a mere boy, was led in. When the tyrant inquired whether <u>he was willing to eat and be released</u>, he said, ¹⁴**"I am younger in age than my brothers, but I am their equal in mind. ¹⁵Since to this end we were born and bred, we ought likewise to die for the same principles. ¹⁶So if you intend to torture me for not eating defiling foods, go on torturing!"** ¹⁷When he had said this, they led him to the wheel. ¹⁸He was carefully stretched tight upon it, his back was broken, and he was roasted from underneath. ¹⁹To his back they applied sharp spits that had been heated in the fire, and pierced his ribs so that his entrails were burned through. ²⁰While being tortured he said, **"O contest befitting holiness, in which so many of us brothers have been summoned to an arena of sufferings for religion, and in which we have not been defeated! ²²I also, equipped with nobility, will die with my brothers, ²³and I myself will bring a great avenger upon you, you inventor of tortures and enemy of those who are truly devout.**

¹⁸After him they brought forward the sixth. And when he was about to die, he said, **"Do not deceive yourself in vain. For we are suffering these things on our own account, because of our sins against our own God. Therefore astounding things have happened. ¹⁹But do not think that you will go unpunished for having tried to fight against God!"**

²⁰The mother was especially admirable and worthy of honorable memory. Although she saw her seven sons perish within a single day, she bore it with good courage because of her hope in the Lord. ²¹She encouraged each of them in the language of their ancestors. Filled with a noble spirit, she reinforced her woman's reasoning with a man's courage, and said to them, ²²**"I do not know how you came into being in my womb. It was not I who gave you life and breath, nor I who set in order the elements within each of you. ²³Therefore the Creator of the world, who shaped the beginning of humankind and devised the origin of all things,** will in his mercy give life and breath back to you again, since you now forget yourselves for the sake of his laws." ²⁴Antiochus felt that he was being treated with contempt, and he was suspicious of her reproachful tone. The youngest brother being still alive, Antiochus not only appealed to him in words, but promised with oaths that he would make him rich and enviable if he would turn from the ways of his ancestors, and that he would take him for his Friend and entrust him with public affairs.

²⁴**We six boys have paralyzed your tyranny.** ²⁵Since you have not been able to persuade us to change our mind or to force us <u>to eat defiling foods,</u> is not this your downfall? ²⁶Your fire is cold to us, and the catapults painless, and your violence powerless. ²⁷For it is not the guards of the tyrant but those of the divine law that are set over us; therefore, unconquered, we hold fast to reason."

¹²⁻¹When he too, thrown into the caldron, had died a blessed death, the seventh and youngest of all came forward. ²Even though the tyrant had been vehemently reproached by the brothers, he felt strong compassion for this child when he saw that he was already in fetters. He summoned him to come nearer and tried to persuade him, saying, ³"You see the result of your brothers' stupidity, for they died in torments because of their disobedience.

^{25}Since the young man would not listen to him at all, the king called the mother to him and urged her to advise the youth to save himself. ^{26}After much urging on his part, she undertook to persuade her son. ^{27}But, leaning close to him, she spoke in their native language as follows, deriding the cruel tyrant: **"My son, have pity on me. I carried you nine months in my womb, and nursed you for three years, and have reared you and brought you up to this point in your life, and have taken care of you. ^{28}I beg you, my child, to look at the heaven and the earth and see everything that is in them, and recognize that God did not make them out of things that existed. And in the same way the human race came into being. ^{29}Do not fear this butcher, but prove worthy of your brothers. Accept death,** so that in God's mercy I may get you back again along with your brothers."

^{30}While she was still speaking, the young man said, **"What are you waiting for? I will not obey the king's command, but I obey the command of the law that was given to our ancestors through Moses. ^{31}But you, who have contrived all sorts of evil against the Hebrews,** will certainly not escape the hands of God. ^{32}**For we are suffering because of our own sins** ^{33}**And if our living Lord is angry for a little while, to rebuke and discipline us, he will again be reconciled with his own servants.**

^{4}You too, if you do not obey, will be miserably tortured and die before your time, ^{5}but if you yield to persuasion you will be my friend and a leader in the government of the kingdom." ^{6}When he had thus appealed to him, he sent for the boy's **mother** to show compassion on her who had been bereaved of so many sons and to influence her to persuade the surviving son to obey and save himself. ^{7}But when his mother had exhorted him in the Hebrew language, as we shall tell a little later, ^{8}he said, **"Let me loose, let me speak to the king and to all his friends that are with him."** ^{9}Extremely pleased by the boy's declaration, they freed him at once. ^{10}**Running to the nearest of the braziers,** ^{11}**he said, "You profane tyrant, most impious of all the wicked, since you have received good things and also your kingdom from God, were you not ashamed to murder his servants and torture on the wheel those who practice religion?** ^{12}**Because of this,** justice has laid up for you intense and eternal fire and tortures, and these throughout all time will never let you go. ^{13}**As a man, were you not ashamed, you most savage beast, to cut out the tongues of men who have feelings like yours and are made of the same elements as you, and to maltreat and torture them in this way? ^{14}Surely they by dying nobly fulfilled their service to God, but you will wail bitterly for having killed without cause the contestants for virtue."** ^{15}Then because he too was about to die, he said, ^{16}**"I do not desert the excellent example of my brothers, ^{17}and I call on the God of our ancestors to be merciful to our nation; ^{18}but on you he will take vengeance both in his present life and when you are dead."** ^{19}After he had uttered these imprecations, he flung himself into the braziers and so ended his life.

³⁴But you, unholy wretch, you most defiled of all mortals, do not be elated in vain and puffed up by uncertain hopes, when you raise your hand against the children of heaven. ³⁵You have not yet escaped the judgment of the almighty, all-seeing God. **³⁶For our brothers after enduring a brief suffering** have drunk of ever-flowing life, **under God's covenant;** but you, by the judgment of God, will receive just punishment for your arrogance. **³⁷I, like my brothers, give up body and life for the laws of our ancestors, appealing to God to show mercy soon to our nation and by trials and plagues to make you confess that he alone is God, ³⁸and through me and my brothers to bring to an end the wrath of the Almighty that has justly fallen on our whole nation."** ³⁹The king fell into a rage, and handled him worse than the others, being exasperated at his scorn. ⁴⁰So he died in his integrity, putting his whole trust in the Lord.

¹³:¹Since, then, the seven brothers despised sufferings even unto death, everyone must concede that devout reason is sovereign over the emotions. ²For if they had been slaves to their emotions and had eaten defiling food, we would say that they had been conquered by these emotions. ³But in fact it was not so. Instead, by reason, which is praised before God, they prevailed over their emotions. ⁴The supremacy of the mind over these cannot be overlooked, for the brothers mastered both emotions and pains. ⁵How then can one fail to confess the sovereignty of right reason over emotion in those who were not turned back by fiery agonies?

⁶For just as towers jutting out over harbors hold back the threatening waves and make it calm for those who sail into the inner basin, ⁷so the seven-towered right reason of the youths, by fortifying the harbor of religion, conquered the tempest of the emotions. ⁸For they constituted a holy chorus of religion and encouraged one another, saying, ⁹**"Brothers, let us die like brothers for the sake of the law; let us imitate the three youths in Assyria who despised the same ordeal of the furnace. ¹⁰Let us not be cowardly in the demonstration of our piety."** ¹¹While one said, **"Courage, brother,"** another said, **"Bear up nobly,"** ¹²and another reminded them, **"Remember whence you came, and the father by whose hand Isaac would have submitted to being slain for the sake of religion."**

¹³Each of them and all of them together looking at one another, cheerful and undaunted, said, **"Let us with all our hearts consecrate ourselves to God, who gave us our lives, and let us use our bodies as a bulwark for the law. ¹⁴Let us not fear him who thinks he is killing us,** ¹⁵for great is the struggle of the soul and the danger of eternal torment lying before those who transgress the commandment of God. ¹⁶**Therefore let us put on the full armor of self-control, which is divine reason.** ¹⁷**For** if we so die, Abraham and Isaac and Jacob will welcome us, and all the fathers will praise us." ¹⁸Those who were left behind said to each of the brothers who were being dragged away, **"Do not put us to shame, brother, or betray the brothers who have died before us."**
¹⁹You are not ignorant of the affection of family ties, which the divine and all-wise Providence has bequeathed through the fathers to their descendants and which was implanted in the mother's womb.

²⁰There each of the brothers spent the same length of time and was shaped during the same period of time; and growing from the same blood and through the same life, they were brought to the light of day. ²¹When they were born after an equal time of gestation, they drank milk from the same fountains. From such embraces brotherly-loving souls are nourished; ²²and they grow stronger from this common nurture and daily companionship, and from both general education and our discipline in the law of God. ²³Therefore, when sympathy and brotherly affection had been so established, the brothers were the more sympathetic to one another. ²⁴Since they had been educated by the same law and trained in the same virtues and brought up in right living, they loved one another all the more.
²⁵A common zeal for nobility strengthened their goodwill toward one another, and their concord, ²⁶because they could make their brotherly love more fervent with the aid of their religion. ²⁷But although nature and companionship and virtuous habits had augmented the affection of family ties, those who were left endured for the sake of religion, while watching their brothers being maltreated and tortured to death.

¹⁴:¹Furthermore, they encouraged them to face the torture, so that they not only despised their agonies, but also mastered the emotions of brotherly love. ²O reason, more royal than kings and freer than the free! ³O sacred and harmonious concord of the seven brothers on behalf of religion! ⁴None of the seven youths proved coward or shrank from death, ⁵but all of them, as though running the course toward immortality, hastened to death by torture.

⁶Just as the hands and feet are moved in harmony with the guidance of the mind, so those holy youths, as though moved by an immortal spirit of devotion, agreed to go to death for its sake. ⁷O most holy seven, brothers in harmony! For just as the seven days of creation move in choral dance around religion, ⁸so these youths, forming a chorus, encircled the sevenfold fear of tortures and dissolved it. ⁹Even now, we ourselves shudder as we hear of the suffering of these young men; they not only saw what was happening, not only heard the direct word of threat, but also bore the sufferings patiently, and in agonies of fire at that. ¹⁰What could be more excruciatingly painful than this? For the power of fire is intense and swift, and it consumed their bodies quickly.

¹¹Do not consider it amazing that reason had full command over these men in their tortures, since the mind of woman despised even more diverse agonies, ¹²for the mother of the seven young men bore up under the rackings of each one of her children. ¹³Observe how complex is a mother's love for her children, which draws everything toward an emotion felt in her inmost parts. ¹⁴Even unreasoning animals, as well as human beings, have a sympathy and parental love for their offspring. ¹⁵For example, among birds, the ones that are tame protect their young by building on the housetops, ¹⁶and the others, by building in precipitous chasms and in holes and tops of trees, hatch the nestlings and ward off the intruder. ¹⁷If they are not able to keep the intruder away, they do what they can to help their young by flying in circles around them in the anguish of love, warning them with their own calls.

[18]And why is it necessary to demonstrate sympathy for children by the example of unreasoning animals, [19]since even bees at the time for making honeycombs defend themselves against intruders and, as though with an iron dart, sting those who approach their hive and defend it even to the death? [20]But sympathy for her children did not sway the mother of the young men; she was of the same mind as Abraham.

[15.1]O reason of the children, tyrant over the emotions! O religion, more desirable to the mother than her children! [2]Two courses were open to this mother, that of religion and that of preserving her seven sons for a time, as the tyrant had promised. [3]She loved religion more, the religion that preserves them for eternal life according to God's promise. [4]In what manner might I express the emotions of parents who love their children? We impress upon the character of a small child a wondrous likeness both of mind and of form. Especially is this true of mothers, who because of their birth pangs have a deeper sympathy toward their offspring than do the fathers. [5]Considering that mothers are the weaker sex and give birth to many, they are more devoted to their children. [6]The mother of the seven boys, more than any other mother, loved her children. In seven pregnancies she had implanted in herself tender love toward them, [7]and because of the many pains she suffered with each of them she had sympathy for them; [8]yet because of the fear of God she disdained the temporary safety of her children. [9]Not only so, but also because of the nobility of her sons and their ready obedience to the law, she felt a greater tenderness toward them. [10]For they were righteous and self-controlled and brave and magnanimous, and loved their brothers and their mother, so that they obeyed her even to death in keeping the ordinances.

¹¹Nevertheless, though so many factors influenced the mother to suffer with them out of love for her children, in the case of none of them were the various tortures strong enough to pervert her reason. ¹²But each child separately and all of them together the mother urged on to death for religion's sake. ¹³O sacred nature and affection of parental love, yearning of parents toward offspring, nurture and indomitable suffering by mothers! ¹⁴This mother, who saw them tortured and burned one by one, because of religion did not change her attitude. ¹⁵She watched the flesh of her children being consumed by fire, their toes and fingers scattered on the ground, and the flesh of the head to the chin exposed like masks.
¹⁶O mother, tried now by more bitter pains than even the birth pangs you suffered for them! ¹⁷O woman, who alone gave birth to such complete devotion! ¹⁸When the firstborn breathed his last, it did not turn you aside, nor when the second in torments looked at you piteously nor when the third expired; ¹⁹nor did you weep when you looked at the eyes of each one in his tortures gazing boldly at the same agonies, and saw in their nostrils the signs of the approach of death. ²⁰When you saw the flesh of children burned upon the flesh of other children, severed hands upon hands, scalped heads upon heads, and corpses fallen on other corpses, and when you saw the place filled with many spectators of the torturings, you did not shed tears. ²¹Neither the melodies of sirens nor the songs of swans attract the attention of their hearers as did the voices of the children in torture calling to their mother. ²²How great and how many torments the mother then suffered as her sons were tortured on the wheel and with the hot irons! ²³But devout reason, giving her heart a man's courage in the very midst of her emotions, strengthened her to disregard, for the time, her parental love.

²⁴Although she witnessed the destruction of seven children and the ingenious and various rackings, this noble mother disregarded all these because of faith in God. ²⁵For as in the council chamber of her own soul she saw mighty advocates – nature, family, parental love, and the rackings of her children – ²⁶this mother held two ballots, one bearing death and the other deliverance for her children. ²⁷She did not approve the deliverance that would preserve the seven sons for a short time, ²⁸but as the daughter of God-fearing Abraham she remembered his fortitude. ²⁹O mother of the nation, vindicator of the law and champion of religion, who carried away the prize of the contest in your heart! ³⁰O more noble than males in steadfastness, and more courageous than men in endurance! ³¹Just as Noah's ark, carrying the world in the universal flood, stoutly endured the waves, ³²so you, O guardian of the law, overwhelmed from every side by the flood of your emotions and the violent winds, the torture of your sons, endured nobly and withstood the wintry storms that assail religion.

¹⁶:¹If, then, a woman, advanced in years and mother of seven sons, endured seeing her children tortured to death, it must be admitted that devout reason is sovereign over the emotions. ²Thus I have demonstrated not only that men have ruled over the emotions, but also that a woman has despised the fiercest tortures. ³The lions surrounding Daniel were not so savage, nor was the raging fiery furnace of Mishael so intensely hot, as was her innate parental love, inflamed as she saw her seven sons tortured in such varied ways.

⁴But the mother quenched so many and such great emotions by devout reason. ⁵Consider this also: If this woman, though a mother, had been fainthearted, she would have mourned over them and perhaps spoken as follows: ⁶"O how wretched am I and many times unhappy! After bearing seven children, I am now the mother of none! ⁷O seven childbirths all in vain, seven profitless pregnancies, fruitless nurturings and wretched nursings! ⁸In vain, my sons, I endured many birth pangs for you, and the more grievous anxieties of your upbringing. ⁹Alas for my children, some unmarried, others married and without offspring. I shall not see your children or have the happiness of being called grandmother.
¹⁰Alas, I who had so many and beautiful children am a widow and alone, with many sorrows. ¹¹And when I die, I shall have none of my sons to bury me." ¹²Yet that holy and God-fearing mother did not wail with such a lament for any of them, nor did she dissuade any of them from dying, nor did she grieve as they were dying. ¹³On the contrary, as though having a mind like adamant and giving rebirth for immortality to the whole number of her sons, she implored them and urged them on to death for the sake of religion. ¹⁴O mother, soldier of God in the cause of religion, elder and woman! By steadfastness you have conquered even a tyrant, and in word and deed you have proved more powerful than a man. ¹⁵For when you and your sons were arrested together, you stood and watched Eleazar being tortured, and said to your sons in the Hebrew language,

[16]"My sons, noble is the contest to which you are called to bear witness for the nation. Fight zealously for our ancestral law. [17]For it would be shameful if, while an aged man endures such agonies for the sake of religion, you young men were to be terrified by tortures. [18]Remember that it is through God that you have had a share in the world and have enjoyed life, [19]and therefore you ought to endure any suffering for the sake of God. [20]For his sake also our father Abraham was zealous to sacrifice his son Isaac [Gen. 22:10], the ancestor of our nation; and when Isaac saw his father's hand wielding a knife and descending upon him, he did not cower. [21]Daniel the righteous was thrown to the lions [Dan. 6], and Hananiah, Azariah, and Mishael were hurled into the fiery furnace and endured it for the sake of God [Dan. 3].
[22]You too must have the same faith in God and not be grieved. [23]It is unreasonable for people who have religious knowledge not to withstand pain." [24]By these words the mother of the seven encouraged and persuaded each of her sons to die rather than violate God's commandment. [25]They knew also that those who die for the sake of God live to God, as do Abraham and Isaac and Jacob and all the patriarchs [Exod. 3:6].

[17:1]Some of the guards said that when she also was about to be seized and put to death she threw herself into the flames so that no one might touch her body. [2]O mother, who with your seven sons nullified the violence of the tyrant, frustrated his evil designs, and showed the courage of your faith! [3]Nobly set like a roof on the pillars of your sons, you held firm and unswerving against the earthquake of the tortures. [4]Take courage, therefore, O holy-minded mother, maintaining firm an enduring hope in God.

⁵The moon in heaven, with the stars, does not stand so august as you, who, after lighting the way of your star-like seven sons to piety, stand in honor before God and are firmly set in heaven with them **[Dan. 12:3?]**. ⁶For your children were true descendants of father Abraham. ⁷If it were possible for us to paint the history of your religion as an artist might, would not those who first beheld it have shuddered as they saw the mother of the seven children enduring their varied tortures to death for the sake of religion? ⁸Indeed it would be proper to inscribe on their tomb these words as a reminder to the people of our nation:

⁹"Here lie buried an aged priest and an aged woman and seven sons, because of the violence of the tyrant who wished to destroy the way of life of the Hebrews. ¹⁰They vindicated their nation, looking to God and enduring torture even to death." ¹¹Truly the contest in which they were engaged was divine, ¹²for on that day virtue gave the awards and tested them for their endurance. The prize was immortality in endless life. ¹³Eleazar was the first contestant, the mother of the seven sons entered the competition, and the brothers contended. ¹⁴The tyrant was the antagonist, and the world and the human race were the spectators. ¹⁵Reverence for God was victor and gave the crown to its own athletes. ¹⁶Who did not admire the athletes of the divine legislation? Who were not amazed? ¹⁷The tyrant himself and all his council marveled at their endurance, ¹⁸because of which they now stand before the divine throne and live the life of eternal blessedness. ¹⁹For Moses says, "All who are consecrated are under your hands." **[Deut. 33:3]**

[20]These, then, who have been consecrated for the sake of God, are honored, not only with this honor, but also by the fact that because of them our enemies did not rule over our nation, [21]the tyrant was punished, and the homeland purified – they having become, as it were, a ransom for the sin of our nation. [22]And through the blood of those devout ones and their death as an atoning sacrifice, divine Providence preserved Israel that previously had been mistreated. [23]For the tyrant Antiochus, when he saw the courage of their virtue and their endurance under the tortures, proclaimed them to his soldiers as an example for their own endurance, [24]and this made them brave and courageous for infantry battle and siege, and he ravaged and conquered all his enemies.

[18:1]O Israelite children, offspring of the seed of Abraham, obey this law and exercise piety in every way, [2]knowing that devout reason is master of all emotions, not only of sufferings from within, but also of those from without. [3]Therefore those who gave over their bodies in suffering for the sake of religion were not only admired by mortals, but also were deemed worthy to share in a divine inheritance. [4]Because of them the nation gained peace, and by reviving observance of the law in the homeland they ravaged the enemy. [5]The tyrant Antiochus was both punished on earth and is being chastised after his death. Since in no way whatever was he able to compel the Israelites to become pagans and to abandon their ancestral customs, he left Jerusalem and marched against the Persians.
[6]The mother of seven sons expressed also these principles to her children [7]**"I was a pure virgin and did not go outside my father's house; but I guarded the rib from which woman was made [Gen. 2:22].**

⁸No seducer corrupted me on a desert plain, nor did the destroyer, the deceitful serpent [Gen. 3:1-7], defile the purity of my virginity. ⁹In the time of my maturity I remained with my husband, and when these sons had grown up their father died. A happy man was he, who lived out his life with good children, and did not have the grief of bereavement. ¹⁰While he was still with you, he taught you *the law and the prophets*. ¹¹He read to you about Abel slain by Cain [Gen. 4:8], and Isaac who was offered as a burnt offering [Gen. 22], and about Joseph in prison [Gen. 39:7-23]. ¹²He told you of the zeal of Phinehas [Num. 25:7-13], and he taught you about Hananiah, Azariah, and Mishael in the fire [Dan. 3]. ¹³He praised Daniel in the den of the lions [Dan. 6] and blessed him. ¹⁴He reminded you of the scripture of Isaiah, which says, 'Even though you go through the fire, the flame shall not consume you' [Isa. 43:2]. ¹⁵He sang to you songs of the psalmist David, who said, 'Many are the afflictions of the righteous' [Ps. 34:19 (LXX, 33:20)]. ¹⁶He recounted to you Solomon's proverb, 'There is a tree of life for those who do his will' [Prov. 3:18]. ¹⁷He confirmed the query of Ezekiel, 'Shall these dry bones live?' [Ezek. 37:2-3] ¹⁸For he did not forget to teach you the song that Moses taught, which says, ¹⁹'I kill and I make alive: this is your life and the length of your days.' [Deut. 32:39, 47; 30:20]"

²⁰O bitter was that day – and yet not bitter – when that bitter tyrant of the Greeks quenched fire with fire in his cruel caldrons, and in his burning rage brought those seven sons of the daughter of Abraham to the catapult and back again to more tortures, ²¹pierced the pupils of their eyes and cut out their tongues, and put them to death with various tortures.

4. Wisdom and Philosophical Literature 133

⁴¹Last of all, the mother died, after her sons. ⁴²Let this be enough, then, about the eating of sacrifices and the extreme tortures.

²²For these crimes divine justice pursued and will pursue the accursed tyrant. ²³ But the sons of Abraham with their victorious mother are gathered together into the chorus of the fathers, and have received pure and immortal souls from God, ²⁴to whom be glory forever and ever. Amen.

Reading these two accounts of the seven brothers and their mother, it becomes apparent that the author of *4 Maccabees* has taken some liberties when using this account to serve his theological-philosophical goal rather than attempting to giving a "historically-accurate" account of the events and dialogues that took place. This being the case, it also brings into question the historical accuracy of the dialogues in 2 Maccabees 7. Could the author of 2 Maccabees also have been driven by a larger theological agenda which would have shaped his account of the events? Is it even possible for a theological-philosophical text to be completely historically accurate? Would the theological-philosophical argument be weakened if the author treats the account of the events too freely? Does it even matter if the events and the dialogues described by the author even took place?

The most significant difference between these two versions of the story is the view of the afterlife. Table 10 outlines the view presented in 2 Maccabees 7 and *4 Maccabees* 8–18. It is organized according to the dialogues, bolded text states the reward of the martyr/righteous while the italicized text states the destiny of the tyrant/wicked.

Table 10. The final destiny of the righteous and the wicked in 2 Maccabees 7 and *4 Maccabees* 8–18

	2 Maccabees 7	*4 Maccabees* 8–18
	Martyrs/Righteous vs. *Tyrant/Wicked*	**Martyrs/Righteous vs.** *Tyrant/Wicked*
Introduction		• Because of our religion, do not suppose that you can injure us by torturing us (9:7) • **They will gain the prize of virtue and be with God (9:8)** • *Eternal torment by fire (9:9)*
First Brother	• **Compassion on his servants (v.6)**	• **Martyrdom → immortality (9:22)**

Second Brother	• **Will be raised up to an everlasting renewal of life (v. 9)**	• *Will be judged and receive the divine wrath (9:32)*
Third Brother	• **I hope to get my limps back again (v. 11)**	• **Their body can be tortured but the soul cannot be touched (10:4)** • *Will undergo unceasing torments (10:11)*
Fourth Brother	• **Will be raised by God again (v. 14a)** • *No resurrection to life for the wicked (v. 14b)*	• **Everlasting life of the pious (10:15b)** • *Eternal destruction (10:15a)*
Fifth Brother	• *God's mighty power will torture you and your descendants (v. 17)*	• *Will incur punishment form the heavenly justice for the crimes (11:3)*
Sixth Brother	• **Don't think God will not punish those who have tried to fight him (v. 19)**	• *The brother himself will bring a great avenger upon him if killed (11:23)*
Mother's Speech I	• **God in his mercy will give life and breath back to her sons (v. 23)**	
Mother's speech II Seventh Brother	• **In God's mercy, she may get him and her other sons back again (v. 29)** • **The brothers have drunk of ever-flowing life (v. 36)** • *Will certainly not escape the hands of God (v. 31)* • *Not escape the judgment of the almighty all-seeing God (v. 35)* • *By the judgment of God, he will receive just punishment for his arrogance (v. 36)*	• *Justice has laid up for him an intense and eternal fire and tortures, and these throughout all times will never let him go (12:12)* • *God will take vengeance both in this present life and when dead (12:18)*

4. Wisdom and Philosophical Literature 135

Philosophical Remarks			• If they so die, Abraham and Isaac and Jacob will welcome them, and all the fathers will praise them (13:17) • Running the course toward immortality (14:5) • Religion that preserves them for eternal life according to God's promise (15:3) • She disregarded all these deaths because of faith in God (15:24) • Giving rebirth for immortality imploring them onto death (16:13) • Those who die for the sake of God live to God, as do Abraham and Isaac and Jacob and all the patriarchs (16:25) • Star-like seven sons to piety stand in honor before God and are firmly set in heaven with them (17:5) • Prize was immortality in endless life (17:12) • Reverence for God was victory and gave the crown to its own athletes (17:15) • Deemed worthy to share in a divine inheritance (18:3) • *Great struggle of the soul and the danger of eternal torment lying before those who transgress the commandment of God (13:15)* • *Punished on earth and is being chastised after his death (18:5)*

Conclusion		• **Gathered together into the chorus of the fathers, and have received pure and immortal souls from God (18:23)** • *Divine justice pursued and will pursue the accursed tyrant (18:22)*

Comparing these two accounts of the final destiny of the righteous and the wicked, it becomes clear that the main emphasis of the author of *4 Maccabees* seems to be the reward in store for the righteous (see the Introduction and Philosophical Remark section). Similarly, it should also be noted that the mother's two speeches in 2 Maccabees 7 also focuses on the reward in store for the righteous.

The most significant change relevant for this study is the systematic modification made to the dialogues, turning the martyrdom account in 2 Maccabees from a bodily resurrection text into an account which has no need for a resurrection since the soul of the righteous and the wicked receives its deserved destiny upon death. Hugh Anderson observes: "His [the author's] espousal of the Greek doctrine of the immortality of the soul is clear-cut and striking; he consistently omits the passages in his primary source, 2 Maccabees, that testify unreservedly to the Jewish belief in the resurrection of the body (7:9, 11, 14, 22f.)."[11]

In the introduction section of this martyr account (*4 Macc.* 8:1–9:10), the author makes plain the two destinies in store for everyone when he states:

> If you can take our lives for the sake of our religion, do not think you can harm us with your torments. By our suffering and endurance we shall obtain the prize of virtue and shall be with God, on whose account we suffer. But you, because of our foul murder, will suffer at the hand of divine justice the everlasting torment by fire you deserve. (*4 Macc.* 9:7-9)

The author is clear that this life is not all there is, death is not final, and those who are righteous will receive their reward and be with God while those who are wicked will be tormented by an everlasting fire. This is the main framework of God's theodicy. The other "resurrection" passages expand and add a few more details.

---

11. Hugh Anderson, "4 Maccabees: A New Translation and Introduction," *OTP* 2:539.

Commenting on the torture sequence of the first brother, the author may have had the refiner's fire on the day of judgment (Mal. 3:2-3) in mind when stating that this brother was stoic throughout the torture "as though he were being transformed into incorruption by the fire" (*4 Macc.* 9:22). This suggests that the transition from this life to life after death will be instantaneous, which is further supported by the author's report that instead of being filled with grief by the death of her sons, the mother "implored them and urged them on to death for the sake of religion" as if she was "giving rebirth for immortality to the whole number of her sons" (*4 Macc.* 16:13). She saw only two roads before her sons (15:2, 26) – one would give them instant deliverance, but would be short-lived, since it would ultimately lead to eternal death (15:3, 27), while the other would uphold piety but would lead to instant death. However, this road would preserve them "to eternal life according to God's word" (15:3).

Several passages liken the trials experienced by the martyrs to a race in which a great reward is in store for them if they persevere (*4 Macc.* 9:8; 14:5, 6; 17:12; 18:3, 23), one of these states: "but all, as though running on the highway to immortality, hurried on to death by torture…as if impelled by the deathless soul of piety" (14:5, 6). The author also notes that "the world and the life of men were the spectators" (17:14).[12] Other passages emphasize the invulnerable nature of the soul of the righteous. The tyrant may think he can harm them (9:7; 13:14), but they cannot touch their soul (10:4) since they will be receiving the reward of immortality (9:8; 13:17).[13]

The author's celebration of the mother notes that her "hope of endurance is secure with God (*4 Macc.* 17:4), likening her to the moon in heaven among her star-like sons (17:5), an image alluded to Dan. 12:3 (see highlighted words in gray).[14]

---

12. A similar image is used by Paul, who writes: "Don't you know that the runners in a stadium all race, but only one receives the prize? Run in such a way to win the prize. Now everyone who competes exercises self-control in everything. However, they do it to receive a crown that will fade away, but we a crown that will never fade away. Therefore I do not run like one who runs aimlessly or box like one beating the air. Instead, I discipline my body and bring it under strict control, so that after preaching to others, I myself will not be disqualified" (1 Cor. 9:24-27, CSB). Paul is also referring to the Apostles as becoming "a spectacle to the world and to angels and to men" (1 Cor. 4:9).

13. Jesus had a similar view, noting a person should not fear those who can kill the body, but only he who can kill the soul and body in Gehenna (Mt. 10:28; Lk. 12:5-6).

14. A similar image appears in Joseph's second dream in Gen. 37:9, where his father Jacob is likend to the sun, his mother to the moon, and his brothers to the stars.

4 Maccabees 17:5	Daniel 12:3
οὐχ οὕτως σελήνη κατ' οὐρανὸν σὺν **ἄστροις** σεμνὴ καθέστηκεν, ὡς σὺ τοὺς ἰσαστέρους ἑπτὰ παῖδας φωταγωγήσασα πρὸς τὴν εὐσέβειαν ἔντιμος καθέστηκας θεῷ καὶ ἐστήρισαι σὺν αὐτοῖς **ἐν οὐρανῷ**	καὶ οἱ συνιέντες φανοῦσιν ὡς φωστῆρες τοῦ οὐρανοῦ καὶ οἱ κατισχύοντες τοὺς λόγους μου ὡσεὶ **τὰ ἄστρα τοῦ οὐρανοῦ** εἰς τὸν αἰῶνα τοῦ αἰῶνος
Not so much has the moon in heaven among **the stars** been made to stand as revered as you, who lit the path toward piety for the seven star-like children, have been made <u>to stand honored in God's presence</u> and firmly fixed with them **in the heavens**.	And the wise shall shine as the brightness of the firmament, and *some* of the many righteous as **the stars of heaven** <u>for ever and ever</u>.

This statement fully acknowledges the role the mother played in helping her sons by "lighting the way of piety" for them. Thus, she will also be honored by God by being "firmly set in heaven" (*4 Macc.* 17:5).

The author of *4 Maccabees* notes that the endurance, demonstrated by the brothers during their torment, even impressed the tyrant. Their perseverance and loyalty to God's Torah gave them victory "on account of which they now stand before the divine throne and live throughout the blessed eternity" (*4 Macc.* 17:18). This assurance of a life after death is supported by quoting Deut. 33:3 (highlighted in gray):

4 Maccabees 17:17-21	Deuteronomy 33:3
¹⁷Αὐτός γέ τοι ὁ τύραννος καὶ ὅλον τὸ συμβούλιον ἐθαύμασαν αὐτῶν τὴν ὑπομονήν ¹⁸<u>δι' ἣν καὶ τῷ θείῳ νῦν παρεστήκασιν θρόνῳ καὶ τὸν μακάριον βιοῦσιν αἰῶνα</u> ¹⁹καὶ γάρ φησιν ὁ Μωυσῆς **καὶ πάντες οἱ ἡγιασμένοι ὑπὸ τὰς χεῖράς σου**. ²⁰καὶ οὗτοι οὖν ἁγιασθέντες διὰ θεὸν τετίμηνται, οὐ μόνον ταύτῃ τῇ τιμῇ, ἀλλὰ καὶ τῷ δι' αὐτοὺς τὸ ἔθνος ἡμῶν τοὺς πολεμίους μὴ ἐπικρατῆσαι ²¹καὶ τὸν τύραννον τιμωρηθῆναι καὶ τὴν πατρίδα καθαρισθῆναι, ὥσπερ ἀντίψυχον γεγονότας τῆς τοῦ ἔθνους ἁμαρτίας	καὶ ἐφείσατο τοῦ λαοῦ αὐτοῦ **καὶ πάντες οἱ ἡγιασμένοι ὑπὸ τὰς χεῖράς σου** καὶ οὗτοι ὑπὸ σέ εἰσιν, καὶ ἐδέξατο ἀπὸ τῶν λόγων αὐτοῦ

¹⁷Even the tyrant himself and the whole council admired their moral excellence and endurance, ¹⁸<u>on account of which they now stand before the divine throne and live throughout the blessed eternity</u>. ¹⁹For indeed Moses says, **"And all the sanctified are under your hand."** ²⁰And they themselves, then, having been sanctified {on account of God} have been honored not only with this honor, but also in that, on account of them, the enemies did not conquer our nation, ²¹and the tyrant was punished, and the homeland purified, they having become, as it were, a life-in-exchange for the sin of the nation

And he spared his people, **and all his sanctified ones** *are* **under thy hands**; and they are under thee; and he received of his words

The author notes that all God's sanctified are in His hands, supporting the claim that the brothers are now with God. Importantly, their death is also viewed as having a redemptive function for the people of Israel. Their righteous death prevented their nation from being conquered, the tyrant was punished, and their homeland was purified. Their deaths functioned as an atonement for the sins of the nations. Thus, he states: "they have become, as it were, a life-in-exchange for the sin of the nation" (*4 Macc.* 17:21).

(1) *Mother's Speech to Her Sons*. In the mother's speech to her sons (*4 Macc.* 18:6-19), she expresses key life principles and provides a summary of the crucial teaching her deceased husband had taught them from the Law and the Prophets while growing up, which would be of special comfort to them now when they were facing martyrdom. The first part of her husband's teaching (*4 Macc.* 18:10-13) contains a list of six examples from the Law and the book of Daniel, which have great relevance for the situation they were facing. Table 11 lists the six examples with a suggested explanation for how this specific narrative could be helpful to observe.

Table 11. Helpful examples to remember (*4 Macc.* 18:11-13)

v. 11	Abel slain by Cain	Gen. 4:1-6, 8	Abel represents the pious whose gift is accepted by God. This story also represents the hostility experienced by those who please God, which may even lead to death.
	Isaac offered as a burnt offering	Gen. 22:1-19	Isaac was willing to be sacrificed as a burnt offering, in order to be loyal to God. God saved his life and gained the promises.
	Joseph in prison	Gen. 39:7-23; 40:3	Joseph refused to commit adultery, which ultimately led to his imprisonment. However, he was later greatly rewarded by God.
v. 12	Zeal of Phineas	Num. 25:6-13	Phineas actively addressed the problem of idolatry and assimilation among the people of Israel thereby ending God's wrath. God blessed him by giving him and his descendants the priesthood.
	Hananiah, Azariah, and Mishael in the fire	Dan. 3:1-30	Daniel's friends would rather die than worship an idol (Dan. 3:18). They were loyal to God in the face of certain death. God saved them miraculously and they received great rewards from the king.
v. 13	Daniel in the lion's den	Dan. 6:1-28	Daniel continued to bring his requests to God despite the prohibition that only the king could receive such requests. He was willing to die in order to stay loyal to God. God saved him and he was richly rewarded by the king.

The second part of her husband's teaching gives a list of five quotes from the Septuagint. deSilva observes that this list of quotations is not random. He writes, "The order of the quotations appears to be not haphazard but highly significant, as the author builds up a 'case' on the strength of written authorities that would support a person facing, and choosing, endurance of hardship for the sake of covenant loyalty."[15] A reader will note that these texts support the view of an afterlife. deSilva also provides a detailed discussion of these five quotations – the following

---

15. deSilva, *4 Maccabees*, 260.

brief comments summarize his main observations.[16] To help the reader better understand the immediate context of these five quotes, the quoted section of the verse is highlighted in gray, while words missing from the quoted verse are bolded in the text. The first link in the chain is Isa. 43:2.

4 Maccabees 18:14	**Isaiah 43:2**
ὑπεμίμνησκεν δὲ ὑμᾶς καὶ τὴν Ησαιου γραφὴν τὴν λέγουσαν Κἂν διὰ πυρὸς διέλθῃς, φλὸξ οὐ κατακαύσει σε.	καὶ ἐὰν διαβαίνῃς δι' ὕδατος μετὰ σοῦ εἰμι, καὶ ποταμοὶ οὐ συγκλύσουσίν σε καὶ ἐὰν διέλθῃς διὰ πυρός **οὐ μὴ κατακαυθῇς** φλὸξ οὐ κατακαύσει σε.
And he would call to mind also the writings of Isaiah that says, "Even if you pass through fire, a flame will not consume you."	And if thou pass through water, I am with thee; and the rivers shall not overflow thee: and if thou go through fire, **thou shalt not be burned**; the flame shall not burn thee.

It should be noted that the author of *4 Maccabees* has made some subtle changes to the quoted text. The most obvious change is the words that are left out, which are bolded in the text. A second difference is the word order, the words διὰ πυρός, "through fire," in the phrase διέλθῃς διὰ πυρός in Isaiah has been changed to διὰ πυρὸς διέλθῃς in *4 Maccabees*, possibly for the sake of emphasis. This verse recalls the fifth example in the first part of the husband's teaching (*4 Macc.* 18:12), regarding Hananiah, Azariah, and Mishael who were faced with certain death by an all-consuming fire, yet, by God's direct intervention, they walked through the fire without being burned and survived. Afterward they received great rewards from the pagan king. Thus, the mother of the seven sons, by recollecting their father's teaching, ensures them that if they stay loyal to God, they will also be saved "from the fire and be preserved for eternal life in God's presence."[17] deSilva concludes with this comment on the first link: "The catena, then, begins with a verse that acknowledges the reality of the fiery trials that come even upon the faithful, but also gives assurance that, in some sense, those fiery trials do not threaten the ultimate integrity of the faithful person's being, which is kept by God."[18]

---

16. For a detailed discussion of these five quotations, see ibid., 260–5.
17. Ibid., 261.
18. Ibid.

The second link in the chain is Ps. 34:20, which also makes an association with the first part of the father's teaching. Isaac, Joseph, Hananiah, Azariah, Mishael, and Daniel were all faced with trials, which confronted them with a life or death situation. However, they were all delivered by God from their dire situations.

4 Maccabees 18:15	**Psalm 34:20**
τὸν ὑμνογράφον ἐμελῴδει ὑμῖν Δαυιδ λέγοντα Πολλαὶ αἱ θλίψεις τῶν δικαίων.	πολλαὶ αἱ θλίψεις τῶν δικαίων καὶ ἐκ πασῶν αὐτῶν ῥύσεται αὐτούς
He would sing to you David the psalmist who said, "Many are the trials of the just."	Many are the afflictions of the righteous: but out of them all Lord will deliver them.

Although the author of *4 Maccabees* does not cite the entire verse, most devout Jews of that period would probably have been able to finish this stanza of the psalm in their minds: "but out of them all Lord will deliver them."[19] Psalm 34 presents a God of justice, who will deliver the righteous and will punish and destroy the wicked by erasing all memory of them upon the earth (Ps. 34:16), a very comforting message indeed to a person who is facing an imminent death by the hands of the wicked. deSilva makes the following important observation: "This logic leads the listener to firmly anticipate God's rescue of the righteous in one form (temporal safety) or another (reward beyond death), explicating God as the source of the guarantee made by Isaiah (the rescue from fire) and thereby focusing attention on maintaining one's relationship with God inviolable as the path to deliverance."[20]

The third link in the chain is Prov. 3:18, which describes Wisdom as a tree of life (ξύλου ζωῆς) for those who possess her.

---

19. It is interesting to note that the proceeding verse promises that: "He protects all his bones; not one of them is broken," something which did not prove to be true in the case of the seven sons. This illustrates that although the overall message of the psalm may fit the author's agenda, some of the specific details may not, and are thus ignored. In some way, this comes close to a proof-text approach to the Scriptures. It is applying and claiming promises given to someone else in a different situation, but brings some comfort to the person claiming the promise. deSilva considers this lack of fear that this verse could destroy the promise in v. 20 as an indication that the readers had no problem considering the fulfillment of this promise as something that could take place after death. Thus, demonstrating a strong belief in life beyond death (deSilva, *4 Maccabees*, 263).

20. Ibid., 262.

4 Maccabees 18:16	Proverbs 3:18
τὸν Σαλωμῶντα ἐπαροιμίαζεν ὑμῖν λέγοντα Ξύλον ζωῆς ἐστιν τοῖς ποιοῦσιν αὐτοῦ τὸ θέλημα.	ξύλον ζωῆς ἐστι πᾶσι τοῖς ἀντεχομένοις αὐτῆς καὶ τοῖς ἐπερειδομένοις ἐπ᾽ αὐτὴν ὡς ἐπὶ κύριον ἀσφαλής
He made proverbial [the saying of] Solomon, who said "There [or, He] is a tree of life for the ones who keep doing His will."	She is a tree of life to all that lay hold upon her; and she is *a* secure *help* to all that stay themselves on her, as on the Lord.

The phrase "a tree of life," ξύλου ζωῆς, appears only in one additional passage apart from these two cases. It is in Rev. 22:2, which describes the New Jerusalem in the world to come. It should be noted that the definite form of this phrase, "the tree of life," τὸ ξύλον τῆς ζωῆς (Gen. 2:9; Rev. 22:14) and τοῦ ξύλου τῆς ζωῆς (Gen. 3:22, 24; Isa. 65:22; Rev. 2:7; 22:19), also appear in either the Eden Narrative (Gen. 2–3) or when describing the New Jerusalem and the New Earth. Apart from Gen. 2:9, the focus of the Eden Narrative is that humans should not have access to it due to their rebellion, however, one of the rewards for the righteous is to regain access to it. Therefore, there is a strong association between the wisdom in Prov. 3:18 and the tree of life in the Garden of Eden and in the New Jerusalem. In the larger context of Proverbs 3 and the introduction of the book, a strong association is made between following God's instruction and fearing God and gaining wisdom: "The fear of the Lord is the beginning of wisdom" (Prov. 1:7, LXE). The association between wisdom and adhering to God's Torah is already seen in the Wisdom of Sirach: "The fear of the Lord is all wisdom; and in all wisdom is the performance of the law, and the knowledge of his omnipotency" (Sir. 19:20, KJA; cf. Sir. 1:26; 24:23). An association between the tree of life and God's instructions is attested in the *Targum Pseudo-Jonathan* on Gen. 3:24 and in Pirkei Avot 6:7.[21]

---

21. This Targum significantly expands on Gen. 3:24, the relevant section has been highlighted in gray. "And He drave out the man from thence where He had made to dwell the glory of His Shekina at the first between the two Kerubaia. Before He had created the world, He created the law; He prepared the garden of Eden for the righteous, that they might eat and delight themselves with the fruit of the tree; because they would have practiced in their lives the doctrine of the law in this world, and have maintained the commandments: (but) he prepared Gehinnam for the wicked, which is like the sharp, consuming sword of two edges; in the midst of it He hath prepared flakes of fire and burning coals for the judgment of the wicked who rebelled in their life against the doctrine of the law. To serve the law is better than (to eat of) the fruit of the tree of life, (the law) which the Word of the Lord prepared, that man in keeping it might continue, and walk in the paths of the way of life in the world to

In *4 Macc.* 18:6, the author states that there is a tree of life, i.e. a future place in the world to come, for those who keep on doing God's will, i.e. who follow God's Torah. Thus, the mother of the seven sons encourages them to stay true to God's Torah, even if they will suffer death, since there is a tree of life in store for them on the other side.

The fourth link in the chain is Ezek. 37:2-3, which describes Ezekiel's vision of the valley of the bones, a text most often associated with a bodily resurrection. deSilva states: "the author comes close to making room for the resurrection of the dead in his discourse, which is even muted here in deference to the author's predilection for speaking instead of the immortality of the soul."[22]

4 Maccabees **18:17**	**Ezekiel 37:2-3**
τὸν Ιεζεκιηλ ἐπιστοποίει τὸν λέγοντα Εἰ ζήσεται τὰ ὀστᾶ **τὰ ξηρὰ** ταῦτα;	²καὶ περιήγαγέν με ἐπ' αὐτὰ κυκλόθεν κύκλῳ, καὶ ἰδοὺ πολλὰ σφόδρα ἐπὶ προσώπου τοῦ πεδίου **ξηρὰ** σφόδρα ³καὶ εἶπεν πρός με Υἱὲ ἀνθρώπου, εἰ ζήσεται τὰ ὀστᾶ ταῦτα; καὶ εἶπα Κύριε σὺ ἐπίστῃ ταῦτα
He used to confirm Ezekiel, who said: "will these **dry** bones live?"	²And he led me round about them every way: and, behold, *there were* very many on the face of the plain, very **dry**. ³And he said to me, Son of man, will these bones live? and I said, O Lord God, thou knowest this.

The principal part of the quote comes from the question asked in Ezek. 37:3 (highlighted in gray) with a minor addition from the preceding verse (underlined text). Again, these words are meant as encouragement for her

come" (Gen. 3:24, PJE). The following statement is taken form *Pirkei Avot*: "Great is Torah, for it gives life to its doers in this world and in the next world, as it is written: 'For they [the teachings of the Torah] give life to those who find them and healing to all flesh' (Prov. 4:22). It also says: 'Healing will it be for your flesh and marrow for your bones' (Prov. 3:8). It also says: 'It is a tree of life to those who take hold of it, and those who support it are fortunate' (Prov. 3:18). And it says: 'They are a graceful garland for your head and necklaces for your throat' (1:9). And it says: 'It will give your head a graceful garland; it will provide you a crown of glory' (Prov. 4:9). And it says: 'For in me [the Torah] will you lengthen days, and years of life will be added to you' (Prov. 9:11). And it says: 'Length of days in its right hand; in its left are wealth and honor' (Prov. 3:16). And it is written: 'For length of days, years of life, and peace will they [the Torah's teachings] increase for you' (Prov. 3:2)."

22. deSilva, *4 Maccabees*, 264.

seven sons. Even when they only see death around them and see no hope, like the dry bones, there is still hope. God has not forgotten them, and death is not the end, as God will give them eternal life. The conclusion of Ezekiel's vision declares:

> Look how they say, "Our bones are dried up, and our hope has perished; we are cut off." [12]Therefore, prophesy and say to them: This is what the Lord GOD says: I am going to open your graves and bring you up from them, My people, and lead you into the land of Israel. [13]You will know that I am the LORD, My people, when I open your graves and bring you up from them. [14]I will put My Spirit in you, and you will live, and I will settle you in your own land. Then you will know that I am the LORD. I have spoken, and I will do it. (Ezek. 37:11-14, CSB)

The fifth and final link in the chain is the Song of Moses (Deut. 32:1-43), which functions as the climax to their father's teaching and provides their ultimate encouragement by giving a deeper meaning and purpose to their martyrdom. Much like Isaac's willingness to be obedient until death, Joseph staying true to his father's teaching as a result experiencing suffering, or the show of loyalty of the three friends, this demonstration of their commitment to God and his Torah brought great blessing to the people of Israel.

4 Maccabees **18:18-19**	**Deuteronomy 32:39, 47; 30:20 (LXT/LXE)**
[18] ᾠδὴν μὲν γάρ, ἣν ἐδίδαξεν Μωυσῆς, οὐκ ἐπελάθετο διδάσκων τὴν λέγουσαν [19] Ἐγὼ ἀποκτενῶ καὶ ζῆν ποιήσω, **αὕτη ἡ ζωὴ ὑμῶν καὶ** <u>ἡ μακρότης τῶν ἡμερῶν</u>.	ἴδετε ἴδετε ὅτι ἐγώ εἰμι καὶ οὐκ ἔστιν θεὸς πλὴν ἐμοῦ ἐγὼ ἀποκτενῶ καὶ ζῆν ποιήσω πατάξω κἀγὼ ἰάσομαι καὶ οὐκ ἔστιν ὃς ἐξελεῖται ἐκ τῶν χειρῶν μου ὅτι οὐχὶ λόγος κενὸς οὗτος ὑμῖν ὅτι **αὕτη ἡ ζωὴ ὑμῶν καὶ** ἕνεκεν τοῦ λόγου τούτου μακροημερεύσετε ἐπὶ τῆς γῆς εἰς ἣν ὑμεῖς διαβαίνετε τὸν Ιορδάνην ἐκεῖ κληρονομῆσαι αὐτήν ἀγαπᾶν κύριον τὸν θεόν σου, εἰσακούειν τῆς φωνῆς αὐτοῦ καὶ ἔχεσθαι αὐτοῦ ὅτι τοῦτο **ἡ ζωή** σου **καὶ** <u>ἡ μακρότης τῶν ἡμερῶν</u> σου κατοικεῖν σε ἐπὶ τῆς γῆς ἧς ὤμοσεν κύριος τοῖς πατράσιν σου Αβρααμ καὶ Ισαακ καὶ Ιακωβ δοῦναι αὐτοῖς

¹⁸ For he did not neglect teaching you the song which Moses taught, that says, ¹⁹ "I will kill and I will cause to live. **This is your life and** <u>the length of days</u>."	Behold, behold that I am *he*, and there is no god beside me: I kill, and I will make to live: I will smite, and I will heal; and there is none who shall deliver out of my hands. For this *is* no vain word to you; **for it *is* your life, and** because of this word ye shall live long upon the land, into which ye go over Jordan to inherit it. to love the Lord thy God, to hearken to his voice, and cleave to him; for this *is* thy **life, and** <u>the length of thy days</u>, that thou shouldest dwell upon the land, which the Lord sware to thy fathers, Abraam, and Isaac, and Jacob, to give to them.

The Song of Moses reveals the history of Israel, with its ups and downs, but it concludes with a message of hope for the people of Israel. The first part of the quote is taken from Deut. 32:29 (highlighted in gray), the middle section is quoting from Deut. 32:47 and Deut. 30:20 (bolded text), while the final section is taken from Deut. 30:20 (underlined text). deSilva indicates that the word order of the first part of the quote is highly significant, suggesting that the author understood them as "a temporal sequence rather than merely as a balanced expression of God's power to give life and take away life: 'I kill and [then] I make alive' becomes support for the belief in the resurrection of the martyred faithful."[23] This is the final reason the mother of the seven sons gives for why they have nothing to fear. Even if they do die in the fire, as long as they stay true to God's Torah, he will deliver them. Thus, there will be a tree of life for them, a future eternity. The reference to Deut. 32:47 and 30:20 emphasizes the message that their loyalty to God and His Torah will bring them life and length of days, once more suggesting that there will be life after death. It should be noted that the author understood the last two quotes to go beyond the literal land of Israel. Rather, he considers the promised land as a reference to the World to Come, as noted by deSilva: "'life and length of days' is no longer limited to 'living in the land' located across the Jordan, but transferred to immortal life in the presence of God."[24]

---

23. Ibid., 264–5.
24. Ibid., 265.

c. Concluding Remarks

Although the author of *4 Maccabees* has gone to great lengths to amend the account of the martyrdom of the seven sons and their mother in 2 Maccabees 7, to remove the bodily resurrection hope by replacing it with an instant reward for the soul upon death, the speech of encouragement given to her sons at the conclusion of the book still hints at a bodily resurrection. Interestingly, it could be argued that the father's teachings to his sons, as summarized by the mother, could also be used to support a universal eschatological resurrection. The following figure (Fig. 4) gives an overview of the death and afterlife view presented in *4 Maccabees*. The eternal destiny of a person is based on the present life, if he/she has conquered his/her passion by making piety their primary concern (*4 Macc.* 7:18). Following the point of death, the soul parts from the body to receive either eternal reward (9:8; 10:15b) or eternal punishment (9:9; 10:15a), which would imply a personal judgment. Thus, the author of *4 Maccabees* does not need an eschatological universal judgment or bodily resurrection to solve the question of theodicy.

Figure 4. Death and Resurrection in *4 Maccabees*

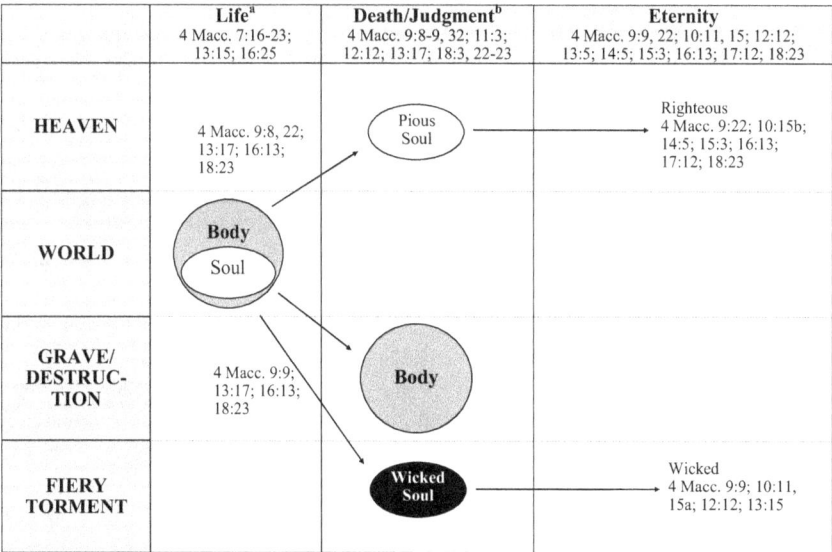

[a] The eternal destiny of a person is based on this life, if they have conquered their passion of the flesh by making piety their primary concern (*4 Macc.* 7:18). The pious will gain everlasting life (9:8; 10:15b; 14:5; 15:3; 16:25; 17:15) while the wicked will receive eternal destruction (10:15) by eternal tormenting fire (9:9; 12:12; 13:15).

ᵇ Following the point of death, the soul parts from the body to receive either eternal reward (*4 Macc.* 9:8; 10:15b) or eternal punishment (9:9; 10:15a), thus, there is neither a need for an eschatological bodily resurrection nor an eschatological universal judgment. However, a personal judgment is implied in which a decision is made regarding the eternal destiny of the soul (9:8, 32; 10:15; 11:3; 12:12; 18:22).

~ ~ ~

2. Pseudo-Phocylides

Pseudo-Phocylides[25] was written in Greek by an unknown Hellenistic Jewish poet who may have lived in Alexandria,[26] sometime between 50 BCE and 50 CE.[27] This book contains a 230-line long didactic Wisdom poem, a *gnomology*.[28] The poem contains a "mixture of biblical and nonbiblical ethical rules," with the purpose "to make clear that biblical and Greek ethics are not incompatible" since "even the famous Phocylides propagated biblical ethics."[29] Walter T. Wilson suggests that these maxims

---

25. The prologue identifies the author as Phocylides (v. 2), who was a sixth-century BCE Greek gnomic poet who lived in Miletus in Ioncia (west coast Anatolia in Asia Minor). By ancient sources, "he was regarded as a great authority concerning ethical matters and correct behavior in daily living (K. D. Clarke, "Pseudo-Phocylides," *DNTB* 868). However, the generally accepted view is this book is a pseudepigraphal book written by an unknown Jewish poet (see the discussion in Pieter W. van der Horst, *The Sentences of Pseudo-Phocylides* [Leiden: Brill, 1978], 55–63), hence the title *Pseudo-Phocylides*.

26. The identification of Alexandria as the setting of this book is based on a possible reference to the act of dissecting a human body (*Ps.-Phoc.* 102) for the purpose of anatomical research. Indeed, Alexandria was the only known place in ancient time for such practices (see van der Horst, *The Sentences of Pseudo-Phocylides*, 82). However, John J. Collins questions this assumption and argues that line 102 may instead refer to "the Jewish practice of secondary burial" which took place in Palestine during this time. However, he concludes, "the Sentences certainly come from a Greek-speaking environment. Egypt remains the most likely candidate" (John J. Collins, "Life after Death in *Pseudo-Phocylides*," in *Jewish Cult and Hellenistic Culture*, JSJSup 100 [Leiden: Brill, 2005], 139, 142).

27. For a discussion of the providence of this poetic work, see Clarke, "*Pseudo-Phocylides*," 868; van der Horst, *The Sentences of Pseudo-Phocylides*, 81–3; Walter T. Wilson, *The Sentences of Pseudo-Phocylides*, CEJL (Berlin: de Gruyter, 2005), 5–8.

28. For a discussion on the genre of this poem, see van der Horst, *The Sentences of Pseudo-Phocylides*, 77–80.

29. Pieter W. van der Horst, "Pseudo-Phocylides, Sentences," in Feldman, Kugel, and Schiffman, eds., *Outside the Bible*, 3:2353. See also van der Horst, *The Sentences of Pseudo-Phocylides*, 70–6.

are not randomly presented but are grouped into the following topical paragraphs:[30]

  1-2   Prologue
- 3-8   Summary of the Decalogue
- 9-21   Exhortations to Justice
- 22-41   Admonitions to Mercy
- 42-47   Love of Money and its Consequences
- 48-58   Honesty, Modesty, and Self-Control
- 59-69   Moderation in All Things
- 70-96   The Danger of Envy and Other Vices
- 97-115   Death and After-life
- 116-121   The Instability of Life
- 122-131   Speech and Wisdom, Man's Distinction
- 132-152   Avoidance of Wickedness and Virtuous Life
- 153-174   The Usefulness of Labour
- 175-227   Marriage, Chastity and Family Life

  Epilogue

a. Death and Afterlife (*Ps.-Phoc.* 97-115)

Van der Horst has observed that most scholars find the death and afterlife section of this poem (*Ps.-Phoc.* 97-115) difficult to interpret since there seems to be more than one view presented on the afterlife. The text seems to present a bodily resurrection view (103-104) while, at the same time, it states that the soul is immortal (115). Scholars also debate the relationship between body ($\sigma\tilde{\omega}\mu\alpha$), soul ($\psi\upsilon\chi\alpha\grave{\iota}$), and spirit ($\pi\nu\epsilon\tilde{\upsilon}\mu\alpha$), whether the poet held a tripartite (body–soul–spirit) or a bipartite (body–soul/spirit) anthropological view.[31]

This section of the poem begins with a set of instructions regarding proper mourning and burial practices (*Ps.-Phoc.* 97-102), noting that one should mourn in moderation (97-98) and show proper respect for the dead, by emphasizing the importance of proper burial and noting

---

30. Wilson, *The Sentences of Pseudo-Phocylides*, 23. The outline uses the headings appearing in van der Horst's commentary (*The Sentences of Pseudo-Phocylides*), with the relevant section for this study in gray.

31. Collins, "Life after Death in *Pseudo-Phocylides*," 129–30; Pieter W. van der Horst, "Pseudo-Phocylides on the Afterlife: A Rejoinder to John J. Collins," *JSJ* 35 (2004): 70. It should be noted that Collins and van der Horst represent the two different sides of this debate. Collins defends the tripartite view while van der Horst the bipartite view. Collins' interpretation seems to provide a consistent view on the afterlife in contrast to the interpretation given by van der Horst.

that divine anger would be stirred up against whoever would disturb the deceased by digging up their grave and unearthing the dead (99-101). The poet states that "it is not good to dissolve the human frame" (102), perhaps referring to the practice of exhuming and dissecting cadavers in Alexandria for the purpose of anatomical research.[32] However, the poet may be warning against corpse desecration in general, or perhaps he was alluding to the Palestinian practice of secondary burial during late Second Temple period Judaism, in which the dead were initially placed in a burial cave while the flesh decomposed in order for the bones of the deceased to be collected and placed in an ossuary at a later time.[33] The next two lines of the poem (*Ps.-Phoc.* 103-104) provide the underlying rationale for why corpses should be respected and for the instruction that dead loved ones should not be mourned excessively.

Verses 103-104

| [103] καὶ τάχα δ' ἐκ γαίης ἐλπίζομεν ἐς φάος ἐλθεῖν [104] λείψαν' ἀποιχομένων· ὀπίσω δὲ θεοὶ τελέθονται. | [103-104a] For in fact we hope that the remains of the departed will perhaps come to the light again out of the earth. [104b] **And afterwards they become gods**. |

These two lines (*Ps.-Phoc.* 103-104a) present a bodily resurrection hope (highlighted in gray) in which the very remains of the dead will once more come to light, "out of the earth." In other words, the corpses need to be treated with respect because, due to a belief in a bodily resurrection, the body will be needed in the future. The Greek adverb τάχα, based on the larger context, could either be translated as "perhaps, possibly, probably" (cf. Wis. 13:6; 14:19; Rom. 5:7; Phil. 1:15) or "soon" (as used in Classical Greek writing from Herodotus down).[34] Collins argues for the former (τάχα = "perhaps"), emphasizing the hope aspect of the statement, suggesting the poet may not have considered this future resurrection to be universal in nature,[35] while Horst argues for the latter view (τάχα =

---

32. For this interpretation, see van der Horst, *The Sentences of Pseudo-Phocylides*, 183–4.

33. See Collins, "Life after Death in *Pseudo-Phocylides*," 142.

34. Henry George Liddell and Robert Scott, "τάχα," in *A Greek–English Lexicon; Machine Readable Texts* (Oxford: Trustees of Tufts University, 1940), http://perseus.uchicago.edu/cgi-bin/philologic/getobject.pl?c.73:4:27.LSJ.

35. This view would be in line with Dan. 12:2, which seems to present a limited eschatological resurrection.

"soon"), stressing the urgency and the strong conviction held by the poet in his resurrection hope.³⁶

Following the bodily resurrection, the poet states that they will become gods (*Ps.-Phoc.* 104b, bolded text). This seems to support a non-universal eschatological resurrection view since, if universal, both the righteous and the wicked would become gods, a view which was unprecedented in Second Temple period Jewish literature, since it would not solve the problem of theodicy. Instead, the poet must be describing the elevation of the righteous which will take place after the eschatological resurrection of the righteous, who will be elevated in a special way.³⁷ This elevation, becoming gods, may be a variant of Dan. 12:3 and *1 En.* 104:2-6 (where the righteous are elevated to heaven to become like stars, shining for all eternity), or become like or actually be companions of the angels.³⁸ Perhaps it alludes to the Adam tradition, which suggests that God will grant Adam his wish to become god following his resurrection (*T. Adam* 3:3-5).³⁹

---

36. See van der Horst, "*Pseudo-Phocylides* on the Afterlife," 72–3; Collins, "Life after Death in *Pseudo-Phocylides*," 132, 140.

37. If the poet describes a limited eschatological resurrection, it would, although not mentioned in the poem, require a pre-resurrection judgment, since it would be necessary to determine who should be a part of this resurrection. The alternative interpretation is nicely presented by Wilson. He writes: "What is surprising is that, for our author, resurrection appears to have no judiciary function or aspect whatsoever, as it does in most all Jewish or Christian writings that express this hope. The text projects a scenario in which the remains of all people, not just the worthy, are deified" (Wilson, *The Sentences of Pseudo-Phocylides*, 145).

38. Collins observes that in contemporary Jewish literature, like the Dead Sea Scrolls, angels were often referred to as אלהים, "gods" (Collins, "Life after Death in *Pseudo-Phocylides*," 133). Also see John J. Collins, "Powers in Heaven, Gods and Angels in the Dead Sea Scrolls," in *Religion in the Dead Sea Scrolls*, ed. J. J. Collins and R. A. Kugler (Grand Rapids: Eerdmans, 2000), 1–28.

39. The poet may have expanded on several biblical statements. The psalmist notes that humans were created a little lower than God (וַתְּחַסְּרֵהוּ מְּעַט מֵאֱלֹהִים) and were honored and glorified by him (Ps. 8:6, MT); the Creation account states that humans were created in the image and likeness (בְּצַלְמוֹ בְּצֶלֶם) of God (Gen. 1:26-27); in the Eden Narrative God observes that humans have become/were like one of us (הָאָדָם הָיָה כְּאַחַד מִמֶּנּוּ) following the fall (Gen. 3:22). If this was the position of humans in the beginning, it would very likely also be the case following the resurrection. This elevated position of humans as "lesser gods" following their creation appears in the *Books of Adam and Eve*, and was the case for Satan's rebellion (*LAE* 12:1–17:2).

One of the main questions of interpretation in the next four lines of the poem (*Ps.-Phoc.* 105-108) is, does the poet present a tripartite (body–soul–spirit) or a bipartite (body–soul/spirit) anthropological view? Does the poet perceive ψυχαὶ (soul) and πνεῦμα (spirit) as synonyms, or as two different parts of a human being? The answer to this question will affect the overall understanding of "the death and afterlife" section of this poem.

Verses 105-108

¹⁰⁵ ψυχαὶ γὰρ μίμνουσιν ἀκήριοι ἐν φθιμένοισιν.	¹⁰⁵ **For** the souls remain unharmed among the dead.
¹⁰⁶ πνεῦμα γάρ ἐστι θεοῦ χρῆσις θνητοῖσι καὶ εἰκών·	¹⁰⁶ **For** the spirit is a loan from God to mortals, and his image.
¹⁰⁷ σῶμα γὰρ ἐκ γαίης· ἔχομεν κἄπειτα πρὸς αὖ γῆν ¹⁰⁸ λυόμενοι κόνις ἐσμέν· ἀὴρ δ' ἀνὰ πνεῦμα δέδεκται.	¹⁰⁷ **For** we have a body out of earth, and when afterwards we are resolved ¹⁰⁸ again into earth we are but dust; but the air has received our spirit.

It is important to note that soul, spirit, and body are introduced in the same way by the author (noun – conjunction), suggesting he viewed them as three separate entities: ψυχαὶ γὰρ (*Ps.-Phoc.* 105), πνεῦμα γάρ (106), and σῶμα γὰρ (107). Upon death, the poem reveals the destiny of each entity.

Regarding the soul (ψυχαὶ), this poem is unambiguous in its immortality of the soul view (*Ps.-Phoc.* 105, 115). However, the important question is what happens to the soul when the person dies. The author states that death will not affect the soul itself, noting it will remain unharmed (μίμνουσιν ἀκήριοι), but it is not quite clear what he has in mind when he states that the soul remains unharmed ἐν φθιμένοισιν? Van der Horst seems to suggest that the soul will remain alive in the dead body. However, he acknowledges that his reading creates an inconsistency in the poem (he argues that the poet does not present a consistent view) when attempting to harmonize this statement with the latter statement, ἀὴρ δ' ἀνὰ πνεῦμα δέδεκται, "but the air has received our spirit" (*Ps.-Phoc.* 108b), suggesting a different location for the soul/spirit, assuming the author has used these two words as synonyms.[40] According to Collins, a better translation of the phrase ἐν φθιμένοισιν, is "among the dead," suggesting the soul parts for Hades when a person dies, which seems to harmonize with the poet's description of Hades (*Ps.-Phoc.* 111-113).

---

40. Van der Horst, *The Sentences of Pseudo-Phocylides*, 188–9.

Regarding the Spirit (πνεῦμα), the poet reveals two important details. First, the Spirit is only on loan (χρῆσις) from God, as such, it will be returned to the lender upon death (*Ps.-Phoc.* 106). Second, the Spirit (πνεῦμα) is associated with God's image (εἰκών). The idea that the Spirit is on loan from God is not a foreign concept in Judaism, it may derive from an interpretation of Gen. 2:7 and Gen. 6:3 and Eccl. 12:7 (see the highlighted keywords in the following texts).

Ecclesiastes 12:7 (LXT/WTT/LXE)	Genesis 2:7 (LXT/WTT/LXE)
καὶ ἐπιστρέψῃ ὁ χοῦς ἐπὶ τὴν γῆν ὡς ἦν καὶ τὸ πνεῦμα ἐπιστρέψῃ πρὸς τὸν θεόν ὃς ἔδωκεν αὐτό	καὶ ἔπλασεν ὁ θεὸς τὸν ἄνθρωπον χοῦν ἀπὸ τῆς γῆς καὶ ἐνεφύσησεν εἰς τὸ πρόσωπον αὐτοῦ πνοὴν ζωῆς καὶ ἐγένετο ὁ ἄνθρωπος εἰς ψυχὴν ζῶσαν
וְיָשֹׁב הֶעָפָר עַל־הָאָרֶץ כְּשֶׁהָיָה וְהָרוּחַ תָּשׁוּב אֶל־הָאֱלֹהִים אֲשֶׁר נְתָנָהּ׃	וַיִּיצֶר יְהוָה אֱלֹהִים אֶת־הָאָדָם עָפָר מִן־הָאֲדָמָה וַיִּפַּח בְּאַפָּיו נִשְׁמַת חַיִּים וַיְהִי הָאָדָם לְנֶפֶשׁ חַיָּה׃
and the dust also return to the earth as it was, and the spirit return to God who gave it.	And God formed the man *of* dust of the earth, and breathed upon his face the breath of life, and the man became a living soul.

In the Eden Narrative, the first human was created from the dust of the earth and the breath of life (πνοὴν ζωῆς/נִשְׁמַת חַיִּים) from God, in order to become a living soul (ψυχὴν ζῶσαν/לְנֶפֶשׁ חַיָּה). In Ecclesiastes, the "breath of life" has been turned into the Spirit (τὸ πνεῦμα/רוּחַ) when it describes death, the reversal of the creation process. In fact, Ecclesiastes states that the Spirit returns to God who gave it (Eccl. 12:7). A similar thought appears in Gen. 6:3 when God declares that his Spirit (τὸ πνεῦμά μου/רוּחַ) will not dwell in the humans forever (ἐν τοῖς ἀνθρώποις τούτοις εἰς τὸν αἰῶνα/בָּאָדָם לְעֹלָם), suggesting that God will, at one point, repossess his belonging, his Spirit. The concept that life is on loan from God, as described by *Pseudo-Phocylides*, also appears in Wis. 15:8 and Lk. 12:20 (see highlighted phrases).

Luke 12:20	Wisdom 15:8 (LXT/KJA)	Genesis 6:3
εἶπεν δὲ αὐτῷ ὁ θεός· ἄφρων, ταύτῃ τῇ νυκτὶ τὴν ψυχήν σου **ἀπαιτοῦσιν** ἀπὸ σοῦ· ἃ δὲ ἡτοίμασας, τίνι ἔσται;	καὶ κακόμοχθος θεὸν μάταιον ἐκ τοῦ αὐτοῦ πλάσσει πηλοῦ ὃς πρὸ μικροῦ ἐκ γῆς γενηθεὶς μετ' ὀλίγον πορεύεται ἐξ ἧς ἐλήμφθη τὸ τῆς ψυχῆς **ἀπαιτηθεὶς χρέος**	καὶ εἶπεν κύριος ὁ θεὸς οὐ μὴ καταμείνῃ τὸ πνεῦμά μου ἐν τοῖς ἀνθρώποις τούτοις εἰς τὸν αἰῶνα διὰ τὸ εἶναι αὐτοὺς σάρκας, ἔσονται δὲ αἱ ἡμέραι αὐτῶν ἑκατὸν εἴκοσι ἔτη
		וַיֹּאמֶר יְהוָה לֹא־יָדוֹן רוּחִי בָאָדָם לְעֹלָם בְּשַׁגַּם הוּא בָשָׂר וְהָיוּ יָמָיו מֵאָה וְעֶשְׂרִים שָׁנָה:
"But God said to him, 'You fool! This very night your life is **demanded** of you. And the things you have prepared—whose will they be?'	And employing his labours lewdly, he maketh a vain god of the same clay, even he which a little before was made of earth himself, and within a little while after returneth to the same, out when his life which was lent him **shall be demanded**.	And the Lord God said, My Spirit shall certainly not remain among these men for ever, because they are flesh, but their days shall be an hundred and twenty years.

In both these accounts, death is described as God reclaiming his loan, demanding the return of the person's life (bolded text). The technical word, "debt/loan," used in this context, χρῆσις (*Ps.-Phoc.* 106) parallels χρέος in Wis. 15:8 (both words are underlined). The word χρέος also appears in the TaNaKh in the context of forgiving debt (Deut. 15:2-3 – debt forgiveness every Sabbatical year) or a loan/life given to God (1 Sam. 2:20).

The second detail regarding the spirit (πνεῦμα), is its association with the image (εἰκών) of God, a clear allusion to the Creation of the first human couple (Gen. 1:26-27). See the highlighting in the following text.

[26a] καὶ εἶπεν ὁ θεός ποιήσωμεν ἄνθρωπον κατ' εἰκόνα ἡμετέραν καὶ καθ' ὁμοίωσιν ... [27] καὶ ἐποίησεν ὁ θεὸς τὸν ἄνθρωπον κατ' εἰκόνα θεοῦ ἐποίησεν αὐτόν ἄρσεν καὶ θῆλυ ἐποίησεν αὐτούς

[26a]וַיֹּאמֶר אֱלֹהִים נַעֲשֶׂה אָדָם בְּצַלְמֵנוּ כִּדְמוּתֵנוּ [27]וַיִּבְרָא אֱלֹהִים אֶת־הָאָדָם בְּצַלְמוֹ בְּצֶלֶם אֱלֹהִים בָּרָא אֹתוֹ זָכָר וּנְקֵבָה בָּרָא אֹתָם:

[26a] And God said, Let us make man according to our image and likeness... [27] And God made man, according to the image of God he made him, male and female he made them.

[26a] Then God said, "Let Us make man in Our image, according to Our likeness..." [27] So God created man in His own image; He created him in the image of God; He created them male and female.

By reading the two creation accounts of the origin of the first humans (Gen. 1:26-27; 2:7), in light of each other, it could be possible to see an association between God's image in the first account with that of God's breath of life (נִשְׁמַת חַיִּים or רוּחַ, according to Gen. 6:3 and Eccl. 12:7) in the second. If a human being is a compound of dust of the ground and the breath of life, and if humans were also created in the image of God, it stands to reason that it is God's breath of life (and not the dust of the ground), the only element, according to Genesis 2, which was uniquely given to the humans, that makes them into God's image.[41] According to Collins, Philo makes this very point regarding the image of God and the breath of life[42] when he writes: οὐδὲν ἦν ἕτερον ἢ πνεῦμα θεῖον, "he means nothing else than the divine spirit" (Philo, *Opi.* 1:135 [PHI/PHE]). Philo also notes that it is the possession of this Spirit that makes us into a being who is in God's image and likeness, in contrast to the animals who do not possess God's Spirit (Philo, *Opi.* 1:137, 139), showing a distinction between Spirit (πνεῦμα) and Soul (ψυχή).

In light of the distinction shown between Spirit (πνεῦμα) and Soul (ψυχή) in both *Pseudo-Phocylides* and Philo, the tripartite anthropological view is evident in Second Temple period Jewish literature. This view is also evident in the writings of the early Church fathers such as Justine Martyr,[43] Tation,[44] Origen,[45] and Irenæus.[46] This being the case, a tripartite view should not too readily be ruled out in New Testament texts such as:

---

41. Unlike the Eden Narrative which suggests that only humans received the Spirit from God, Ecclesiastes suggests that both humans and animals have a Spirit (πνεῦμα τοῦ κτήνους) which will part the body upon death (Eccl. 3:21).

42. Collins, "Life after Death in *Pseudo-Phocylides*," 135.

43. Justine Martyr writes in "Fragments on the Lost Work on Justine on the Resurrection" (*ANF*, 1:298): "For the body is the house of the soul; and the soul the house of the spirit."

44. Tation writes in "Address of Tation to the Greeks" (*ANF*, 2:70): "We recognise two varieties of spirit, one of which is called the soul (ψυχή), but the other is greater than the soul, an image and likeness of God: both existed in the first men."

45. Origen writes in "De Principiis" (*ANF*, 4:289): "Into the hands of His Father He commends not His soul, but His spirit; and when He says that the flesh is weak, He does not say that the soul is willing, but the spirit: whence it appears that the soul is something intermediate between the weak flesh and the willing spirit."

46. Irenæus writes in "Irenæus against Heresies" (*ANF*, 1:534 [cf. 1:532]): "Now, spiritual men shall not be incorporeal spirits; but our substance, that is, the union of flesh and spirit, receiving the Spirit of God, makes up the spiritual man."

1 Thessalonians 5:23 (BNT/CSB)	**Hebrews 4:12** (BNT/CSB)
Αὐτὸς δὲ ὁ θεὸς τῆς εἰρήνης ἁγιάσαι ὑμᾶς ὁλοτελεῖς, καὶ ὁλόκληρον ὑμῶν τὸ πνεῦμα καὶ ἡ ψυχὴ καὶ τὸ σῶμα ἀμέμπτως ἐν τῇ παρουσίᾳ τοῦ κυρίου ἡμῶν Ἰησοῦ Χριστοῦ τηρηθείη	Ζῶν γὰρ ὁ λόγος τοῦ θεοῦ καὶ ἐνεργὴς καὶ τομώτερος ὑπὲρ πᾶσαν μάχαιραν δίστομον καὶ διϊκνούμενος ἄχρι μερισμοῦ ψυχῆς καὶ πνεύματος ἁρμῶν τε καὶ μυελῶν, καὶ κριτικὸς ἐνθυμήσεων καὶ ἐννοιῶν καρδίας·
Now may the God of peace Himself sanctify you completely. And may your spirit, soul, and body be kept sound and blameless for the coming of our Lord Jesus Christ.	For the word of God is living and effective and sharper than any double-edged sword, penetrating as far as the separation of soul and spirit, joints and marrow. It is able to judge the ideas and thoughts of the heart.

Regarding the body (σῶμα), the author states that it will return to the substance it was originally taken (*Ps.-Phoc.* 107-108a), dust of the earth, alluding to the Eden Narrative (Gen. 2:7; 3:19b) and Ecclesiastes (Eccl. 3:20; 12:7). In the same way, the author reasons, the Spirit (πνεῦμα/רוּחַ) will return to the substance from which it was taken (ἀήρ, "air"). Thus, the earth receives the body, the air receives the Spirit, while Hades receives the Soul – the only part which survives death since it is immortal (*Ps.-Phoc.* 115). Based on this perspective, the author makes the following exhortation to the rich:

Verses 109-110

¹⁰⁹ Πλούτου μὴ φείδου· μέμνησ' ὅτι θνητὸς ὑπάρχεις· ¹¹⁰ οὐκ ἔνι δ' εἰς Ἀιδην ὄλβον καὶ χρήματ' ἄγεσθαι.	¹⁰⁹ When you are rich do not be sparing; remember that you are mortal. ¹¹⁰ It is impossible to take riches and money with you **into Hades**.

The rich should not hoard their wealth but should instead share it generously, remembering they are but mortal, since their riches will not be of any use for them when they die.[47] The rich cannot bring their wealth with them to Hades. The author continues with:

---

47. Jesus makes a similar exhortation when he urges his listeners to save up treasures in heaven: "'Don't collect for yourselves treasures on earth, where moth and rust destroy and where thieves break in and steal. But collect for yourselves treasures in heaven, where neither moth nor rust destroys, and where thieves don't break in and steal'" (Mt. 6:19-20). Jesus expands on this concept when he tells the rich man to sell all that he has and then become his disciple: "go, sell your belongings and give

Verses 111-113

¹¹¹ πάντες ἴσον νέκυες· ψυχῶν δὲ θεὸς βασιλεύει. ¹¹² κοινὰ μὲν ἆθλα, τέλη δ' αἰώνια· καὶ πατρὶς Ἀιδης, ¹¹³ ξυνὸς χῶρος ἅπασι, πένησί τε καὶ βασιλεῦσιν.	¹¹¹ All alike are corpses, but God rules over the souls. ¹¹² Their shared, eternal home and fatherland is Hades, ¹¹³ a common place for all, both poor and kings.

All are on an equal footing, since all are corpses, and everyone will die. However, the soul (ψυχῶν) survives and dwells in Hades, the common "eternal home and fatherland" for all. Whatever station a person possessed while living, it will have no meaning in Hades. In fact, there seems to be no distinction made between the righteous or the wicked souls either, indicating that immortality is not considered a reward for a righteous life. The author declares that God rules over all the souls, both the righteous and the wicked. Therefore, God is also the God of the dead, he is in sole control of all spheres of human existence, even when a person is dead. This, as pointed out by Collins, leaves the possibility open for a future resurrection which would include whomever God wishes since their souls have been kept intact and are, as such, readily available to God who rules over all the souls.[48] The author concludes his statement on "Death and Afterlife" with a last observation:

Verses 114-115

¹¹⁴ οὐ πολὺν ἄνθρωποι ζῶμεν χρόνον, ἀλλ' ἐπὶ καιρόν· ¹¹⁵ ψυχὴ δ' ἀθάνατος καὶ ἀγήρως ζῇ διὰ παντός.	¹¹⁴ We humans live not a long time but for a season. ¹¹⁵ But our soul is immortal and lives ageless forever.

While humans may only live for a short while, their souls are immortal and will, therefore, live ageless forever. Whether a person lives an ethical life or not, upon death, all bodies will turn back to dust, all spirits will turn back to the air, and all souls will dwell in Hades under God's rulership. However, the author leaves the possibility open for some of these souls to be reunified with their former bodies and spirits, and become gods, who

---

to the poor, and you will have treasure in heaven" (Mt. 19:21, CSB; cf. Mk 10:21; Lk. 12:33). Paul claims that good deeds also adds to the person's treasures in heaven: "Instruct them to do what is good, to be rich in good works, to be generous, willing to share, storing up for themselves a good reserve for the age to come, so that they may take hold of life that is real" (1 Tim. 6:18-19, CSB).

48. Collins, "Life after Death," 137–8.

will dwell in Heaven for all eternity. Figure 5 gives an overview of the death and resurrection view presented by the author of *Pseudo-Phocylides*.

Figure 5. Death and Resurrection in *Pseudo-Phocylides*

	Life[a]	Death[b] Ps.-Phoc., 105-108, 110, 112-113	(Judgment?) Resurrection[c] Ps.-Phoc., 103-104a	Eternity[d] Ps.-Phoc., 104b, 115
GOD		Spirit[e]		Ps.-Phoc., 115
WORLD	Body / Soul / Spirit	Ps.-Phoc., 106, 108b Ps.-Phoc., 107-108a	Body / Soul / Spirit	Ps.-Phoc., 104b
EARTH	Ps.-Phoc., 105	Body	Ps.-Phoc. 103-104	
HADES		Soul Ps.-Phoc., 110, 112-113		Ps.-Phoc., 115

[a] The "Death and Afterlife" section appears in a didactic wisdom-poem in which the writer suggests a proper way for behaving in a number of life situations. The prologue of this work states: "These counsels of God by His holy judgments." This and other references to God (*Ps.-Phoc.* 8, 11, 17, 29, 54, 98?, 106, 111, 125) indicate a certain ethical behavior is expected by God. *Pseudo-Phocylides* 11 states: "If you judge evilly, God will judge you thereafter."

[b] The author of *Pseudo-Phocylides* presents a tripartite view on anthropology, consisting of spirit–soul–body. Upon death, these three parts separate, the spirit goes back to God who lent it to the person (*Ps.-Phoc.* 106b, 108a), both the righteous and the wicked souls go to Hades (105), and the body is buried in the ground and returns to dust (107-108a).

[c] Only a limited eschatological bodily resurrection seems to be suggested in the text (*Ps.-Phoc.* 103-104a), which would also imply the necessity of a pre-resurrection judgment (*Ps.-Phoc.* 11?) to determine who will participate in this eschatological resurrection. Although the author only mentions the body as being a part of this resurrection, it could be assumed that both the soul and the spirit would also be involved, since resurrection would be a reversal of death, when the spirit–soul–body separated and went to separate places.

[d] *Pseudo-Phocylides* 115 states the soul (χυχή) is "immortal and lives ageless forever," *Pseudo-Phocylides* 105, 110, and 112-113 suggest the soul will dwell in Hades, while *Pseudo-Phocylides* 104b suggests resurrected persons (body–soul–spirit) will become gods. Thus, it could be argued that the two possible locations for eternity are either with God as gods or a shadowy existence in Hades.

ᵉ *Pseudo-Phocylides* 106a suggests that the spirit (πνεῦμα) goes back to God, the lender, following a person's death. *Pseudo-Phocylides* 108 states that the body returns to the substance it was taken from (dust of the earth) and the spirit (πνεῦμα/רוּחַ) returns to the substance from which it was taken (ἀήρ, "air").

~ ~ ~

Chapter 5

PRAYERS, PSALMS, AND ODES

The book of Psalms in the TaNaKh was not the only important collection of psalms, hymns, and prayers for the Jews during the Second Temple period and the first two centuries of the common era. David Flusser observes the majority of these extra-biblical prayers were "put into the mouths of biblical persons who figure in these apocryphal works and it is clear that at least in their present form the primary purpose was not liturgical. Rather, such prayers and hymns were composed by the author as parts of their literary output."[1] This section will consider three collections which contain the resurrection hope. The following table (Table 12) provides a list of the resurrection passages contained in three of the collections belonging in this category, *Psalms of Solomon*, *Hellenistic Synagogal Prayers*, and *Odes of Solomon*.

Table 12. Resurrection texts in *Prayers*, *Psalms*, and *Odes*

Passage		Notes	Resurrection		Classification			
			Imp.	Stat.	Ref.	Allude	Phil.	Assum.
Psalms of Solomon	2:31-35	Judgment/ Resurrection	×			×		×
	3:11-12	Righteous → Eternal life		×				×
	14:9-10	Righteous → Eternal life	×					×
	15:10-13	Judgment/ Resurrection	×					×

---

1. David Flusser, "Psalms, Hymns and Prayers," in Stone, ed., *Jewish Writings of the Second Temple Period*, 551.

Passage		Notes	Resurrection		Classification			
			Imp.	Stat.	Ref.	Allude	Phil.	Assum.
Hellenistic Synagogue Prayers	3:24-27	"Loosed the boundary of death"		×				×
	7:11	God's act of redemption		×				×
	12:46-50	The two ways theology		×		×	×	×
	16:7-9	Funeral prayer for the dead Rest || Death		×		×		×
Odes of Solomon	17:12-15	Jesus' work → Gift to the righteous		×				×
	22:8-12	Christ speaks		×	×			×
	42:11-20	Resurrection of Jesus and the many		×				×

1. *Psalms of Solomon*

Psalms of Solomon dates to the mid-first century BCE[2] and is a collection of 18 pseudonymous psalms. These psalms were most likely composed by several authors who belonged to the same Jewish community, perhaps residing in Jerusalem. Although scholars have traditionally argued for a Pharisaic or more recently an Essenes background,[3] it is probably safer to consider the psalms as a product of an unknown Jewish community. These psalms were originally written in Hebrew, but have only survived in their Greek and Syriac translations.[4]

In *Psalms of Solomon*, God is presented as the righteous judge (*Pss. Sol.* 2:18; 4:24-25; 9:5; 17:10) who will destroy the wicked (2:31, 34-35; 3:11-12a; 9:5; 13:6a, 11b; 14:9-10; 15:8-9, 12; 16:5c). He will also give

---

2. This date is based on allusions made in these psalms to both national Jewish concerns and broader international events (Pompey's invasion and death), see M. Lattke, "Psalms of Solomon," *DNTB* 855; Robert B. Wright, *The Psalms of Solomon: A Critical Edition of the Greek Text*, JCT 1 (New York: T&T Clark International, 2007), 1–7; and R. Wright, "Psalms of Solomon," *OTP* 2:640–1.

3. Lattke, "Psalms of Solomon," 855; Wright, *The Psalms of Solomon*, 7–11; and Wright, "Psalms of Solomon," 2:641–2.

4. Wright, *The Psalms of Solomon*, 11–13.

glory and eternal life (3:12; 13:11; 14:3) to the righteous in his eschatological judgment (2:32-35; 14:9-10; 15:12-13). The following four passages refer or allude to the resurrection hope, 2:31; 3:11-12; 14:9-10; 15:10-13 (see Table 12).

a. *Psalms of Solomon* 2:31

The first allusion to the eschatological judgment and resurrection of the righteous appears toward the end of *Psalms of Solomon* 2, a psalm most likely pertaining to the military invasion of Jerusalem by the Roman general Pompey in 63 BCE and to his assassination in Egypt in 48 BCE. This psalm presents the two destinies in store for the righteous and the wicked. The righteous will be raised up to glory (*Pss. Sol.* 2:31), shown mercy (2:33b, 34a, 36a), and be kept from the humiliation which is in store for the sinners (2:35), while the sinners will be put to sleep for eternal destruction in dishonor (2:31b), be repaid according to their actions (2:34b), and for what they did toward the righteous (2:35b), because they did not know God (2:31c).

The allusion to the resurrection hope, voiced by the righteous (*Pss. Sol.* 2:31a), carries several parallel ideas with the clear resurrection statement in Daniel 12 and has been highlighted in the two passages. The contrast in the psalm is between glory and dishonor, while in Daniel it is between life and shame (see boxes). Both passages contain the "sleep" element (bolded), though in the psalm "sleep" is also considered a part of the punishment of the sinners (2:31b). Both texts contain the "raising" aspect (highlighted in gray); however, it seems only to include the righteous in the psalm while both righteous and wicked will partake in the resurrection in Daniel, though it is still limited in nature. Both passages emphasize the "eternal aspect" (underlined) of the two destinies and the shame in store for the sinners/wicked (italics).

Psalms of Solomon 2:31	Daniel 12:2 (LXX/LXE)
ὁ ἀνιστῶν ἐμὲ εἰς δόξαν καὶ **κοιμίζων** ὑπερηφάνους εἰς ἀπώλειαν αἰῶνος ἐν ἀτιμίᾳ, ὅτι οὐκ ἔγνωσαν αὐτόν.	καὶ πολλοὶ τῶν **καθευδόντων** ἐν τῷ πλάτει τῆς γῆς ἀναστήσονται, οἱ μὲν εἰς ζωὴν αἰώνιον οἱ δὲ εἰς ὀνειδισμὸν οἱ δὲ εἰς διασπορὰν καὶ αἰσχύνην αἰώνιον.
He is the one who raises me up into glory, and who brings down the arrogant **to sleep**, to their *dishonorable* destruction for <u>forever</u>, because they did not know him.	And many of them that **sleep** in the dust of the earth shall awake, some to <u>everlasting</u> life, and some to reproach and <u>everlasting</u> *shame*.

One important difference between these two resurrection passages is the scope of the resurrection. While Daniel 12 presents a limited resurrection for the most righteous and the most wicked, in which most dead will not experience a resurrection, the psalm seems to suggest that only the righteous will participate in the eschatological resurrection, while the sinners will continue in their sleep, to "their dishonorable destruction forever." It is not clear from the psalm if the judgment that will "separate the righteous and the sinners" (*Pss. Sol.* 2:34a) and will repay the sinners for their wicked deeds (2:34b, 35b) requires an eschatological resurrection of the sinners, or if God has already measured out their punishment in full by their "eternal destruction in dishonor" (2:31c).

b. *Psalms of Solomon* 3:11-12

The only clear resurrection statement in *Psalms of Solomon* appears at the end of the third psalm, which contrasts the behavior of the righteous (*Pss. Sol.* 3:3-8) with that of the sinners (3:9-10) and their respective destiny (3:11-12). This passage, like the previous (*Pss. Sol.* 2:31), also alludes to Dan. 12:2. The word ἀναστήσονται, "will cause to stand up," appears in both passages (highlighted in gray),[5] in addition to the phrase εἰς ζωὴν αἰώνιον, "to everlasting life" (in italics or bolded). Both passages also mention the eternal destruction/shame of the sinner/wicked (underlined).

Songs of Solomon 3:11-12	Daniel 12:2
¹¹ ἡ ἀπώλεια τοῦ ἁμαρτωλοῦ εἰς **τὸν αἰῶνα**, καὶ οὐ μνησθήσεται, ὅταν ἐπισκέπτηται δικαίους. ¹² αὕτη ἡ μερὶς τῶν ἁμαρτωλῶν εἰς **τὸν αἰῶνα**· οἱ δὲ φοβούμενοι τὸν κύριον ἀναστήσονται εἰς ζωὴν **αἰώνιον**, καὶ ἡ ζωὴ αὐτῶν ἐν φωτὶ κυρίου καὶ οὐκ ἐκλείψει ἔτι.	² καὶ πολλοὶ τῶν καθευδόντων ἐν τῷ πλάτει τῆς γῆς ἀναστήσονται οἱ μὲν εἰς ζωὴν **αἰώνιον** οἱ δὲ εἰς ὀνειδισμὸν οἱ δὲ εἰς διασπορὰν καὶ αἰσχύνην **αἰώνιον**

---

5. This verb in its future indicative middle form also appears in Isa. 26:19 and Hos. 6:2, in the context of a bodily resurrection. In addition, the "life" aspect appears in Hos. 6:2, but only in the Hebrew version of Isa. 26:19 (יִחְיוּ, "they will live"). Thus, the poet could also be alluding to these passages.

¹¹ The destruction of the sinner is **forever**, and [the Lord] will not remember him when he looks after the righteous.
¹² This is the portion of sinners **forever**; *but those* who fear the Lord will rise to **eternal** *life*, and their *life* [will be] in the light of the Lord, and will come to an end no more.

² And many of them that sleep in the dust of the earth shall awake, some to **everlasting** *life*, and some to reproach and **everlasting** shame.

Similar to the previous psalm, this psalm does not mention the resurrection of the sinners, it only speaks about their eternal destruction. The righteous, in contrast, will be resurrected, if dead, receive eternal life, and be in "the light of the Lord," a possible allusion to Isa. 2:5; 60:1; and Prov. 20:27, noting that the righteous will be in God's presence forever.

c. *Psalms of Solomon* 14:9-10

An allusion to the eschatological resurrection also appears in *Psalms of Solomon* 14, which is, according to Kenneth Atkinson, a Midrash on the biblical Psalm 1.[6] Like *Psalms of Solomon* 3, this psalm also expands on the difference in behavior and attitude between the righteous (*Pss. Sol.* 14:1-5) and the sinners (14:6-8), and their eternal destiny (14:9-10). The key section of the psalm seems to expand on Ps. 1:5-6, which refers to the eschatological resurrection and judgment. The reader learns that the final destiny of the sinners is "Hades and darkness and destruction" (*Pss. Sol.* 14:9a) which probably expands on the statement regarding the destruction of the ungodly in Ps. 1:6b (underlined). This psalm also makes a clear statement that the sinners "will not be found in the day when the righteous obtain mercy" (*Pss. Sol.* 14:9b), a possible allusion to Ps. 1:5a which states that the ungodly will not participate in the resurrection to stand in the judgment (bolded).[7] However, the author of *Psalms of Solomon* notes the righteous will resurrect, receive mercy, and inherit life with joy (highlighted in gray).

---

6. Kenneth Atkinson, *An Intertextual Study of the Psalms of Solomon: Pseudepigrapha*, SBEC 47 (Lewiston, NY: Mellen, 2001), 275.

7. Psalm 1:5a uses the word ἀναστήσονται, "will cause to stand up," which is the same word used in *Pss. Sol.* 3:12; Dan. 12:2; Isa. 26:19, and Hos. 6:2, when describing the eschatological bodily resurrection of the righteous.

Psalms of Solomon 14:9-10	Psalm 1:5-6
⁹ διὰ τοῦτο ἡ κληρονομία αὐτῶν <u>ᾅδης καὶ σκότος καὶ ἀπώλεια</u>, **καὶ οὐχ εὑρεθήσονται ἐν ἡμέρᾳ ἐλέους δικαίων·** ¹⁰ οἱ δὲ ὅσιοι κυρίου κληρονομήσουσιν ζωὴν ἐν εὐφροσύνῃ.	⁵ διὰ τοῦτο οὐκ ἀναστήσονται **ἀσεβεῖς ἐν κρίσει οὐδὲ ἁμαρτωλοὶ ἐν βουλῇ δικαίων** ⁶ ὅτι γινώσκει κύριος ὁδὸν δικαίων καὶ ὁδὸς ἀσεβῶν <u>ἀπολεῖται</u>.
⁹ Therefore their inheritance [is] <u>Hades and darkness and destruction</u>, **and they will not be found in the day when the righteous [obtain] mercy.** ¹⁰ But the pious ones of the Lord will inherit life with joy.	⁵ Therefore **the ungodly shall not rise in judgment, nor sinners in the counsel of the just.** ⁶ For the Lord knows the way of the righteous; but the way of the ungodly <u>shall perish</u>.

d. *Psalms of Solomon* 15:10-13

The final allusion to the resurrection is found in *Psalms of Solomon* 15, a psalm revealing the final destiny of the righteous (15:1-7, 13) and the sinners (15:8-12). The righteous are marked for salvation (15:6a), and as such, they are protected by God from evil and have nothing to fear in the eschatological judgment, since they will be shown mercy (15:13), alluding to an eschatological resurrection for the righteous. However, the sinners have received the mark of destruction on their forehead (15:9b), and thus, will not escape the Lord's judgment (15:8b). They will inherit "destruction and darkness, and their lawless actions shall pursue them below into Hades" (15:10). The sinners will "perish forever in the day of the Lord's judgment" (15:12a, 13c), when "God oversees the earth at his judgment" (15:12b). In contrast, the righteous will live by the mercy of their God (15:13b), suggesting a future eternal life with God.

This psalm is unclear as to the nature of the eschatological resurrection or who will be a part of it. The mark of salvation placed on the righteous seems to suggest that the righteous dead will be resurrected on the day of the eschatological judgment to receive the mercy of God. The mark of destruction, however, may not include the necessity of a future resurrection of the sinners, since they are already experiencing their punishment in Hades, an everlasting destruction (*Pss. Sol.* 15:8b-11). The judgment of the sinners mentioned in the psalm (15:12a), may only refer to the sinners who are still alive when the eschatological judgment takes place. In other words, when the eschatological judgment has ended, there will be no more sinners, only the righteous will be alive by the mercy of their God.

e. Concluding Remarks

Assuming *Psalms of Solomon* represents the complete death and afterlife view held by the community which produced them, and that each resurrection passage describes various aspects of said view, the following two observations could be made regarding death and the eschatological resurrection. First, there is no indication in these psalms that humans have an immortal soul, or a soul that can exist independently from the body. Wright concludes: "the psalmist conceives of man as essentially embodied and the occasional use of the term 'soul' corresponds to its use in the psalter to mean 'person.' He posits no body/soul dualism and is not in the least 'otherworldly' in his thinking. The cosmos and the nature of humanity are undivided."[8] Secondly, the dead sinners seem to have no part in the eschatological resurrection. The following figure (Fig. 6) gives an overview of the death and resurrection view presented by the community who produced the *Psalms of Solomon*. Comparing this figure with the other resurrection views presented in the Apocrypha and the Pseudepigrapha, it becomes clear that it has the most in common with the view of 2 Maccabees (see Fig. 2, in the companion volume, *Afterlife and Resurrection Beliefs in the Apocrypha and Apocalyptic Literature*).

Figure 6. Death and Resurrection in the *Psalms of Solomon*

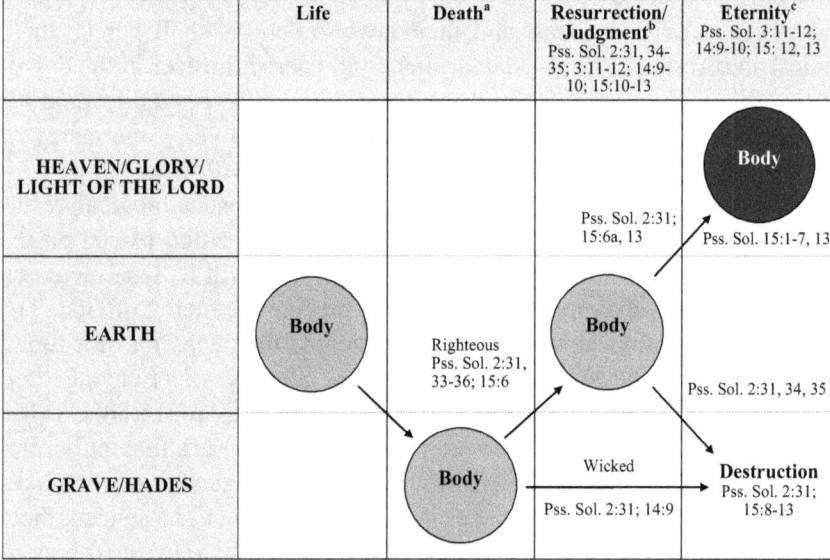

---

8. Wright, "*Psalms of Solomon*," *OTP* 2:645.

ᵃ There are no indications in these psalms that humans have an immortal soul, or a soul that can exist independently from the body. Upon death, the body is buried in the ground where it will remain until the day of the eschatological resurrection of the righteous and the judgment of the righteous and the wicked who are alive at this point in time.

ᵇ In the eschatological resurrection, the righteous will be raised up to glory (*Pss. Sol.* 2:31), and be brought to the judgment. God is presented as the righteous judge (2:18; 4:24-25; 9:5; 17:10), who will destroy the wicked (2:31, 34-35; 3:11-12a; 9:5; 13:6a, 11b; 14:9-10; 15:8-9, 12; 16:5c). The righteous will be shown mercy (2:33b, 34a, 36a), given glory and eternal life (3:12; 13:11; 14:3), and be kept from the humiliation which is in store for the sinners (2:35). The sinners, on the other hand, will be put to sleep for eternal destruction in dishonor (2:31b), be repaid according to their actions (2:34b), and for what they did towards the righteous (2:35b) because they did not know God (2:31c). The judgment of the sinners mentioned in *Pss. Sol.* 15:12a, may only refer to the sinners who are still alive when the eschatological judgment takes place.

ᶜ It is not clear where the righteous will spend their eternity. However, the most likely place is heaven as the righteous will be raised up to glory (*Pss. Sol.* 2:31), and their life will be "in the light of the Lord" (3:12).

~ ~ ~

2. Hellenistic Synagogal Prayers

Hellenistic Synagogal Prayers are found among the *Apostolic Constitution*, a Christian collection of liturgy. These sixteen prayers appear in books seven and eight of the collection. However, there is some scholarly disagreement if all sixteen should be considered of Jewish origin.[9] Van der Horst notes that only the first six prayers should be considered to have been adopted from Jewish prayers "in a Christianized form in order to be used in Church services," since they seem to be based on the Seven Benedictions for Sabbath morning (*Avoth, Gevuroth, Kedushat ha-Shem, Kedushat ha-Yom, Avodah, Hoda'a, Birkat Shalom* – the first and last three benedictions from the *Amidah* and a special Sabbath/festival benediction in the middle).[10] David Fiensy holds a more liberal view and believes all sixteen "may be remnant of Jewish Synagogal prayers,"[11] noting the lack

---

9. For an overview of the history of research on these Synagogal prayers, see Pieter W. van der Horst and Judith H. Newman, *Early Jewish Prayers in Greek*, CEJL (Berlin: de Gruyter, 2008), 9–22, 27–9.

10. Pieter van der Horst, "Greek Synagogal Prayers," in Feldman, Kugel, and Schiffman, eds., *Outside the Bible*, 2:2110.

11. D. A. Fiensy, "Hellenistic Synagogal Prayers," *OTP* 2:671.

of peculiar Christian context, while it contains a distinctly Jewish context. He adds the distinct Christian elements in these prayers are often "only loosely – often awkwardly – connected to the context," which suggests these elements are Christian interpolations.[12]

Regarding dating and provenance of these prayers, they were probably composed either in Alexandria or in Syria where the *Apostolic Constitution* was compiled, sometime during the second and third century CE. Van der Horst suggests that these prayers were composed in Hebrew and were later translated into Greek and expanded to serve the synagogues in the Jewish Diaspora. He then suggests that Judaizing Christians adopted these prayers in fourth-century Syria and were added into the *Apostolic Constitutions* by an anonymous compiler "in Antioch in the 380s CE."[13]

A brief consideration will be given to the four clear resurrection passages in these prayers. The first two resurrection passages appear in the Synagogal prayers that are based on the Seven Benedictions for Sabbath morning, while the last two appear among the last ten prayers of the collection. The passages to be treated are: *Hel. Syn. Pr.* 3:24-27; 7:11; 12:46-50; 16:7-9.

a. *Hellenistic Synagogal Prayers* 3:24-27

The first resurrection text appears in the context of the Creation Story, Genesis 1–3, in which the author expands on the Gen. 1:26 – "Let us make man according to our image and likeness." From this expansion, we learn that God gave humans a "soul out of non-being" (*Hel. Syn. Pr.* 3:21), a possible reference to Gen. 2:7, contrasting the earth and the breath of God aspect of the human being.[14] The prayer also notes that God intended the humans to have immortal lives (probably alluding to Gen. 2:17). However, due to their disobedience (alluding to Gen. 3), God took their eternal lives away so they would experience death, though he promised that it would not be forever (*Hel. Syn. Pr.* 3:24-25). The prayer ends with the resurrection promise that they will only have to sleep for a little while

---

12. Ibid., 2:672–3.

13. Van der Horst, "Greek Synagogal Prayers," 2110. See also Fiensy, "Hellenistic Synagogal Prayers," 2:673; Van der Horst and Newman, *Early Jewish Prayers in Greek*, 22–7.

14. Van der Horst suggests that God also provided humans with a spirit which could control the soul, noting that "the idea here is that the rational part of the soul, namely the spirit, enables humankind to take control over the irrational parts, the senses and their perceptions, that might otherwise lead to sin" ("Greek Synagogal Prayers," 2:2121).

before they will be "called forth to new birth," since God has "loosed the boundary of death" and is "the Maker of life for the dead" (*Hel. Syn. Pr.* 3:27). This promise may refer to Dan. 12:2 or to the promise mentioned in *Life of Adam and Eve* tradition discussed earlier; however, the author may have seen the resurrection promise in Gen. 3:19b as attested in the *Targum Pseudo-Jonathan* expansion and in *Sib. Or.* 8.96-99.

b. *Hellenistic Synagogal Prayers* 7:11

The second resurrection passage appears in a thanksgiving prayer celebrating God's act of redemption and gift to human beings. In this prayer, the author marvels that God brings forth from the womb a rational and complex creature, just from a little drop, which he has also given an immortal soul (*Hel. Syn. Pr.* 7:9). This prayer considers God the creator of every human, paralleling the creation account in Gen. 2:7, and he is still actively forming and shaping new life and giving everyone his "breath of life." It should be noted that the prayer reveals that an immortal soul has been given to everyone, even before a person is shown to be righteous or wicked.

This thanksgiving prayer is also praising God for his instructions and ordinances which have cleansing powers (*Hel. Syn. Pr.* 7:10), assuming from the effect of sins which introduced death, despite the immortal spirit. However, God has promised that the dissolution will be temporary, due to the promised resurrection (7:11), referring to the same promise as mentioned in the first resurrection passage (3:26). Although this prayer does not specifically state whether this resurrection will be universal, it could be assumed it will only contain the righteous dead, those who were cleansed by the God-given ordinances.

c. *Hellenistic Synagogal Prayers* 12:46-50

The third resurrection passage is similar to the first as both place the promise of a future resurrection in the context of the creation-rebellion narrative (Gen. 1–3), the latter prayer expanding even further on the biblical account. In the following two parallel prayers, similar elements are highlighted, and the underlined words are clear Christian interpolations. Relevant references to the Creation Story (Gen. 1–3) and the New Testament have been added within square brackets.

Hel. Syn. Pr. 3:19b-27 (AC 7.34.6-8)	Hel. Syn. Pr. 12:35-52 (AC 8.12.16-21)
	³⁵⁽¹⁶⁾And you not only made the world, but you also made the world citizen in it, declaring him (to be) a (micro-)cosm of the cosmos.
¹⁹ᵇ⁽⁶⁾*Let us make man according to our image and likeness* [Gen. 1:26]; ²⁰having declared him a (micro-)cosm of cosmos,	³⁶For you said by your Wisdom, *Let us make man according to our image, and according to (our) likeness; and let them rule the fish of the sea, and the winged birds of the heaven* [Gen. 1:26].
having formed for him the body **out of the four elements**; ²¹and having prepared for him the soul out of non-being, [Gen. 2:7]	³⁷⁽¹⁷⁾Therefore also you have made him out of immortal soul, and out of a body that may be scattered; [Gen. 2:7] ³⁸ the one indeed out of that which is not, but the other **out of the four elements**.
and having given to him **fivefold perception**, and having placed over the perceptions a mind, the holder of the reins of the soul.	³⁹And you have indeed given to him, with reference to the soul, rational discrimination, distinguishing of piety and impiety, observation of right and wrong.
²²⁽⁷⁾And in addition to all these things, O Master, Lord, who can worthily describe the movement of rain-producing clouds, the flashing forth of lightning, the clashing of thunders; ²³ for the supplying of appropriate nourishment, and the blending of complex atmospheres?	⁴⁰While with reference to the body, you have given (him) **five senses**, and the movement involving change of place.

	⁴¹⁽¹⁸⁾For you, O God Almighty, <u>through Christ</u>, planted a paradise in Eden, eastward [Gen. 2:8a], with all manner of edible foods, in (proper) order; ⁴²and into it, as if into a very expensive home, you brought him [Gen. 2:8b-9, 15]. ⁴³And indeed, you have given to him an implanted law to do [Rom. 2:14f.], so that form himself, and by himself, he might have the seeds of divine knowledge.
	⁴⁴⁽¹⁹⁾So, having brought (him) into the paradise of luxury, you allowed him the right to partake of all things [Gen. 1:29, 16]. ⁴⁵But of only one thing did you refuse him the taste [Gen. 2:17]; in hope of greater things, in order that, if he should keep the commandment [Gen. 2:15], he might receive immortality as a reward for this [Gen. 2:9‖Gen. 3:22, 24 – access to the Tree of Life].
²⁴⁽⁸⁾But when man was disobedient, You took away his deserved life. [Gen. 3:22, 24]	
²⁵You did not make it disappear absolutely, but for a time,	⁴⁶⁽²⁰⁾But, having cared nothing for the commandment, and having tasted of the forbidden fruit, by trickery of a serpent, and by the counsel of a woman [Gen. 3:1-7], you indeed rightly thrust him out from paradise [Gen. 3:23]. ⁴⁷Yet in goodness, you did not overlook him who was perishing forever, for he was your work of art. ⁴⁸ But, having subjected to him the creation [Gen. 1:26, 28], You have given to him, through sweat and hard labors [Gen. 3:17-19], to provide by himself the nourishment for his own family, while you are causing all things to grow, and to ripen. ⁴⁹And in time, having caused him to fall asleep for a while, you called (him) by an oath to new birth; ⁵⁰having dissolved the boundaries of death, you promised life by resurrection! [Gen. 3:19b]
²⁶having put (him) to sleep for a little (while), by an oath you have called (him forth) to new birth [Gen. 3:19b]. ²⁷You have loosed the boundary of death,	

	⁵¹⁽²¹⁾And not only this; but also those who poured forth from him, to become an innumerable multitude – ⁵² those
You who are the Maker of life for the dead,¹⁵ through Jesus Christ, our hope! [1 Tim. 1:1]	who continued with you, you glorified, while those who separated from you, you punished.

The additional elements appearing in the expanded version are qualifiers regarding God-given immortality. Although it is implied in the shorter version (*Hel. Syn. Pr.* 3:24), the expanded version draws a specific link between obedience and receiving immortality as a reward for keeping the commandment (12:45). Thus, suggesting the immortal soul bestowed upon humans at the point of creation (12:37) was conditional, it, rather, carried the potential for immortality as long as humans adhered to God's instructions. The obedience–immortality relationship is emphasized once more when stating the resurrection promise that God would not let them perish forever, but he will instead dissolve the boundaries of death and bring the first human couple, and their descendants, back to life – "an innumerable multitude" (12:47, 49-50). The first resurrection passage (3:24-27) does not clearly state who will be included in this promised resurrection, but the expanded version does. It states that those who continue their relationship with God, he will glorify, "while those who separated from you [God] you punished" (12:52). Thus, only the righteous are included in the promise of the future resurrection and will be glorified by God and receive immortality.

d. *Hellenistic Synagogal Prayers* 16:7-9

The fourth resurrection passage appears in the last prayer of the *Hellenistic Synagogal Prayers* collection, in a funeral prayer for the dead. In this prayer, the congregation begs God to receive the soul of the dead person and "forgive him every sin – voluntary and involuntary" and place him "among the godly ones," the patriarchs and those of old who God found

---

15. Van der Horst translates the phrase, ὁ ζωοποιὸς τῶν νεκρῶν, as "you reviver of the dead," a phrase from the *Gevurot*, the second prayer of the Amidah, which states: "You, O Lord, are mighty forever, You are the Reviver of the dead, You are greatly able to save. You sustain the living in lovingkindness, You revive the dead with great compassion, You support the falling, heal the sick, set free the bound and keep faith with those who sleep in the dust. Who is like You, O Master of mighty deeds? Who compares to You, a king who puts to death and restores to life, and brings forth salvation? And You are faithful to revive the dead. Blessed are You, O Lord, who revives the dead.

pleasing and "who did his will" (*Hel. Syn. Pr.* 16:2-4, 12-13). Then the prayer addresses God as the immortal artisan creator of humans who promised him the resurrection (16:7), who saved both Enoch and Elijah from death (16:8a), and expands on Exod. 3:6 – "God of Abraham, and Isaac, and Jacob, not as of the dead, but as God of the living, are you. Because, with you, all souls are alive [πάντων αἱ ψυχαὶ παρὰ σοὶ ζῶσιν], and the spirit of the righteous are in your hands [τῶν δικαίων τὰ πνεύματα ἐν τῇ χειρί σού εἰσιν]" (*Hel. Syn. Pr.* 16:9).[16] The prayer concludes the way it started with a request to forgive the sins of the dead person and place him with "favorable angels" and "the patriarchs, and the prophets" (16:12), in a place "where there cannot be grief, and pain, and moaning, but a free place of godly ones, and a land of upright ones, set up for you" (16:14).

There are several new elements added in this last prayer regarding the afterlife and resurrection hope. Unlike the previous resurrection passages in this prayer collection, this prayer states specifically that the soul of the dead is truly immortal (*Hel. Syn. Pr.* 16:9) and exists apart from the body upon death. The prayer states that the soul returns to God (16:3a), and the spirit of the righteous will be under God's protection (16:9b) – soul and spirit are probably used as synonyms. God assigns a place for the soul as it awaits the day of resurrection when it will once more be unified with the body.

It also seems like the communal prayer given on behalf of the dead is believed to have some effect on the soul's afterlife, since the prayer is begging God for forgiveness on behalf of the dead (*Hel. Syn. Pr.* 16:3b, 12a), and is asking for a favorable placement with good angels (16:12b) and with the patriarchs and prophets (16:4b-d, 12c-13). Little is revealed regarding the destiny of the souls of the wicked, or whether the wicked will also be a part of the eschatological resurrection. However, the text does infer that the souls of the righteous and the wicked will be treated differently. It mentions the placement of the righteous souls with the godly ones, the patriarchs, prophets, and the faithful (16:4, 12-13), in a place where "pain and grief and moaning have fled away" (16:4e, 14a), where anguish will not touch the righteous (16:9b), since they will be under God's hand (16:10) and be "received into another sphere" (16:11), in "a land of upright ones" (16:14). The reader could, therefore, assume that the wicked souls would be placed in a very different place, with other sinners,

---

16. Exodus 3:6 is also the text Jesus expands upon when arguing for a future bodily resurrection (Mt. 22:32; Lk. 20:38). However, the author of this prayer understands Exod. 3:6 as referring to the soul and spirit of the patriarchs, who are thus alive and with God.

in a place where pain, grief, moaning, and anguish are found since they are not under God's hand.

e. Concluding Remarks

In this collection of *Hellenistic Synagogal Prayers*, humans are presented with a soul (*Hel. Syn. Pr.* 3:21; 12:37; 16:3, 9) which is separate from the body. These resurrection passages also consider the soul or human as intended for immortality (*Hel. Syn. Pr.* 3:24b; 7:9b; 12:37a, 45c). Though their disobedience led to their "temporary" death (3:26a; 7:11a; 12:47a, 49; 16:7b), God promised resurrection (3:26b; 7:11b; 12:50b; 16:7b). However, the author gives the impression that it is only the righteous who will participate in the resurrection, those who have been cleansed by God's law and ordinances (7:10-11), showing little interest in the destiny of the wicked. It could be argued that due to the close relationship between obedience and immortality shown in these resurrection passages, the soul of the wicked should be considered mortal, thus having no future hope, destiny, or life after death. Apart from the Prayer for the Dead (*Hel. Syn. Pr.* 16), no interest is shown regarding the whereabouts of the soul of the righteous between the time of death and the future resurrection.

3. *Odes of Solomon*

The *Odes of Solomon* is a late first- to early second-century[17] Jewish-Christian Pseudepigraphical work, most likely composed in Syriac or Aramaic.[18] It is not clear where these odes originated, but "Ephesus, Antioch, or western Syria"[19] are good candidates. This collection consists of 42 odes and functioned as lyrical-books or a hymnal for the early Christian church.

Charlesworth suggests these odes contain neither the Greek immortality belief, in which a soul transmigrates from one body to another, nor the Jewish bodily resurrection view. Instead, the Odist "exults in his salvation and experience of immortality," stating "emphatically

---

17. James H. Charlesworth, *Critical Reflections on the Odes of Solomon*. Vol. 1, *Literary Setting Textual Studies, Gnosticism, the Dead Sea Scrolls and the Gospel of John*, JSPSup 22 (Sheffield: Sheffield Academic, 1998), 22–3; *idem*, "Odes of Solomon," *OTP* 2:726–7; *idem*, "Odes of Solomon," *DNTB* 749; Michael Lattke, *Odes of Solomon: A Commentary*. Hermeneia, ed. Harold W. Attridge, trans. Marianne Ehrhardt (Minneapolis: Fortress, 2009), 6–10.

18. For a discussion on the original language of the *Odes*, see Charlesworth, *Critical Reflections on the Odes of Solomon*, 78–136.

19. Ibid., 23.

that his immortality is geographically here and chronologically now."[20] However, Michael Novak makes a convincing case that these odes are also apocalyptic in nature and "are set in the wider imaginative world of apocalypticism."[21] Novak suggests that "transformation, resurrection, eternal life, otherworldly journeys and guides – dominates the *Odes*,"[22] all motifs associated with apocalyptic literature. According to Novak's analysis, the only apocalyptic motif missing in these odes is *ex eventu* prophecies.[23] Apart from *Odes* containing judgment events and the destruction of the wicked (*Odes* 5; 7; 11; 17-18; 23-25; 29), cosmic transformations (1; 3-15; 17-23; 25; 27; 29-33; 35-37; 39; 41-42), and other forms of afterlife (3; 5-11; 15; 17; 20-21; 26; 28-29; 31; 33-34; 38; 40), Novak considers the four odes to contain a resurrection hope: *Odes* 17; 22; 28; 42.[24] However, none of these resurrection statements or allusions seem to describe an eschatological universal resurrection. Perhaps, as noted by Charlesworth, the focus of the *Odes* is the immortality already experienced by the community members; therefore, a future bodily resurrection is less relevant.

a. Resurrection in the *Odes of Solomon*

The Odist seems to speak as Christ in some of these resurrection passages (*Odes* 17:12-15; 22:8-12; 42:11-20), referring to Christ's act of salvation which even extended to those who were already dead, a possible interpretation of 1 Pet. 3:18-22 and Acts 2:22-27. According to these three *Odes* passages, Christ entered the realm of the dead, gave them knowledge and "resurrection,"[25] and sowed his fruits in their hearts which transformed them, so "they received my blessing and lived, and they were gathered to me and were saved" (*Odes* 17:13-15). *Odes of Solomon* 22:4-12 expands on Christ's work of salvation and alludes to Ezek. 37:1-10 when referring to his act of resurrection (*Odes* 22:8-10). Both passages have the subject

20. Charlesworth, "Odes of Solomon," 2:731.
21. Michael A. Novak, "The Odes of Solomon as Apocalyptic Literature," *VC* 66 (2012): 548.
22. Ibid., 547.
23. See Novak's use of Collin's analysis diagrams for Apocalyptic literature (see Table 17) on the *Odes of Solomon* in ibid., 538–9.
24. There are a number of resurrection allusions in the *Odes of Solomon*, but this section will only consider the specific resurrection passages. For a list of these resurrection allusions and an anthology of these passages, see the section titled "Prayers, Psalms, and Odes" in Table 25 of Appendix A.
25. Charlesworth, "Odes of Solomon," 2:751 n. f. It is suggested that the literal "my prayer" became a reference to the resurrection.

of the dead or very dry bones (underlined), and a reversal is taking place in which the bones are once more covered in flesh (bolded). The same observation is made in both passages, that without God's energy of life (italicized), or God's breath (Ezek. 37:8-10), the body remains motionless, still dead. It is only when the breath enters the dead body that it becomes a living being (highlighted in gray). This is the reversal of the dying process when the breath went back to God and the body returns to dust (Gen. 3:19b; Eccl. 3:19-20; 12:7), paralleling God's act of creating humans from the dust of the earth and giving them his breath of life (Gen. 2:7).

Odes 22:8-10 (*OTP*)	Ezekiel 37:1-6 (CSB)
[8]And it chose them from the graves, and separated them from the dead ones. [9]It took dead bones and **covered them with flesh**. [10]But *they were motionless, so it gave (them) energy for life*.	[1] The hand of the LORD was on me, and He brought me out by His Spirit and set me down in the middle of the valley; it was full of bones. [2] He led me all around them. There were a great many of them on the surface of the valley, and they were very dry. [3] Then He said to me, "Son of man, can these bones live?" I replied, "Lord GOD, only You know." [4] He said to me, "Prophesy concerning these bones and say to them: Dry bones, hear the word of the LORD! [5] This is what the Lord GOD says to these bones: I will cause breath to enter you, and you will live. [6] I will put tendons on you, **make flesh grow on you, and cover you with skin**. I will put breath in you so that you come to life. Then you will know that I am the LORD."

In *Odes* 42:11-20, the Odist gives more details regarding the response of the dead who heard Christ's words when he entered Sheol and "made a congregation of living among his dead" (42:14). They begged Christ for pity, mercy, and resurrection since they recognized that death had no power over him (42:15-17). They also recognized Christ as the Savior and asked if they could be saved (42:18), and then he placed his name on their heads and claimed them as his possession (42:18, 20). However, it is not clear from the text when this resurrection would take place: whether it was instantaneous, whether these dead were resurrected together with Christ, or whether they would have to be patient and wait for an eschatological resurrection.

b. Concluding Remarks

Although the *Odes of Solomon* uses resurrection language in several passages, even alludes to and presents a bodily resurrection view, it is not clear from these resurrection passages when this resurrection event will take place. Similarly, we have no indication of its nature.

Chapter 6

THE POSTHUMOUS BODY AND THE SOUL

This chapter will briefly consider the nature of the posthumous body and the soul appearing in the Apocrypha and the Pseudepigrapha and highlight aspects of these views with relevant afterlife and resurrection passages from the New Testament. It will draw upon the afterlife and resurrection passages discussed in this monograph and the companion volume, *Afterlife and Resurrection Beliefs in the Apocrypha and Apocalyptic Literature*.

1. Description of the Disembodied Souls

Richard C. Steiner makes a compelling case suggesting there are several passages in the TaNaKh that present the נפש, "soul," as something separate from the body, the clearest being Ezek. 13:17-21.[1] In this passage, Ezekiel condemns the women sorceresses who trap dream-souls with pillow casings (Ezek. 13:17-21), turning them into bird-souls who await the "imminent demise of their owners, unless the latter agree to ransom them."[2] Steiner notes that although Ezekiel "clearly condemns the *behavior* of the women" there is no indication that he rejected the underlying belief.[3] Based on this key passage, Steiner argues that several additional passages may also reflect a belief in a disembodied נפש, soul (e.g. Gen. 35:18; 1 Sam. 25:29; Ps. 116:7; Song 5:6).[4] Steiner concludes, "in the light of all

---

1. Richard C. Steiner, *Disembodied Souls: The Nefesh in Israel and Kindred Spirits in the Ancient Near East, with an Appendix on the Katumuwa Inscription*, ANEM 11 (Atlanta: SBL Press, 2015).
2. Ibid., 66.
3. Ibid., 66–7.
4. See Steiner's discussion, ibid., 68–100. He also notes the pentateuchal idiom וַיֵּאָסֶף אֶל־עַמָּיו, "and is gathered unto his people" (Gen. 25:8-9, 17; 35:29; 49:29, 33 [cf. 50:13]; Num. 20:24; 27:13; 31:2; Deut. 32:50), "refer to something that occurs after death but before burial – either right before burial (Isaac) or long before burial (Jacob)" (ibid., 94), implying "the existence of the soul or spirit that leaves the body

this evidence, it is no longer possible to insist that the Hebrew was unable to conceive of a disembodied נפש. If anything, the opposite now appears to be true. The evidence suggests that a belief in the existence of disembodied souls was a part of the common religious heritage of the people of the Ancient Near East."[5] Saliently, Steiner suggest that the disembodied soul could still possess a bodily form or shape, adding that the Hebrews may have had a hard time conceiving "souls in the shape of anything but a body – a body resembling their own."[6]

This monograph and the companion volume lend support to Steiner's observation regarding a soul existing independently from the body, a concept that became the norm in the Apocrypha and the Pseudepigrapha. Table 13 provides a list of all the literary works of the Apocrypha and the Pseudepigrapha that mention the pre-resurrected disembodied soul and the resurrected soul (in the cases which do not require a bodily resurrection) and lists the relevant references. It provides a brief description of the details each literary work reveals regarding the righteous and/or wicked soul. The table also indicates whether the literary work provides a physical description of the disembodied soul. The no description (No Desc.) label indicates the work does not provide details regarding the soul's physical nature. It does not imply the soul mentioned in this literary work is not physical in nature, that it does not resemble the dead person, or could be identified as the dead person.

---

at death, before interment, and continues to exist in disembodied form" (ibid., 97). Steiner finds Jacob Milgrom's suggestion that the punishment כָּרֵת, as in the formula וְנִכְרְתוּ הַנְּפָשׁוֹת הָעֹשׂת מִקֶּרֶב עַמָּם, "and the souls who are doing [so] shall be cut off from the midst of the people" (Lev. 18:29), is the idiom's antonym (Jacob Milgrom, *Leviticus 1–16: A New Translation with Introduction and Commentary*, AB 3 [New York: Doubleday, 1991], 459–60), "attractive and potentially very important" (ibid., 99) as these two archaic expressions provide evidence "that ideas about disembodied souls and their punishment in the afterlife were current among the Israelites far earlier than generally assumed" (ibid., 100).

5. Ibid., 127.
6. Ibid., 123.

180   *Afterlife and Resurrection Beliefs in the Pseudepigrapha*

Table 13. Description of the disembodied soul – pre-resurrected and resurrected

Literary work	Ref.	Pre-Resurrection: Disembodied Soul		Resurrected Soul	Physical/ No Desc.
Wisdom of Solomon	3:1-4	Righteous • Will be in the hand of God • No torment will ever touch them • They are at peace			No desc.
4 Ezra	7:75-101	Righteous • Will see with great joy the glory of him who receives them • They shall have rest in their chambers and be guarded by angels in profound quiet • They will rejoice, be confident and glad	Wicked • Will not enter into habitations • Will wander about in torments • Will always be grieving and sad • Will utterly waste away in confusion and be consumed with shame		No desc.
Book of Watchers (*1 En.* 1–36)	22:2-3, 9-13	Righteous • Will be in God's presence	Wicked • Will suffer great torment		No desc.

6. *The Posthumous Body and the Soul*   181

Literary work	Ref.	Pre-Resurrection: Disembodied Soul		Resurrected Soul	Physical/ No Desc.
		Righteous	Wicked		
Book of the Epistle of Enoch (1 En. 91–105)	102:4- 103:4 103:5-8	• Will experience grief/ sorrow	• Will experience great anguish • Will experience evil and great tribulation • Will dwell in darkness, in a trap, and in a burning flame • Will have no peace		No desc.
1 Enoch – Appendices (1 En. 106–108)	108:6-7	Wicked • Will experience Hellfire • They will be weeping, crying, lamenting, and be in strong pain			No desc.
2 Enoch	J58:6	• A single soul will not perish until the great judgment.			No desc.
3 Enoch	15:1; 28:7-10; 43:2; 44:5-6	1. The soul becomes disembodied following a three-day purification process, when the soul is resurrected and brought before God to be judged.		2. The resurrected soul has a bodily form	No Desc Physical
Sibylline Oracles	2.199-200, 217-218, 227-237 8.350- 358, 401	• There is an implacable Hades and a heavenly vault • Will lead all the souls of men from the murky dark to judgment • Mournful forms (μορφή)		• The souls of the wicked will suffer in the eternal fire	No desc.

Literary work	Ref.	Pre-Resurrection: Disembodied Soul		Resurrected Soul		Physical/ No Desc.
Apocalypse of Zephaniah	4:7 7:1–9:5; 10:4-9, 12-14	• Everyone goes through the "Trial of Hades" upon death when their souls will be judged and both the righteous and wicked will be weighed in a balance • The souls deemed righteous will cross over the crossing place on a boat • The wicked souls have a physical form and will remain in Hades to be severely punished.		Righteous • Will be clothed in angelic garments • Will be recognizable	Wicked • Will remain in Hades for eternity unless they repent before the Day of Judgment	Physical
Greek Apocalypse of Ezra	4:6-24 5:20-28; 6:3, 17, 21; 7:2-3	• Souls are entrusted to humans by God, and at the point of death God demands the soul back.		The soul of the Christian righteous are brought to Heaven upon death, while the souls in the Bowel of Hades/ Gehenna/Tartarus will be reunified with the body in the eschatological resurrection. At that point, the righteous and uncorrupted will be brought to Heaven suggesting the righteous souls who are already there would also have a physical body.		Physical
		Righteous • The soul parts with the body for Heaven where it will receive a crown • The righteous who are in Hades are identifiable and will be brought out by God	Wicked • Will experience physical punishment			

6. The Posthumous Body and the Soul

Literary work	Ref.	Pre-Resurrection: Disembodied Soul	Resurrected Soul	Physical/No Desc.
Vision of Ezra	1.1-59	• Upon death, each person is brought down to the infernal regions to be judged. The wicked will be punished in the Hellfire while the righteous will pass through unscathed on their way to Heaven • The soul of the righteous and the wicked are physical and appear like a body.		Physical
Question of Ezra	A10, 19-21 B2, 5-9	**Righteous** • Are taken to a place of honor • The soul shines • The soul sparkles • They experience light, rest, and eternal life	**Wicked** • Are taken to a place of punishment/ • Endure unending torture • The soul is darkened	No desc.
Apocalypse of Sedrach	2:5; 4:1; 9:1; 10:1-4; 11:11; 14:5, 9; 15:5; 16:3, 6	Upon death, a person's soul "ascends where the Lord calls" it, while the wretched body goes away for judgment" (11:11). The righteous soul, like Sedrach, is brought to Paradise/Third Heaven (2:5; 9:1; 16:6), God's Kingdom (15:5), or the "bosom of Abraham" (14:5); to "be with the just ones in a place of refreshment and rest" (16:3). The soul of the wicked, however, will "see the place of punishment" (4:1; 14:9; 16:3).		No desc.
2 Baruch	21:23-24; 30:1-2	Upon death, the body is deposited in the earth/dust (*2 Bar.* 42:8; 50:2 and the soul is stored in the treasuries (*2 Bar.* 14:12; 21:23; 24:1; 30:2; 76:2). At the time of the universal resurrection, the souls will join their former body and be judged.		No desc.

Literary work	Ref.	Pre-Resurrection: Disembodied Soul	Resurrected Soul	Physical/No Desc.
Apocalypse of Elijah	(C) 4:25	• The Lord will receive the spirits and the souls of the righteous	No desc.	No desc.
	(H)	• Upon death, the soul undergoes a painful judgment, each one in accordance with its deeds		
Testament of the 12 Patriarchs	T. Dan 5:11 T. Levi 3:1-2	• The souls of the righteous are imprisoned by Belial until the messianic age • "The spirits of those dispatched to achieve the punishment of mankind" are kept in the lowest heaven		No desc.
Testament of Job	47:11 52:6, 10	Job's soul separated from his body upon death and was brought to Heaven.		No desc.
Testament of Abraham	A11:1– 13:5; A14:16	Upon death, the soul separates from the body and is brought to the place of judgment where it will be led through one of two gates, either for punishment or reward.		No desc.
	B7:15-16	The soul of Abraham is taken to heaven upon his death. The soul will once more unite with the body at the end of the seven thousand ages.		No desc.
Martyrdom and Ascension of Isaiah	4:16; 8:14-15; 9:7-9	This apocalypse does not mention the soul specifically; however, it does mention the "robes of flesh" and the "robes of above," indicating that something lives on that is separate from the "robes" or "body." It could be assumed that there will be a short moment where the righteous will exist without robe, following death and judgment and before he/she is brought to Heaven to receive his/her heavenly robes. The text does not reveal the type of "robes" the wicked will have after death.		No desc.

6. *The Posthumous Body and the Soul* 185

Literary work	Ref.	Pre-Resurrection: Disembodied Soul	Resurrected Soul	Physical/ No Desc.
Life of Adam and Eve	Gr. **13**:6; **37**:5; **43**:2-3 *Vita* **51**:2	• The soul of Eve is mentioned in connection with her funeral as passing away from the earth • Adam's soul is brought to the 3rd Heaven • The souls of the wicked are not mentioned • The states that following the resurrection, the soul and body will be joined together for all eternity		No desc.
Pseudo-Philo	**16**:3; **23**:6, 13; **28**:10; **31**:7; **36**:4; **38**:4; **44**:10; **51**:5; **63**:4	Upon death, the soul parts from the body and the soul is judged based on the person's decisions in the present world. Based on this judgment, the soul will either join the souls of the righteous or the souls of the wicked in the underworld. The souls of the righteous will experience peace and the souls of the wicked will be punished for their sins until God's eschatological visitation, the time of the universal resurrection and judgment.		No desc.
4 Maccabees	**9**:8-9; **10**:15	Following the point of death, the soul parts from the body to receive either eternal reward or eternal punishment; thus, there is no need for an eschatological bodily resurrection or an eschatological universal judgment.		No desc.
Pseudo-Phocylides	97-115	According to this tripartite view of anthropology, the spirit goes back to God, the soul enter Hades, and the body returns to dust.		No desc.

Literary work	Ref.	Pre-Resurrection: Disembodied Soul	Resurrected Soul	Physical/ No Desc.
Hellenistic Synagogal Prayers	**3:24-27; 7:9-11; 12:46-50; 16:7-9**	In this collection, humans are presented with a soul which is separate from the body. These resurrection passages also consider the soul or human as intended for immortality, though their disobedience led to their "temporary" death, God promises resurrection. Apart from the Prayer for the Dead (*Hel. Syn. Pr.* 16), no interest is shown regarding the whereabouts of the soul of the righteous between the time of death and the future resurrection.		No desc.
Odes of Solomon	**42:11-20**	The dead in Sheol begged Christ for pity, mercy, and resurrection, since they recognized that death had no power over him. They also recognized Christ as the Savior and asked if they could be saved, and then he placed his name on their heads and claimed them as his possession.		Physical

It becomes clear from Table 13 that the majority of the literary works do not show great interest in the physicality of disembodied souls. Only five of these works provide details regarding the soul's bodily form, describing anatomical features and appearance (*3 Enoch, Apocalypse of Zephaniah, Greek Apocalypse of Ezra, Vision of Ezra, Odes of Solomon*). Apart from *Odes of Solomon*, these literary works are found among the apocalyptic texts of the Pseudepigrapha and are discussed in the companion volume, *Afterlife and Resurrection Beliefs in the Apocrypha and Apocalyptic Literature*.

The earliest work, the *Apocalypse of Zephaniah*, does not present a bodily resurrection view as the soul receives its reward and punishment and transitions from Hades to the heavenly city if deemed worthy. The righteous cross over the crossing place on a boat (*Apoc. Zeph.* 7:9; 8:1) in order to enter the heavenly realm (2:7; 5:1-6; 9:4-5) and receive a celestial body (8:3). The wicked soul, however, remains in Hades to be severely punished. The author of the *Apocalypse of Zephaniah* describes the wicked souls sinking into the sea. Some souls have their hands bound to their neck, "with their hand and feet being fettered," other souls were "covered with mats of fire," some souls were blind and others had hair (10:4-9, 12-14). This very graphic punishment scene also appears in the *Greek Apocalypse of Ezra* and the *Vision of Ezra*, when describing the destiny of the wicked souls, a sight which even made Ezra weep and beg God for his mercy (*Gk. Apoc. Ezra* 4:6-24; 5:23-28; *Vis. Ezra* 1.8-55, 61).

3 Enoch does not present an eschatological resurrection and judgment view either, as God sits on the throne of judgment every day passing judgment on those who have just died (*3 En.* 28:10; 32:2; 44:3). Based on this judgment of the souls, they are divided into three categories: the righteous, the wicked, and the in-between. The resurrected souls will receive "spiritual bodies" with human form. The righteous souls will have bodies like eagles (*3 En.* 44:5a, i.e. like angels; cf. *3 En.* 2:1; 24:11; 26:3), the intermediate souls will be gray (or greenish) since they are tainted by sin (*3 En.* 44:5b), and the wicked will be black as "the bottom of a pot" due to their wickedness (*3 En.* 44:6).[7] The belief that the resurrected souls will have bodies which are different than the earthly body, is also supported by *3 En.* 15:1, which describes the transformation Enoch experienced before he could be taken to heaven. Table 14, describes the bodily forms of the soul, as presented by *3 Enoch*.

---

7. The *Question of Ezra* also presents the view that the souls of the righteous and the wicked will have different qualities – the souls of the righteous will shine and sparkle while the wicked will darken (*Ques. Ezra* A19-21). However, this literary work does not go into details regarding the physicality of the soul.

Table 14. The bodily forms of the soul[8]

15:1	Righteous	Forthwith my flesh was changed into flames, my sinews into flaming fire, my bones into coals of burning juniper, the light of my eye-lids into splendor of lightnings, my eye-balls into fire-brands, the hair of my head into hot flames, all my limbs into wings of burning fire and the whole of my body into glowing fire.
43:2		And he lifted me up to his side, took me by his hand lifted me up near the Throne of Glory by the place of the *Shekina*; and he revealed the Throne of Glory to me, and he showed me the spirits that have been created and had returned: and they were flying above to Throne of Glory before the Holy One, blessed be He.
44:5	Intermediate	And behold the appearance of their faces (and, lo, it was) as the appearance of children of men, and their bodies like eagles. And not only that but (furthermore) the color of the countenance of the intermediate was like pale grey on account of their deeds, for there are stains upon them until they have become cleaned from their iniquity in the fire.
44:6	Wicked	And the color of the wicked was like the bottom of a pot on account of the wickedness of their doings.

In the relevant passage in the *Odes of Solomon*, Christ is described as visiting the dead in Sheol following his crucifixion (42:11-20), to make "a congregation of living among his dead" (42:14). Seeing Christ, the dead ran towards him, begging for pity and mercy, asking him to bring them out "from the chains of darkness," and open the door so they can escape, because they recognized that death had no power over him (42:15-17). The Odist concludes his account by noting that Christ heard their plea and claimed them has his possessions by placing his name upon their heads (42:20). This seems to be an interpretation of Peter's statement that Jesus, upon his death, "went and made a proclamation to the spirits (πνεύμασιν) in prison," who had died in their disobedience "in the days of Noah" (1 Pet. 3:19-20) and to Peter's declaration of faith in Acts 2:22-27.[9]

---

8. Table 14 also appears in the companion volume, *Afterlife and Resurrection Beliefs in the Apocrypha and Apocalyptic Literature*.

9. This event is also alluded to in *Odes* 17:12-15; 22:8-12 and *Sib. Or.* 1.378; 8.310-311.

2. Disembodied Souls, Ghosts, and the New Testament

The New Testament presents two narratives involving what the disciples believed was a ghost – a spirit or soul of a dead human being. The first ghost story is recorded in the parallel accounts of Mt. 14:25-27 and Mk 6:48-50, following the feeding of the five thousand men, in addition to their wives and children (Mt. 14:13-23; Mk 6:31-46). In this story, the disciples found themselves battered by waves and strong winds in the middle of the Sea of Galilee (Mt. 14:24; Mk 6:47-48), when they saw what they believed was a ghost walking on the water, coming towards them. In their horror, they cried out in fear, but Jesus was quick to reveal his identity and told them not to be afraid.

Matthew 14:25-27 (BYZ/NAS)	Mark 6:48-50 (BYZ/NAS)
²⁵<u>Τετάρτῃ δὲ φυλακῇ τῆς νυκτὸς</u> ἀπῆλθεν πρὸς αὐτοὺς ὁ Ἰησοῦς, περιπατῶν ἐπὶ τῆς θαλάσσης. ²⁶ Καὶ ἰδόντες αὐτὸν οἱ μαθηταὶ **ἐπὶ τὴν θάλασσαν περιπατοῦντα** ἐταράχθησαν, λέγοντες ὅτι Φάντασμά ἐστιν· καὶ ἀπὸ τοῦ φόβου ἔκραξαν. ²⁷Εὐθέως δὲ ἐλάλησεν αὐτοῖς ὁ Ἰησοῦς, λέγων, Θαρσεῖτε· ἐγώ εἰμι· μὴ φοβεῖσθε.	⁴⁸Καὶ εἶδεν αὐτοὺς βασανιζομένους ἐν τῷ ἐλαύνειν, ἦν γὰρ ὁ ἄνεμος ἐναντίος αὐτοῖς, <u>καὶ περὶ τετάρτην φυλακὴν τῆς νυκτὸς</u> ἔρχεται πρὸς αὐτούς, **περιπατῶν ἐπὶ τῆς θαλάσσης**· καὶ ἤθελεν παρελθεῖν αὐτούς. ⁴⁹Οἱ δέ, ἰδόντες αὐτὸν περιπατοῦντα ἐπὶ τῆς θαλάσσης, ἔδοξαν φάντασμα εἶναι, καὶ ἀνέκραξαν· ⁵⁰πάντες γὰρ αὐτὸν εἶδον, καὶ ἐταράχθησαν. Καὶ εὐθέως ἐλάλησεν μετ' αὐτῶν, καὶ λέγει αὐτοῖς, Θαρσεῖτε· ἐγώ εἰμι, μὴ φοβεῖσθε.
²⁵<u>And in the fourth watch of the night</u> He came to them, walking on the sea. ²⁶And when the disciples saw Him **walking on the sea**, they were frightened, saying, "It is a ghost!" And they cried out for fear. ²⁷But immediately Jesus spoke to them, saying, "Take courage, it is I; do not be afraid."	⁴⁸And seeing them straining at the oars, for the wind was against them, <u>at about the fourth watch of the night</u>, He came to them, **walking on the sea**; and He intended to pass by them. ⁴⁹But when they saw Him walking on the sea, they supposed that it was a ghost, and cried out; ⁵⁰for they all saw Him and were frightened. But immediately He spoke with them and said to them, "Take courage; it is I, do not be afraid."

It is of great importance that this narrative event took place during the fourth watch of the night, between 3:00 and 6:00 in the morning, when night turns into dawn. Jason Combs notes that "contrary to some depictions in modern media, in antiquity it was believed that ghosts did not glow; therefore, a minute amount of light was required for them to be seen."[10] This pre-dawn time element would also address the question of how Jesus would have been able to see the boat from the shore (Mk 6:48), or how he was able to find them (Mt. 14:24).

Perhaps the most surprising element of this ghost story is that the ghost was the walking on the sea. Combs writes that walking on water is the one thing ghosts are not capable of. This is probably why a boat was necessary to transport the soul in the *Apocalypse of Zephaniah*. Combs states, "the Jewish and Greco-Roman audience…would have been particularly dumbfounded by the disciples' misunderstanding. If, in addition to this, one considers the research of Yarbro Collins, then the disciples' misunderstanding becomes even more shocking. Yarbo Collins, as noted previously, reviews a wealth of Greco-Roman sources that describe divine men and gods walking on water."[11] In other words, if the disciples were aware of the Greco-Roman ghost-tradition, they should have known that it could not have been a ghost. Rather, they should have concluded it was a divine person or God who was walking towards them. Be that as it may, this narrative illustrates that the disciples believed in ghosts and that ghosts were something they were afraid of.

In the second ghost-narrative, the main characters are also the disciples and Jesus. This time, following Jesus' resurrection and manifestation to the two apostles on the way to Emmaus, he was thought to be a ghost when he suddenly appeared among his followers in Jerusalem in Lk. 24:36-43.

---

10. Jason Robert Combs, "A Ghost on the Water? Understanding an Absurdity in Mark 6:49-50," *JBL* 127, no. 2 (2008): 351.

11. Ibid., 358.

Luke 24:36-43 (BYZ/NAS)

³⁶Ταῦτα δὲ αὐτῶν λαλούντων, αὐτὸς ὁ Ἰησοῦς ἔστη ἐν μέσῳ αὐτῶν, καὶ λέγει αὐτοῖς, Εἰρήνη ὑμῖν. ³⁷Πτοηθέντες δὲ καὶ ἔμφοβοι γενόμενοι ἐδόκουν πνεῦμα θεωρεῖν. ³⁸Καὶ εἶπεν αὐτοῖς, Τί τεταραγμένοι ἐστέ, καὶ διὰ τί διαλογισμοὶ ἀναβαίνουσιν ἐν ταῖς καρδίαις ὑμῶν; ³⁹Ἴδετε τὰς χεῖράς μου καὶ τοὺς πόδας μου, ὅτι αὐτὸς ἐγώ εἰμι· ψηλαφήσατέ με καὶ ἴδετε, ὅτι πνεῦμα σάρκα καὶ ὀστέα οὐκ ἔχει, καθὼς ἐμὲ θεωρεῖτε ἔχοντα. ⁴⁰Καὶ τοῦτο εἰπὼν ἐπέδειξεν αὐτοῖς τὰς χεῖρας καὶ τοὺς πόδας. ⁴¹Ἔτι δὲ ἀπιστούντων αὐτῶν ἀπὸ τῆς χαρᾶς καὶ θαυμαζόντων, εἶπεν αὐτοῖς, Ἔχετέ τι βρώσιμον ἐνθάδε; ⁴²Οἱ δὲ ἐπέδωκαν αὐτῷ ἰχθύος ὀπτοῦ μέρος, καὶ ἀπὸ μελισσίου κηρίου. ⁴³Καὶ λαβὼν ἐνώπιον αὐτῶν ἔφαγεν.

³⁶And while they were telling these things, He Himself stood in their midst. ³⁷But they were startled and frightened and thought that they were seeing a spirit. ³⁸And He said to them, "Why are you troubled, and why do doubts arise in your hearts? ³⁹"See My hands and My feet, that it is I Myself; touch Me and see, for a spirit does not have flesh and bones as you see that I have." ⁴⁰*And when He had said this, He showed them His hands and His feet.* ⁴¹And while they still could not believe *it* for joy and were marveling, He said to them, "Have you anything here to eat?" ⁴²And they gave Him a piece of a broiled fish; ⁴³and He took it and ate *it* before them.

It was only after Jesus encouraged the disciples to touch him and they saw him eat food that they were convinced he was not a ghost but that he had truly resurrected from the dead. The important element in this story is that ghosts are not physical; they do not have flesh and bones. This suggests there was a conception that ghosts, even though they resembled the deceased, were immaterial, and as such, could not be touched or consume food. This narrative also suggests it was believed that ghosts could communicate with the living.

These two ghost narratives demonstrate a belief in ghosts and disembodied souls was present among the followers of Christ. The parable of the rich man and Lazarus (Lk. 16:19-31) may add further support to this observation. In this parable, both the rich man and Lazarus can communicate and recognize each other following their death. Although it is not specifically stated, it could be assumed that it is the disembodied souls who are communicating and are experiencing their reward and punishment. This is further supported by the rich man's request that Lazarus should return to the land of the living, to warn his five brothers in the hope that they would repent, thus avoiding the punishment of the wicked – believing that if "someone goes to them from the dead, they will repent" (Lk. 16:30, NAS).

There is also a reference to disembodied souls in Rev. 6:9-11, following the opening of the fifth seal by the Lamb.

Revelation 6:9-11 (BYZ/NAS)

⁹Καὶ ὅτε ἤνοιξεν τὴν πέμπτην σφραγῖδα, εἶδον ὑποκάτω τοῦ θυσιαστηρίου τὰς ψυχὰς τῶν ἐσφαγμένων διὰ τὸν λόγον τοῦ θεοῦ, καὶ διὰ τὴν μαρτυρίαν τοῦ ἀρνίου ἣν εἶχον, ¹⁰ καὶ ἔκραξαν φωνῇ μεγάλῃ, λέγοντες, "Ἕως πότε, ὁ δεσπότης, ὁ ἅγιος καὶ ἀληθινός, οὐ κρίνεις καὶ ἐκδικεῖς τὸ αἷμα ἡμῶν ἐκ τῶν κατοικούντων ἐπὶ τῆς γῆς; ¹¹ Καὶ ἐδόθη αὐτοῖς ἑκάστῳ στολὴ λευκή, καὶ ἐρρέθη αὐτοῖς ἵνα ἀναπαύσωνται ἔτι χρόνον, ἕως πληρώσωσιν καὶ οἱ σύνδουλοι αὐτῶν καὶ οἱ ἀδελφοὶ αὐτῶν καὶ οἱ μέλλοντες ἀποκτένεσθαι ὡς καὶ αὐτοί.

⁹And when He broke the fifth seal, I saw underneath the altar the souls of those who had been slain because of the word of God, and because of the testimony which they had maintained; ¹⁰and they cried out with a loud voice, saying, "How long, O Lord, holy and true, wilt Thou refrain from judging and avenging our blood on those who dwell on the earth?" ¹¹And there was given to each of them a white robe; and they were told that they should rest for a little while longer, until the number of their fellow servants and their brethren who were to be killed even as they had been, should be completed also.

This passage mentions the laments of the souls of the Martyrs coming from under the altar, demanding justice. It describes God clothing these righteous souls in white robes and notes that they are asked to wait for justice until the number of the martyrs were filled. Although this passage appears in an apocalyptic text with highly symbolic language, the depictions of the righteous disembodied souls are similar to the images appearing in the Apocrypha and the Pseudepigrapha.

3. Description of the Eschatological Resurrected Body

The remaining part of this chapter briefly considers the description of the eschatological resurrected body appearing in the afterlife and resurrection passages of the Apocrypha and the Pseudepigrapha as discussed in greater detail in other sections of this monograph and the companion volume. Table 15 provides a list of the literary works of the Apocrypha and the Pseudepigrapha that describe an eschatological resurrected body. It provides relevant textual references in these literary works and a brief description of the eschatological resurrected body described in each of these literary works. Finally, the table indicates the final destiny of the resurrected righteous, if their dwelling will be terrestrial (T) or outer-worldly (O). It should be noted that a question mark (?) follows the location indicator to show that this is the most likely location based on the circumstantial evidence appearing in the literary work.

Perhaps the most interesting observation is the importance of the final destination of the resurrected righteous. If the eternal dwelling will be terrestrial, the literary work seems to emphasize the link between the pre-death body and the post-resurrected body. However, if the eternal dwelling will be outer-worldly, the literary work seems to emphasize the need for a celestial body. There also seems to be a relationship between an incorruptible body and the need for a renewal or glorification of the pre-death body which is being resurrected. As such, there is a strong link between the pre-death body and the post-resurrected body for terrestrial dwelling, but this new body is not quite the same as the old one. Some of these literary works also emphasize the importance of recognizing the resurrected, as a part of the reward and punishment process.

Table 15. Description of the eschatological resurrected body

Literary Work	Ref.	Description of the Eschatological Resurrected Body	Location T/O
2 Maccabees	7:9, 11b, 36; 12:44-45; 14:46	Presents a belief in a bodily resurrection in which every limb of the body, even if completely destroyed by fire, will be restored.	T
Wisdom of Solomon	2:21-22; 3:7-13, 18; 4:16; 4:20–5:14	"In the time of their visitation they will shine forth, and will run like sparks through the stubble. They will govern nations and rule over peoples, and the Lord will reign over them forever" (3:7-8, NRSV). The unrighteous will recognize those they persecuted, suggesting the resurrected bodies resemble the pre-death bodies.	T
4 Ezra	7:31-44; 14:35	"The earth shall give up those who are asleep in it, and the dust those who rest there in silence; and the chambers shall give up the souls that have been committed to them" (7:32, NRSV). "It is shown them [the righteous] how their face is to shine like the sun, and how they are to be made like the light of the stars, being incorruptible from then on" (7:97, NRSV; cf. 7:125). The author seems to draw a close relationship between the pre-death body and the resurrected body, noting the body of the righteous will be glorified when being made incorruptible.	T

Literary Work	Ref.	Description of the Eschatological Resurrected Body	Location T/O
Book of Watchers (*1 En.* 1–36)	1:7, 9; 5:7-10; 22:3-4, 13 24:2–25:6	"Then they shall be glad and rejoice in gladness, and they shall enter into the hole (place); its fragrance shall (penetrate) their bones, long life will they live on earth, such as your father lived in their days" (*OTP* 1:26). The author reveals little about the resurrected body following the resurrection of the righteous soul and the eschatological judgment when they will be rewarded with "light, joy, and peace, and they shall inherit the earth" (5:7).	T
Book of Parables (*1 En.* 37–71)	51:1-5; 61:1-5; 62:13-16	The author considers the dead bodies (and souls?) as great treasures which were only placed in the earth or in *Sheol* (51:1a-b) for safekeeping awaiting the eschatological judgment ("in those days"), or as a great debt which needs to be repaid in full (51:1c) whenever God decides to collect what belongs to him. Following the eschatological judgment, the righteous will be rewarded with a bodily existence that will never end. "The righteous and elect ones shall rise from the earth and shall cease being of downcast face. They shall wear the garments of glory. These garments of yours shall become the garments of life from the Lord of the Spirits. Neither shall your garments wear out, nor your glory come to an end before the Lord of the Spirit." (62:15-16). The author seems to draw a strong connection between the pre-death body and the resurrected body. However, the eschatological body is described as having a garment of glory.	T

6. The Posthumous Body and the Soul 195

Literary Work	Ref.	Description of the Eschatological Resurrected Body	Location T/O
Book of Dream Visions (*1 En.* 83–90)	**89**:36-38, 75; **90**:20-37	The term "sleep" is used in the dream vision, suggesting death is temporary and the dead will resurrect. The author also describes the eschatological judgment and the new age. The wicked will be judged and "thrown into that fiery abyss" to be burned (90:26-27). The description of the new age includes a new temple which will be able to house all God's righteous sheep. The dream vision concludes by noting that the new age will be filled with peace and all the sheep, the wild beasts, and all the birds of heaven were changed and became white cattle (90:34-38). This suggests that the new earth will include both Jews and Gentiles and a bodily transformation into the primordial condition.	T
1 Enoch – Appendices (*1 En.* 106–8)	**108**	Those who have their name written in the book of life will have their spirits resurrected (v. 11), transformed (into shining lights, v. 12a), manifested (shining like stars, v. 12), and exalted (heavenly enthronement, v. 12b) by this vindication. The author seems to suggest a physical reality of the righteous in heaven, more like a bodily experience. The saved will sit on the throne of their honor (v. 12b) and they will shine like the righteous in Dan. 12:3. This may suggest that they will receive "new" bodies which radiate light in contrast to the old ones which were buried in the earth.	O

Literary Work	Ref.	Description of the Eschatological Resurrected Body	Location T/O
2 Enoch	J32:1; **39**:5; 42:7; J65:6	The author perceives a resurrection hope in Gen. 3:19, noting that although a body will return to earth at the point of death, the person will once more be recreated from this earth at the second coming (J32:1). The righteous will receive their eternal inheritance in Paradise, located in the third Heaven (8:1–9:1; 42:3-14; 44), receiving glorious bodies (22:8) and becoming like the angels (22:10; 66:7).	O
Sibylline Oracles	**2**.221-251	The resurrection passage begins by noting the central role God holds in the resurrection process since He will give "souls and breath and voice to the dead" (2.221-222) which, according to Gen. 2:7, are the crucial divine elements required to create life. The opening statement is followed by a detailed description of the resurrection process itself, taken from Ezek. 37:1-10, concluding that the universal resurrection will happen in a single day (2.226). In the Christian addition to this Oracle (2.238-250), Moses will be present at the eschatological judgment, after he has put on flesh (2.245-246), perhaps suggesting that he had a non-bodily existence before the time of judgment, or a non-earthly body. The use of Ezek. 37:1-10, creates a strong link between the pre-death body and the resurrected body as the resurrection is depicted as the reversal of the dying process.	T

6. *The Posthumous Body and the Soul* 197

Literary Work	Ref.	Description of the Eschatological Resurrected Body	Location T/O
	4.179-92	Like the resurrection passage in 2.221-226, *Sib. Or.* 4.181 uses the imagery of Ezek. 37:1-10 with the same emphasis on God as the initiator, although this is a significantly abbreviated reference: "God himself will again fashion the bones and ashes of men and he will raise them up mortals again as they were before" (4.181-182). The righteous will be rewarded with a pleasant life on a fertile earth (4.45-46, 187) while the impious will be punished in the fire of Gehenna (4.43-44, 184-186). This passage makes a strong link between the pre-death body and the resurrected body, noting the resurrected will be as they were before.	T
	7.144-145	Following the bodily resurrection, the wicked will "burn in spirit by their perishing flesh for the years of ages forever" (7.126-128) while the righteous will be provided for by God on a recreated world (7.144-151).	T
	8.82-83, 226-228, 413-416	The author might allude to Isa. 29:18-19 and 35:4-7 when describing the eschatological resurrection event and the changes that will take place – the blind will see, the death will hear, and those who cannot speak will speak (8.205-212). This passage suggests the resurrected body will not be identical to the pre-death body as the resurrected body will be renewed. The second half of the book states Jesus will resurrect the dead by breaking the gates of Hades (8.226-228), suggesting a strong link between the pre-death body and the resurrected body.	T

Literary Work	Ref.	Description of the Eschatological Resurrected Body	Location T/O
Greek Apocalypse of Ezra	1:23; 2:26; 4:36-43	The righteous will rise up uncorrupted (4:36) and brought to Paradise. The text does not reveal whether the resurrected body will be different from the pre-death body, although it must resemble it since the righteous are recognized by the prophet when brought to Paradise (5:22).	O
Question of Ezra	A5, 10; B3, 12-14	In the eschatological resurrection, the souls "come and are united each with its body which had been returned to dust and which the sound of the trumpet had built and aroused and renewed" (B13). The author seems to suggest that the resurrected body is the same as the pre-death body, although it has been renewed.	O
Apocalypse of Sedrach	1:21	The dominant view is that the soul parts the body upon death to receive its reward or punishment (9:1; 11:11; 16:5-6). The righteous souls are brought to Paradise/Third Heaven/God's Kingdom/"bosom of Abraham" (2:5; 9:1; 14:5; 15:5; 16:6). However, there is one resurrection statement in the Christian sermon on love which states that the "son of God" came down, thus, "death was trampled down, Hades was made captive, Adam was recalled (from death), and through love one flock was made thereafter of angels and men" (1.21). The Christian text seems to suggest that the pre-death and resurrected body is the same as it is liberated from captivity in Hades.	O

Literary Work	Ref.	Description of the Eschatological Resurrected Body	Location T/O
2 Baruch	30:1-5; 42:8; 49–52; 57:2	The eschatological resurrection is depicted as universal. The soul of the dead will once more join their former body, the body from the earth and the soul from the treasuries. Both the righteous and the wicked will be resurrected with the same body/form as when they died, so everyone will be able to be recognized. During the eschatological judgment process, both the righteous and the wicked will experience a transformation which will expose their true character. The righteous will be glorified and the shape of their faces will be changed into "the light of their beauty" (51:3), "into the splendor of angels" (51:5) and they will be "like the angels and be equal to the stars" (51:10). The wicked, upon seeing the transformation of the righteous, will also be transformed. Their "shapes will be made more evil" (51:2), "into startling vision and horrible shapes; and they will waste away even more" (51:5). At the conclusion of the judgment, the righteous will enter Paradise, the world to come, while the wicked will be sent to the place of torment. The righteous seem to experience a second transformation while in Paradise. From being like and equal to the angels, and having the ability to "change into any shape which they wished" (51:10), they will become greater than the angels (51:12).	O?

Literary Work	Ref.	Description of the Eschatological Resurrected Body	Location T/O
Apocalypse of Elijah	(C) 1:8-10; **4**:5, 15, 27; **5**:2-6	The apocalypse reveals that the righteous, those who are sealed with God's name on their forehead and his seal on their right hand (1:9), will receive thrones and crowns in heaven (1:8) and walk with the angels up to the city of God (1:10). When the righteous die, their spirit and their soul will return to God while their body will turn into rock to protect it from being eaten by wild animals (4:25-26). On the last day of the great judgment, the righteous will be resurrected and receive their reward. There will be one reward for those who died as martyrs and a different reward for those who fled into the wilderness to escape martyrdom, the first group will be in the kingdom of Christ (4:27-29) while the second will be raised up and to receive a place of rest (4:27a). The resurrected righteous "will see the sinners and those who persecuted them and those who handed them over to death in their torments," suggesting the resurrected bodies resemble the pre-death bodies. Upon the final destruction of the Antichrist, the righteous will dwell on a newly created earth with Christ for a thousand years (5:36-39).	O/T

Literary Work	Ref.	Description of the Eschatological Resurrected Body	Location T/O
	(H)	The apocalypse depicts the resurrection process as the reversal of death, in which the dust of the dead is reshaped and "made like (the forms they had) when they were formerly alive." This resurrection act is supported by quoting Deut. 32:29 and Ezek. 37:8. In Elijah's resurrection vision, God's angels play an active role. They are the ones who open the tombs, inject the dead righteous "with their 'animating breaths'" so they will revive, and help the newly resurrected with standing with their feet. The resurrection passages describe the Garden with the great tree, the New Jerusalem, and the houses which have been prepared for the righteous.	T
T12P	Sim. **6**:7; Levi **18**:14; Jud. **25**; Zeb. **10**:1-3; Dan **5**:7-13; Benj. **10**:4-11	These testaments contain several allusions to the eschatological resurrection in eight of the "death and burial" sections of the book. In these passages the word "sleep" is used as a metaphor for death which implies that, at one point in the future, they will be woken up from their sleep and regain life. The "limited resurrection" passages focus on the eschatological resurrection of the patriarch and the saints, while the destiny of the wicked is mostly ignored. Following the resurrection of the patriarchs, they "will once more be chiefs among the people" (*T. Jud.* 25:1). The universal resurrection passage of this collection mentions that everyone will be changed, "some destined for glory, others "for dishonor" (*T. Benj.* 10:8) as a result of the eschatological judgment (*T. Benj.* 10:10) – borrowing phraseology from Dan. 12:2.	O?

Literary Work	Ref.	Description of the Eschatological Resurrected Body	Location T/O
T. Job	**33**:2-3; **39**:4-11; **40**:1-6; **46**:1–53:8	The dead bodies of Job's children were "taken up into haven by the Creator their King" (39:11), suggesting a bodily resurrection, but in this case, not an eschatological one. Job asks his wife and his friends to "look up with your eyes to the east and see my children crowned with the splendor of the heavenly one (40:1). This suggests their earthly bodies were taken to heaven, however, in the case of Job's death, his body was buried while his soul was brought to heaven. At the day of the eschatological resurrection, it could be assumed Job's soul would once more join his body.	O
T. Abraham	A13:6; B7:15-16	A bodily resurrection is only specifically mentioned in Recension B of the testament, although it is implied in Recension A. This resurrection will take place at the end of the seven thousand ages, when the soul will once more unite with the body (B7:15-16). The resurrection of Recension B would easily be harmonized with Recension A as it would fit between the first and the following two judgments. If this eschatological resurrection is indeed a unique element in Recension B, there seems to be little reason for the soul to be reunified with the body prior to the eschatological and universal second judgment which will be presided over by the twelve tribes of Israel.	O

Literary Work	Ref.	Description of the Eschatological Resurrected Body	Location T/O
T. Adam	3:3-5	As far as the prophecy is concerned, Adam's body (and that of his posterity) will be buried in the grave, be consumed by maggots and worms (3:2), and become food for the serpent (3:3). However, God will not let Adam (and his posterity) be left to "waste away in Sheol" forever (3:3), but in his grace, he will resurrect Adam's body when he comes into this world (3:3-4) and, it could be assumed, the bodies of his posterity at the end of the world (3:5). God will make Adam into a god, placing him at "the right hand of my divinity" and restore to Adam and his posterity "that which is the justice of heaven" (3:4).	O
Martyrdom and Ascension of Isaiah	4:14-18	At the point of death, it could be assumed a judgment of the soul takes place as the righteous soul leaves the "robe of flesh" behind and is brought to the seventh heaven to receive the "robes of above" and be with the saints (4:16; 8:14-15; 9:7-9). The hosts of saints who accompany God and his angels at the Second Coming, when descending from the seventh heaven, is the resurrection of the righteous, as they will once more be clothed in the "robes of flesh" and become a part of the earthly messianic kingdom. The period of the earthly messianic kingdom concludes with the resurrection and the judgment of the wicked. The wicked will be destroyed by the fire while the righteous will return to the seventh heaven, leaving their "robes of flesh" behind and receiving their "robes of above" (4:18-19).	O

Literary Work	Ref.	Description of the Eschatological Resurrected Body	Location T/O
Life of Adam and Eve	Gr. **10**:2; **13**:3-5; **28**:4; **37**:5; **39**:2-3; **41**:1-3; **43**:2-3 Vita **42**:1-5; **47**:3; **51**:2	In the bodily resurrection, the soul will once more return to the body. One of the resurrection passages seems to suggest everyone will be made into a holy person through a process of removing their evil heart and replacing it with a heart that understands good and worships God alone. Thus, they will not sin anymore. It is also suggested that, following the resurrection, they will have full access to the Garden and God will be in their midst. This literary composition presents a strong link between the pre-death body and the resurrected body.	T?
Pseudo-Philo	**3**:9; **16**:3; **19**:12-13, 15; **23**:13; **26**:12; **48**:1	At the time of the eschatological visitation (19:12-13), God will resurrect all the dead in order to bring them to judgment. The souls will once more be unified with their bodies and they will be judged as a unit (3:9-10; 19:12-13; 25:7). Those who are deemed righteous will gain eternal life and dwell in happiness with God in the world-to-come (19:12-13; 23:13). Samuel, when brought back to life, looked different than the dead Philistines that the witch of Endor had resurrected during her 40-year-long career. She describes Samuel as a divine being clothed in a white robe with a mantle placed over it, escorted by two angels (64:6). The witch description suggests the righteous dead, when brought back to life, look different than those who are wicked.	T
Lives of the Prophets	**2**:11-19; **3**:10-12	The author views the resurrection hope in light of Ezek. 37:1-14, giving the passage a dual interpretation – both national and personal (3:12).	T

Literary Work	Ref.	Description of the Eschatological Resurrected Body	Location T/O
4 Baruch	6:6-10; 9:12-14	The author states that God will reward those who love him, and he will "raise them in their tabernacles" (bodies). Just like he preserved the figs in the basket for sixty-six years, he will also preserve the flesh of those who do the things commanded by the angel of righteousness (6:6-10). He also draws a parallel between Jeremiah's ecstatic faint and the eschatological resurrection. In the same way Jeremiah's soul left his tabernacle or body at the beginning of his ecstatic faint, so does the soul of a person leave the body upon death. Jeremiah's soul returned to his body after the three-day-long ecstatic faint, and so too will a person will return to life in the eschatological resurrection. The composition makes a strong connection between the pre-death body and the resurrected body.	O
Pseudo-Phocylides	103-104a	Regardless whether a person lives an ethical life or not, upon death, all bodies will turn back to dust, all spirits will turn back to the air, and all souls will dwell in Hades under God's rulership. However, the author leaves the possibility open for some of these souls to be reunified with their former bodies and spirits, and become gods, who will dwell in Heaven for all eternity.	O

Literary Work	Ref.	Description of the Eschatological Resurrected Body	Location T/O
Psalms of Solomon	2:31, 34-35; 3:11-12; 14:9-10; 15:1-7, 10-13	In the eschatological resurrection, the righteous will be raised up to glory, and be brought to the judgment. The righteous will be shown mercy and be kept from the humiliation which is in store for the sinner. It is not clear where the righteous will spend their eternity. However, the most likely place is heaven as the righteous will be "raised up to glory" (2:31), and their life will be "in the light of the Lord" (3:12).	O?
Hellenistic Synagogal Prayers	3:24-27; 7:11; 12:46-50; 16:7-9	The righteous are promised that they will only have to sleep for a little while before they will be "called forth to new birth" (3:27), a possible allusion to Gen. 3:19b. The righteous will be glorified and receive immortality (12:45, 52).	O?
Odes of Solomon	22:4-12; 42:11-20	The author seems to view the resurrection in light of Ezek. 37:1-10, as the dead are described as heaving very dry bones, and a reversal is taking place in which the bones are once more covered in flesh. However, it is only when God's breath enters the motionless body that it becomes alive. Thus, resurrection is the reversal of the dying process and parallels God's original act of creating humans out of dust. Jesus is also described as entering Sheol to speak to the dead. The dead begged Christ for pity, mercy, and resurrection, because they recognized that death had no power over him (42:15-17) and he had the power to save (42:18). In response, Christ placed his name on their heads and claimed them as his possession (42:18, 20).	T

4. The Eschatological Resurrected Body and the New Testament

There are several New Testament accounts of a bodily resurrection from death where the resurrected continues their previous mortal life. In these passages, the resurrected person is identical in all ways to the pre-death self, apart from the medical condition which caused their death in the first place. The most well-known account is the account of Lazarus (Jn 11:1-45). For a list of resurrection texts appearing in the New Testament, see Appendix B.

A bodily resurrection to an eternal life is quite different. This is hinted at in the narrative taking place on the Mount of Transfiguration, in which Jesus is transfigured before the disciples' eyes – "His face shone like the sun (or his face became different – Lk. 9:29), and His garments became as white as light" (Mt. 17:1, NAS) or "radiant and exceedingly white" (Mk 9:3, NAS). The narrative adds that both Elijah and Moses appeared with him (Mt. 3; Mk 9:5; Lk. 9:30), a prophet who had cheated death (2 Kgs 2) and a prophet who had been brought (resurrected) to Heaven at one point after death (an event possibly alluded to in Jude 1:9). The changing nature of the resurrected incorruptible body is also hinted at when Jesus was not immediately recognized by his followers (Lk. 24:13-21 – thought to be a fellow traveler; Jn 20:11-18 – thought to be a gardener; Jn 21:1-13 – thought to be a stranger at the shore). The resurrected Jesus is presented in the Gospels as a "spirit being" who could suddenly appear and disappear (Lk. 24:36-51; Jn 20:26-29).

In conclusion, the most relevant text regarding a resurrection to immortality is 1 Corinthian 15, where the questions of how the dead are raised and what kind of body they will have (1 Cor. 15:35) are addressed. Paul uses the analogy of a seed which only grows or "resurrects" after it has been buried or "died" in the ground to describe the nature of the resurrected body. This analogy is also used in early rabbinic Judaism to support and illustrate a resurrection belief (*b. Ketub.* 111b; *b. Sanh.* 90b; *Eccl. Rab.* 1:6-7; 3:11; cf. *Gen. Rab.* 28:3; *Lev. Rab.* 18:1; *Eccl. Rab.* 12:5). Paul makes the case that the resurrected body (seedling) is different than the buried body (seed), although the seedling comes from the seed. The resurrected body of the righteous is incorruptible, glorious, powerful, spiritual, and is ready for an eternal life, while the current body is corruptible and will therefore die (1 Cor. 15:42-44). However, Paul makes it clear that the righteous who are not dead when God returns will be changed and transformed so they also can partake in the heavenly Paradise (1 Cor. 15:51-54). Paul's description parallels several aspects of the death and resurrection view presented in *2 Baruch* (see Table 18 and its associated discussion in the companion volume, *Afterlife and Resurrection*

Beliefs in the Apocrypha and Apocalyptic Literature). However, unlike *2 Bar.* 50:2-4, Paul is only concerned with the future of the righteous.[12] Table 16 outlines Paul's contrasts between the corruptible terrestrial body and the incorruptible, outer-worldly body – that is spiritual and required by the heavenly realm. Paul's understanding, therefore, is in line with the general observation emerging from the Apocrypha and the Pseudepigrapha, which is perhaps best illustrated in the *Martyrdom and Ascension of Isaiah*, with the "robe of flesh" and the "robe of above."

Table 16. The nature of the eschatological resurrected body in 1 Corinthians 15

Reference	Body that is Buried	Eschatological Resurrected Body
15:36-42a	Dead body likened to a seed sown in the ground	Resurrected body likened to a seedling emerging from the ground
15:42b	Sown as a perishable body	Raised as an imperishable body
15:43a	Sown in dishonor	Raised in glory
15:43b	Sown in weakness	Raised in power
15:44	Sown a natural body	Raised a spiritual body
15:45-48	The first Adam (Gen. 2:7) Became a living soul From the earth	The last Adam (Christ) Became a life-giving spirit From heaven
15:49	Bears the image of the earthy	Bears the image of the heavenly
15:50	Flesh and blood Perishable	Imperishable
15:52-56	Perishable Mortal Death Sin	Raised imperishable – put on the imperishable Put on immortality Victory over death (No more sin)

---

12. Jesus also uses this analogy when referring to his own death and the result of his sacrifice which will bring life to all who believe in him (Jn 12:23-26). For further reading regarding Paul's discussion on the nature of the resurrected body, see David Hodgens, "Our Resurrection Body: An Exegesis of 1 Corinthians 15:42-49," *MJT* 17, no. 2 (2001): 65–91.

Chapter 7

SUMMARY AND CONCLUSION

This chapter functions as the summary and conclusion both for this monograph and the companion volume, *Afterlife and Resurrection Beliefs in the Apocrypha and Apocalyptic Literature*. This being the case, for ease of reference, figures from the companion volume will be prefixed with "1-," while figures from the current monograph will be prefixed with "2-." The resurrection passages appearing in the Apocrypha and Pseudepigrapha, present very diverse views. Each literary work containing a "life-after-death" view seems to present a unique perspective, even those compositions presenting scant details regarding the events following death and the eschatological time. This study identified eighteen distinct and complete views (from death to eternity)[1] regarding life-after-death with varying degrees of complexity ranging from the basic view of *2 Maccabees* (Fig. 1-2) and *Psalms of Solomon* (Fig. 2-6) to the more complex views of the *Book of Watchers* (Fig. 1-6) and *2 Baruch* (Fig. 1-15). Considering this literature, it becomes apparent that there is no progression from a basic to a more complex death and resurrection view as multiple levels of complexity are attested throughout this period. Thus, there is no linear development of the resurrection belief; rather, multiple views co-existed, although an eschatological bodily resurrection belief became the central tenet for both Rabbinic Judaism and the Early Christian Church. Moreover, there seems to be no evidence in this literature that supports a shift in focus from a bodily resurrection toward

---

1. These eighteen distinct and complete views are found in: *2 Maccabees* (Fig. 1-2); *Wisdom of Solomon* (Fig. 1-3); *4 Ezra* (Fig. 1-5); *Book of Watchers* (Fig. 1-6); *Book of the Epistle of Enoch* (Fig. 1-7); *2 Enoch* (Fig. 1-8); *3 Enoch* (Fig. 1-9); *Apocalypse of Zephaniah* (Fig. 1-10); *Greek Apocalypse of Ezra* (Fig. 1-11); *Vision of Ezra* (Fig. 1-12); *Question of Ezra* (Fig. 1-13); *2 Baruch* (Fig. 1-15); *Testament of Abraham* (Fig. 2-1); *Martyrdom and Ascension of Isaiah* (Fig. 2-2); *Pseudo-Philo* (Fig. 2-3); *4 Maccabees* (Fig. 2-4); *Pseudo-Phocylides* (Fig. 2-5); and *Psalms of Solomon* (Fig. 2-6).

the immortality of the soul, as the fate of both the body and soul seem to be of great interest to the authors and the communities to which they belonged. From this study, it could also be concluded that just because Jewish and/or Christian texts borrowed terms or concepts also present in Greek philosophical texts, it does not necessarily mean the whole philosophical framework was accepted. Rather, this study has shown these terms and concepts were adapted to fit into the theological framework of the composition.

1. Human Anthropology

One of the primary elements impacting these diverse resurrection views is the understanding of human anthropology. Figure 2-7 shows the three positions present in the Apocrypha and the Pseudepigrapha. The first (Body) considers a living human being as only consisting of a body and life-giving-breath from God. Following death, the body returns to dust while the breath returns to God. Thus, the person ceases to exist as there is no element of that person existing past the physical death of the body. The second (Body + Soul) is a bipartite view which suggests a person is both a body and a soul – a soul which lives on after the physical death of the person. The third (Body + Soul + Spirit) is a tripartite view which suggests a person consists of a body, soul, and spirit, the latter two components existing beyond death. The books appearing in grey, in these three categories of Figure 2-7, do not clearly state the anthropological view, although details provided in these literary works make their suggested placement the most likely. From Figure 2-7, it becomes clear that the predominant view appearing in the Apocrypha and the Pseudepigrapha is the bipartite view (Body + Soul), while only a handful of books seem to belong to the first category (Body). Only one book belongs to the tripartite category (Body + Soul + Spirit). The view that humans have a soul that exists independently from the body after the point of death, therefore, is by far the majority position presented by these books. As such, if a Jewish or Christian document dated to the Second Temple period seemingly presents a bipartite view, strong evidence from the larger context needs to be provided by the exegete if a different anthropological view is argued. It could also be argued that if the anthropological view of a certain text is not specifically stated, the reader could assume the writer held a bipartite view, unless there is evidence in the text to the contrary. This raises an important question for a New Testament scholar. If Jesus seems to present a bipartite view in the parable of the rich man and Lazarus (Lk. 16:19-31), or in his warning against the one who can kill both the body and soul

(Mt. 10:28), could it be assumed this view of the afterlife and anthropology represent Jesus' personal theological view? If this is the case, Jesus' personal view would certainly be in line with the majority view appearing in Second Temple period literature (see Fig. 2-7).

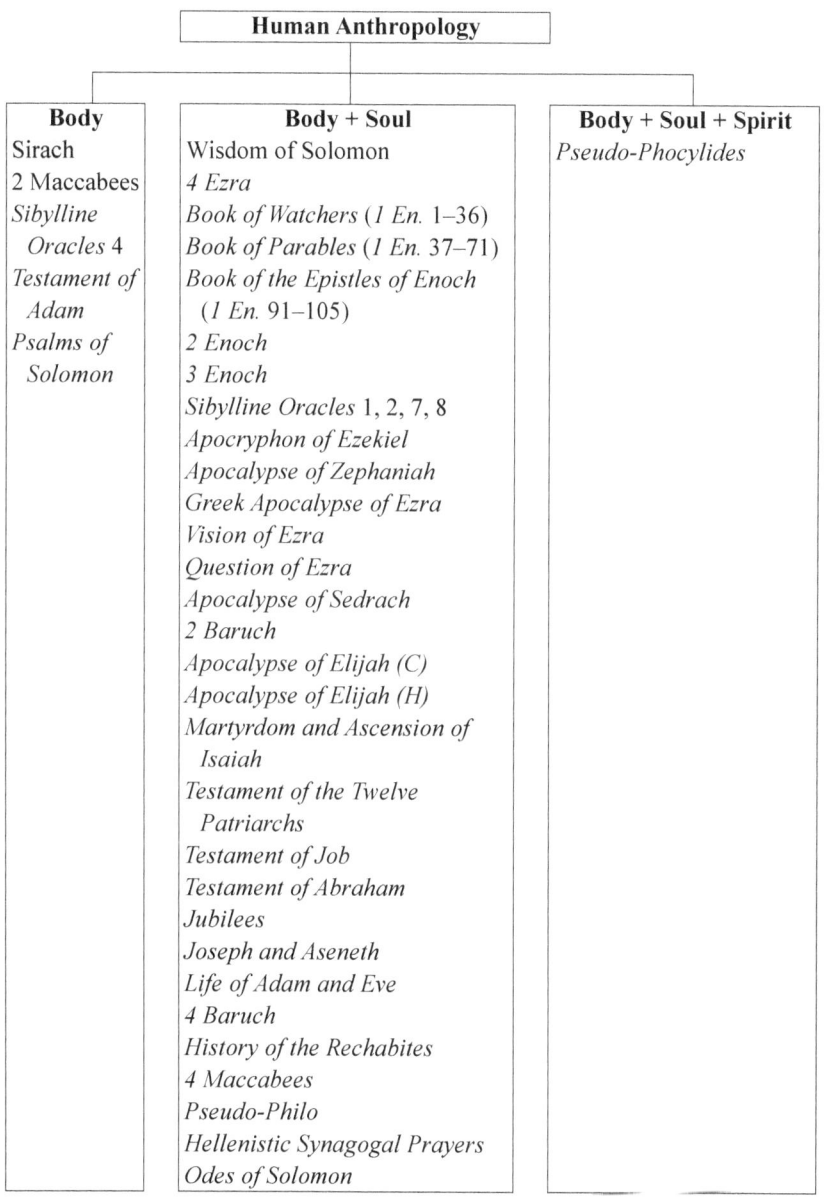

Figure 7. Human Anthropology – The Apocrypha and Pseudepigrapha

Conversely, if Jesus does not hold a bipartite view, an alternative explanation is warranted for his statements. With regard to parables, could a parable present an overarching theological framework (e.g. in the case of the Rich Man and Lazarus, upon death the soul leaves the body, the righteous are brought to Paradise for their reward while the wicked are brought to Hades for their punishment, and there is a possibility of a resurrection) which contradicts the personal view of the person recounting the parable – making the main theological point of the parable true, yet the overall theological framework false? Although this is an important question, this issue is outside the scope of this study.[2]

The bi- and tripartite view of human anthropology introduces several additional elements impacting the death and resurrection view. First, what is the nature of this soul: is it mortal or immortal? Second, where does it go when parting from the body? Third, does the soul of the righteous and the wicked face a different fate following the physical death? If it does, it would require a postmortem evaluation of the soul – a judgment of the soul. Fourth, will the soul be reunified with the body in the eschatological future? An option requiring a bodily resurrection. Fifth, will the soul be in a conscious or an unconscious state while awaiting this eschatological reunification? The literature belonging to the Apocrypha and the Pseudepigrapha provides a different answer to these questions, hence the diversity in resurrection views (see Table 17). Table 17 lists the destination of the disembodied soul of the righteous and the wicked, indicated the state of the soul while disembodied (conscious/unconscious), and notes whether the soul will experience its reward or punishment while in this state. A question mark indicates the literary work does not provide a clear answer. The righteous and the wicked soul have been given the abbreviation R and W respectively.

---

2. It might be helpful to consider Brad Young's observation that although parables "are designed to portray a reality," they only give "a pictorial representation" of said reality, and as such, careful consideration needs to be shown regarding the relationship between the picture and the portrayed reality. He notes there may be multiple "points of contact," but suggests a parable only "communicates a single message" in order to "elicit a response" from the audience (*The Parables: Jewish Tradition and Christian Interpretation* [Peabody, MA: Hendrickson, 1998], 14). For a discussion regarding this parable, see, e.g., Kenneth E. Bailey, *Jesus through Middle Eastern Eyes: Cultural Studies in the Gospels* (Downers Grove, IL: InterVarsity, 2008), 378–96; Amy-Jill Levine, *Short Stories by Jesus: The Enigmatic Parables of a Controversial Rabbi*, pbk ed. (New York: HarperOne, 2015), 267–96; and Klyne R. Snodgrass, *Stories with Intent: A Comprehensive Guide to the Parables of Jesus* (Grand Rapids: Eerdmans, 2008), 419–35.

7. Summary and Conclusion 213

Table 17. The disembodied souls

Literary Work	Disembodied Soul		State of the Soul		Experiences its Reward/ Punishment
	Righteous (R)	Wicked (W)	Conscious	Unconscious	
Wisdom of Solomon	God	?			
4 Ezra	Return to God for 7 days before sent to a holding chamber		R/W		R/W
Book of Watchers	Holding chambers		R/W		R/W
Book of the Epistle of Enoch	Sheol		R?/W	R?	
2 Enoch	?	?			
3 Enoch	3 days in the grave → judgment before God's throne		R/W		
Sibylline Oracles	Heavenly Vault	Hades, the Murky dark	R/W		R/W
Apocalypse of Zephaniah	3 days in the air → judgment in Hades Righteous → Heaven Wicked → remains in Hades		R/W		R/W
Greek Apocalypse of Ezra	Heaven/Paradise	Bowel of Hades	R/W		R/W
Vision of Ezra	Infernal Regions				R/W
Question of Ezra	Higher Atmosphere	Lower Atmosphere	R/W		R/W
Apocalypse of Sedrach	Third Heaven/Paradise God's Kingdom Bosom of Abraham	Place of Punishment	R/W		R/W

Literary Work	Disembodied Soul		State of the Soul		Experiences its Reward/ Punishment
	Righteous (R)	Wicked (W)	Conscious	Unconscious	
2 Baruch	Treasuries for the Souls			R/W	R/W
Apocalypse of Elijah	Western Region		R?/W		R/W
Testament of the Twelve Patriarchs	Captivated by Beliar			R/W	
Testament of Job	Heaven	Hades			
Testament of Abraham	Judgment at the first gate of Heaven Righteous → Paradise In-betweens → Limbo Wicked → Destruction		R/W		R/W
Martyrdom and Ascension of Isaiah	Seventh Heaven	Sheol	R	W?	R
Life of Adam and Eve	Third Heaven?	?		R?/W?	
Pseudo-Philo	Underworld		R/W		R/W
4 Maccabees	Heaven	Fiery torment	R/W		R/W
Pseudo-Phocylides	Spirit → God Soul → Hades			R/W	
Odes of Solomon	Sheol		R/W		

It should be noted that this reunification at the time of the eschatological resurrection and judgment, presented in most of these resurrection passages of this period, does not support the Platonic or Gnostic notion that the soul ("the spiritual") is pure while the body ("the physical or material") is impure (the source of evil which has imprisoned the soul), because the righteous will spend eternity in their bi- or tripartite state. Moreover, the soul described in these writings, at times, seems to have a very literal and physical depiction,[3] as the reward and punishment experienced by the soul requires a "body." The *Vision of Ezra* (Fig. 1-12) serves as a good example.

2. The Nature of the Soul

Figure 2-8 shows the three categories pertaining to the nature of the wicked soul. It is not helpful to consider the souls of the righteous as they will experience immortality as a part of their reward. The focus should be on the soul of the wicked as their fate is where one would naturally see significant variation in the views relating to the immortality of the soul. The first category of books presents the view that the soul is mortal in the sense that the wicked (Body + Soul) will be completely annihilated. The second category of books present the soul as having a beginning, but no end. Therefore, the souls of the wicked will also exist throughout eternity. Unlike the righteous, who will receive their eternal reward, the wicked will experience their eternal punishment. The third category of books presents the soul as being truly immortal in that the soul has neither a beginning nor an end – they pre-existed life on earth and they will experience an eternity of reward or punishment. The books appearing in grey in these three categories do not clearly state the destiny of the wicked souls, although details provided in these literary works make their suggested placement the most likely. It should also be noted that several books belonging to Second Temple period literature do not seem to show

---

3. Using physical terminology when describing a disembodied soul is not unique to these texts. Richard C. Steiner remarks that "in a number of cultures, free souls of the living and/or spirits of the dead are depicted as ethereal miniature replicas of their owners" (*Disembodied Souls*, 121–2), noting "the Greek ψυχή, the Egyptian *ba*, and (less certainly) the Mesopotamian *etemmu* possessed a bodily form, and yet they fit the dictionary definition of *disembodied*: they had no material existence, and after death they were freed from their owner's body" (ibid., 123). He concludes that "it may well be that the Hebrews, Egyptians, and Greeks could not conceive of their souls in the shape of anything but a body – a body resembling their own" (ibid.).

much interest in the final destiny of the wicked but focus instead on the reward in store for the righteous, therefore making it difficult to determine the nature of the soul in those books.

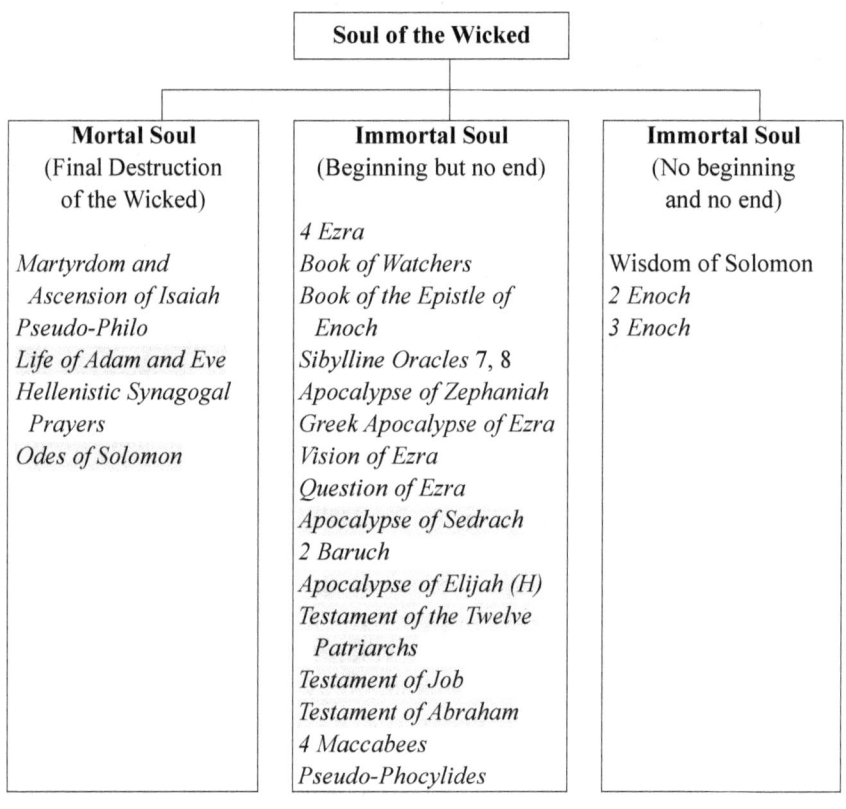

Figure 8. Human Anthropology – The Souls of the Wicked.

3. Scope of the Resurrection

The diverse resurrection views appearing in the Apocrypha and the Pseudepigrapha also differ in their scope, ranging from a universal resurrection to a more limited one. The limited resurrection views consider the resurrection as the eschatological reward of the righteous (Figs. 1-2, 2-5, and 2-6), while views containing a resurrection, both of the righteous and the wicked, seem to emphasize God's theodicy, in which the righteous are rewarded for their loyalty and the wicked are punished or destroyed due to their disloyalty to God and His instructions. Although most of the resurrection views in the Apocrypha and the Pseudepigrapha contain a dual resurrection, they are not always universal in nature, as demonstrated by the *Book of Watchers* (Fig. 1-6) in which only some of the wicked are resurrected to receive punishment. Most of the resurrection views also consider the dual resurrection of both the righteous and the wicked as an important aspect of the reward and punishment process. A portion of the reward of the righteous is to see the punishment given to their former persecutors and enemies, while a portion of the punishment of the wicked is to see rewards bestowed upon the righteous and those they previously persecuted (only one book, *Martyrdom and Ascension of Isaiah*, presents a view similar to the book of Revelation, introducing a time gap between the resurrection of the righteous and the wicked [Fig. 2-2]). The question of the nature of the resurrected body then becomes important – will their body look the same as before they died or different? If seeing what happens to "the others" is a part of the reward or punishment, then it becomes very important that they recognize "the others." Otherwise, who cares? This is the resurrection view presented in *2 Baruch* (Fig. 1-15).

4. Number and Function of the Judgments

There is also variation in resurrection views when it comes to the function and the number of judgments. If considering the 18 unique and complete death and resurrection views outlined in this study, it becomes apparent that most of these views present an eschatological judgment (Judgment II), in which the righteous will receive their reward and the wicked their punishment. It also becomes apparent that many of these views also have a judgment of the soul following the physical death of a person. This judgment determines whether the soul is righteous, neutral, or wicked, and their immediate and/or future fate (Judgment I). In the case of resurrection being a reward for the righteous, it would also require a pre-resurrection judgment to determine who these righteous are. The *Testament of Abraham* presents an additional Judgment process (Judgment III) which will also take place in the eschatological time and will be universal in nature (Fig. 2-1). Table 18 outlines the number of judgments presented in these 18 unique views – brackets indicate the given judgment is not clearly mentioned in the literary work, although it is certainly implied. It should also be noted that Judgment I is an ongoing judgment as it judges the newly dead until the time of the eschatological resurrection and judgment. Thus, *Apocalypse of Zephaniah* (Fig. 1-10) and *Questions of Ezra* (Fig. 1-13) allow for repentant wicked souls to move to the category of the righteous souls. The neutral souls of the *Testament of Abraham*, those who are in need of an additional righteous deed to be counted among the righteous, are described as being in a state of limbo until the day of eschatological judgment unless someone intercedes on their behalf, an act deemed to push them over the line (Fig. 2-1). *3 Enoch* also describes "intermediate souls" who are purified from sin in Sheol until they are deemed pure and can then join the "righteous" souls in heaven. However, *3 Enoch* does not describe an eschatological resurrection and judgment. Instead, it describes a daily ongoing judgment, leaving a potential category for in-between souls (Fig. 1-9).

Table 18. Number of judgments presented in the 18 unique resurrection views of the Apocrypha and the Pseudepigrapha

Literary Work	Judgment I Death/Judgment	Judgment II Resurrection/ Judgment	Judgment III
2 Maccabees	×		
Wisdom of Solomon	×	×	
4 Ezra	×	×	
Book of Watchers	×	×	
Epistles of Enoch		×	
2 Enoch		×	
3 Enoch	×	×	(×)
Apocalypse of Zephaniah	×	×	
Greek Apocalypse of Ezra	×	×	
Vision of Ezra	×		
Questions of Ezra	×	×	
2 Baruch	(×)	×	
Testament of Abraham	×	×	×
Martyrdom and Ascension of Isaiah	(×)	× ×	
Pseudo-Philo	×		
4 Maccabees	×		
Pseudo-Phocylides		(×)	
Psalms of Solomon	(×)	(×)	

The relationship between resurrection and judgment within the context of the question of theodicy raises an interesting hermeneutical and theological question. This study shows that a resurrection belief also requires a belief in a judgment as there is a need to determine who will be resurrected and/or evaluate who is righteous or wicked since they will receive a different destiny. However, does a promise of a future judgment in Second Temple period literature, and by extension in biblical literature, imply there will also be a form of afterlife and a possible future resurrection, even if this belief is not explicitly stated? Further research into the relationship between a future judgment and implied afterlife is warranted.[4] Based on the reverse relationship noted in this study, a tentative suggestion could be made. The context and the nature of the future judgment would probably be the determining factor. If the future judgment seems to be personal and is mentioned in a composition which also promotes a set of ethical behaviors for an individual to adopt (or provides a list of behaviors to avoid), it could be assumed an individual's actions will be evaluated at a future judgment, thus implying some type of afterlife. Otherwise, what would be the purpose of the judgment? Alternatively, if the future judgment is mentioned in the context of the nation of Israel, the judgment

---

4. Two potentially fruitful biblical passages to explore regarding a future judgment after death and an implied afterlife are Eccl. 11:9–12:14 and Heb. 9:27-28. The author of the concluding words of Ecclesiastes urges the target audience to "fear God and keep His commandments" as "God will bring every work into judgment, including every secret thing, whether good or evil" (Eccl. 12:13-14, NKJV). The concept יְרָא אֶת־הָאֱלֹהִים, "fear God," appears in five additional passages in this wisdom book (Eccl. 3:14; 5:6; 7:18; 8:12) which, together with the expectation of divine judgment, forms the two great themes of the concluding words and provides an interpretative framework for the composition as a whole. In this book, a contrast is also made between two classes of people, "the righteous" (using terms like God-fearers [Eccl. 3:14; 5:6; 7:18; 8:12; 12:13]; righteous [Eccl. 3:17; 7:15-16, 20; 8:14; 9:2]; good [Eccl. 9:2]; and the wise [e.g. Eccl. 10:2]) and "the wicked" (using terms like sinners [Eccl. 2:26; 7:26; 8:11; 9:2, 18]; wicked [Eccl. 3:17; 7:15; 8:10, 12-14; 9:2]; and fool [e.g. Eccl. 5:2]). For further study into the eschatological and universal nature of the concluding chapter of Ecclesiastes, see Jacques B. Doukhan, *Ecclesiastes: All Is Vanity* (Nampa, ID: Pacific, 2006), 119–28. From this, it could be argued that unless there is some form of afterlife in which a person receives some form for reward or punishment based on their good or evil behavior, the warning of a pending judgment would be meaningless. However, the author does not reveal the nature of this implied afterlife.

The link between judgment and some form of afterlife is also implied in Heb. 9:27-28, in the context of Christ's sacrifice (Heb. 9:23-28). The author states: "And as it is appointed for men to die once, but after this the judgment, so Christ was offered once to bear the sins of many" (Heb. 9:27-28a), suggesting there will be a judgment in store for everyone following death. Though this passage states all humans are faced with certain death, Leon Morris notes this is not "the complete and the final end." He adds, "death is more serious than that because it is followed by judgment. Men are accountable, and after death they will render account to God" ("Hebrews," in *The Expositor's Bible Commentary*, ed. Frank E. Gæbelein [Grand Rapids: Zondervan, 1981], 93). This text is ambiguous regarding the nature of this judgment (if it will be an instant personal judgment at the point of death, or an eschatological universal judgment) and the nature of the implied afterlife.

may probably not imply a personal afterlife but may instead provide a hope for the survival of the nation.[5]

5. Final Destiny of the Righteous and the Wicked

The final destiny of the righteous and the wicked also impacts a death and resurrection view, as the wicked may be annihilated or punished for all eternity. The final destiny of the righteous also affects the type of body needed to live in that location. If the righteous will spend eternity on earth/new earth, they would only need an earthly body. However, if the righteous will be brought to heaven following the eschatological resurrection and judgment, they would need a "heavenly body" as described

---

5. The vivid resurrection vision in Ezek. 37:1-14 serves as a good example of a belief in a life after death following God's catastrophic "judgment" of exile. Based on a rhetorical criticism on Ezekiel's vision of the *Valley of the Bones*, Michael V. Fox, notes "it would be a misinterpretation of Ezekiel 37 to see there a concept of individual resurrection, but that misinterpretation would be rooted in Ezekiel's own rhetoric." He suggests this vision "contributed to the formulation of the later doctrine of corporeal resurrection." He adds "the resurrection that he [Ezekiel] is really interested in is not from actual death but from figurative death. Yet his image does offer a new perspective on the life–death polarity, one in which death is not seen as final" (Michael V. Fox, "The Rhetoric of Ezekiel's Vision of the Valley of the Bones," *HUCA* 51 [1980]: 12). Fox concludes that Ezekiel's vision regarding the nation of Israel goes beyond a mere promised rebirth and restoration since God will fundamentally restructure its psychology with his "breath of life" (ibid., 15). Moshe Greenberg notes that this "resurrection metaphor of national restoration" was later interpreted literally by early Jewish and Christian interpreters as relating to the universal eschatological resurrection (see Moshe Greenberg, *Ezekiel 21–37: A New Translation with Introduction and Commentary*, AB 22A [Garden City, NY: Doubleday, 1997], 749–51). The net effect was Ezekiel's vision was either interpreted figuratively or literally – referring to a national restoration or an individualized revivification.

This study noted several resurrection or personal afterlife passages appearing in the Pseudepigrapha which alluded or referred to the *Valley of the Bones* vision (*Sib. Or.* 2.221-226; 4.181-182; *Apoc. Elij.* [H]; *Liv. Proph.* 3:12; *4 Macc.* 18:17; *Odes* 22:8-10). The most interesting in this context is the case in *Lives of the Prophets* as this passage shows a dual understanding of Ezekiel's vision, giving it both a personal and a corporate interpretation. It seems Ezekiel would argue that both the nation of Israel and the individual person will have a "future." The enemy may think they will be able to defeat or the destroy the nation of Israel; however, this will only be a temporary defeat since the nation will have a "future" in the present age and will be restored. The same is true on a personal level: though individuals are killed, through their resurrection they will have a "future" in the age to come.

in *2 Baruch*, *Martyrdom and Ascension of Isaiah*, and *Psalms of Solomon* (Figs. 1-15, 2-2, and 2-6). This view is best described in the *Martyrdom and Ascension of Isaiah* (Fig. 2-2), which describes the "robes-of-flesh" intended for earthly dwelling and the "robes-of-above" necessary for dwelling in heaven. Table 19 shows the final destination of the righteous and the wicked as outlined in this study. Some of the resurrection passages considered in this work did not provide a full resurrection picture, as they only focused on either the fate of the righteous or the wicked, and did not reveal the final destiny of the other group, or only alluded to their final destination. This ambiguity or uncertainty has been indicated by the use of "?" in the following table.

Table 19. Final destiny of the righteous and the wicked

Book	Righteous	Wicked
Sirach	World?	Fire and worms
2 Maccabees	World	Grave
Wisdom of Solomon	World	Grave
4 Ezra	World	Hades/Hell
Book of Watchers	World	Fiery Abyss
Book of Parables	Earth to Come/ Dwell with God	Condemnation?
Book of Dream Visions	New Age	Fiery Abyss
Book of Epistles of Enoch	Heaven	Hell
2 Enoch	Paradise (Third Heaven)	Hell (Fifth Heaven)
3 Enoch	God's Throne	Gehinnom
Sibylline Oracles 2	Recreated world	Destruction by fire
Sibylline Oracles 4	Pleasant life on a fertile earth	Punished in the fire of Gehenna
Sibylline Oracles 7	Recreated world	Burn in spirit by their perishing flesh
Sibylline Oracles 8	Recreated world?	Punished by a torturous fire forever
Sibylline Oracles Frag. 1	Paradise	Burned with torches all day, forever
Apocalypse of Zephaniah	Heavenly City	Hades
Greek Apocalypse of Ezra	Heaven/Paradise	Hades/Gehenna
Vision of Ezra	Heaven/Paradise	Infernal Regions/Hellfire
Question of Ezra	God's throne/Upper Atmosphere	Place of Punishment
Apocalypse of Sedrach	Paradise/Third Heaven/God's Kingdom/Bosom of Abraham	Place of Punishment

2 Baruch	Heaven/Paradise/World to come	Place of torment/Fire
Apocalypse of Elijah (C)	Heaven Recreated world	?
Apocalypse of Elijah (H)	New Jerusalem, Earth	Punishment
Testament of the Twelve Prophets	Paradise/Presence of the Lord	Destroyed by eternal fire
T. Job	Heaven	Hades
T. Abraham	Paradise	Destruction and eternal punishment
T. Moses	?	Gehenna
T. Adam	Heaven	Sheol
Jubilees	Heaven	Sheol
Martyrdom and Ascension of Isaiah	Seventh Heaven	Destruction
Joseph and Aseneth	Seventh Heaven	?
Life of Adam and Eve	Garden of Eden with God	Condemned to Death
Pseudo-Philo	World-to-Come	Annihilation
Lives of the Prophets	World-to-Come	?
4 Baruch	Heavenly Jerusalem	?
4 Maccabees	Heaven	Fiery Torment
Pseudo-Phocylides	God	Hades
Psalms of Solomon	Haven/Glory/Light of the Lord	Destruction
Hellenistic Synagogal Prayers	Paradise (regained)	?
Odes of Solomon	New World	Destruction

In the light of the profusion of views regarding the afterlife in the literature of the Second Temple period, a reader of the New Testament is faced with the following crucial question: Is it reasonable to assume that the New Testament presents a harmonized view of the resurrection and afterlife (see Figure 2-9 for an example of a harmonized resurrection view)? Or, should the reader instead be open to New Testament writers holding various views, thus being more sensitive to the differences between the differing eschatological accounts?[6]

---

6. Jan A. Sigvartsen, "The Afterlife in the Apocalyptic Literature of Second Temple Period Judaism," paper presented at the Midwest Region Society of Biblical Literature, Olivet Nazarene University, Bourbonnais, IL, 8 February 2015.

7. *Summary and Conclusion* 223

Figure 9. A Harmonized Resurrection View

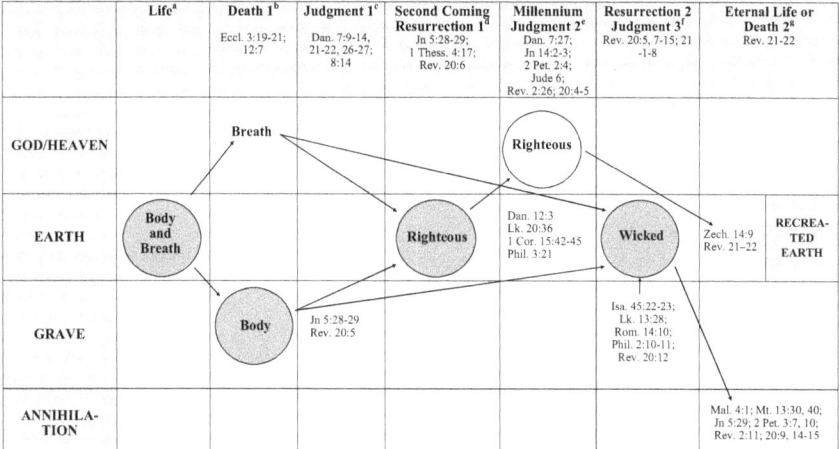

ᵃ This life determines a person's future destiny (Jn 5:29). A righteous person will participate in the first resurrection which will take place at the Jesus' Second Coming. The righteous dead, together with the righteous living, are transformed and brought to Heaven (Jn 5:28-29; 1 Cor. 15:42-45; 1 Thess. 4:15-17; Phil. 3:21; Rev. 20:6). At the end of the Millennium, the righteous will return to a renewed earth where they will spend eternity. The wicked dead, will be joined by the wicked at the Second Coming and will "sleep" in their graves until the resurrection of the wicked at the end of the Millennium – at that point, they will be judged and suffer eternal destruction (Jn 5:29; Rev. 2:11; 20:14-15).

ᵇ A living being consists of body and God's breath as described in the creation story (Gen. 2:7). Death is the reversal of God's creation act, the body returns to dust while the breath returns to God who gave it (Gen. 3:19; Eccl. 3:19-21; 12:7). The breath of life should not be confused with a "soul" that lives on independently from the body upon death.

ᶜ Before the second coming, there will be an investigative judgment (Dan. 7:9-14, 21-22, 26-27; 8:14) which will determine who will be a part of the resurrection of the righteous and who are numbered among the righteous living – those who Jesus will bring to Heaven for the Millennium.

ᵈ The first general resurrection takes place at the Second Coming and includes all the righteous dead. Following the resurrection, all the righteous will be transformed and be "clothed in immortality" and become like the angels before they are brought to Heaven to be with God during the Millennium (Lk. 20:36; 1 Cor. 15:42-45; Phil. 3:21; Rev. 20:4-6). There will be a "special" and limited resurrection of those who killed Jesus (and the most wicked) which will take place before the Second Coming and the resurrection of the righteous (Mt. 26:64; Rev. 1:7), following the Second Coming they will die a second time and await their final annihilation at the end of the Millennium. The wicked, however, will be destroyed (Mt. 24:37-39; Lk. 17:28-30; Rev. 19:18-21) and be dead until the resurrection of the wicked at the end of the Millennium.

ᵉ During the Millennium, the earth will be desolate (Jer. 4:23-25 || Gen. 1:2), only Satan will be roaming the earth (Rev. 20:2-3), while the righteous are in Heaven reigning with God (Dan. 7:27; Rev. 2:26; 20:4) and "judging the wicked" (1 Cor. 6:2-3; 2 Pet. 2:4; Jude 6; Rev. 20:4) before the resurrection and sentencing of the wicked.

ᶠ The resurrection of the wicked takes place at the end of the Millennium when the righteous have returned to the earth with God and the New Jerusalem. Following the sentencing of the wicked, the wicked will be cast into the lake of fire (Rev. 20:7-15; 21:1-8).

ᵍ The righteous will live on a recreated earth with God for all eternity while the wicked are completely annihilated (Rev. 21–22).

~ ~ ~

This raises an important theological question regarding inspiration. If the Holy Spirit inspired the New Testament writers,[7] could they hold different views regarding the resurrection belief? Is it possible to have a high view of Scripture while at the same time making allowance for different resurrection views? Could it be argued that the New Testament writers are in agreement on the main theological points (the big picture), that this life is not all there is? They suggest there is a life after death where the righteous will be rewarded and the wicked will be punished, although they may have different views regarding some of the finer details of this afterlife. Would such a consideration be regarded as an abandonment of the Reformation principles of *Sola Scriptura*, *Tota Scriptura*, *Prima Scriptura*, and the *Analogy of Scripture* by scholars belonging to a Protestant tradition?

6. Use of the TaNaKh in Support of the Resurrection Belief

A careful reading of all the resurrection passages appearing in the Apocrypha and the Pseudepigrapha reveal that most of the distinct views on life after death, regardless of their complexity, are often supported by several key passages from the books that later became a part of the TaNaKh or shared motifs with these books. Future analysis of these key passages from the TaNaKh may shed further light on how the literary works from this period interpreted, understood, used, and reused the "TaNaKh." It may even determine whether the resurrection belief is

---

7. This assumes the Greek phrase πᾶσα γραφὴ θεόπνευστος, "all Scriptures is God-breathed" (2 Tim. 3:16a), is not only referring to the Scriptures in the TaNaKh but is also applicable to the New Testament writings – even those books written after this statement was written.

indeed present in these texts (based on good exegesis) or if this belief was read into these texts by Second Temple period authors (an example of eisegesis). Based on preliminary observations, some of these resurrection concepts seem to derive naturally from the "TaNaKh," while others seem to be based on an interpretation or a more elaborate exegesis. Yet, other usages seem a bit more forced, and in those cases the TaNaKh appears to be considered a source of proof-texts, seemingly often disregarding the larger context of the text quoted or alluded to. Early Second Temple period resurrection texts seem to be supported by a creative use of the TaNaKh, while late Second Temple period texts, early Christian, and Rabbinic texts seem to utilize more proof-texting. A good example is the conclusion of *4 Maccabees*, which gives a list of important texts in support of an afterlife and the instant reward in store for the soul of the righteous, a view excluding the need for a bodily resurrection which is in stark contrast to the parallel narrative of 2 Maccabees 7. Interestingly, it may be argued that these proof-texts could easily be utilized to support a universal eschatological resurrection belief, and this study shows that some of these passages were indeed used by other literary works in support of their unique perspective on the afterlife. For Christian writers, the main support for the resurrection belief was found in Jesus' resurrection. Thus, questioning the bodily resurrection belief was equated with questioning the historicity of Jesus' resurrection, the guarantor for the Christians' salvation hope. Hence, the Christian interpolations found in the Pseudepigrapha do not add much additional support from the TaNaKh in support of the resurrection belief. In Rabbinic Judaism, questioning that the resurrection belief did not derive from the Torah would disqualify the person from any share in the world to come – thus their propensity to find proof-texts from the Torah, as attested in the *Babylonian Talmud* (*b. Sanh.* 90a-92b). An awareness of Second Temple period literature is helpful for gaining a better understanding of the death and afterlife views presented in the New Testament and Early Rabbinic literature, as it shows they are a part of the larger discussion taking place during this critical period. Table 20 provides a list of "resurrection passages" from the TaNaKh which were referred or alluded to in the context of the resurrection statements surveyed from the Apocrypha and the Pseudepigrapha. However, "Resurrection Scripture Clouds" are not included in this table.[8] Table 21

---

8. A "Resurrection Scripture Cloud" is a combination of passages carefully strung together to form a resurrection argument which individually would not necessarily support a resurrection belief. Several examples of such "Scripture Clouds" appear in Table 21, in which *Book of Watchers* and *4 Maccabees* serve as great examples. These "Scripture Clouds" have been explored and discussed in the previous chapters.

centers on the 18 distinct afterlife views and indicates which views are supported by the TaNaKh – references and allusions to the TaNaKh are bolded as a contrast to shared concepts. These two tables will give an indication of the number of TaNaKh texts that were perceived as resurrection texts and the texts that were most often referred or alluded to. The reader should keep in mind that the profusion of afterlife views continued beyond the close of the Second Temple period[9] and has survived into present time. This is reflected by the diverse beliefs held by the many Christian denominations.

Table 20. List of the TaNaKh passages referred or alluded to in the context of the resurrection statements surveyed from the Apocrypha and the Pseudepigrapha.

TaNaKh	Apocrypha and Pseudepigrapha
Gen. 3:19	*2 En.* J32:1; *Sib. Or.* 8:96-99; *Apoc. Mos.* 41:1-2; *Hel. Syn. Pr.* 3:25-26; 12:49-50
Exod. 3:6	*4 Macc.* 7:18-19; *Hel. Syn. Pr.* 16:7-9
Deut. 30:19-20	*4 Ezra* 7:129; *4 Macc.* 18:18-19
Deut. 32:29	*2 Macc.* 7:6; *Apoc. Elij. (H)*
Deut. 32:29, 47	*4 Macc.* 18:18-19
Deut. 33:3	*4 Macc.* 17:17-21
1 Sam. 28:7-20	*Ps.-Philo* 64:5-8
Isa. 26:19-21	*2 Macc.* 7:23; *4 Ezra* 7:97; *Apoc. Ezek.* Frag. 1
Isa. 35:4-7	*Sib. Or.* 8:205-212
Isa. 49:6	*Sir.* 48:1-11
Isa. 52–53	*2 Macc.* 7:23; *Wis.* 3:5-6
Isa. 52:1-2	*1 En.* 62:15a
Isa. 54:8-10	*2 Macc.* 7:28-29
Isa. 56:1	*2 Macc.* 7:28-29
Isa. 64:4-11	*2 Macc.* 7:28-29
Isa. 65:17	*Ps.-Philo* 3:10
Isa. 66:22-24	*Sir.* 7:17b; *Ps.-Philo* 3:10; *Apoc. Elij. (H)*
Ezek. 34	*1 En.* 90:33
Ezek. 37:1-14	*1 En.* 90:33; *Sib. Or.* 2.211-226; 4.181-182; *Apoc. Elij. (H)*; *Liv. Proph.* 3:12; *4 Macc.* 18:17; *Odes* 22:8-10
Hos. 6:2	*3 En.* 28:7-10
Mal. 4:1-6	*Sir.* 48:1-11; *T. Zeb.* 9:8
Ps. 1:5-6	*Pss. Sol.* 14:9-10
Ps. 50:1-6	*Apoc. Ezek.* Frag. 1

9. For a study on the multiple resurrection views held in the early Christian Church, see Eliezer Gonzalez, *The Fate of the Dead in Early Third Century North African Christianity: The Passion of Perpetua and Felicitas and Tertullian*, STAC 83 (Tübingen: Mohr Siebeck, 2014).

7. Summary and Conclusion

Prov. 3:18	*4 Macc.* 18:16
Job 42:17 LXX	*T. Job* 4:4-11
Dan. 7:18, 22	Wis. 3:7-8
Dan. 12:1-3	*1 En.* 51:1-5; 102:4–104:8
Dan. 12:1-2	*T. Benj.* 10:8
Dan. 12:2-3	*4 Ezra* 7:32-33; *2 Bar.* 49–51; *T. Mos.* 10:9-14
Dan. 12:2	2 Macc. 7:9b, 14b; *Mart. Ascen. Isa.* 4:14-18; *Ps.-Philo* 3:10; *Pss. Sol.* 2:31; 3:11-12
Dan. 12:3	Wis. 3:7-8; *2 En.* 22:8, 10; 66:7; *4 Macc.* 17:5; *Ps.-Philo* 33:1-5; *Ps.-Phoc.* 104b
Dan. 12:13	Wis. 3:5-6; *T. Mos.* 10:9-14

Table 21. The 18 distinct afterlife views and the TaNaKh.

2 Maccabees	**Gen. 1** [*ex nihilo*]; **Deut. 28–32** [**32:29**]; **Isa. 26; 52–53; Eccl. 12:13**
Wisdom of Solomon	**Isa. 5:24; 52–53; Obad. 18; Dan. 7:18, 22; 12:1-3, 13**
4 Ezra	**Deut. 30:11-20; Isa. 26:19; Dan. 7:9-10; 12:2-3**
Book of Watchers (*1 En.* 1–36)	**Gen. 2:7; 4:9-10; 9:4-6; Eccl. 12:7**
Book of the Epistle of Enoch (*1 En.* 91–105)	Dan. 12:1-3
2 Enoch	**Gen. 3:19b**
3 Enoch	**Hos. 6:2; Dan. 4** [celestial beings]; **Dan. 7:9-10, 27**
Apocalypse of Zephaniah	-
Greek Apocalypse of Ezra	-
Vision of Ezra	-
Question of Ezra	-
2 Baruch	**Gen. 1:8; Exod. 35:29-30; Dan. 2; 7; 12:1-3, 13**
Testament of Abraham	**Deut. 19:15** [the need for three witnesses ‖ judgments]
Martyrdom and Ascension of Isaiah	**Dan. 2; 7; 12** [**Dan. 12:12** – 1335-day prophecy]
Pseudo-Philo	Exod. 34:29-35; Josh. 7; **1 Sam. 28:12-19**; Isa. 65:17; 66:22; Dan. 12:2-3
4 Maccabees	**Gen. 3:24; 4:1-6, 8; 22:1-19; 39:7-23; 40:3; Exod. 3:6; Num. 25:6-13; Deut. 30:20; 32:1-43; 32:39, 47; 33:3; Isa. 43:2; Ezek. 37:1-14; Mal. 3:2-3; Ps. 34:20; Prov. 3:18; Dan. 3:1-30; 6:1-28; 12:3**
Pseudo-Phocylides	**Gen. 1:26-27; 2:7; 3:19b, 22; 6:3;** Deut. 15:2-3; 1 Sam. 2:20; **Ps. 8:6** [MT]; **Eccl. 3:20; 12:7;** Dan. 12:3
Psalms of Solomon	Isa. 2:5; 60:1; **Ps. 1:5-6;** Prov. 20:27; **Dan. 12:2**

Appendix A:
Classification and Anthology of Resurrection Texts

Appendix A gives a survey of the resurrection passages compiled from the Testament (often with apocalyptic sections), Expansion on Stories and Legends, Wisdom and Philosophical Literature, and Prayers, Psalms, and Odes sections of Charlesworth's two-volume Pseudepigrapha. For a survey of the resurrection passages compiled from the Apocrypha and the apocalyptic and related works section of the Pseudepigrapha, see Appendix A in the companion volume, *Afterlife and Resurrection Beliefs in the Apocrypha and Apocalyptic Literature*. For a survey of the resurrection passages from the Dead Sea Scrolls, Josephus, New Testament, and Early Rabbinic Period, see Appendix B.

Table 22 – Resurrection Texts in the Testaments, Table 23 – Resurrection Texts in Expansions on Stories and Legends, Table 24 – Resurrection Texts in Wisdom and Philosophical Literature, and Table 25 – Resurrection Texts in Prayers, Psalms, and Odes, are followed by an anthology of the resurrection passages listed in the Table. This is to show the larger context of the resurrection statement and provide the general reader convenient access to these resurrection texts which are discussed in this monograph.[1] Chapters two through five of this monograph examine the passages listed in the tables of this Appendix which are either referring or alluding to texts from the TaNaKh in support of a resurrection belief.

The following list shows the different categories used when analyzing and classifying these resurrection texts and provides a short explanation of

---

1. The relevant passages for the anthologies are collected from: *Revised Standard Version* (RSV)/*New Revised Standard Version* (NRSV); James H. Charlesworth, ed., *The Old Testament Pseudepigrapha*, 2 vols. (New York: Doubleday, 1983–85); George W. E. Nickelsburg and James C. VanderKam, *1 Enoch: The Hermeneia Translation* (Minneapolis: Fortress, 2012); John C. Reeves, *Trajectories in Near Eastern Apocalyptic: A Postrabbinic Jewish Apocalypse Reader* (Atlanta: Society of Biblical Literature, 2005); Michael E. Stone and Matthias Henze, *4 Ezra and 2 Baruch: Translations, Introductions, and Notes* (Minneapolis: Fortress, 2013).

each category. Since the books appearing in the Testament, Expansion on Stories and Legends, Wisdom and Philosophical Literature, and Prayers, Psalms, and Odes sections of the Pseudepigrapha were composed, edited and even redacted during a period ranging several centuries (second century BCE–seventh century CE) it becomes helpful to include a suggested dating for each book in these four Tables for a proper evaluation of the resurrection passage since it may also shed some light on the developmental stages of the resurrection belief.[22] Appendix B provides similar table of categories to show the relevant categories when classifying and evaluating resurrections texts found in the Dead Sea Scrolls, Josephus, New Testament, Jewish Liturgy texts, and in early rabbinic literature.

Category		Explanation
Date		Date the book was written.
Passage		Passage reference.
Notes		Author's notes.
Resurrection	Implied	A resurrection belief is implied in the passage.
	Stated	A resurrection belief is stated clearly in the passage.
Classification	Reference	The resurrection passage refers to a resurrection text in the TaNaKh.
	Allusion	The resurrection passage alludes to a resurrection text in the TaNaKh.
	Philosophical	Resurrection passage uses a philosophical argument as a proof for a resurrection belief.
	Assumed	Since the resurrection belief is assumed, no attempt is made to prove biblically or philosophically that there will be a resurrection.

The relevant sections referring directly or indirectly to a resurrection belief have been highlighted in gray for emphasis in the anthologies. The reader will also notice that these anthologies have placed these resurrection statements in the larger context, a decision made to better understand the underlying reasoning behind each statement. Additionally, references and allusions to the TaNaKh, Apocrypha, Pseudepigrapha, Dead Sea Scrolls,

---

2. The suggested dates given for the literary works belonging to the Pseudepigrapha are mostly based on Charlesworth's two-volume work, *The Old Testament Pseudepigrapha* and to a lesser degree on Evans, *Ancient Texts for New Testament Studies*. Additionally, the dating of each literary work is considered in chapter two through five when discussing the resurrection passages appearing in these literary works.

Rabbinic Literature, and the New Testament (most of these references appears in the margin and in the footnotes of Charles'[3] and Charlesworth's collections of Pseudepigraphical writings) are placed in a smaller font and in [brackets in 8pt] in the resurrection passage. References and allusions to the TaNaKh, alluding or directly supporting a resurrection belief have also been **bolded** for emphasis. It should be noted that many of these references are cross-references referring to synonymous or related thoughts found in the larger body of Second Temple period texts and as such, does not necessarily reflect or suggest a dependency between the passage and the given reference. Obvious Christian interpolation in an original Jewish text has been <u>underlined</u> in the anthology.

---

3. R. H. Charles, ed., *The Apocrypha and Pseudepigrapha of the Old Testament in English* (Oxford: Clarendon Press, 1913).

Resurrection Texts in the Testaments

Table 22. Resurrection texts in the *Testaments*

Date	Passage		Notes	Resurrection			Classification		
				Implied	Stated	Ref.	Allude	Phil.	Assum.
2nd cent. CE	*Testament of the Twelve Patriarchs*	Simeon 6	Arise in joy		×		×		×
		8:1	Sleep ‖ Death	×					
	Levi	18:14	Patriarchs share in the eschatological blessings	×					
	Judah	25	Resurrection of Patriarchs		×		×		
		26:4	Sleep = Death	×					
	Issachar	7:9	Sleep ‖ Death	×				×	×
	Zebulun	10:1-7	Righteous/Wicked		×				×
	Dan	5:7-13	The work of the dual Messiah		×				×
		7:1	Sleep ‖ Death	×				×	
	Gad	8:1	Sleep ‖ Death	×					×
	Asher	8:1	Sleep ‖ Death	×					×
	Joseph	20:4	Sleep ‖ Death	×					×
	Benjamin	10:4-10	Resurrection of patriarchs/transformation/Judgment		×	×			×

Appendix A 231

232 *Appendix A*

Date	Passage		Notes	Resurrection		Classification			
				Implied	Stated	Ref.	Allude	Phil.	Assum.
1st cent. CE	*Testament of Job*	4:9	Regarding the impending calamities		x	x			x
		33; 41:4	Job's throne in Heaven	x					x
		39:12	The children have been taken up to heaven	x					x
		43	The two ways	x					x
		47:11; 52; 53	Coming for the immortal Soul Death ‖ Sleep	x					x
1st to 2nd cent. CE	*Testament of the Three Patriarchs*	*Testament of Abraham* B7:16	Resurrection after 7000 ages are fulfilled		x			x	
1st cent. CE	*Testament of Moses*	1:15	Death = Sleep	x					x
		10:9	The End-time	x		x		x	
		10:14	Death = Sleep	x				x	
2nd to 5th cent. CE	*Testament of Adam*	3:2	Created in God's image	x				x	x
		3:4	Resurrection/ 2nd Adam	x		x		x	

Testament of the Twelve Patriarchs
Sleep || Death

Simeon 8:1-2 –	**He fell asleep** with his fathers at the age of one hundred and twenty years.
(*OTP* 1:787)	They placed him in a wooden coffin in order to carry his bones up to Hebron.
Judah 26:4 –	**Judah fell asleep** and his sons did everything as he had instructed them, and they buried
(*OTP* 1:802)	him in Hebron with his fathers.
Issachar 7:9 –	And he stretched his legs and died at a good old age – the fifth son, with all his members
(*OTP* 1:804)	sound and still strong; **he slept the eternal sleep**.
Zebulun 10:6 –	When he had said this, **he fell into a beautiful sleep**, and his sons placed him in a coffin.
(*OTP* 1:807)	
Dan 7:1 –	When he had said this, he kissed them and **slept an eternal sleep**. And his sons buried
(*OTP* 1:810)	him and later they carried his bones to be near Abraham, Isaac, and Jacob.
Gad 8:1 –	He drew up his feet and **fell asleep in peace**. And after five years they took him up and
(*OTP* 1:816)	buried him in Hebron with his fathers.
Asher 8:1 –	After he had said these things he gave instructions, saying, "Bury me in Hebron." And he
(*OTP* 1:818)	died, **heaving fallen into a beautiful sleep**.
Joseph 20:4-5 –	And after he had said this he stretched out his feet and **fell into a beautiful sleep.** And all
(*OTP* 1:825)	Israel and all Egypt mourned with great lamentation.

Simeon 6 *OTP* **1:787**

[1] "See, I have told you everything, so that I might be exonerated with regard to your sin.

[2] "If you divest yourselves of envy and every hardness of heart,
my bones will flourish as a rose [cf. Isa. 35:1; Hos. 14:5-7; Song 2:1] in Israel,
and my flesh as a lily in Jacob,

>   My odor shall be like the odor of Lebanon;
>   Holy ones shall be multiplied from me forever and ever,
>   and their branches shall extend to a great distance.
> 3   Then the seed of Canaan will be destroyed,
>   and there will be no posterity of Amalek,
>   All the Cappadocians (1QapGen 21:23 vs. Gen. 14:9) shall be destroyed,
>   and all the Hittites shall be wholly obliterated.
> 4   The land of Ham shall be wanting,
>   and all that people shall perish.
>   Then the whole earth shall be at rest from trouble,
>   and everything under heaven shall be free from war.

⁵"Then Shem shall be glorified; because God the Lord, the Great One in Israel, will be manifest upon the earth [as a man]. By himself will he save Adam. ⁶Then all the spirits of error shall be given over to being trampled underfoot. And men will have mastery over the evil spirits. ⁷**Then I shall arise in gladness [Dan. 12:2** – however, both the just and unjust] and I shall bless the Most High for his marvels, [because God has taken a body, eats with human beings, and saves human beings].

Levi 18:1-14   *OTP* 1:794-95

¹⁸:¹When vengeance will have come upon them from the Lord, the priesthood will lapse.
²And then the Lord will raise up a new priest [cf. Ps. 110]
to whom all the words of the Lord will be revealed.
He shall effect the judgment of truth over the earth for many days.
³And his star [Num. 24:17] shall rise in heaven like a king;
kindling the light of knowledge as day is illumined by the sun.
And he shall be extolled by the whole inhabited world.
⁴This one will shine forth like the sun in the earth;
he shall take away all darkness form under heaven,
and there shall be peace in all the earth.
⁵The heaven shall greatly rejoice in his days
and the earth shall be glad [Isa. 44:23];
the clouds will be filled with joy
and the knowledge of the Lord will be poured out on the earth like the water of the seas [Isa 11:9].
And the angels of glory of the Lord's presence will be made glad by him.
⁶The heavens will be opened,
and from the temple of glory sanctification will come upon him,
with a fatherly voice, as from Abraham to Isaac.
⁷And the glory of the Most High shall burst forth upon him.
And the spirit of understanding and sanctification
shall rest upon him [in the water] [Isa. 11:2 | Mk 1:9-11].
⁸For he shall give the majesty of the Lord to those who are his sons in truth forever.
And there shall be no successor for him from generation to generation forever.
⁹And in his priesthood the nations shall be multiplied in knowledge on the earth,

and they shall be illumined by the grace of the Lord,
but Israel shall be diminished by her ignorance
and darkened by her grief.
In his priesthood sin shall cease
and lawless men shall rest from their evil deeds,
and righteous men shall find rest in him.
¹⁰And he shall open the gates of paradise [Gen. 3:24];
he shall remove the sword that has threatened since Adam,
¹¹and he will grant to the saints to eat of the tree of life [Gen. 2:9 | Rev. 22:2, 4, 19].
The spirit of holiness shall be upon them.
¹²And Beliar shall be bound by him [Isa. 24:22-23 | cf. Mk 3:27; Lk. 10:19; 11:14-22].
And he shall grant to his children the authority to trample on wicked spirits.
¹³And the Lord will rejoice in his children;
he will be well pleased by his beloved ones forever.
¹⁴**Then Abraham, Isaac, and Jacob will rejoice** [cf. Mt. 8:11; Jn 8:56]**,
and I shall be glad, and the saints shall be clothed in righteousness.**

Judah 25   *OTP* 1:801-2

¹**And after these things shall Abraham and Isaac and Jacob arise unto life**, and I and my brethren shall be chiefs of the tribes [of Israel]: Levi first, I the second, Joseph third, Benjamin fourth, Simeon fifth, Issachar sixth, and so all in order. ²And the Lord blessed Levi, and the Angel of the Presence, me; the powers of glory, Simeon; the heaven, Reuben; the earth, Issachar; the sea, Zebulun; the mountains, Joseph; the tabernacle, Benjamin; the luminaries, Dan; **Eden**, Naphtali; the sun, Gad; the moon, Asher.
³And ye shall be the people of the Lord [cf. Jn 17:22; Eph. 4:4], and have one tongue [Gen. 11:1-9 | cf. *Jub.* 3:28];
And there shall be there no spirit of deceit of [Beliar],
For he shall be cast into the fire for ever [Rev. 20:2, 14].
⁴**And they who have died in grief shall arise [in joy],
[And they who were poor for the Lord's sake shall be made rich],
And they who are put to death for the Lord's sake shall awake [to life]** [Dan. 12:2 | Rev. 12:11; 20:4].
⁵And the harts of Jacob shall run [joyfulness],
And the eagles of Israel shall fly [in gladness] [Isa. 40:28-31];
And all the people shall glorify the Lord for ever.

Zebulun 10:1-7   *OTP* 2:332

¹And now, my children, grieve not that I am dying, nor be cast down in that I am coming to my end. ²**For I shall rise again in the midst of you, [as a ruler in the midst of his sons]; and I shall rejoice in the midst of my tribe**, as many as shall keep the law of the Lord, [and the commandments of Zebulun their father]. ³But upon the ungodly shall the Lord bring eternal fire, and destroy them throughout all generations [cf. Gen. 19:24; Ps. 11:5-7]. ⁴But I am now hastening away to my rest, as did also my fathers. ⁵But do ye fear the Lord [our God with all your strength all

the days of your life]. ⁶And when he had said these things he fell asleep, [at a good **old age**]. ⁷And his sons laid him in a [wooden] coffin. And afterwards they carried him up and buried him in Hebron, with his fathers.

Dan 5:7-13   *OTP* 1:809-10

⁷My sons will draw close to Levi,
will participate with them in all manners of sins;
and with the sons of Judah they will share in greed,
like lions snatching what belongs to others.
⁸Accordingly you will be led off with them into captivity;
there you will receive all the plagues of Egypt,
and all the evils of the gentiles.
⁹Therefore when you turn back to the Lord, you will receive mercy,
and he will lead you into his holy place, proclaiming peace to you.
¹⁰And there shall arise for you from
the tribe of Judah
    and (the tribe of) Levi the Lord's salvation.
He will make war against Beliar;
he will grant the vengeance of victory as our goal.
¹¹**And he shall take from Beliar the captives, the souls of the saints**;
and he shall turn the hearts of the disobedient ones to the Lord,
and grant eternal peace to those who call upon him.
¹²And the saints shall refresh themselves in Eden;
the righteous shall rejoice in the New Jerusalem,
which shall be eternally for the glorification of God.
¹³And Jerusalem shall no longer undergo desolation [Dan. 9:2],
nor shall Israel be led into captivity,
because the Lord will be in her midst [living among human beings].
The Holy One of Israel will rule over them in humility and poverty,
and he who trusts in him shall reign in truth in the heavens.

Benjamin 10:2-11   *OTP* 1:828

¹⁰:²After he had spoken these things to them he said, "You know then, my children, that I am dying. Do the truth, each of you to his neighbor; ³keep the Law of the Lord and his commandments, ⁴for I leave you these things instead of an inheritance. Give them, then, to your children for an eternal possession; this is what Abraham, Isaac, and Jacob did. ⁵They gave us all these things as an inheritance, saying, 'Keep God's commandments until the Lord reveals his salvation to all the nations.' ⁶**And then you will see Enoch and Seth and Abraham and Isaac and Jacob being raised up at the right hand in great joy [Dan. 12:2]. ⁷Then shall we also be raised [ibid.], each of us over our tribe [cf. Mt. 19:28-30], and we shall prostrate ourselves before the heavenly king. ⁸Then all shall be changed** [1 Cor. 15:51], **some destined for glory, others for dishonor**, for the Lord first judges Israel for the wrong she has committed ⁹and then he shall do the same for all the nations. ¹⁰Then he shall judge Israel by the chosen gentiles as he tested Esau by the Medianites who loved their

brothers. You, therefore, my children, may your lot come to be with those who fear the Lord. **¹¹Therefore, my children, if you live in holiness, in accord with the Lord's commands, you shall again dwell with me in hope; all Israel will be gathered to the Lord** [Rom. 11:26].

Testament of Job

Testament of Job 4:3-11   *OTP* 1:841

³Again he said, "Thus says the Lord: ⁴If you attempt to purge the place of Satan, he will rise up against you with wrath for battle. But he will be unable to bring death upon you. He will bring in you many plagues, ⁵he will take away for himself your goods, he will carry of your children. ⁶But if you are patient, I will make your name renowned in all generations of the earth till the consummation of the age [Not in LXX | cf. Mt. 13:39; Heb. 9:26]. ⁷And I will return you again to your goods. It will be repaid to you doubly, ⁸so you may know that the Lord is impartial – rendering good things to each one who obeys. ⁹*And you shall be raised up in the resurrection* [**Job 42:17a (LXX)**]. ¹⁰For you will be like a sparring athlete, both enduring pains and winning the crown. ¹¹Then will you know that the Lord is just, true, and strong, giving strength to his elect ones."

Testament of Job 33; 41:4   *OTP* 1:855-56, 860-61

³³˙¹After Eliphas finished wailing while his fellow kings responded to him all in a great commotion, ²when the uproar died down, I said to them, "Quiet! Now I will show you my throne with the splendor of its majesty, **which is among the holy ones**.

> ³ "**My throne is in the upper world**, and its splendor and majesty come from the right hand [Mt. 26:64; Mk 16:19; Lk. 22:69; Acts 2:33; Eph. 1:17, 20; Heb. 1:3; 8:1] of the Father [Isa. 63:16; 64:8; Mal. 1:6; 2:10].
>
> ⁴The whole world shall pass away [1 Cor. 7:31; 1 Jn 2:17]
>
> and its splendor shall fade. And those who heed it shall share in its overthrow.
>
> ⁵**But my throne is in the holy land** [cf. Zech. 3:2], **and its splendor is in the world of the changeless one**.
>
> ⁶*Rivers will dry up* [Job 14:11],
>
> and the arrogance of their waves goes down into the depths of the abyss.
>
> ⁷**But the rivers of my land, where my throne is, do not dry up nor will they disappear,**
>
> **but they will exist forever** [the term "forever" is only used in Heb. 7:3; 10:1, 12, 14].
>
> ⁸These kings will pass away, and rulers come and go; but their splendor and boast shall be as in a mirror [1 Cor. 13:12; Jas 1:23].
>
> ⁹**But my kingdom is forever and ever, and its splendor and majesty are in the chariots of the Father**."

⁴¹:⁴But I [Elihu] will not hold on. From the start I too made lamentation for him [Job], remembering his former prosperity. And here now he speaks out in boastful grandeur, **saying he has his throne in heave.**

Testament of Job 39:8-12   *OTP* 1:859

⁸But she [Sitis, Job's wife] began to beg them [Job's friends], saying, "I plead with you, order your soldiers to dig through the ruins of the house that fell on my children so that at least their bones might be preserved as a memorial ⁹since we cannot because of the expense. Let us see them, even if it is only their bones. ¹⁰Have I the womb of cattle or of a wild animal that my ten children have died and I have not arranged the burial of a single one of them?"

¹¹And they left to dig, but I forbade it, saying, "Do not trouble yourselves in vain. ¹²**For you will not find my children, since they were taken up into heaven by the Creator their King.**"

Testament of Job 43   *OTP* 1:861-63

¹Then when Eliphas, Baldad, and Sophar knew that the Lord had showed them favor regarding their sin – but had not considered Elihu worthy – ²Eliphas replied and spoke up with a hymn ³while the other friends and their troops sang to him in response near the altar. ⁴Eliphas spoke in this manner:

"Our sins were stripped off, and our lawlessness buried.

⁵Elihu, Elihu – the only evil one – will have no memorial among the living.

His quenched lamp lost its luster [Job 18:5],

⁶and the splendor of his lantern will flee from him into condemnation.

For this one is the one of darkness and not of light.

And the doorkeepers of darkness shall inherit his splendor and majesty.

⁷His kingdom is gone, his throne is rotted.

And the honor of his tent lies in Hades.

⁸He loved the beauty of the snake and the scales of the dragon.

Its venom and poison shall be his food.

⁹He did not take to himself the Lord, nor did he fear him.

But even his honored ones he provoked to anger.

¹⁰The Lord has forgotten him, and the holy ones abandoned him.

¹¹But wrath and anger shall be his tent.

He has no hope in his heart, nor peace in his body.

¹²He had the poison of asps in his tongue.

¹³Righteous is the Lord, true are his judgments.

With him there is no favoritism. **He will judge us all together**.

¹⁴Behold the Lord has come! Behold his holy ones are prepared,

while crowns lead the way with praises.

¹⁵Let the holy ones rejoice, let them leap for joy in their hearts,

¹⁶**for they have received the splendor they awaited**.

¹⁷Gone is our sin, cleansed is our lawlessness.

And the evil one Elihu has no memorial among the living."

Testament of Job **47:11; 52; 53:7**   *OTP* **1:865, 867-68**

⁴⁷:¹¹Rise then, gird yourselves with them [the three multicolored cords] before I die in order that you may be able to see **those who are coming for my soul**, in order that you may marvel over the creatures of God."

⁵²:¹After three days, as Job fell ill on his bed (without suffering or pain, however, since suffering could no longer touch him on account of the omen of the sash he wore), ²after those three days he saw those **who had come for his soul**. ³And rising immediately he took a lyre and gave it to his daughter Hemera. ⁴To Kasia he gave a censer, and to Amaltheia's Horn he gave a kettle drum, ⁵so that they might bless those who had come for his soul. ⁶And when they took them, they saw the gleaming chariots [Gen. 5:24; 2 Kgs 2:11] which **had come for his soul**. ⁷And they blessed and glorified God each one in her own distinctive dialect.
⁸After these things the one who saw in the great chariot got off and greeted Job ⁹as the three daughters and their father himself looked on, though certain others did not see. ¹⁰And taking **the soul** he flew up, embracing it, and mounted the chariot and set off for the east. ¹¹But this **body, prepared for burial**, was borne to the tomb as his three daughters went ahead girded about and singing hymns to God.

⁵³:⁸But after three days they laid him **in the tomb in a beautiful sleep**.

Testament of the Three Patriarchs

Testament of Abraham **B7:13-17**   *OTP* **1:898-99**

¹³When the radiant man said these things, I saw the sun of my house going up into heaven, but I saw that crown no more. ¹⁴That sun was like you, my father." ¹⁵And Michael said to Abraham, "Your son Isaac has spoken the truth; for you are (the sun), and you will be taken up into the heavens, ¹⁶**while your body remains on the earth until seven thousand ages are fulfilled. For then all flesh will be raised.** ¹⁷Now, therefore, Abraham, make a will (governing) the things of your household and concerning your sons, for you have heard completely the dispensation concerning you."

Testament of Moses

Testament of Moses **10:1-10**   *OTP* **1:931-32**

¹Then his kingdom will appear throughout his whole creation.
Then the devil will have an end.
Yea, sorrow will be led away with him.

²Then will be filled the hands of messenger,
    who is in the highest place appointed.
Yea, he will at one avenge them of their enemies [Dan. 10:13, 21; 12:1].

³For the Heavenly One will arise from his kingly throne.
Yea, he will go forth from his holy habitation [Deut. 26:15; Isa. 63:15; Jer. 25:30; Mic. 1:3]
    With indignation and wrath on behalf of his sons.

⁴And the earth will tremble, even to its ends shall it be shaken.
And the high mountains will be made low.
Yea, they will be shaken, as enclosed valleys will they fall.

⁵The sun will not give light.
And in darkness the horns of the moon will flee.
Yea, they will be broken in pieces.

It will be turned wholly into blood.
Yea, even the circle of the stars will be thrown into disarray.

⁶And the sea all the way to the abyss will retire,
    to the sources of waters which fail.
Yea, the rivers will vanish away.

⁷For God Most High will surge forth,
    the Eternal One alone.
In full view will he come to work vengeance on the nations [cf. Deut. 32:11-13; Josh. 10:24; Isa. 40:31].
Yea, all their idols will he destroy.

⁸Then will you be happy, O Israel!
And you will mount up above the necks and the wings of an eagle.
Yea, all things will be fulfilled.

⁹**And God will raise you to the heights.**
Yea, he will fix you firmly in the heaven of the stars [Dan. 12:3],
    in the place of their habitations.

¹⁰And you will behold from on high.
Yea, you will see your enemies on the earth.

And recognizing then, you will rejoice.
And you will give thanks.
Yea, you will confess your creator.

Testament of Adam

Testament of Adam 3:2-4   *OTP* 1:994

²He spoke to me about this in Paradise after I picked some of the fruit in which death was hiding: "Adam, Adam do not fear. You wanted to be a god [Gen. 3:4, 22]; I will make you a god [cf. Jn 10:33-36], not right now, **but after a space of many years. I am consigning you to death, and the maggot and the worm will eat your body.**" ³And I answered and said to him, "Why, my Lord?" And he said to me, "Because you listened to the words of the serpent, you and your posterity will be food for the serpent. **But after a short time there will be mercy on you because you were created in my image [Gen. 1:27], and I will not leave you to waste away in Sheol.** For you sake I will be born of the Virgin Mary. For your sake I will taste death and enter the house of the dead. For your sake I will make a new heaven, and I will be established over your posterity. ⁴**And after three days, while I am in the tomb, I will raise up the body I received from you. And I will set you at the right hand of my divinity [Ps. 110:1], and I will make you a god just like you wanted. And I will receive favor from God, and I will restore to you and to your posterity that which is the justice of heaven.**"

Resurrection Texts in Expansions on Stories and Legends

Table 23. Resurrection texts in expansions on stories and legends

Date		Passage	Notes	Resurrection			Classification		
				Imp.	Stat.	Ref.	Allude	Phil.	Assum.
2nd cent. BCE	*Jubilees*	4:24	Judgment Texts (Implied Resurrection)	x					x
		5:10						x	
		10:17							
		23:11							
		30:23							
		36:10-11							
		37:19							
		39:6							
		10:15; 23:1; 36:18; 45:15	Sleep ‖ Death	x					x
		23:27-31	Bones rest in the earth, Spirits will increase joy	x					x
2nd cent. BCE– 4th cent. CE	*Martyrdom and Ascension of Isaiah*	1:3-5	Hezekiah's vision	x					x
		3:18	Faith → salvation	x					
		4:14-22	2nd Coming		x				x
		7:4; 8:14, 23, 27; 11:35	Rope of Flesh Rope of Angels	x					x
		9:7-11	Saints in Heaven	x					x
		9:16-18	Resurrection of Jesus and the Saints	x					x

Appendix A

Date	Passage		Notes	Resurrection			Classification		
				Imp.	Stat.	Ref.	Allude	Phil.	Assum.
1st cent. BCE–2nd cent. CE	*Joseph and Aseneth*	8:(10)–(11)	Joseph's blessing of Aseneth	×			×		
		12:(12)	God's gift	×					×
		15:3-6, (7), 12×, 16:(8)	The Book of Life	×					×
		16:21-23	Resurrection of bees		×				×
		20:7	God is the life giver		×				×
		22:(9)	Aseneth's place of rest	×					×
		27:10	The immortality of the Soul	×					×
1st cent. CE	*Apocalypse of Moses (Life of Adam and Eve)*	10:2	Eve's woe		×				×
		13:2-6	Michael's words to Seth		×		×		×
		28:4	If you are righteous → resurrection → immortality		×			?	×
		37:5	Adam taken to Paradise	×					×
		39:2-3	Promise given to Adam	×					×
		41	Promised resurrection		×	×			×
		43:2-3	Burial practice Body → earth Soul → after 7 days back to heaven		×				×
1st cent. CE	*Vita (Life of Adam and Eve)*	47:2-3	Resurrection/judgment	×		×			×
		51:2	The Sabbath is a sign of the resurrection		×				×

Date		Passage	Notes	Resurrection			Classification		
				Imp.	Stat.	Ref.	Allude	Phil.	Assum.
1st cent. CE	Pseudo-Philo	3:10	Resurrection/judgment		×				×
		16:3	Rebellion of Korah	×					×
		19:2, 6	Death = sleep	×					×
		19:12-13	Resurrection of Moses		×				×
		23:13	The righteous		×	×			×
		25:7	Repentance → resurrection		×				×
		28:10	Death = sleep	×					×
		29:4	Death = sleep	×					×
		33:2-3	No repentance after death		×				×
		33:6	Death = Sleep	×					×
		35:3	Death = sleep	×					×
		48:1	Ascension of Phinehas	×					×
		62:9	The souls will know each other	×					×
		64:6-9	Samuel's resurrection caused by Saul		×	×			×
1st cent. CE	Lives of the Prophets	2:11-19	The ark will appear at the resurrection		×				×
		3:10-12	Hope for Israel		×				×
c. 1st cent. CE	Ladder of Jacob	7:21	Resurrection of Eve		×				×
1st to 2nd cent. CE	4 Baruch	6:6-10	Promise to Abimelech	×					×
		7:18	Resurrection of the dead man		×				×
		9:12-14	Jesus the resurrector		×				×
1st to 4th cent. CE	History of the Rechabites	14-16	Soul		×				×
			Body						

Jubilees

Jubilees 23:27-31   *OTP* 2:101-2

[22] And there will be a great plague upon the deeds of the generation from the Lord and he will give them to the sword and to judgment and to captivity and pillage and destruction. [23] And he will rouse up against them the sinners of the nations who have no mercy or grace for them and who have no regard for any persons old or young or anyone [Ezek. 9:6]. For (they will be) cruel and powerful so that they will act more evilly than any of the sons of men.

And they will cause turmoil in Israel and sin against Jacob;
and much blood will be shed upon the earth;
and there will be no one who will gather and no one who will bury [Jer. 8:2].
[24] In those days, they will cry out and call and pray
to be saved form the hand of the sinners, the gentiles,
but there will be none who will be saved,
[25] and the heads of children will be white with gray hairs,
and an infant three weeks old will look aged
like one whose years (are) one hundred,
and their stature will be destroyed by affliction and torment.
[26] And in those days, children will begin to search the law,
and to search the commandments
and to return to the way of righteousness.
[27] And the days will begin to increase and grow longer
among those sons of men, generation by generation,
and year by year, until
their days approach a thousand years,
and to a great number of years than days.
[28] And there (will be) no old men and none who is full of days [Isa. 60:20].
Because all of them will be infants and children.
[29] And all of their days they will be complete
and live in peace and rejoicing
and there will be no Satan and no evil (one) who will destroy,
because all of their days will be days of blessing and healing.
[30] **And then the Lord will heal his servants,**
and they will rise up and see great peace.
And they will drive out their enemies,
and the righteous ones will see and give praise,
and rejoice forever and ever with joy;
and they will see all of their judgments and all of their curses among their enemies.
[31] **And their bones will rest in the earth,**
and their spirits will increase joy.
And they will know that the Lord is an executor of judgment;
but he will show mercy to hundreds and thousands,
to all who love him.

Martyrdom and Ascension of Isaiah

Martyrdom and Ascension of Isaiah 1:3-5   *OTP* 2:156-57

[2]He [Hezekiah] summoned him [Manasseh] in the presence of Isaiah, the son of Amoz, the prophet, and in the presence of Josab the son of Isaiah, in order to hand over to him the words of righteousness which the king himself had seen, [3]and (the words concerning) **the eternal judgments, and the torments of Gehenna**, and the prince of this world, and his angels, and his authorities, and his powers [Eph. 6:12; 1 Pet. 3:22], [4]and the words concerning faith in the Beloved [Mt. 12:18; Mk 1:11; 9:7; Eph. 1:6] which he himself had seen in the fifteenth year of his reign during his sickness. [5]And he handed to him the written words which Samnas the secretary had written out, and also those which Isaiah the son of Amoz had given to him, and to the prophets also, that they might write out and store up with him what he himself had seen in the house of the king **concerning the judgment of the angels, and concerning the destruction of this world, and concerning the robes of the saints and their going out, and concerning their transformation and the persecution and ascension of the Beloved** which he himself had seen in the fifteenth year of his reign during his sickness [cf. 2 Kgs 20:1-11; Isa. 38; 2 Chron. 32:24].

Martyrdom and Ascension of Isaiah 3:15b-20   *OTP* 2:160

[15b]And the angel of the Holy Spirit [16]and Michael, the chief of the holy angels, will open his [Christ's] gave on the third day, [17]and that Beloved, sitting on their shoulders, will come forth and send out his twelve disciples, [18]and they will teach all nations and every tongue **the resurrection of the Beloved, and those who believe in his cross will be saved**, and in his ascension to the seventh heaven from where he came; [19]and that many who believe in him will speak through the Holy Spirit, [20]and there will be many sings and miracles in those days.

Martyrdom and Ascension of Isaiah 4:14-22   *OTP* 2:162-63

[14]And after [one thousand] three hundred and thirty-two days [Dan. 12:12] the Lord will come with his angels and with the hosts of the saints [1 Thess. 3:13; 2 Thess. 1:7; Jude 14] from the seventh haven, with the glory of the seventh heaven, and will drag Beliar, and his hosts also, into Gehenna [Rev. 19:20]. [15]And he will **give rest** to the pious whom he finds in the body in this world, but *the sun will be ashamed* [Isa. 24:23], [16]and (to) all who because of their faith in him have cursed Beliar and his kings. But the saints will come with the Lord [1 Thess. 3:13] with their robes which are stored up in the seventh heaven above; with the Lord will come those whose spirits are clothed [1 Thess. 4:14; Rev. 20:4], they will descend and be present in the world, and the Lord will strengthen those **who are found in the body**, together with the saints in the robes of the saints, and will serve those who have kept watch in this world [Lk. 12:37]. [17]And after this they will be turned in their robes upwards, and their body will be left in the world [1 Cor. 15:50-53; 2 Cor. 5:1-4; Phil. 3:21]. [18]Then the voice of the Beloved will reprove in anger this heaven, and this earth, and the mountains, and the hills, and the cities, and the desert, and the trees, and the angel of the sun, and that of the moon, and everywhere that Beliar has appeared

and acted openly in this world. **There will be a resurrection and a judgment in their midst in those days** [Rev. 20:11-15], **and the Beloved will cause fire to rise from him, and it will consume all the impious** [Isa. 11:4 | 2 Thess. 1:8; 2:8], **and they will become as if they had not been created** [Eth. Job 10:19]. [19]And the rest of the words of the vision are written in the vision of Babylon [LXX Isa. 13:1, 19-22]. [20]And the rest of the vision about the Lord, behold it is written in parables in the words of mine that are written in the book which I prophesied openly. And the descent of the Beloved into Sheol [Isa. 53:8 (LXX)], behold it is written in the section where the Lord says, "*Behold, my son shall understand*" [Isa. 52:13 (LXX)] And all these things, behold they are written in the Psalms, in the parables of David the son of Jesse, and in the Proverbs of Solomon his son, and in the words of Korah [e.g. Pss. 42; 44] and of Ethan [Ps. 89 (LXX 88)] the Israelite, and in the words of Asaph [Pss. 50; 73–83], and in the rest of the psalms which the angel of the spirit has inspired, [22](namely) in those which have no name written, and in the words of Amos my father and of Hosea the prophet, and Micah, and of Joel, and of Nahum, and of Jonah, and of Obadiah, and of Habakkuk, and of Haggai, and of Zephaniah, and of Zechariah, and of Malachi, and in the words of the righteous Joseph, and in the words of Daniel.

Martyrdom and Ascension of Isaiah 9:6-11   *OTP* 2:170
[6]**And he took me up into the seventh heaven, and there I saw a wonderful light, and also angels without number.** [7]**And there I saw all the righteous from the time of Adam onwards.** [8]**And there I saw the holy Abel and all the righteous.** [9]**And there I saw Enoch and all who (were) with him, stripped of (their) robes of the flesh; and I saw them in their robes of above** [cf. 2 Cor. 5:1-4; Rev. 3:4f.; 6:11; 7:9, 13f.], **and they were like the angels who stand there in great glory.** [10]But they were not sitting on their thrones [Mt. 19:28; Lk. 22:30; Rev. 3:21; 4:4], nor were their crowns of glory [1 Cor. 9:25; 2 Tim. 4:7f. Jas 1:12; 1 Pet. 5:4; Rev. 2:10; 3:11; 4:4] on them. [11]And I asked the angel who (was) with me, "How is it that they have received these robes, but are not on (their) thrones nor in (their) crowns?"

Martyrdom and Ascension of Isaiah 9:16-18   *OTP* 2:170
[16]"**And when he has plundered the angel of death**, he will rise on the third day and will remain in that world for five hundred and forty-five days. [17]**And the many of the righteous will ascend with him, whose spirits do not receive (their) robes until the Lord Christ ascends and they ascend with him**. [18]Then indeed they will receive their robes and their thrones and their crowns, when he has ascended into the seventh heaven."

Joseph and Aseneth

Joseph and Aseneth 8:(10)-(11)   *OTP* 2:213
[9]And he [Joseph] lifted up his right hand and put it upon her [Aseneth] head and said:

(10)Lord God of my father Israel,
the Mist High, the Powerful One of Jacob,
who gave life to all (things)
and called (them) from the darkness to the light,
and from the error to the truth,
and **from the death to the life** [cf. Lk. 15:24, 32; Jn 5:24; 1 Jn 3:14];
you, Lord, bless this virgin,
(11)and renew her by your spirit,
and form her anew by your hidden hand,
and **make her alive again by your life** [cf. Exod. 17:16 (LXX)],
and let her eat your bread of life,
and drink your cup of blessing,
and number her among your people
that you have chosen [cf. Ps. 33:12; Eph. 1:4] before all (things) came into being,
and **let her enter your rest**
which you have prepared for your chosen ones [cf. Ps. 95:11 (LXX rather than MT) | Heb. 3:7–4:13],
and live in your eternal life [e.g. Dan. 12:2 | Mt. 25:46; Jn 3:5; Rom. 5:21]
for ever (and) ever.

Joseph and Aseneth 12:15(12)　　　　　　　　　　　　　　　　　　　*OTP* 2:222
15What father (is) as sweet as you, Lord,
and who (is as) long-suffering toward our sins as you, Lord?
(12)For behold, all the gifts of my father Pentephres,
which he gave me as an inheritance, are transient [cf. Mt. 6:19-31; 2 Cor. 4:18 || 1 Pet. 1:4; Jas 1:17] and obscure;
　　　but the gifts of your inheritance, Lord, are incorruptible and eternal
[Mk 10:17-31 || Heb. 10:34].

Joseph and Aseneth 15:2b-6, (7), (12×); 16:(8)　　　　*OTP* 2:226, 227, 229
15:2bAnd the man said to her, "Courage, Aseneth, chaste virgin. Behold, I have heard all the words of your confession and your prayer. 3Behold, I have also seen the humiliation and the affliction of the seven days of your want (of food). Behold, from your tears and these ashes, plenty of mud has formed before your face. 4 (3)Courage, Aseneth, chaste virgin. **For behold, your name was written in the book of the living** [cf. e.g. Exod. 32:32f.; Ps. 87:6 | Lk. 10:20; Rev. 20:12, 15] **in heaven; in the beginning of the book, as the very first of all, your name was written by my finger, and it will not be erased forever.** 5 (4)Behold, from today, you will be renewed and formed anew and made alive again [1 Cor. 2:3; 4:9; Eph. 2:5; 3:6], and you will eat blessed bread of life, and drink a blessed cup of immortality, and anoint yourself with blessed ointment of incorruptibility. 6 (5)Courage, Aseneth, chaste virgin. Behold, I have given you today to Joseph for a bride, and he himself will be your bridegroom for ever (and) ever.

(7)For Repentance is in the heavens, an exceedingly beautiful and good daughter of the Most High. And she herself entreats the Most High God for you at all times and for all who repent in the name of the Most High God, because he is (the) father of Repentance. And she herself is guardian of all virgins, and loves you very much, and is beseeching the Most High for you at all times **and for all who repent she prepared a place of rest in the heaven** [cf. Jn 14:2f.]. And she will renew all who repent, and wait on them herself for ever (and) ever.

(12x)What is your name, Lord; tell me in order that I may praise and glorify you for ever (and) ever." And the man said to her, "Why do you seek this, my name, Aseneth? My name is in the heavens in the book of the Most High, written by the finger of God in the beginning of the book before all (the others), because I am chief of the house of the Most High. **And all names written in the book of the Most High are unspeakable, and man is not allowed to pronounce nor hear them in this world, because those names are exceedingly great and wonderful and laudable.**"

16:8For this comb is (full of the) spirit of life. And the bees of the paradise of delight have made this from the dew of the roses of life that are in the paradise of God. And all the angels of God eat of it and all the chosen of God and all the sons of the Mist High [e.g. Ps. 89:7], because this is **a comb of life, and everyone who eats of it will not die for ever (and) ever**.

Joseph and Aseneth 16:21-23   *OTP* 2:230

21And all the bees rose and flew and went away into heaven. 22 (16)And those who wanted to injure Aseneth fell to the ground and died. (17)**And the man stretched out his staff over the dead bees and said to them, "Rise you, too, and go away to your place."** 23**And the bees who had died rose** and went into the court adjoining Aseneth's house and sought shelter on the fruit-bearing trees.

Joseph and Aseneth 20:6-8   *OTP* 2:234

6 (5)And her father and mother and his whole family came from the field which was their inheritance. And they saw Aseneth like (the) appearance of light, and her beauty was like heavenly beauty. And they saw her sitting with Joseph and dressed in a wedding garment. 7And they were amazed at her beauty and rejoiced and **gave glory to God** [cf. Mt. 5:16; 1 Pet. 2:12] **who gives life to the dead** [**Amidah 2**]. 8And after this they ate and drank and celebrated [e.g. 1 Kgs 4:20 | Lk. 12:19. Could this be a conversion meal? cf. Mk 2:15; Lk. 15:23; Acts 16:34].

Joseph and Aseneth 22:(8)-(9)   *OTP* 2:239

13 (8)And Aseneth grasped Levi's hand. And Aseneth loved Levi exceedingly beyond all of Joseph's brethren, because he was one who attached himself to the Lord, and he was a prudent man and a prophet of the Most High and sharp-sighted with (9)his eyes, and he used to see letters written in heaven by the finger of God and he knew the unspeakable (mysteries) of the Most High God and revealed them to Aseneth in secret, because he himself, Levi, would love Aseneth very much, and **see her place**

of rest in the highest [cf. Isa. 66:1 (LXX ?)], and her walls like adamantine eternal walls, and her foundations founded upon a rock of the seventh heaven.

Joseph and Aseneth 27:9-10   OTP 2:245

$^{9\,(8)}$And they came toward Aseneth holding their swords drawn, full of blood. ^{10}And Aseneth saw them and was exceedingly afraid and said:
Lord my God, **who made me alive again**
and rescued me [cf. Isa. 49:7, 26; 54:5, 8] from the idols and the corruption of death, who said to me, "**Your soul will live for ever**,"
rescue me from the hands of these wicked men.

Apocalypse of Moses

Apocalypse of Moses 10   OTP 2:273

$^{10:1}$And Seth and Eve went into the regions of Paradise. As they were going, Eve saw her son and a wild beast attacking him. ^{2}And Eve wept, saying, "Woe is me! **For when I come to the day of resurrection**, all who have sinned will curse me, saying that Eve did not keep the command of God." ^{3}And Eve cried out to the beast and said, "O you evil beast, do you not fear to attack the image of God [Gen. 1:26, 28]? How was your mouth opened? How did your teeth grove strong? How did you not remember your subjection, for you were once subjected to the image of God? [ibid.]"

Apocalypse of Moses 13   OTP 2:275

^{1}And Seth went with his mother Eve near to Paradise. And they wept there, praying God that he would send his angel to give them the oil of mercy. ^{2}And God sent Michael the archangel, and he said to them, "Seth, man of God, do not labor, praying with this supplication about the tree from which the oil flows, to anoint your father Adam; it shall not come to be yours now (but at the end of times. ^{3}**Then all flesh from Adam up to that great day shall be raised, such as shall be the holy people; ^{4}then to them shall be given every joy of Paradise and God shall be in their midst, ^{5}and there shall not be any more sinners before him, for the evil heart shall be removed from them, and they shall be given a heart that understands the good and worship God alone** [Jer. 31:33; Ezek. 18:31; 36:26].) ^{6}But you go again to your father, since the measure of his life is fulfilled, that is, in three days. And as his soul departs, you are sure to witness its fearful upward journey."

Apocalypse of Moses 28   OTP 2:285

^{1}And the LORD turned and said to Adam, "From now on I will not allow you to be in Paradise." ^{2}And Adam answered and said, "LORD, give me from the tree of life that I might eat before I am cast out." ^{3}Then the LORD spoke to Adam, "You shall not now take from it; for it was appointed to the cherubim and the flaming sword which turns to guard it [Gen 3:24] because of you, that you might not taste of it and be immortal forever, but that you might have the strife which the enemy has placed in you. ^{4}But when you come out of Paradise, if you guard yourself from all evil, preferring death to it, **at the time of the resurrection I will raise you again**, and then there shall be given to you from the tree of life, and you shall be immortal forever."

Apocalypse of Moses 37 — OTP 2:289, 291

¹While Seth was speaking to his mother, an angel sounded the trumpet and the angels who were lying on their faces stood up and cried out with a fearful voice, saying, ²"Blessed be the glory of the LORD over his works; he has had mercy on Adam, the work of his hands." ³When the angels had shouted out these things, one of the six-winged seraphim came and carried Adam off to the Lake of Acheron and washed him three times in the presence of God. ⁴He lay three hours, and so the LORD of all, sitting on his holy throne, stretched out his hands and took Adam and handed him over to the archangel Michael, saying to him, ⁵"Take him up into Paradise, to the third heaven [2 Cor. 12:2], and leave (him) there **until that great and fearful day which I am about to establish for the world**." ⁶And the archangel Michael took Adam and brought him away and left him, just as God told him at the pardoning of Adam.

Apocalypse of Moses 39 — OTP 2:291

¹Now the body of Adam was lying on the ground in Paradise, and Seth was mourning greatly over him. And the LORD God said, "Adam, why did you do this? If you had kept my commandment, those who brought you down into this place would not have rejoiced. ²**Yet now I tell you that their joy shall be turned into sorrow, but your sorrow shall be turned into joy; and when that happens, I will establish you in your dominion on the throne of your seducer**. ³But that one shall be cast into this place, so that you might sit above him. Then he himself and those who listen to him shall be condemned, and they shall greatly mourn and weep when they see you sitting on his glorious throne."

Apocalypse of Moses 41 — OTP 2:293

¹And God called Adam and said, "Adam, Adam." And the body answered from the ground and said, "Here I am." ²And the LORD said to him, "I told you that *you are dust and to dust you shall return* [**Gen. 3:19b**]. ³**Now I promise to you the resurrection; I shall raise you on the last day in the resurrection with every man of your seed**."

Apocalypse of Moses 43 — OTP 2:295

¹When she died, the archangel Michael stood by, and three angels came and took her body and buried it where the body of Abel was. ²And the archangel Michael said to Seth, "Thus you shall prepare for burial each man who dies **until the day of resurrection**. ³And do not mourn more than six days; on the seventh day rest and be glad in it, for on that day both God and we angels rejoice in the migration form the earth of a righteous soul" [**Sabbath || resurrection**]. ⁴And when he had said these things, the angel went up into heaven, glorifying (God) and saying, "Alleluia, to whom be glory and power forever and ever."

Vita

Vita 47 — OTP 2:290

¹And all the angels sounded the trumpets and said, "Blessed are you, LORD, who has pitied your creature." ²Then Seth saw the extended hand of the LORD holding Adam, and he handed him over to Michael, saying, ³"Let him be in your custody **until the day of dispensing punishment at the last years, when I will turn his sorrow into joy. Then he shall sit on the throne of him who overthrew him.**"

Vita 51 — OTP 2:294

¹After this, all her children buried her [Eve] with great weeping. ²Then, when they had mourned for four days, the archangel Michael appeared to them and said to Seth, "Man of God, do not prolong mourning your dead more than six days, **because the seventh day is a sign of the resurrection, the rest of the coming age, and on the seventh day the LORD rested from all his work**" [Gen. 2:2] ³Then Seth made the tablets.

Pseudo-Philo

Pseudo-Philo 3:9-10 — OTP 2:306–7

⁹And God said, "*I will never again curse the earth on man's account, for the tendency of man's heart is foolish from his youth; and so I will never destroy all living creatures at one time as I have done* [Gen. 8:21]. But when those inhabiting the earth sin, I will judge them by famine or by the sword or by fire or by death; and there will be earthquakes, and they will be scattered to uninhabited places. But no more will I destroy the earth by the water of the flood. And *in all the days of the earth, seedtime and harvest, cold and heat, spring and fall will not cease day and night* [Gen. 8:22] until I remember those who inhabit the earth, until the appointed times are fulfilled. ¹⁰"But when the years appointed for the world have been fulfilled, then the light will cease and the darkness will fade away. And **I will bring the dead to life and raise up those who are sleeping form the earth. And hell will pay back its debt, and the place of perdition will return its deposit so that I may render to each according to his works and according to the fruit of his own devices, until I judge between soul and flesh**. And the earth will not be without progeny or sterile for those inhabiting it; and **no one who has been pardoned by me will be tainted. And there will be another earth and another heaven, an everlasting dwelling place.**"

Pseudo-Philo 16:3 — OTP 2:324

³And now the thoughts of men are very corrupt; behold I command the earth, and it will swallow up the body and soul together. And their dwelling place will be in darkness and the place of destruction; and they will not die but melt away **until I remember the world and renew the earth**. And then they will die and not live, and their life will be taken away from the number of all men. And **hell will no longer spit them back**, and their destruction will not be remembered, and their passing will be like that of those tribes of nations of whom I said: 'I will not remember them,'

that is, the camp of the Egyptians and the race that I destroyed with the water of the flood. And the earth will swallow them up, and I will do no more.

Pseudo-Philo 19:12-13   OTP 2:328

¹²Now I will take you [Moses] from here and glorify you with your fathers, and I will give you rest in your slumber and bury you in peace. And all the angels will mourn over you, and the heavenly hosts will be saddened. But neither angel *nor man will know your tomb* [Deut. 34:6] in which you are to be buried **until I visit the world. And I will raise up you and your fathers from the land of Egypt in which you sleep and you will come together and dwell in the immortal dwelling place that is not subject to time.** ¹³But this haven will be before me like a fleeting cloud and passing like yesterday. And when the time draws near to visit the world, I will command the years and order the times and they will be shortened [e.g. Mk 13:20 (Mt. 24:22)], and the stars will hasten and the light of the sun will hurry to fall and the light of the moon will not remain; **for I will hurry to raise up you who are sleeping in order that all who can live may dwell in the place of sanctification I showed you**.

Pseudo-Philo 23:12-13   OTP 2:333

¹²And now, if you listen to your fathers, I will set my heart among you forever and overshadow you, and your enemies will fight against you no more. And your land will be renowned over all the earth, and your seed special among all the peoples, who will say, "Behold a faithful people! Because they believed in the LORD, therefore the LORD freed them and planted them." And so I will plant you like a desirable vine and tend you like a lovable flock; and I will command the rain and the dew, and they will be abundant for you during your lifetime. ¹³**But also at the end the lot of each one of you will be life eternal, for you and your seed, and I will take your souls and store them in peace until the time allotted the world be complete. And I will restore you to your fathers and your fathers to you [Mal. 4:6 (MT 3:24)], and they will know through you that I have not chosen you in vain**. These are the words that the LORD spoke to me this night.

Pseudo-Philo 25:7   OTP 2:335

¹⁷And Kenaz brought them out and said to them, "Behold now you know how Achan confessed when he came out in the lot and how he declared everything he had done. And now declare to us your wicked deeds and schemes. **And who knows that if you tell the truth to us, even if you die now, nevertheless God will have mercy on you when he will resurrect the dead?**"

Pseudo-Philo 33:1-3   OTP 2:347-48

¹And when the days of her [Deborah's] death drew near, she sent and gathered all the people and said to them, "Listen now, my people. Behold I am warning you as a woman of God and am enlightening you as one from the female race; and obey me like your mother and heed my words as people who will also die. ²*Behold I am going today on the way of all flesh* [Josh. 23:14], on which you also will come. **Only**

direct your heart to the LORD your God during the time of your life, because after your death you cannot repent of those things in which you live. ³For the death is sealed up and brought to an end, and the measure and the time and the years have returned their deposit. For even if you seek to do evil in hell after your death, you cannot, because the desire for sinning will cease and the evil impulse will lose its power, **because even hell will not restore what has been received and deposited to it unless it be demanded by him who has made the deposit to it.** Now therefore, my sons, obey my voice; while you have the time of life and the light of the Law, make straight your ways." ⁴ And while Deborah was saying these words, all the people raised up their voice together and wept and said, "Behold now, Mother, you will die, and to whom do you commend your sons whom you are leaving? Pray therefore for us, and after your departure your soul will be mindful of us forever." ⁵ And Deborah answered and said to the people, "While a man is still alive he can pray for himself and for his sons, but after his end he cannot pray or be mindful of anyone. Therefore do not hope in your fathers. For they will not profit you at all unless you be found like them. **But then you will be like the stars of the heaven, which now have been revealed among you.**"

Pseudo-Philo **48:1**　　　　　　　　　　　　　　　　　　　　　　　　*OTP* 2:362

¹And in that time Phinehas laid himself down to die, and the LORD said to him, "Behold you have passed the 120 years that have been established for every man [Gen. 6:3]. And now rise up and go from here and dwell in Danaben on the mountain and dwell there many years. And *I will command* my eagle, and *he will nourish you there* [1 Kgs 17:4], and you will not come down to mankind until the time arrives and you be tested in that time; and you will shut up the heaven then, and by your mouth it will be opened up [ibid., 1]. **And afterward you will be lifted up into the place where those who were before you were lifted up, and you will be there until I remember the world. Then I will make you all come, and you will taste what is death.**"

Pseudo-Philo **62:9**　　　　　　　　　　　　　　　　　　　　　　　　*OTP* 2:375

⁹And Jonathan answered and said to David, "Come to me, my brother David, and I will tell you of your righteousness. My soul will pine away in sadness over you, because we are now separated from each other. And our sins have caused this, that we should be separated from each other; but let us be mindful of one another night and day while we live. **Even if death separates us, I know that our souls will know each other**. For yours is a kingdom in this world, and from you is the beginning of a kingdom which will come in its own time.

Pseudo-Philo **64:6-9**　　　　　　　　　　　　　　　　　　　　　　　*OTP* 2:377

⁶*And Saul said to her, "What is his appearance?"* She said, "You are asking me about *divine beings* [1 Sam. 28:13f.]. For behold his appearance is not the appearance of a man. For he is clothed in a white robe with a mantle placed over it, and two angels are leading him." And Saul remembered the mantle that Samuel tore when he was alive [1 Sam. 15:27], and he struck his hand *on the ground* and pounded

it. ⁷*And Samuel said to* **him, "Why have you disturbed me by raising me up? [1 Sam. 28:14-15] I thought that the time for being rendered the rewards of my deeds have arrived**. And so do not boast, King, nor you, woman; for you have not brought me forth, but that order that God spoke to me while I was still alive, that I should come and tell you that you have sinned now a second time in neglecting God. **Therefore after rendering up my soul my bones have been disturbed so that I who am dead should tell you what I heard while I was alive.** ⁸Now therefore *tomorrow you and your sons will be with me* [in death] when *the people* have been delivered *into the hands of the Philistines* [ibid., 19]; and because your insides were eaten up with jealousy, what is yours will be taken from you." ⁹And Saul heard the words of Samuel and grew faint and said, "Behold I am going to die with my sons; perhaps my destruction will be an atonement for my wickedness." *And* Saul *rose up and went away* from there [ibid., 25].

Lives of the Prophets

Lives of the Prophets 2:11-19   *OTP* 2:388

¹¹This prophet [Jeremiah], before the capture of the Temple, seized the ark of the Law and the things in it, and made them be swallowed up in a rock. ¹²And to those standing by he said, "The Lord has gone away from Zion into heaven and will come again in power. ¹³And this will be for you a sign of his coming, when all the gentiles worship a piece of wood." ¹⁴And he said, "This ark no one is going to bring out except Aaron, and none of the priests or prophets will any longer open the tablets in it except Moses, God's chosen one. ¹⁵**And in the resurrection the ark will be the first to be resurrected and will come out of the rock and be placed on Mount Sinai, and all the saints will be gathered to it there as they await the Lord and flee from the enemy who wishes to destroy them.**" ¹⁶In the rock with his finger he set as a seal the name of God, and the impression was like a carving made with iron, and a cloud covered the name, and no one knows the place nor is able to read the name to this day and to the consummation. ¹⁷And the rock is in the wilderness, where the ark was at first, between the two mountains on which Moses and Aaron lie. ¹⁸And at night there is a cloud like fire, just like the ancient one, for the glory of God will never cease from his Law. ¹⁹And God bestowed this favor upon Jeremiah, that he might himself perform the completion of his mystery, so that he might become a partner of Moses, and they are together to this day [cf. Mt. 16:14].

Lives of the Prophets 3:10-12   *OTP* 2:389

¹⁰Through prayer he [Ezekiel] furnished them of his own accord with an abundant supply of fish, and for many who were at the point of dying he entreated that life should come from God. ¹¹When the people was being destroyed by its enemies, he went to the (enemy) leaders and, terrified by the prodigies, they ceased. ¹²He used to say this to them: **"Are we lost? Has our hope perished?" and in the wonder of the dead bones [Ezek. 37:1-14] he persuaded them that there is hope for Israel both here and in the coming (age).**

Ladder of Jacob

Ladder of Jacob 7:10-25   *OTP* 2:410-11

¹⁰"Then the earth will be glorified, receiving heavenly glory. ¹¹What was above will be below also. ¹²And from your seed will bloom a root of kings; ¹³it will emerge and overthrow the power of evil. ¹⁴And he himself will be the Savior for every land and rest for those who toil, and a cloud shading the whole world form the burning heat. ¹⁵For otherwise the uncontrolled will not be controlled. ¹⁶If he does not come, the lower (things) cannot be joined with the upper. ¹⁷At his coming the idols of brass, stone, and any sort of carving will give voice for three days. They will give wise men news of him and let them know what will be on earth. ¹⁹By a star, those who wish to see on earth him whom the angels do not see above will find the way to him. ²⁰Then the Almighty will be on earth in body, and, embraced by corporeal arms, he will restore human matter. ²¹**And he will revive Eve, who died by the fruit of the tree**. ²²Then the deceit of the impious will be exposed and all the idols will fall face down. ²³For they will be put to shame by a dignitary. ²⁴For because (they were) lying by means of hallucinations, henceforth they will not be able to rule or to prophesy. ²⁵Honor will be taken from them and they will remain without glory.

4 Baruch

4 Baruch 6:1-10   *OTP* 2:421

¹After these things Abimelech went outside the city and prayed to the LORD. ²And behold, an angel of the LORD came and, taking hold of his right hand, brought him back to the place where Baruch was sitting, and he found him in a tomb. ³And when they saw each other, both (of them) wept, and they kissed each other. ⁴And looking up, Baruch saw with his (own) eyes the figs sheltered in Abimelech's basket. ⁵And raising his eyes to heaven, he prayed, saying, ⁶**"You are the God who bestows a reward (on) those who love you. Prepare yourself, my heart; rejoice and be glad in your tabernacle, saying to your fleshly dwelling, 'Your sorrow has been turned to joy.' For the Mighty One is coming and will raise you in your tabernacle, for sin has not taken root in you. ⁷Be refreshed within your tabernacle, in your virgin faith, and believe that you will live. ⁸Look at this basket of figs; for behold, they are sixty-six years old and they have not withered nor do they stink, but they are dripping with milk. ⁹Thus will it be for you, my flesh, if you do the things commanded you by the angel of righteousness. ¹⁰He who preserved the basket of figs, the same one again will preserve you by his power."**

4 Baruch 7:12-21   *OTP* 2:422

¹²Then the eagle took flight, having the letter around his neck, and departed for Babylon. And when he arrived (there), he rested in a certain tree outside the city in a deserted place. ¹³And he was silent until Jeremiah came by, for he and certain other people were coming out to burry a dead man outside the city. ¹⁴For Jeremiah had made a request of King Nebuchadnezzar, saying, "Give me a place where I may bury the dead of my people." And the king had given (it) to him. ¹⁵And as the were

going out with the dead man and weeping, they passed by the eagle. ¹⁶And the eagle cried in a loud voice, saying, "I say to you, Jeremiah, chosen one of God, go! Gather the people and come here that they may hear a letter which I have brought you from Baruch and Abimelech." ¹⁷And when Jeremiah heard, he glorified God, and he went out and gathered the people with (their) wives and children, and he came to where the eagle was. ¹⁸**And the eagle descended upon the one who had died, and he came back to life**. ¹⁹This happened that they might believe. ²⁰And all the people marveled at what had happened, saying, "Is this the God who appeared to our fathers in the wilderness through Moses (who) has now also appeared to us through this eagle?" ²¹And the eagle said, "I say to you, Jeremiah, come untie this letter and read it to the people." So, untying the letter, he read it to the people.

4 Baruch 9:1-14   *OTP* 2:424

¹And those who were with Jeremiah continued for nine days rejoicing and offering up sacrifices for the people. ²But on the tenth (day) Jeremiah alone offered up a sacrifice. ³And he prayed a prayer, saying, "Holy, holy, holy [Isa. 6:3], incense of the living trees, true light that enlightens me [Jn 1:9] until I am taken up to you; ⁴for your mercy I plead, for the sweet voice of the two seraphim I plead, for another fragrant odor of incense. ⁵And may Michael, the archangel of righteousness who opens the gates for the righteous, be (the object of) my attention until he leads the righteous in. ⁶I implore you, Almighty LORD of all creation, unbegotten and incomprehensible, in whom all judgment was hidden before these things existed." ⁷And as Jeremiah said these things, while standing at the altar with Baruch and Abimelech, he became as one of those who have given up their soul. ⁸And Baruch and Abimelech remained weeping and crying in a loud voice, "Who to us, because our father Jeremiah has left us; the priest of God has departed." ⁹And all the people heard their weeping, and they all ran to them and saw Jeremiah lying on the ground as though dead. ¹⁰And they tore their garments and put dust on their heads and wept bitterly. ¹¹And after these things, they prepared themselves to bury him. ¹²**And behold, there came a voice saying, "Do not bury one still living, for his soul is coming into his body again."** ¹³**And because they heard the voice, they did not bury him but remained in a circle around his tabernacle for three days, saying, "At what hour is he going to rise?"** ¹⁴**And after three days, his soul came into his body and he lifted up his voice in the midst of (them) all and said, "Glorify God with one voice [Rom. 15:6]! All (of you) glorify God, and the Son of God who awakens us, Jesus Christ the light of all the aeons, the inextinguishable lamp, the life of faith!**

History of the Rechabites

History of the Rechabites 14-16   *OTP* 2:458-60

14 ¹And again we announce to you, O brothers, that among us there is no sickness, pain, fatigue to our bodies, mutilation, weariness, or temptations; not even Satan's power can touch us, for there is not among us rage, jealousy, evil desire, or hateful thoughts. But (we experience only) quietness and gladness; and (exhibit) love and affection toward God and each other. ²**And the soul of each of us is not wearied**

or sorrowful or wishes to stay behind when the angels of God come to guide it from the body. But we are glad and rejoice and the holy angels (rejoice) with us when they are sent out after the soul of each of us.

³As the bride rejoices over her betrothed bridegroom, so the soul rejoices at the good news of the holy angels. For they (the angels) say to it nothing except this alone: "O pure soul, your Lord is calling you to come to him." ⁴Then the soul with great rejoicing leaves the body to meet the angel. And seeing that pure soul, which has (just) left the body, all the holy angels unfold (for it) their shining stoles. ⁵And they receive it with joy, saying, "Blessed are you, O pure soul, and blest, for you have thoroughly done the will of God, your Lord." ⁵ᵃAnd this (is how) he brings his providence to each one of us:

15 ⁽¹⁻³⁾⁴(The soul) discerns and knows the day of its departure through a revelation from holy angels. ⁴ᵃAnd we live an extremely long time; and the extent of our life (is) not brief and short as with you. ⁴ᵇWhen the holy angels are sent among us, in this beautiful order (of which) we have informed you, they visit among us. ⁽⁵⁾⁴ᶜHowever, first they come to our elders; and when they blessed elders see the angels who have come, they immediately with joy entreat (so that) all the blessed brothers assemble. ⁶And when all the people have assembled, immediately with praise we come with the angels to the place **in which bodies are buried**. ⁷And because we have nothing to use for digging, the angels themselves make a sepulcher for the bodies. ⁷ᵃAnd again when all of these (souls) have completed (their time), then they are separated from our assembly; and (each) departs with great joy. ⁸And all of us with exultation come near to it and offer it peace in the kiss of the LORD while it is being conducted and led (to the grave) by the holy angels. ⁹And then the soul of our blessed brother leaves the body in which it had settled; ⁹ᵃand with joy far removed from mourning it approaches and comes to the holy angels and ascends up to God with joy. ¹⁰But we with one accord see the soul when it leaves the body clearly and plainly; **the appearance of the soul when it leaves the body is the likeness of a glorious light, and formed and imprinted in the likeness and type of the body, and it is spiritually flying**.

16 ¹And while we are looking at that holy and spotless soul, the holy angels carry it away and salute it, and thus it ascends and goes up form us in glory. And after is ascends with them and passes into the region of the power of the highest heavens, then other orders (of angels) receive it with joy. ¹ᵃAnd the archangels salute it; and afterward they stretch out to it (their hands and lead it) to the thrones and dominions that (are) above them. And thus it goes up and ascends until it enters (before) and worships the LORD. ¹ᵇAnd when the highest order of cherubim and seraphim receive it, they rise to the gate of the holy Trinity. ²Then the Son of God receives that soul from their hands and brings it (forward) so that it may worship the father. ⁽³,⁴⁾⁵And when the soul falls down upon its face to worship before God, then the revelation is revealed to us, (and) all of us fall upon the land and worship the LORD with the soul. ⁶And when God makes that soul rise from its worship, we also rise to our feet. ⁽⁷⁾⁷ᵃ**And then God sends that soul to a stately mansion**

(to await) the day of resurrection for (the rest of our) community. ⁷ᵇThen we also go away form the body of that soul of our brother to our (own) assembly and complete the service through praises to the Holy Spirit. ⁸And so we have engraved (upon) these tablets and sent (them) to you through the hands of our brother Zosimus.

⁽³⁾⁸ᵃAnd again God, our Creator, has given us this (privilege): we hear the voices of the spirits and the praises of the angles, the hosts, and the heavenly orders, who continually praise God. ⁽³⁾⁸ᵇWhen they praise (God), so also we in our land praise (him).

⁸ᶜAnd the angels receive and transmit our prayers and our praises (by) entering and worshiping in love before that divine and mystic throne, (which) knows secrets. ⁸ᵈAnd thus by the aid of the angels and the heavenly hosts our prayers pass on and find entrance before God. ⁸ᵉThis is all of our manner (of life). And we are truly called the Blessed Ones, because we experience the benevolence of God. ⁸ᶠAnd we write and send (these tablets) to you, O people who dwell in that world of vanity, through the hands of this our brother Zosimus, who entered among us for your sake through the mercies (of God) and remained with us (for) seven days. ⁸ᵍAnd accompanying him we traveled with him until (we came) to the shores of the great ocean.

Resurrection Texts in Wisdom and Philosophical Literature

Table 24. Resurrection texts in wisdom and philosophical literature

Date	Passage		Notes	Resurrection			Classification		
				Imp.	Stat.	Ref.	Allude	Phil.	Assum.
1st cent. CE	*4 Maccabees*	7:18-19	Conquer the passion of the flesh → resurrection	x				?	x
		9:8-9, 22	The reward for virtue	x					x
		10:2-4	"Cannot touch my soul"	x					x
		13:9-18	"Our forefathers will receive us"	x					x
		14:4-6	Righteous' death → immortality	x					x
		15:3-4, 27	Righteous' death → immortality	x					x
		16:12-13, 25	Righteous' death → immortality	x					x
		17:4-5	Hope of endurance	x					x
		17:11-12, 17-21	Prizes for victory	x			x		x
		18:3	Martyrs → worthy of the divine portion	x					x
		18:10-23	The Father's teaching		x	x			x
1st cent. BCE– 1st cent. CE	*Pseudo-Phocylides*	91-115	Death and afterlife; Immortality of the soul		x		x		x

4 Maccabees

***4 Maccabees* 7:16-23** *OTP* 2:553

[16]If, therefore, an old man despised torments unto the death on account of his piety, we must admit that devout reason is leader over the passion. [17]But some may contend that not all men are masters of the passions, because not all men possess enlightened reason. [18]Only those who with all their heart make piety their first concern are able to conquer the passions of the flesh, [19]**believing that to God they do not die, as our patriarchs Abraham, Isaac. And Jacob died not, but live to God** [Mk 12:26; Rom. 6:10; 14:8; Gal. 2:19]. [20]Accordingly, the validity of our argument is not impaired by the fact that some men seem to be ruled by their passions because of the weakness of their reason. [21]For what philosopher is there, who lives by the whole rule of philosophy and believes in God [22]and knows that it is blessed to endure every pain for the sake of virtue, who could fail to master his passions for the sake of piety? [23]Only the wise and courageous man is ruler of the passions.

***4 Maccabees* 9:7-9, 21-22** *OTP* 2:554, 555

[7]Put us to the test then, tyrant; and if you take our lives for the sake of our religion, do not think you can harm us with your torments. [8]**By our suffering and endurance we shall obtain the prize of virtue and shall be with God, on whose account we suffer**. [9]**But you, because of our foul murder, will suffer at the hand of divine justice the everlasting torment by fire you deserve**.

[21]Even when his bodily frame was all dissevered, the great-souled youth, a true son of Abraham, uttered not a groan. [22]**As though he were being transformed into incorruption by the fire** [Mal. 3:2-3], he nobly endured the torments.

***4 Maccabees* 10:1-4** *OTP* 2:555

[1]When he had bravely met his illustrious death, the third son was brought forward amid fervent exhortations from many people to taste of the food and save himself. [2]But he cried aloud and said, "Do you not know that the very same father begot both me and my dead brothers, and the same mother bore us all, and **I was brought up on the same doctrines**? [3]I do not abjure the noble bond of brotherhood. [4]Therefore, if you have any means of torture, apply it to my body, **for my soul you cannot touch even if you would**."

***4 Maccabees* 13:8-18** *OTP* 2:558

[8]They formed a holy choir of piety as they encouraged each other with the words, [9]"Let us die like brothers all, brothers, for the Law's sake. Let us follow the example of the tree youths in Assyria, who despised the same trial by ordeal in the furnace [Dan. 3]. [10]Let us not be pusillanimous in the demonstration of true piety." [11]"Courage, brother!" said one, and another, "Hold on nobly!" [12]And another, recalling the past, said, "Remember whence you came and at the hand of what father Isaac gave himself to be sacrificed for piety's sake" [Gen. 22]. [13]Each one severally and all together, looking at each other with most cheerful mien, aglow with courage,

said, "With all our hearts let us consecrate ourselves unto God, who gave us our souls, and let us expend our bodies for the custodianship of the Law. [14]Let us have no fear of him **who thinks he kills** [Mt. 10:28]. [15]Great is the ordeal and peril of the soul that lies in wait in eternal torment for those who transgress the commandment of God. [16]Let us then arm ourselves with the control over the passions which comes from divine reason. [17]**After our death in this fashion Abraham and Isaac and Jacob will receive us, and all our forefathers will praise us.**" [18]And to each one of the brothers as they were dragged away, those who were left said, "Do not shame us, brother, nor be traitor to our brothers who have already died."

4 Maccabees **14:2-6**   *OTP* **2:559**

[2]O reason, more kingly than kings, more free than freemen! [3]How holy and harmonious the concord of the seven brothers for piety's sake! [4]Not one of the seven lads turned coward, nor cowered away from death, [5]**but all, as though running on the highway to immortality**, hurried on to death by torture. [6]Just as hands and feet move in unison with the promptings of the soul, so did those holy youths, as if impelled by the deathless soul of piety, go in harmony to the death for piety's sake.

4 Maccabees **15:2-4, 25-28**   *OTP* **2:559, 560**

[2]When two options lay before her, namely piety or the instant deliverance of her seven sons according to the tyrant's promise, [3]she loved piety better, **which preserves to eternal life according to God's word**. [4]How can I possibly express the deep love of parents for their children? On the tender nature of the child we impress a wonderful likeness of **soul** and **form**, and especially mothers, who are more affectionate in their own feelings toward their children than fathers.

[25]In the council chamber of her own heart, so to speak, she saw clever advocates, nature and parenthood and maternal love and the torment of her children – [26]a mother holding two votes in regard to her children, one to consign them to death and the other to preserve them alive; [27]**but she did not decide on the safe course that would preserve her sons for a little while**, [28]but like a true daughter of God-fearing Abraham called to mind Abraham's unflinching bravery.

4 Maccabees **16:12-13, 24-25**   *OTP* **2:561, 562**

[12]But the holy and God-fearing mother lamented none of them with any such dirge, nor urged any of them to avoid death, nor grieved over them in the moment of their death. [13]Rather, as though she had a mind of adamant **and were this time bringing her brood of sons to birth into immortal life**, she encouraged them and pled with them to die for piety's sake.

[24]With these words the mother of the seven exhorted each one and persuaded them to die rather than transgress the commandment of God, [25]and **they knew full well themselves that those who die for the sake of God live unto God, as do Abraham and Isaac and Jacob and all the patriarchs** [Exod. 3:6 | Mk 12:26f.].

4 Maccabees 17:4-6   *OTP* 2:562

[4]**Be of good cheer, therefore, mother of holy souls, whose hope of endurance is secure with God.** [5]Now so majestic stands the moon in heaven as you stand, lighting the way to piety for **your seven starlike sons [Dan. 12:3]**, honored by God and firmly set with them in heaven. [6]For your childbearing was from our father Abraham.

4 Maccabees 17:11-12, 17-21   *OTP* 2:562, 563

[11]Truly divine was the contest in which they were engaged. [12]On that day virtue was the umpire and the test to which they were put was a test of endurance. [12]**The prizes for victory was incorruption in long-lasting life.** [13]The first to enter the contest was Eleazar, but the mother of the seven sons competed also, and the brothers as will took part. [14]The tyrant was the adversary and the world and the life of men were the spectators [1 Cor. 4:9].

[17]The tyrant himself and his whole council were astonished at their endurance, [18]**on account of which they now stand beside the divine throne and live the life of the age of blessing.** [19]**For Moses says,** *All the holy ones are under your hands* **[Deut. 33:3 (LXX)]. These then, having consecrated themselves for the sake of God, are now honored not only with this distinction** but also by the fact that through them our enemies did not prevail against our nation, [21]and the tyrant was punished and our land purified, since they became, as it were, a ransom for the sin of our nation. [22]Through the blood of these righteous ones and through the propitiation of their death the divine providence rescued Israel, which had been shamefully treated.

4 Maccabees 18:3-5   *OTP* 2:563

[3]Those men who surrendered their bodies to suffering for piety's sake were in return not only admired by mankind **but were also deemed worthy of the divine portion.** [4]And it was because of them that our nation enjoyed peace – they revived the observance of the Law in their land and repulsed their enemies' siege. [5]And the tyrant Antiochus was punished on earth and continues to suffer punishment in death. For when he had failed absolutely to compel the people of Jerusalem to adopt the pagan way of life, and to forsake the customs of their fathers, he departed from Jerusalem and marched away against the Persians.

4 Maccabees 18:10-23   *OTP* 2:563-64

[10]He [your father] while he was still with you, taught you the Law and the Prophets. [11]He read to you of Abel, slain by Cain [Gen. 4:8], of Isaac, offered as a burnt offering [Gen. 22], and of Joseph, in prison [Gen. 39:7-23]. [12]He spoke to you of the zeal of Phineas [Num. 25:7-13], and taught you about Hananiah, Azariah, and Mishael in the fire [Dan. 3:6]. [13]He sang the praises of Daniel in the lions' den and called him blessed. [14]He reminded you of the scripture of Isaiah which says, *Even though you walk through fire, the flame shall not burn you* [Isa. 43:2]. [15]He sang to you the psalm of David which says, *Many are the afflictions of the righteous* [Ps. 34:19].

¹⁶**He recited the proverbs of Solomon which says,** *He is a tree of life* [referring to God instead of wisdom] *to those who do his will* [Prov. 3:18]. ¹⁷**He affirmed the word of Ezekiel,** *Shall these dry bones live?* [Ezek. 37:2] ¹⁸**Nor did he forget the son that Moses taught which says,** ¹⁹*I kill and I make alive* [Deut. 32:39], for this is your life and the length of your days."

²⁰Ah! bitter was the day and yet no bitter when the cruel tyrant of the Greeks quenched fire with fire in his fierce braziers, and in a furious rage brought to the catapult and back again to his tortures those seven sons of the daughter of Abraham; ²¹he pierced the pupils of their eyes, their tongues he cut out, and slew them with all kinds of torment. ²²And for these acts the divine justice has pursued and will pursue the accursed tyrant. ²³**But the sons of Abraham, together with their mother, who won the victor's prize, are gathered together in the choir of their fathers, having received pure and deathless souls from God, to whom be glory forever and ever.** Amen.

Pseudo-Phocylides

Pseudo-Phocylides 97-115   OTP 2:577-78
Death and afterlife

⁹⁷Sit not in vain at the fire, weakening your heart.

⁹⁸Be moderate in your grief; for moderation is the best.

⁹⁹Let the unburied dead receive their share of the earth [Jer. 16:4; 22:19].

¹⁰⁰Do not dig up the grave of the deceased, nor expose to the sun.

¹⁰¹what may not be seen, lest your stir up the divine anger.

¹⁰²It is not good to dissolve the human frame;

¹⁰³**for we hope that the remains of the departed will soon come to the light (again)**

¹⁰⁴**out of the earth** [cf. Isa. 26:19; Dan. 12:2]; **and afterward they will become gods.**

¹⁰⁵For the souls remain unharmed among the deceased.

¹⁰⁶For the spirit is a loan of God to mortals, and (his) image.

¹⁰⁷**For we have a body out of earth, and when afterward we are resolved again into earth** [Gen. 3:19; Eccl. 12:7]

¹⁰⁸**we are but dust; and then the air has received our spirit.**

¹⁰⁹When you are rich, do not be sparing; remember that you are mortal.

¹¹⁰It is impossible to take riches and money (with you) into Hades [Job 1:21; 3:19; Ps. 49:18f.; Eccl. 5:15].

¹¹¹All alike are corpses, but God rules over the souls.

¹¹²Hades is (our) common eternal home [Eccl. 12:5] and fatherland.

¹¹³a common place for all, poor and kings.

¹¹⁴We humans live not a long time but for a season [Job 14:1f.].

¹¹⁵But (our) soul is immortal and lives ageless forever.

Resurrection Texts in *Prayers*, *Psalms*, and *Odes*

Table 25. Resurrection texts in *Prayers*, *Psalms*, and *Odes*

Date	Passage		Notes	Resurrection		Classification			
				Imp.	Stat.	Ref.	Allude	Phil.	Assum.
1st cent. BCE	*Psalms of Solomon*	2:31-35	Judgment/Resurrection	×			×		×
		3:11-12	Righteous → Eternal life		×				×
		14:9-10	Righteous → Eternal life	×					×
		15:10-13	Judgment/Resurrection	×					×
2nd to 3rd cent. CE	*Hellenistic Synagogue Prayers*	3:24-27	"Loosed the boundary of death"		×				×
		7:11	God's act of redemption		×				×
		12:46-50	The two ways theology		×		×	×	×
		16:7-9	Funeral prayer for the dead Rest ∥ Death		×		×		×

Date		Passage	Notes	Resurrection			Classification		
				Imp.	Stat.	Ref.	Allude	Phil.	Assum.
Late 1st to early 2nd cent. CE	*Odes of Solomon*	3:8-9	Jesus → Life	×					×
		9	God's will/written in the book	×					×
		10:2, 6	Walk in the way of Jesus	×					×
		11:2, 12, 16, 18	God's work for the righteous	×					×
		15:8-10	God's work for the righteous	×					×
		17:12-15	Jesus' work → Gift to the righteous		×				×
		20:7-9	God's grace	×					×
		21:2	God's grace	×					×
		22:8-12	Christ speaks		×	×			×
		25:8-9	God's work		×				×
		28:6-8	Life giving spirit	×					×
		29:3-4	God's work	×					×
		31:4, 6-7, 13	Jesus' work	×					×
		33:8-12	Jesus' work	×					×
		36:1	The work of the Spirit of the Lord	×					×
		38:3	Truth → immortal life	×					×
		40:6	Jesus → immortal life	×					×
		41:11	Jesus, the life giver	×					×
		42:11-20	Resurrection of Jesus and the many		×				×

The *Psalms of Solomon*

The *Psalms of Solomon* 2:18, 28-35   *OTP* 2:653-54

^{18}God is a righteous judge and he will not be impressed by appearances [Deut. 10:17].

^{28}He did not consider that he was a man,
for the latter
do not consider (this).
^{29}He said, "I shall be lord of land and sea";
and he did not understand that it is God who is great,
powerful in his great strength.
^{30}He is king over the heavens,
    judging even kings and rulers,
^{31}**Raising me up to glory,**
but putting to sleep the arrogant for eternal destruction in dishonor,
because they did not know him.
^{32}And now, officials of the earth, see the judgment of the Lord [Ps. 2:10],
    that he is a great and righteous king, judging what is under heaven.
^{33}Praise God, you who fear the Lord with understanding,
    for the Lord's mercy is upon those who fear him with judgment.
^{34}**To separate between the righteous and the sinner**
    to repay sinners forever according to their actions
^{35}And to have mercy on the righteous (keeping him) from the humiliation of the sinner,
    and **to repay the sinner for what he has done to the righteous.**

The *Psalms of Solomon* 3:11-16   *OTP* 2:655

$^{11(9)}$The sinner stumbl**eth** and curs**eth** his life,
The day when he was begotten, and his mother's travail.
$^{12(10)}$He add**eth** sins to sins, while he liveth (?) [Isa. 30:1];
^{13}He fall**eth**—verily grievous is his fall—and ris**eth** no more.
$^{(11)}$ The destruction of the sinner is for ever,
^{14}And he shall not be remembered, when the righteous **is visited**.
$^{(12)}$ ^{15}This is the portion [e.g. Pss. 49:13; 81:15] of sinners for ever.
^{16}**But they that fear the Lord shall rise to life eternal** [see. Dan. 12:2; Job 33:29f.],
And their life (shall be) in the light of the Lord, and shall come to an end no more.

The *Psalms of Solomon* 14:6-10   *OTP* 2:663-64

^{6}But not so are sinners and criminals,
    who love (to spend) the day in sharing their sin.
^{7}Their enjoyment is brief and decaying,
    and they do not remember God.

⁸For the ways of men are known before him always,
    and he knows the secrets of the heart before they happen.
⁹Therefore their inheritance is Hades, and the darkness and destruction;
    and they will not be found on the day of mercy for the righteous,
¹⁰But the devout of the Lord will inherit life in happiness.

The *Psalms of Solomon* 15:7-13   OTP 2:664

⁷Famine and sword and death shall be far from the righteous;
    for they will retreat from the devout like those pursued by famine.
⁸But they shall pursue sinners and overtake them,
    for those who act lawlessly shall not escape the Lord's judgment.
⁹They shall be overtaken as by those experienced in war,
    for on their forehead (is) the mark of destruction.
¹⁰And the inheritance of sinners is destruction and darkness,
    and their lawless actions shall pursue them below into Hades.
¹¹Their inheritance shall not be found for their children,
    for lawless actions shall devastate the homes of sinners.
¹²And sinners shall perish forever in the day of the Lord's judgment,
    when God oversees the earth at his judgment.
¹³But those who fear the Lord shall find mercy in it
    and shall live by their God's mercy;
    but sinners shall perish for all time.

Hellenistic Synagogal Prayers

Hellenistic Synagogal Prayers 3:19b-27   OTP 2:679-70
3. A Prayer That Meditates upon God's Manifold Creative Power, Which Comes to Sinful Man in Redemption (*Apos. Con.* 7.34.1-8)

¹⁹ᵇ*Let us make man according to our image and likeness* [Gen. 1:26];
²⁰having declared him a (micro-)cosm of cosmos,
having formed for him the body out of the four elements;
²¹and having prepared for him the soul out of non-being,
and having given to him fivefold perception,
and having placed over the perceptions a mind, the holder of the reins of the soul.
²²And in addition to all these things, O Master, Lord,
    who can worthily describe the movement of rain-producing clouds,
    the flashing forth of lightning, the clashing of thunders;
²³   for the supplying of appropriate nourishment,
    and the blending of complex atmospheres?
²⁴But when man was disobedient,
You took away his deserved life.
²⁵You did not make it disappear absolutely, but for a time,
²⁶having put (him) to sleep for a little (while),
by an oath you have called (him forth) to new birth.

²⁷**You have loosed the boundary of death,**
You who are the Maker of life for the dead, <u>through Jesus Christ, our hope</u>!
[1 Tim. 1:1]

Hellenistic Synagogal Prayers 7:9-12   *OTP* 2:686
7. A Prayer of Thanksgiving to God for His Continuing Acts of Redemption in the Past, and Now in Christ; and for His Manifold Gifts to Man, the Rational Animal (*Apos. Cons.* 7.38.1-8)

⁹And all these things you have formed out of a little drop in a womb,
    and after the shaping, you freely give immortal life,
    and you bring forward into light the rational animal, the man.
¹⁰With laws, you have taught (him);
with just ordinances, you have cleansed (him);
¹¹   bringing on dissolution for a little while,
You have promised the resurrection!
¹²Therefore indeed, what manner of life is fully able,
and how great length of ages will be sufficient for men for thanksgiving?

Hellenistic Synagogal Prayers 12:35-52   *OTP* 2:692-93
12. A Prayer of Praise to God, Rehearsing the Grounds in Redemption and in Creation Which Make Praise So Fitting for God's Redeemed Creature, Man (*Apos. Con.* 8.12.6-27)

³⁵⁽¹⁶⁾And you not only made the world,
but you also made the world citizen in it,
declaring him (to be) a (micro-)cosm of the cosmos.
³⁶For you said by your Wisdom,
    Let us make man according to our image,
    and according to (our) likeness;
    and let them rule the fish of the sea,
    and the winged birds of the heaven [Gen. 1:26].
³⁷⁽¹⁷⁾Therefore also you have made him out of immortal soul,
    and out of a body that may be scattered;
³⁸   the one indeed out of that which is not,
    but the other out of the four elements.
³⁹And you have indeed given to him, with reference to the soul,
    rational discrimination,
    distinguishing of piety and impiety,
    observation of right and wrong.
⁴⁰While with reference to the body,
    you have given (him) five senses,
    and the movement involving change of place.
⁴¹⁽¹⁸⁾For you, O God Almighty, <u>through Christ</u>,
    planted a paradise in Eden, eastward [Gen. 2:8],

with all manner of edible foods, in (proper) order;
⁴² and into it, as if into a very expensive home, you brought him.
⁴³And indeed, you have given to him an implanted law to do [Rom. 2:14f.],
   so that form himself, and by himself,
   he might have the seeds of divine knowledge.
⁴⁴⁽¹⁹⁾So, having brought (him) into the paradise of luxury,
you allowed him the right to partake of all things.
⁴⁵But of only one things did you refuse him the taste [Gen. 2:15-17];
   in hope of greater things,
   in order that, **if he should keep the commandment,**
   he might receive immortality as a reward for this [access to the Tree of Life].
⁴⁶⁽²⁰⁾But, having cared nothing for the commandment,
and having tasted of the forbidden fruit,
   by trickery of a serpent,
   and by the counsel of a woman,
you indeed rightly thrust him out from paradise [Gen. 3].
⁴⁷**Yet in goodness, you did not overlook him who was perishing forever,**
   for he was your work of art.
⁴⁸ But, having subjected to him the creation,
   You have given to him, through sweat and hard labors [Gen. 3:17-19], to provide
by himself
   the nourishment for his own family,
   while you are causing all things to grow, and to ripen.
⁴⁹**And in time, having caused him to fall asleep for a while,**
you called (him) by an oath to new birth;
⁵⁰ having dissolved the boundaries of death,
   you promised life by resurrection!
⁵¹⁽²¹⁾And not only this; but also those who poured forth from him,
   to become an innumerable multitude–
⁵² those who continued with you, you glorified,
   while those who separated from you, you punished.

Hellenistic Synagogal Prayers **16**   *OTP* 2:696-97
16. Funeral Prayer for the Dead (*Apos. Cons.* 8.41.2-5)
¹⁽²⁾**And on behalf of those our brothers who are at rest** <u>in Christ</u>,
   let us beg;
² on behalf of the repose of this brother or that sister,
   let us beg;
³ that God, the lover of man, having received his soul,
   may forgive him every sin – voluntary and involuntary;
⁴ and being gracious and favorable,
   may appoint him to a position among the godly ones,
   sent into the embrace of Abraham [Lk. 16:23], and Isaac, and Jacob,
   with all those from of old who were well pleasing, and who did his will;
   where pain and grief and moaning have fled away [Isa. 35:10].

⁵Let us arise! Let us commit ourselves, and one another, to the eternal God,
   through the Word (which was) in the beginning!
⁶⁽³⁾And let the bishop say,
⁽⁴⁾   "O you who are by nature immortal and unending,
through who everything immortal and mortal has come into being;
⁷who with artistic skill made this rational living being, man, the mortal world citizen,
and who promised resurrection;
⁸who did not permit Enoch and Elijah to experience death,
the God of Abraham, and Isaac, and Jacob,
not as of the dead, but as God of the living, are you [Mt. 22:32; Lk. 20:38].
⁹**Because, with you, all souls are alive**,
and the spirits of the righteous are in your hand, whom anguish will not touch.
¹⁰For all those who are set apart are under your hand [Deut. 33:3].
¹¹⁽⁵⁾Also now yourself, look upon this your servant,
   whom you have chosen, and received into another sphere;
¹²and forgiven him, if he has committed any great sin, voluntarily or involuntarily;
and place beside him favorable angels;
and appointed him (a place) in the embrace of the patriarchs, and the prophets, and
¹³   the apostles,
   and of all those who from of old were pleasing to you;
¹⁴where there cannot be grief, and pain, and moaning [Isa. 35:10],
but a free place of godly ones,
and a land of upright ones, set up for you,
   and for those in it who see the glory of Christ;
¹⁵With whom to you be glory, honor, and awe, thanksgiving and worship,
and to the Holy Spirit, forever [possible Christian elements in its resemblances to: Jn 1:1; 22:32; Lk. 20:38]. Amen.

Odes of Solomon

Odes of Solomon 3:7-9   OTP 2:735-36

⁷I have been united (to him), because the lover has found the Beloved,
because I love him that is the Son, I shall become a son.

⁸Indeed he who is joined to him who is immortal,
truly will be immortal [Jn 14:19; 1 Cor. 6:17].
⁹**And he who delights in the Life**
will become living [cf. Jn 11:25; also Jn 1:4; 5:26, 40; 10:10, 28; 14:6].

¹⁰This is the Spirit of the Lord, which is not false [cf. Tit. 1:2],
which teaches the sons of men to know his ways [cf. 1QS 3.13-4.26 | Jn 14:17, 26; 15:26].

¹¹Be wise and understanding and vigilant.

Hallelujah.

***Odes of Solomon* 9** *OTP* 2:743

¹Open your ears,
and I shall speak to you.

²Give my yourself,
so that I may also give you myself;

³The rod of the Lord and his desire,
the holy thought which he has thought concerning his Messiah.

**⁴For in the will of the Lord is your life,
and his purpose is eternal life,
and your perfection is incorruptible.**
⁵Be enriched in God the Father;
and receive the purpose of the Most High.
Be strong and saved by his grace.

⁶For I announce peace to you, his holy ones,
so that none of those who hear will fall in the war.

⁷And also that those who have known him may not perish [Jn 3:16],
and so that those who receive (him) may not be ashamed.

⁸An everlasting crown is Truth;
blessed are they who set it on their head [Ps. 20:4 (LXX; MT 21:3)].

⁹(It is) a precious stone,
for the wars were on account of the crown.

¹⁰But Righteousness has taken it,
and has given it to you.

¹¹Put on the crown in the true covenant of the Lord,
and all those who have conquered will be inscribed in his book.

**¹²For their book is the justification which is for you,
and she sees you before her and wills that you will be saved.**

Hallelujah

***Odes of Solomon* 10:1-2, 5-6** *OTP* 2:743, 744

¹The Lord has directed my mouth by his Word,
and has opened my heart by his Light.

²**And he has caused to dwell in me his immortal life** [Jn 4:14],
and permitted me to proclaim the fruit of his peace.

⁵And the gentiles who had been scattered were gathered together [Jn 11:52],
but I [Christ] was not defiled by my love (for them),
because they had praised me in high places [cf. Mal. 1:11].

⁶And the traces of light were set upon their heart,
and they walked according to my life and were saved,
and they became my people for ever and ever.

Hallelujah.

Odes of Solomon **11:2, 12, 16, 18**   *OTP* 2:744-45
²For the Most High circumcised me by his Holy Spirit,
then he uncovered my inward being toward him,
and filled me with his love.

¹²**And from above he gave me immortal rest** [cf. Ps. 95:11 | Heb. 3:7–4:13];
and I became like the land which blossoms and rejoices in its fruits.

¹⁶**And he took me to his Paradise**,
wherein is the wealth of the Lord's pleasure.

¹⁶ᶜAnd the river of gladness was irrigating them,
and the region round about them **in the land of eternal life**.

¹⁸And I said, blessed, O Lord, are they
who are planted in your land,
and **who have a place in your Paradise**;

Odes of Solomon **15:8-10**   *OTP* 2:748
⁸**I have put on incorruption** [cf. 1 Cor. 15:54f.] **through his name,**
and stripped off corruption by his grace.

⁹**Death has been destroyed before my face,**
and Sheol has been vanquished by my word [Rev 1:18].

¹⁰**And eternal life has arisen in the Lord's land,**
and it has become known to his faithful ones,
and been given without limit to all that trust in him.

Hallelujah.

Odes of Solomon **17:12-16**   *OTP* 2:751
**¹²And I went toward all my bondsmen in order to loose them;
that I might not abandon anyone bound or binding.**
¹³And I gave my knowledge generously,
and my **resurrection** through my love.

¹⁴And I sowed my fruits in hearts,
and transformed them through myself.

**¹⁵Then they received my blessing and lived,
and they were gathered to me and were saved;**

¹⁶Because they became my members,
and I was their head [Jn 15; Rom. 12:4f; Col. 1:15-20].

Odes of Solomon **20:7-9**   *OTP* 2:753
**⁷But put on the grace of the Lord generously,
and come into his Paradise [Rev. 2:7],
and make for yourself a crown from his tree.**

**⁸Then put (it) on your head and be refreshed,
and recline upon his serenity.**

**⁹For his glory will go before you;
and you will receive of his kindness and of his grace [cf. Isa. 58:8];
and you will be anointed in truth with the praise of his holiness.**

Odes of Solomon **21:1-3**   *OTP* 2:754
¹I raised my arms on high
on account of the grace of the Lord.

²Because **he cast off my chains** from me,
and **my Helper raised me according to his grace and his salvation**.
³And I stripped off darkness,
and put on light.

Odes of Solomon **22:8-12**   *OTP* 2:755
**⁸And it chose them from the graves,
and separated them from the dead ones.**

**⁹It took dead bones
and covered them with flesh** [Ezek. 37:1-6].

¹⁰**But they were motionless,
so it gave (them) energy for life**.
¹¹Incorruptible was your way and your face;
you have brought your world to corruption,
that everything might be broken and renewed.

¹²And the foundation of everything is your rock.
And upon it you have built your kingdom [Mt. 16:18],
and it became the dwelling place of the holy ones.

Hallelujah.

Odes of Solomon **25:8-9**　　　　　　　　　　　　　　　　　　　　　　*OTP* 2:758
⁸And I was covered with the covering of your spirit,
and **I removed from me my garments of skin**.

⁹**Because your right hand raised me**,
and caused sickness to pass from me.

Odes of Solomon **28:6-8**　　　　　　　　　　　　　　　　　　　　　　*OTP* 2:760
⁶**Because I am ready before destruction comes,
and have been placed in his incorruptible arms.**

⁷**And immortal life embraced me,
and kissed me.**

⁸**And from that (life) is the Spirit which is within me.
And it cannot die because it is life.**

Odes of Solomon **29:1-4**　　　　　　　　　　　　　　　　　　　　　　*OTP* 2:761
¹The Lord is my hope [Pss. 31:1; 71:1],
I shall not be ashamed in him.

²For according to his praise he made me,
and according to his grace even so he gave to me.

³And according to his mercies **he raised me**,
and according to his great honor **he lifted me up**.

⁴And **he caused me to ascend from the depths of Sheol**,
and **from the mouth of Death he drew me**.

Odes of Solomon 31:4, 6-7, 13   *OTP* 2:762-63
⁴Then he raised his voice toward the Most High,
and offered to him those that had become sons through him [Jn 17:1-9].

⁶Come forth, you who have been afflicted,
and receive joy.

⁷And possess yourselves through grace,
and take unto you immortal life.

¹³And that I might not nullify the promises to the patriarchs [Jn 15:8],
to whom I was promised for the salvation of their offspring.

Odes of Solomon 33:8-12   *OTP* 2:764
⁸**And I will enter into you,**
and bring you forth from destruction,
and make you wise in the ways of truth.

⁹Be not corrupted
nor perish.

¹⁰Hear me and be saved,
for I am proclaiming unto you the grace of God.
¹¹**And through me you will be saved and become blessed.**
I am your judge;

¹²**And they who have put me on will not be rejected,**
but they will possess incorruption in the new world.

Odes of Solomon 36:1-2   *OTP* 2:765
¹I rest on the Spirit of the Lord,
and she raised me up to heaven;
²And caused me to stand on my feet in the Lord's high place,
before his perfection and his glory,
where I continued praising (him) by the composition of his odes.

Odes of Solomon 38:1-3   *OTP* 2:766
¹I went up into the light of Truth as into a chariot,
and the Truth led me and caused me to come [cf. Ps. 43:3].

²And caused me to pass over chasms and gulfs,
and saved me from cliffs and valleys.
³And became for me a heaven of salvation,
and set me on the place of immortal life.

Odes of Solomon **40:4-6** *OTP* 2:769
⁴My face rejoices in his exultation,
and my spirit exults in his love,
and my nature shines in him.

⁵And he who is afraid will trust in him,
and salvation will be established in him.

⁶**And his possession is immortal life,
and those who receive it are incorruptible**.

Hallelujah.

Odes of Solomon **41:11-15** *OTP* 2:770
¹¹And his Word is with us in all our way,
the Savior who gives life [Jn 6:33-37] and does not reject ourselves.

¹²The Man who humbled himself,
but was raised because of his own righteousness [Phil. 2:6-9].

¹³The Son of the Most High appeared
in the perfection of his Father.

¹⁴And light dawned from the Word [Jn 1:1]
that was before time in him.

¹⁵The Messiah in truth is one.
And he was known before the foundations of the world,
that he might give life to persons forever by the truth of his name.

Odes of Solomon **42:11-20** *OTP* 2:771
¹¹**Sheol saw me and was shattered,
and Death ejected me and many with me** [Rev. 20:13f.].

¹²I have been vinegar and bitterness to it,
and I went down with it as far as its depth.

¹³Then the feet and the head it released,
because it was not able to endure my face.
¹⁴**And I made a congregation of living among his dead;
and I spoke with them by living lips;
in order that my word may not fail**.

[15]And those who had died ran toward me;
and they cried out and said, "Son of God, have pity on us.

[16]"And deal with us according to your kindness,
and bring us out from the chains of darkness.

[17]"And open for us the door
by which we may go forth to you [Jn 10:7-10; Rev. 3:7f.],
for we perceive that our death does not approach you.

[18]"May we also be saved with you,
because you are our Savior."

[19]Then I heard their voice,
and placed their faith in my heart.

[20]And I placed my name upon their head,
because they are free and they are mine.

APPENDIX B:
RESURRECTION PASSAGES IN QUMRAN, JOSEPHUS, NEW TESTAMENT, AND EARLY RABBINIC JUDAISM

Appendix B provides an analysis of resurrection passages compiled from the Dead Sea Scrolls (Table 27), Josephus (Table 28), New Testament (Table 29), Jewish Liturgy (Table 30), and early rabbinic literature (Table 31). These tables are tentative and the author does not claim that they are complete, but they do give an indication of how prevalent resurrection beliefs are in texts not discussed in this monograph, although several of these texts have been referenced in this monograph when deemed relevant. In research by the author into the resurrection texts appearing among the Dead Sea Scrolls (Table 27), Josephus (Table 28), and Jewish Liturgy (Table 30),[1] dating will be taken into consideration. However, for

---

1. Dating the various resurrection texts found in Josephus' writings would not be helpful for this study since they were written during a fairly short time-period. Josephus was born towards the end of the Second Temple period, in the year of Gaius Caligula's accession (37/38 CE). His writings dates to the tumultuous political period following the first Jewish Revolt, which effectively ended the Second Temple period. As such, his writings were composed during the latter part of his life: The *Jewish War* (seven books) dates to the late 70s, the *Jewish Antiquities* (twenty books) dates to the mid-90s, and the appendix to *Jewish Antiquities*, *Life*, was completed shortly after 100 CE – falling within a period of about twenty years (Evans, *Ancient Texts for New Testament Studies*, 173–4).

Dating Jewish Liturgy is difficult since "prayers were not written down during the Talmudic times" (David Instone-Brewer, *Prayer and Agriculture*, TRENT 1 [Grand Rapids: Eerdmans, 2004], 95). In the case of the Amidah prayer, it evolved over centuries. According to traditions, *Shemoneh Esreh* originated during the early Second Temple period with the "men of the Great Synagogue" (*b. Ber.* 33a) or the "120 elders, prophets among them" (*b. Meg.* 17b). Instone-Brewer notes that "the timing of the Eighteen [Benedictions] appear to be linked to Temple sacrifices, and it is possible that they were part of the private prayer service by the priest before starting their duties (m. Tam. 5.1.)" (Instone-Brewer, *Prayer and Agriculture*, 107). It was not until the end of the Second Temple period, according to Rabbinic tradition, that the order, number and the wording of the Amidah was fixed by Rabban Gamaliel

the purpose of this appendix, the dates have been excluded. Due to the complicating factor that rabbinical literature tends to contain a non-chronological collection of oral traditions credited to Rabbis living in multiple generations, Table 33, also, does not include the dating of the Rabbinical resurrection passages. These five tables give various categories by which each passage is analyzed and classified (see Table 26). It should be noted that a category only appears in a given table if it is of relevance for the resurrection passages falling within that category. Table 31 shows the uniqueness of the New Testament writings regarding the resurrection belief, since Jesus' death and resurrection functions as proof for the New Testament community.

II of Yavneh and his two disciples, Simeon of Pakula and Shmuel Hakatan (Instone-Brewer, *Prayer and Agriculture*, 108 and Gershom Bader, *Encyclopedia of Talmudic Sages* [Northvale, N.J.: Jason Aronson, 1988], 191).

Table 26. List of categories used in the five resurrection texts tables

Category		Table					Explanation
		27	28	29	30	31	
Date				×			Date the book was written.
Passage		×	×	×	×	×	Passage reference.
Notes			×	×	×	×	Author's notes.
Resurrection	Implied		×	×	×	×	A resurrection belief is implied in the passage.
	Stated		×	×	×	×	A resurrection belief is stated clearly in the passage.
Classification	Reference		×	×	×	×	The resurrection passage refers to a resurrection text in the TaNaKh.
	Allusion		×	×	×	×	The resurrection passage alludes to a resurrection text in the TaNaKh.
	Philosophical		×	×	×	×	Resurrection passage uses a philosophical argument as proof of a resurrection belief.
	Assumed		×	×	×	×	Since the resurrection belief is assumed, no attempt is made to prove biblically or philosophically that there will be a resurrection.
	Jesus				×		Reference to Jesus' resurrection.
	Miracle				×		Jesus resurrects a person.
	Eschatological				×		Eschatological resurrection.
	Jewish/ Christian						Jewish, Christian, or a Jewish-Christian passage [J, C, J/C].

Resurrection Texts in the Dead Sea Scrolls

Table 27. List of resurrection texts: Dead Sea Scrolls

Passage	
1QH (1QHodayot)	XI 19-23
	XII 5-XIII 4
	XIV 34-35
	XV 22-31
	XIX 10-14
1QS (1QRule of the Community)	IV 6-8, 11-14
4Q245 (Pseudo-Daniel ar)	Frag. 2
4Q385 (4QPseudo-Ezekiel[a])	Frag. 1-3, 12
4Q386 (4QPseudo-Ezekiel[b])	Frag. 1 col. i
4Q388 (4QPseudo-Ezekiel[d])	Frag. 8
4Q416 (4QInstruction[b])	Frag. 2 col. iii
4Q418 (4QInstruction[d])	Frag. 69 ii
4Q504 (4QWords of the Luminaries[a])	Frags. 1-2 col. vi
4Q521 (4QMessianic Apocalypse)	Frag. 1 col. ii
	Frag. 2 col. ii-iii
	Frags. 7 + 5 col. ii
4Q548 (4QVisions of Amram[f?] ar)	Frag. 1

Resurrection Texts in Josephus

Table 28. List of resurrection texts: Josephus

	Passage	Notes	Resurrection			Classification		
			Implied	Stated	Ref.	Allude	Phil.	Assume
Antiquities	18.1.3	Pharisees		×				×
	18.1.4	Sadducees						
	18.1.5	Essenes						
Jewish War	2.8.10-11	Essenes	×					×
	2.8.14	Pharisees	×					×
	2.8.14	Sadducees						
	3.8.5	Immortality of the soul/ resurrection		×			×	×

Appendix B 283

Resurrection Texts in the New Testament

Table 29. List of resurrection texts: New Testament

Date	Passage	Notes	Resurrection				Classification				
			Implied	Stated	Ref.	Allude	Phil.	Assume	Jesus	Miracle	Eschatological
40–100	Matthew										
	5:3, 10-12	The Beatitudes	x								x
	5:20	Righteous = enter the kingdom	x								x
	6:19-20	Treasures in Heaven	x								x
	7:13-14	The two ways	x								x
	7:21-23	Day of Judgment	x								x
	8:11-12	Feast in Heaven	x								
	9:18-25	A dead girl / death ∥ sleep		x						x	
	10:8	Jesus sends out the Twelve								x	
	10:28	Body / Soul									
	11:5	John's question		x						x	
	12:38-42	Sign of Jonah		x	x				x		
	13:43	Parable of the Weed			x						x
	16:1-4	Sign of Jonah	x						x		
	16:21-28	Jesus predicts His death		x					x		
	17:2-4	Moses and Elijah	x					x			
	17:22-23	Jesus predicts His death		x					x		

Appendix B

Date		Passage	Notes	Resurrection					Classification			
				Implied	Stated	Ref.	Allude	Phil.	Assume	Jesus	Miracle	Eschatological
40–100	Matthew	19:16-28	Rich young ruler	×								×
		20:17-19	Jesus predicts His death		×					×		
		22:23, 28, 30	Discussion with the Sadducees		×	×						×
		24:29-31	The End of the Age	×		×						×
		25:31-46	The sheep and the goats	×								×
		26:63-64	2nd Coming	×								×
		27:52-53	Resurrection of holy people		×					×	×	
		27:62-66	Guarding the tomb		×					×		
		28:1-15	Jesus resurrection		×					×		
60–70	Mark	5:22, 35-43	Jairus daughter death ‖ sleep		×						×	
		6:14, 16	Believed that John had been raised from dead		×						×	
		8:31	Jesus predicts His death		×					×		
		8:35	He who loses his life will save it	×								
		9:4-5	Moses and Elijah	×					×			
		10:17-31	The rich man	×								×
		10:33-34	Jesus predicts His death		×					×		

Appendix B

Date		Passage	Notes	Resurrection		Classification						
				Implied	Stated	Ref.	Allude	Phil.	Assume	Jesus	Miracle	Eschatological
60–70	Mark	12:18-27	Discussion with the Sadducees		×							×
		13:24-27	Signs of the End of the Age	×								×
		14:62	The Son of Man coming on the clouds of Heaven	×								×
		16:6, 9, 12, 14	Jesus' resurrection		×					×		
60–70	Luke	2:29-32	Simeon's praise	×								×
		3:4-6	John's mission	×								×
		6:22-23	Reward in Heaven	×								×
		7:11-17	Widow's son at Nain		×						×	
		7:18-23	John's question		×		×				×	
		8:40-56	Jairus' daughter		×						×	
		9:7-9, 19	Herod perplexed by potential resurrection		×					×		
		9:22	Jesus predicts his death		×					×		
		9:23-27	He who loses his life will save it	×								×

Appendix B 287

Date	Passage		Notes	Resurrection					Classification			
				Implied	Stated	Ref.	Allude	Phil.	Assume	Jesus	Miracle	Eschatological
60–70	Luke	9:30-33	Moses and Elijah	×					×			
		10:20	Book of Life	×								
		11:29-32	Sign of Jonah		×					×		×
		13:28-29	The feast in Heaven	×								×
		14:12-14	Jesus at the Pharisee's house		×				×			×
		14:15	The Great Banquet	×								×
		16:29-31	Lazarus and the rich man		×				×			
		17:33	He who loses his life will save it	×								×
		18:18-29	The rich ruler	×								×
		18:31-33	Jesus predicts His death		×					×		
		20:27-40	Discussion with the Sadducees		×							×
		21:19, 36	The End of the Ages	×								×
		22:30	Judge the tribes	×								×
		23:42-43	The criminal on the cross	×			×					
		24:6-7, 23, 34, 46-47	Jesus' resurrection		×			×				

Date	Passage	Notes	Resurrection					Classification			
			Implied	Stated	Ref.	Allude	Phil.	Assume	Jesus	Miracle	Eschatological
85–90	John										
	2:18-22	Rebuild temple in three days		×					×		
	3:14-18; 4:36, 14	Belief = eternal life	×					×			×
	5:21-29	Resurrection		×				×			×
	6:33-40, 44, 47, 51, 54	Resurrection		×							×
	10:17-18	Jesus' resurrection predicted	×						×		
	11:24-26, 43-44	Lazarus		×						×	×
	12:1, 9-10	Lazarus		×						×	
	12:23-25	The Seed has to die		×					×		×
	14:1-4	Jesus will prepare a place for his people	×								×
	20:9; 21:14	Jesus' resurrection		×					×		

Appendix B 289

Date		Passage	Notes	Resurrection				Classification				
				Implied	Stated	Ref.	Allude	Phil.	Assume	Jesus	Miracle	Eschatological
Early 60s	Acts	1:22; 2:31-32; 3:15; 4:2, 10, 33; 5:30; 10:40; 13:30, 34, 37; 17:3, 18, 31; 26:23	Jesus' resurrection		×					×		
		9:37, 40-41	Dorcas' resurrection		×				×		×	
		10:42-43	Jesus, the judge	×								×
		13:46	Belief in Jesus ‖ eternal life	×								
		17:32	Resurrection/judgment		×				×	×		×
		20:7-11	Eutychus raised from the dead		×						×	
		23:6-8	Pharisees and Sadducees on resurrection		×							×
		24:15, 21	Resurrection of righteous and wicked		×							×
		26:6-8, 18, 23	Resurrection belief		×				×			

Date	Passage	Notes	Resurrection			Classification					
			Implied	Stated	Ref.	Allude	Phil.	Assume	Jesus	Miracle	Eschatological
56–57	Romans 1:4;	Jesus' resurrection		x					x		
	4:24-25; 5:10; 6:9-10; 7:4; 8:11, 34; 10:5-9; 14:9										
	1:16-17	Righteousness gives life	x								
	2:5-16	Judgment	x								x
	5:18-19	Righteousness brings life	x								
	6:4-5, 8	Jesus sacrifice gives life		x					x		
	8:11	God will give life to mortal bodies	x								
	8:38-39	Nothing can separate us from His love	x								
	14:10-12	Everyone will be judged	x								x
55–56	1 Corinthians 6:14	Resurrection		x				x	x		x
	9:24-27	Win the crown	x				x	x			x
	15:4, 12-28, 21, 42	Jesus' resurrection		x					x		
	15:12-57	General resurrection		x			x		x		x
55–56	2 Corinthians 1:9	God raises the dead	x							x	
	4:14	Resurrection	x			x			x		
	5:1-10	Resurrection/judgment	x				x		x		

Appendix B 291

Date	Passage		Notes	Resurrection				Classification				
				Implied	Stated	Ref.	Allude	Phil.	Assume	Jesus	Miracle	Eschatological
52	Galatians	1:1	Jesus' resurrection		×				×			
60–63	Ephesians	1:15-23	Jesus' resurrection		×				×			
		2:1-10	Made alive in Christ					×		×		
		2:19-22; 3:6	Member of God's household							×		
		4:7-13	Body of Christ					×				
c. 61	Philip-pians	2:6-11	Jesus' resurrection	×						×		
		3:10-11, 14	Resurrection, the Heavenly price		×					×		×
		3:20-21	Citizens of Heaven									×
c. 62	Colos-sians	1:9-14	A part of His kingdom	×						×		
		2:12-13, 20; 3:1-4	Jesus' resurrection our resurrection		×					×		×
50	1 Thessa-lonians	1:10	Jesus' resurrection/judgment		×					×		×
		4:13-18	Resurrection		×				×	×		×
50	2 Thessa-lonians	1:5-10	God's judgment	×				×	×	×		×
62–66	1 Timothy	6:12, 18-19	Eternal life	×					×	×		×
65–67	2 Timothy	1:10-12	Death destroyed	×						×		×
		2:8-13, 18-19	Resurrection		×				×	×		×
		4:7-8	Crown of righteousness	×				×				×
62–66	Titus	2:11-14; 3:7	God, our savior	×					×	×		×

Appendix B

Date		Passage	Notes	Resurrection					Classification			Eschato-logical
				Implied	Stated	Ref.	Allude	Phil.	Assume	Jesus	Miracle	
66–70	Hebrews	2:14-15	Freed from death	×								×
		6:2	Resurrection		×							×
		9:15, 27-28	Promised eternal inheritance	×					×			×
		10:35-39	Receive the promise	×					×			×
		11:4, 6, 10, 13, 16, 19, 35, 39-40	Resurrection		×				×			
		12:22-24, 28-29	Heavenly Jerusalem	×					×	×		×
		13:20	Jesus' resurrection				×			×		
45–50	James	4:10	Sin → Death	×				×	×			×
62–64	1 Peter	1:3-9, 11, 21	Jesus' resurrection → resurrection		×					×		×
		3:18-21	Jesus' resurrection saves		×					×		×
		4:5-6	God judges living and dead	×				×	×			×
		4:13, 16-18	Suffering = reward	×				×		×		×
		5:1, 4	Crown of glory	×					×			×
64–68	2 Peter	1:10-11	Great reward	×					×	×		×
		2:4-22	God's judgment		×			×	×			×
		3:4-13	God's judgment	×				×	×			×
c. 90	1 John	2:17, 25; 4:17; 5:10-13	Belief in Jesus → life	×						×		×

Appendix B 293

Date	Passage	Notes	Resurrection					Classification			
			Implied	Stated	Ref.	Allude	Phil.	Assume	Jesus	Miracle	Eschatological
60–65	Jude										
	6	Judgment	×								×
	9	Moses' death/resurrection	×					×			
	14-15	Judgment	×				×	×			×
	21	Eternal life	×					×	×		×
81–96	Revelation										
	1:18	Keys of death	×						×		×
	2:7; 3:21	The one who conquers will eat from the Tree of Life/sit with Jesus on his throne				×					
	20:4-6, 12-15	The first and second resurrection/judgment		×							×

Resurrection Texts in Jewish Liturgy

Table 30. List of resurrection texts: Jewish liturgy

Classification		Notes	Resurrection		Classification			
			Implied	Stated	Ref.	Allude	Phil.	Assume
Eighteen Benedictions	2nd Benediction	Concerning the resurrection		×		×		
Sanhedrin	12th Benediction	These have Birkat HaMinimno portion in the world to come	×					×

Resurrection Texts in Rabbinic Literature

Table 31. List of resurrection texts: Rabbinic literature

Mishnah

Classification		Notes	Resurrection			Classification		
			Implied	Stated	Ref.	Allude	Phil.	Assume
Sotah	9:15	The Holy Spirit leads to the resurrection which comes through Elijah		x				x
Sanhedrin	10:1-3	These have no portion in the world to come		x	x			x
Berakhot	5:2	Amidah 2		x				x
Avot	4:21-22	"Those who die are [destined] for resurrection"/ Judgment/Theodicy		x			x	x

The Tosefta

Classification		Notes	Resurrection			Classification		
			Implied	Stated	Ref.	Allude	Phil.	Assume
Berakhot	3:9, 24	Prayers		x				
Sanhedrin	13:3-5	Three groups of people		x	x			x

Appendix B

Jerusalem Talmud

Classification		Notes	Resurrection		Classification			
			Implied	Stated	Ref.	Allude	Phil.	Assume
Berakhot	5:2	Amidah 2 Rain ‖ Resurrection		×	×			
Ta'anith	1:1	Amidah 2 Rain ‖ Resurrection		×	×			
Ketubbot	12:3	Rabbi's death and his wishes		×	×			
Sanhedrin	10	All Israelites have a share in the world to come, except…		×	×			

Babylonian Talmud

Classification		Notes	Resurrection		Classification			
			Implied	Stated	Ref.	Allude	Phil.	Assume
Berakhot	15b	The grave and the womb		×	×			
	18b	Regarding prayers		×				×
	26b	Regarding prayers		×				
	29a	Regarding prayers		×				×
	33a	Why the rainfall is mentioned in the benediction of the resurrection		×			×	
	60b	Blessing God for restoring souls to dead corpses		×				
Sabbath	152b	God will open the graves		×	×			
Pesachim	68a	The righteous are destined to resurrect the dead/ God will resurrect		×	×		×	
	118a	Resurrection Psalm		×	×			
Rosh HaShana	17a	Three groups at the Day of Judgment		×	×			
	31a	Resurrection after 1000 or 2000 years		×	×			
	32a	The order of the blessings		×				×

Appendix B 297

Tractate	Folio	Topic						
Megillah	17b	The origin of the Amidah prayer	x					
Chagigah	12b	The dew which will revive the dead		x	x			
Sotah	5a	Arrogant people will not resurrect		x	x			
Kiddushin	39b	Every precept in the Torah depends on the resurrection		x	x			
Baba Bathra	16a	Job denied the resurrection of the dead		x	x			
	16b	Esau denied the resurrection of the dead		x	x			
Ketubbot	111a	Who will resurrect (geographically)		x	x			
	111b	Who will not resurrect (the illiterate)/Resurrection in Jerusalem		x	x			
Sanhedrin	90a	All Israel have a portion in the world to come, except…		x	x			
	90b	Resurrection is derived from the Torah		x	x			
	91a	Can dust come to life?		x	x		x	
	91b	The parable about the lame (body) and the blind (spirit) men/Judgment and the world to come/Resurrection is derived from the Torah		x	x			
	92a	Resurrection is derived from the Torah		x	x			
	92b	The identity of the people whom Ezekiel resurrected		x	x			
	113a	Elijah asked for the keys of resurrection		x				x
Avodah Zarah	18a	No portion in the world to come		x				x
	20b	The holy spirit leads to life eternal		x				x
Chullin	142a	Every precept in the Torah depends on the resurrection		x	x			x
Nidah	70b	What conveys uncleanness		x				x

Midrash Rabbah

Classification		Notes	Resurrection		Classification			
			Implied	Stated	Ref.	Allude	Phil.	Assume
Genesis	13:3-6	Parallel between rain and resurrection		x	x			
	14:5, 8	Two formations, one in this world and one in the next		x	x			
	20:10	You shall return from the dust		x	x			
	21:1	The decree against Adam has a limit		x	x			
	26:2	There will be no death and Sheol will be destroyed	x		x			
	26:6	The righteous will receive a reward while the wicked will burn	x		x			
	28:3	A person will be resurrected from the nut of the spinal column		x			x	
	32:1	The generation of the Flood will neither be resurrected nor judged		x	x			
	35:3	The last blessing is greater than the first		x	x			
	56:1-2	The third day/Resurrection a reward for worshiping		x	x			
	63:11, 14	Esau denied the resurrection		x	x			
	73:4	Three keys belong to God		x	x			
	74:1	The land of the living = resurrection		x	x			
	77:1	All God's deeds have been anticipated: Elijah and Elisha resurrected the dead		x	x			

Book	Ref	Description							
	78:1	Waking up in the morning ‖ resurrection				×	×		
	84:11	Joseph's dream: sun, *moon*, and stars				×	×		
	94	The importance of being buried in Israel				×	×		
	95:1	A person will be resurrected in the same state as he/she died				×	×		
	96:5	The importance of being buried in Israel				×	×		
	102:2	Burial practices				×			×
Exodus	1:1	Esau denied the resurrection				×			×
	15:21	Ten things which God will renew in the Time to Come		×			×		
	32:2	People buried in Israel will resurrect first				×			×
	40:2	The Book of Adam				×			×
	48:2	The day of death is better than the day of birth since closer to the day of resurrection				×	×		
Leviticus	18:1	A person will be resurrected from the nut of the spinal column				×	×		
	27:4	Elijah, Elisha, and Ezekiel resurrected the dead → God will resurrect the dead				×	×		
Numbers	11:2	The Abrahamic promise				×			×
	14:1	God has already revived people				×	×		
	15:13	God has already revived people				×	×		
	19:13	The first wilderness generation also has a share in the world to come				×	×		

Book	Ref	Description									
Deuteronomy	2:9-10	The reason Moses had to die in the wilderness		x	x						
	3:15	Moses counted the patriarchs among the living righteous		x	x						
	7:6	God's three keys/rain ‖ resurrection		x	x						
	10:3	Everything that God does can also be done by the righteous		x	x						
Lamentations	1:45	The women who threw themselves into the sea believed in the resurrection		x	x						
	2:6	God gave a resurrection promise to Daniel		x	x						
	3:8	God renews our life each morning → resurrection		x	x						
Ruth	3:2	Some people will never resurrect		x	x						
	6:2	See Rab. Eccl. 7:17		x	xx						
Ecclesiastes	1:6-7	People will resurrect with their blemishes		x	x						
	1:19-20	As the river returns to its source so will people resurrect from the dead		x	x						
	3:2	Parallel between birth and death		x	x						
	3:18	God has already revived people		x	x						
	5:11, 17	Secret or a public resurrection?/Parallel between birth and death		x	x				x		
	7:16	Reward in the Age to Come		x	x						
	12:5	A person will be resurrected from the nut of the spinal column		x					x		
Esther	9:2	The dead will come alive after three days		x	x						
Song of Songs	1:9	Holy Spirit → resurrection → Elijah		x	x						
	2:2	The hidden bodies in the ground will resurrect		x	x						
	2:18	Acts of kindness → resurrection		x	x						
	7:15	Ezekiel brought the dead to life in the Valley of Dura									

Bibliography

Ahearne-Kroll, Patricia. "Joseph and Aseneth." Pages 2525–89 in vol. 3 of *Outside the Bible: Ancient Jewish Writings Related to Scripture*. Edited by Louis H. Feldman, James L. Kugel, and Lawrence H. Schiffman. Philadelphia: Jewish Publication Society of America, 2013.

Allen, Joel S. "Job 3: History of Interpretation." Pages 361–71 in *Dictionary of the Old Testament: Wisdom, Poetry and Writings*. Edited by Tremper Longman III and Peter Enns. Downers Grove, IL: InterVarsity, 2008.

Anderson, Gary A., and Michael E. Stone, eds. *A Synopsis of the Books of Adam and Eve: Second Revised Edition*. Society of Biblical Literature: Early Judaism and Its Literature 17. Atlanta: Scholars Press, 1999.

Anderson, Gary A. "*Life of Adam and Eve.*" Pages 1331–58 in vol. 2 of *Outside the Bible: Ancient Jewish Writings Related to Scripture*. Edited by Louis H. Feldman, James L. Kugel, and Lawrence H. Schiffman. Philadelphia: Jewish Publication Society of America, 2013.

Andersen, H. "4 Maccabees: A Translation and Introduction." *OTP* 2:531–64.

Atkinson, Kenneth. *An Intertextual Study of the Psalms of Solomon*. Studies in the Bible and Early Christianity 49. Lewiston, NY: Mellen, 2001.

———. "Psalms of Solomon." Pages 1903–23 in vol. 2 of *Outside the Bible: Ancient Jewish Writings Related to Scripture*. Edited by Louis H. Feldman, James L. Kugel, and Lawrence H. Schiffman. Philadelphia: Jewish Publication Society of America, 2013.

———. "Testament of Moses." Pages 1856–68 in vol. 2 of *Outside the Bible: Ancient Jewish Writings Related to Scripture*. Edited by Louis H. Feldman, James L. Kugel, and Lawrence H. Schiffman. Philadelphia: Jewish Publication Society of America, 2013.

Attridge, Harold W. "Testament of Job." Pages 1872–99 in vol. 2 of *Outside the Bible: Ancient Jewish Writings Related to Scripture*. Edited by Louis H. Feldman, James L. Kugel, and Lawrence H. Schiffman. Philadelphia: Jewish Publication Society of America, 2013.

Bader, Gershom. *Encyclopedia of Talmudic Sages*. Northvale, NJ: Jason Aronson, 1988.

Badina, Joel. "The Millennium." Pages 225–42 in *Symposium on Revelation – Book II*. Edited by Frank B. Holbrook. Daniel and Revelation Committee Series 7. Silver Springs, MD: Biblical Research Institute and General Conference of Seventh-day Adventists, 1992.

Bailey, Kenneth E. *Jesus through Middle Eastern Eyes: Cultural Studies in the Gospels*. Downers Grove, IL: InterVarsity, 2008.

Böttrich, Christfried. "Apocalyptic Tradition and Mystical Prayer in the *Ladder of Jacob*." *JSP* 23, no. 4 (2004): 290–306.

Buchanan, George Wesley. "Eschatology and the 'End of Days.'" *JNES* 20, no. 3 (1961): 188–93.

Burchard, C. "Joseph and Aseneth: A New Translation and Interpretation." *OTP* 2:177–247.
Cason, Thomas S. "The Rhetoric of Disablement and Repair in the Testament of Job." PhD diss., Florida State University, 2007.
Charles, Robert H. *The Greek Versions of the Testaments of the Twelve Patriarchs*. Oxford: Oxford University Press, 1960.
―――――, ed., *Commentary on the Pseudepigrapha of the Old Testament*. 2 vols. Oxford: Clarendon, 1913.
Charles, R. H. ed., *The Apocrypha and Pseudepigrapha of the Old Testament in English*. Oxford: Clarendon, 1913.
Charlesworth, James H. *Critical Reflections on the Odes of Solomon. Volume 1, Literary Setting, Textual Studies, Gnosticism, the Dead Sea Scrolls and the Gospels of John*. JSPSup 22. Sheffield: Sheffield Press, 1998.
―――. "Odes of Solomon." Pages 749–52 in *Dictionary of New Testament Background*. Edited by Craig A. Evans and Stanley E. Porter. Downers Grove, IL: InterVarsity, 2000.
―――. "Odes of Solomon: A New Translation and Introduction." *OTP* 2:725–71.
―――. "*History of the Rechabites*: A New Translation and Introduction." *OTP* 2:444.
Clarke, K. D. "Pseudo-Phocylides." Pages 868–9 in *Dictionary of New Testament Background*. Edited by Craig A. Evans and Stanley E. Porter. Downers Grove, IL: InterVarsity, 2000.
Collins, John J. "Life after Death in Pseudo-Phocylides." Pages 130–42 in *Jewish Cult and Hellenistic Culture*. JSJSup 100. Leiden: Brill, 2005.
―――. "Powers in Heaven, Gods and Angels in the Dead Sea Scrolls." Pages 1–28 in *Religion in the Dead Sea Scrolls*. Edited by J. J. Collins and R. A. Kugler. Grand Rapids: Eerdmans, 2000.
―――. "Testament." Pages 325–55 in Michael Stone, ed. *Jewish Writings of the Second Temple Period: Apocrypha, Pseudepigrapha, Qumran Sectarian Writings, Philo, Josephus*. Edited by Michael Stone. Assen: Van Gorcum; Philadelphia: Fortress, 1984.
Combs, Jason Robert. "A Ghost on the Water? Understanding an Absurdity in Mark 6:49–50." *JBL* 127, no. 2 (2008): 345–58.
DeSilva, David Arthur. "3 and 4 Maccabees." Pages 661–6 in *Dictionary of New Testament Background*. Edited by Craig A. Evans and Stanley E. Porter. Downers Grove, IL: InterVarsity, 2000.
―――. "4 Maccabees." Pages 2362–98 in vol. 3 of *Outside the Bible: Ancient Jewish Writings Related to Scripture*. Edited by Louis H. Feldman, James L. Kugel, and Lawrence H. Schiffman. Philadelphia: Jewish Publication Society of America, 2013.
―――. *4 Maccabees: Introduction and Commentary on the Greek Text in Codex Sinaiticus*. Septuagint Commentary Series. Leiden: Brill, 2006.
―――. "Apocrypha and Pseudepigrapha." Pages 58–64 in *Dictionary of New Testament Background*. Edited by Craig A. Evans and Stanley E. Porter. Downers Grove, IL: InterVarsity, 2000.
―――. "Testament of Moses." Pages 1192–9 in *Dictionary of New Testament Background*. Edited by Craig A. Evans and Stanley E. Porter. Downers Grove, IL: InterVarsity, 2000.
Doukhan, Jacques B. *Ecclesiastes: All Is Vanity*. Nampa, ID: Pacific, 2006.
Elledge, C. D. *Resurrection of the Dead in Early Judaism: 200 BCE – CE 200*. Oxford: Oxford University Press, 2017.
Evans, Craig A. *Ancient Texts for New Testament Studies: A Guide to the Background Literature*. Peabody, MA: Hendrickson, 2005.

Feldman, Louis H., James L. Kugel, and Lawrence H. Schiffman, eds. *Outside the Bible: Ancient Jewish Writings Related to Scripture*. 3 vols. Philadelphia: Jewish Publication Society of America, 2013.

Fiensy, D. A. "Hellenistic Synagogal Prayers: Introduction." *OTP* 2:671–6.

Fisk, B. N. "Rewritten Bible in Pseudepigrapha and Qumran." Pages 947–53 in *Dictionary of New Testament Background*. Edited by Craig A. Evans and Stanley E. Porter. Downers Grove, IL: InterVarsity, 2000.

Flusser, David. "Psalms, Hymns and Prayers." Pages 551–77 in Michael Stone, ed. *Jewish Writings of the Second Temple Period: Apocrypha, Pseudepigrapha, Qumran Sectarian Writings, Philo, Josephus*. Edited by Michael Stone. Assen: Van Gorcum; Philadelphia: Fortress, 1984.

Fox, Michael V. "The Rhetoric of Ezekiel's Vision of the Valley of the Bones." *HUCA* 51 (1980): 1–15.

Fritsch, C. T. "Pseudepigrapha." *IDB* 3:960–4.

Gonzalez, Eliezer. *The Fate of the Dead in Early Third Century North African Christianity: The Passion of Perpetua and Felicitas and Tertullian*. Studien und Texte zu Antike und Christentum 83. Tübingen: Mohr Siebeck, 2014.

Greenberg, Moshe. *Ezekiel 21–37: A New Translation with Introduction and Commentary*. Anchor Bible 22A. Garden City, NY: Doubleday, 1997.

Hare, Douglas R. A. "*Lives of the Prophets*." *DNTB* 653.

———. "The *Lives of the Prophets*: A New Translation and Introduction." *OTP* 2:385.

Harrington, Daniel J. "Pseudo-Philo." Pages 864–8 in *Dictionary of New Testament Background*. Edited by Craig A. Evans and Stanley E. Porter. Downers Grove, IL: InterVarsity, 2000.

———. "Pseudo-Philo: A New Translation and Introduction." *OTP* 2:297–377.

Herzer, Jens. *4 Baruch (Paraleipomena Jeremiou)*. Writings from the Greco-Roman World 22. Atlanta: Society of Biblical Literature, 2005.

Hodgens, David. "Our Resurrection Body: An Exegesis of 1 Corinthians 15:42–49." *MJT* 17 (2001): 65–91.

Hollander, Harm W., and Marinus De Jonge. *The Testaments of the Twelve Patriarchs: A Commentary*. SVTP 8. Leiden: Brill, 1985.

Instone-Brewer, David. *Prayer and Agriculture*. TRENT 1. Grand Rapids: Eerdmans, 2004.

Jacobson, Howard. "Pseudo-Philo, Book of Biblical Antiquities." Pages 470–613 in vol. 1 of *Outside the Bible: Ancient Jewish Writings Related to Scripture*. Edited by Louis H. Feldman, James L. Kugel, and Lawrence H. Schiffman. Philadelphia: Jewish Publication Society of America, 2013.

Johnson, M. D. "Life of Adam and Eve: A New Translation and Introduction." *OTP* 2:252.

Johnston, Philip S. *Shades of Sheol: Death and Afterlife in the Old Testament*. Downers Grove, IL: InterVarsity, 2002.

Kee, Howard Clark. "Testament of the Twelve Patriarchs." Pages 1200–5 in *Dictionary of New Testament Background*. Edited by Craig A. Evans and Stanley E. Porter. Downers Grove, IL: InterVarsity, 2000.

Klassen, William. "Joseph and Aseneth." Pages 588–9 in *Dictionary of New Testament Background*. Edited by Craig A. Evans and Stanley E. Porter. Downers Grove, IL: InterVarsity, 2000.

Knibb, M. A. "Martyrdom and Ascension of Isaiah: A New Translation and Introduction." *OTP* 2:143–76.

Knight, Chris H. "The Rechabites Revisited: The History of the Rechabites Twenty-Five Years On." *JSP* 23, no. 4 (2014): 290–306.

Knight, Jonathan M. "Testament of Abraham." Pages 1188–9 in *Dictionary of New Testament Background*. Edited by Craig A. Evans and Stanley E. Porter. Downers Grove, IL: InterVarsity, 2000.

———. *The Ascension of Isaiah*. Guides to the Apocrypha and Pseudepigrapha. Sheffield: Sheffield Academic, 1995.

Kolenkow, Anitra Bingham. "The Genre Testament and the Testament of Abraham." Pages 139–62 in *Studies on the Testament of Abraham*. Edited by George W. E. Nickelsburg. Missoula, MT: Scholars Press, 1976.

Kraft, Robert A. *The Testament of Job According to the SV Text*, Pseudepigrapha Series 4. Missoula, MT: Scholars Press, 1974.

Kugel, James L. "Jubilees." Pages 272–465 in vol. 1 of *Outside the Bible: Ancient Jewish Writings Related to Scripture*. Edited by Louis H. Feldman, James L. Kugel, and Lawrence H. Schiffman. Philadelphia: Jewish Publication Society of America, 2013.

———. "Testament of the Twelve Patriarchs." Pages 1697–855 in vol. 2 of *Outside the Bible: Ancient Jewish Writings Related to Scripture*. Edited by Louis H. Feldman, James L. Kugel, and Lawrence H. Schiffman. Philadelphia: Jewish Publication Society of America, 2013.

Kugler, Robert A. "Testaments." Pages 1295–7 in *The Eerdmans Dictionary of Early Judaism*. Edited by John J. Collins and Daniel C. Harlow. Grand Rapids: Eerdmans, 2010.

———. *The Testament of the Twelve Patriarchs*. Edited by Michael A. Knibb. Guides to Apocrypha and Pseudepigrapha. Sheffield: Sheffield Academic, 2001.

Lattke, Michael. *Odes of Solomon*. Hermeneia. Minneapolis: Fortress Press, 2009.

———. "Psalms of Solomon." Pages 853–7 in *Dictionary of New Testament Background*. Edited by Craig A. Evans and Stanley E. Porter. Downers Grove, IL: InterVarsity, 2000.

Levenson, Jon Douglas. *Resurrection and the Restoration of Israel: The Ultimate Victory of the God of Life*. New Haven: Yale University Press, 2006.

Levine, Amy-Jill. *Short Stories by Jesus: The Enigmatic Parables of a Controversial Rabbi*. Pbk ed. New York: HarperOne, 2015.

Levison, J. R. "Adam and Eve, Literature Concerning." Pages 1–6 in *Dictionary of New Testament Background*. Edited by Craig A. Evans and Stanley E. Porter. Downers Grove, IL: InterVarsity, 2000.

Lunt, H. G. "Ladder of Jacob: A New Translation and Introduction." *OTP* 2:401–11.

Milgrom, Jacob. *Leviticus 1–16: A New Translation with Introduction and Commentary*. AB 3. New York: Doubleday, 1991.

Morris, Leon. "Hebrews." Pages 3–158 in vol. 12 of *The Expositor's Bible Commentary*. Edited by Frank E. Gæbelein. Grand Rapids: Zondervan, 1981.

Nickelsburg, George W. E. "The Bible Rewritten and Expanded." Pages 89–156 in Michael Stone, ed. *Jewish Writings of the Second Temple Period: Apocrypha, Pseudepigrapha, Qumran Sectarian Writings, Philo, Josephus*. Edited by Michael Stone. Assen: Van Gorcum; Philadelphia: Fortress, 1984.

———. "Eschatology in the Testament of Abraham: A Study of the Judgment Scene in the Two Recensions." Pages 23–64 in *Studies on the Testament of Abraham*. Edited by George W. E. Nickelsburg. Missoula, MT: Scholars Press, 1976.

———. *Jewish Literature between the Bible and the Mishnah*. Philadelphia: Fortress, 1981.

———. *Resurrection, Immortality, and Eternal Life in Intertestamental Judaism and Early Christianity.* Harvard Theological Studies 56. Cambridge: Harvard University Press, 2006.

———. "Stories of Biblical and Early Post-Biblical Times." Pages 33–87 in Michael Stone, ed. *Jewish Writings of the Second Temple Period: Apocrypha, Pseudepigrapha, Qumran Sectarian Writings, Philo, Josephus.* Edited by Michael Stone. Assen: Van Gorcum. Philadelphia: Fortress, 1984.

———. "Structure and Message in the Testament of Abraham." Pages 85–93 in *Studies on the Testament of Abraham.* Edited by George W. E. Nickelsburg. Missoula, MT: Scholars Press, 1976.

Nickelsburg, George W. E., and James C. VanderKam. *1 Enoch 2: A Commentary on the Book of 1 Enoch, Chapters 37–82.* Hermeneia. Minneapolis: Fortress, 2012.

Novak, Michael Anthony. "The Odes of Solomon as Apocalyptic Literature." *Vigiliae Christianae* 66 (2012): 527–50.

Orlov, Andrei A. "The Face as the Heavenly Counterpart of the Visionary in the Slavonic *Ladder of Jacob.*" Pages 59–76 in *Of Scribes and Sages.* Edited by C. Evans. London: T&T Clark/Continuum, 2004.

Penner, Ken, and Michael S. Heiser, "Old Testament Greek Pseudepigrapha with Morphology." Bellingham, WA: Lexham Press, 2008.

Philonenko, March, and Howard Kee, *Les interpolations chrétiennes des Testaments des douze patriarches et les manuscrits de Qumrân.* CRHPR 35. Paris: Presses Universitaires de France, 1960.

Priest, John. "Testament of Moses: A New Translation and Introduction." *OTP* 1:919–34.

Reed, Annette Yoshiko. "Testament of Abraham." Pages 1671–96 in vol. 1 of *Outside the Bible: Ancient Jewish Writings Related to Scripture.* Edited by Louis H. Feldman, James L. Kugel, and Lawrence H. Schiffman. Philadelphia: Jewish Publication Society of America, 2013.

Reeves, John C. "Sefer Elijah." *Trajectories in Near Eastern Apocalyptic: A Postrabbinic Jewish Apocalypse Reader.* Resources for Biblical Study 45. Atlanta: Society of Biblical Literature, 2005.

Robinson, Stephen Edward. "4 Baruch: A New Translation and Introduction." *OTP* 2:413–25.

———. "Baruch, Book of 4." Pages 622 in vol. 1 of *Anchor Yale Bible Dictionary.* Edited by David Noel Freedman. New York: Doubleday, 1992.

———. "Testament of Adam: A New Translation and Introduction." *OTP* 1:989–95.

Sailhamer, John H. *The Pentateuch as Narrative: A Biblical-Theological Commentary.* Library of Biblical Interpretation. Grand Rapids: Zondervan, 1992.

Sanders, E. P. "Testament of Abraham: A New Translation and Introduction." *OTP* 1:871–90.

Shea, William. "The Parallel Literary Structure of Revelation 12 and 20." *AUSS* 23 (1985): 47.

Sigvartsen, Jan A. *Afterlife and Resurrection Beliefs in the Apocrypha and the Apocalyptic Literature.* JCT 30. London: Bloomsbury T&T Clark, 2019.

———. *Messiah Son of Joseph: A Type in both Jewish and Christian Traditions.* GlossaHouse Studies in Texts & Language Monograph Series 1. Wilmore, KY: GlossaHouse, 2018.

———. "The Afterlife in the Apocalyptic Literature of Second Temple Period Judaism." Paper presented at the Midwest Region Society of Biblical Literature, Olivet Nazarene University, Bourbonnais, IL, 8 February 2015.

———. "The Creation Order – Hierarchical or Egalitarian?" *AUSS* 53 (2015): 127–42.

Snodgrass, Klyne R. *Stories with Intent: A Comprehensive Guide to the Parables of Jesus.* Grand Rapids: Eerdmans, 2008.

Spero, Shubert. "Sons of God, Daughters of Men?" *JBQ* 40, no. 1 (2012): 15–18.

Spittler, Russel P. "Testament of Job." *Dictionary of New Testament Background*, 1189–92.

———. "Testament of Job." *OTP* 1:829–68.

Steiner, Richard C. *Disembodied Souls: The Nefesh in Israel and Kindred Spirits in the Ancient Near East, with an Appendix on the Katumuwa Inscription.* Society of Biblical Literature: Ancient Near East Monographs 11. Edited by Ehud Ben Zvi. Atlanta: SBL Press, 2015.

Stone, Michael E., and Matthias Henze. *4 Ezra and 2 Baruch: Translation, Introduction, and Notes.* Minneapolis: Fortress, 2013.

Suriano, Matthew J. *A History of Death in the Hebrew Bible.* Oxford: Oxford University Press, 2018.

Van der Horst, Pieter W. "Greek Synagogal Prayers." Pages 2110–37 in vol. 2 of *Outside the Bible: Ancient Jewish Writings Related to Scripture.* Edited by Louis H. Feldman, James L. Kugel, and Lawrence H. Schiffman. Philadelphia: Jewish Publication Society of America, 2013.

———. "Jewish Literature: Historians and Poets." Pages 580–4 in *Dictionary of New Testament Background.* Edited by Craig A. Evans and Stanley E. Porter. Downers Grove, IL: InterVarsity, 2000.

———. "Pseudo-Phocylides: A New Translation and Introduction." *OTP* 2:565–82.

———. "Pseudo-Phocylides on the Afterlife: A Rejoinder to John Collins." *JSJ* 35, no. 1 (2004): 70–5.

———. "Pseudo-Phocylides, Sentences." Pages 2353–61 in vol. 3 of *Outside the Bible: Ancient Jewish Writings Related to Scripture.* Edited by Louis H. Feldman, James L. Kugel, and Lawrence H. Schiffman. Philadelphia: Jewish Publication Society of America, 2013.

———. *The Sentences of Pseudo-Phocylides.* Leiden: Brill, 1978.

Van der Horst, Pieter W., and Judith H. Newman. *Early Jewish Prayers in Greek: A Commentary.* Commentaries on Early Jewish Literature. Berlin: de Gruyter, 2008.

VanderKam, James C. "Jubilees." Pages 600–3 in *Dictionary of New Testament Background.* Edited by Craig A. Evans and Stanley E. Porter. Downers Grove, IL: InterVarsity, 2000.

———. *The Book of Jubilees.* Edited by Michael A. Knibb. Guides to Apocrypha and Pseudepigrapha. Sheffield: Sheffield Academic, 2001.

Walton, John H. "Job 1: Book of." Pages 333–46 in *Dictionary of the Old Testament: Wisdom, Poetry and Writings.* Edited by Tremper Longman III and Peter Enns. Downers Grove, IL: InterVarsity, 2008.

Wilson, Walter T. *The Sentences of Pseudo-Phocylides.* Commentaries on Early Jewish Literature. New York: de Gruyter, 2005.

Wintermute, Orval S. "Jubilees: A New Translation and Introduction." *OTP* 2:35–142.

Wright, N. T. *The Resurrection of the Son of God.* Vol. 3 of Christian Origins and the Question of God. Minneapolis: Fortress, 2003.

Wright, Robert B. *The Psalms of Solomon: A Critical Edition of the Greek Text.* Jewish and Christian Texts in Contexts and Related Studies 1. New York: T&T Clark, 2007.

———. "Psalms of Solomon: A New Translation and Introduction." *OTP* 2:639–70.

Young, Brad. *The Parables: Jewish Tradition and Christian Interpretation.* Peabody, MA: Hendrickson, 1998.

Index of References

Hebrew Bible/Old Testament

Genesis

Ref	Pages	Ref	Pages	Ref	Pages
1–3	168, 169	3:4	241	9:4-6	227
1	55, 227	3:5	45	11:1-9	235
1:2	64, 224	3:6-7	73	11:6-9	23
1:8	227	3:8	73	12:1-3	96
1:16	171	3:9-11	73	14:9	234
1:26-27	46, 151, 154, 155, 227	3:12	73	15:15-16	1
1:26	168, 170, 171, 250, 268, 269	3:13	73	19:24	235
		3:14-15	73	22	132, 261, 263
1:27	241	3:15	45	22:1-19	140, 227
1:28	171, 250	3:16	73	22:10	129
1:29	171	3:17-19	73, 171, 270	25:8-9	178
2–3	46, 143	3:19	77, 79, 80, 156, 169, 171, 176, 223, 226, 227, 251, 264	25:17	178
2	155			28:11-22	96
2:2	252			30:8	17
2:7	70, 153, 155, 156, 168–70, 176, 223, 227			34:25-31	17
				35:16-20	17
		3:22-24	73	35:18	178
		3:22	45, 143, 151, 171, 227, 241	35:29	178
				35:32	16
				37–50	69
		3:23	171	37	17
		3:24	72, 143, 171, 227, 235, 250	37:2	17
2:8-9	171			37:9	137
2:8	171, 269			37:25-28	16
2:9	143, 171, 235			38	17
		4	72	39	17
		4:1–5:5	73	39:7-23	132, 140, 227, 263
2:15-17	270	4:1-6	140, 227		
2:15	171	4:8	132, 140, 227, 263	40:3	140, 227
2:17	45, 77, 168, 171			41:1-36	69
		4:9-10	227	41:39-44	69
2:22	131	5:24	34, 239	41:50-52	69
3	72, 73, 168, 270	6:2	47	41:50	69
		6:3	153-55, 227, 254	42:18-25	16
3:1-7	132, 171			46–47	69
3:1-6	73	6:4	47	47:11	16
3:1	73	8:21	252	49	10, 15
3:3	45, 77	8:22	252		

Genesis (cont.)

49:1	10	15:2-3	154, 227	*1 Samuel*	
49:8-12	11	18:15-18	12	2:20	154, 227
49:22-26	11	19:15	38, 41, 227	15:27	254
49:29	178	26:15	240	25:29	178
49:33	178	27:24	56	28:7-20	89, 226
50:13	178	28–32	227	28:12-19	90, 227
		28:15	42	28:13	254
Exodus		28:16-68	42	28:14-15	255
3:6	108, 109,	30:2	42	28:15	91
	129, 173,	30:3-10	42		
	226, 227,	30:11-20	227	*2 Samuel*	
	262	30:19-20	226	6	4
6:4	109	30:20	132, 145,		
16:31	70		146, 227	*1 Kings*	
16:35	70	31–34	42	4:20	249
17:16	248	31–32	15	6–7	4
19–24	55	31:29	10, 43	17:4	254
19:4	43	32–33	10	17:17-24	94
24:12	55	32:1-43	145, 227		
24:18	55	32:11-13	43, 240	*2 Kings*	
29:38-42	57	32:29	146, 226,	2	207
32:32-33	70		227	2:1	34
32:32	248	32:36	114	2:11	34, 239
34:29-35	89, 227	32:39	132, 145,	4:8-37	94
35:29-30	227		227, 264	13:20-21	94
		32:47	132, 145,	20:1-11	246
Leviticus			146, 226,		
18:29	179		227	*2 Chronicles*	
24:19-20	56	32:50	178	32:24	246
		33:3	130, 138,		
Numbers			226, 227,	*Job*	
20:24	178		263, 271	1–2	28
24:14	10, 12	34:5-6	34	1:3	28
24:17-19	10	34:6	253	1:6	47
24:17	234	34:10	12	1:21	264
25:6-13	140, 227			2:1	47
25:7-13	132, 263	*Joshua*		2:9	28
27:13	178	7	88, 227	3:19	264
28:3-8	57	7:25-26	88	9–16	28
31:2	178	10:24	240	14:1	264
		23–24	88	14:11	237
Deuteronomy		23:14	88, 253	18:5	238
8:3	70			29–31	28
10	89	*Judges*		33:29	267
		3:9-10	88	38:7	47

42:7-17	28	153	8	*Song of Songs*	
42:17	32, 33, 227, 237	154	8	2:1	233
		155	8	5:6	178
Psalms		*Proverbs*		*Isaiah*	
1	164	1:7	143	2:5	164, 227
1:5-6	164, 165, 226, 227	3	143	5:24	227
		3:18	132, 142, 143, 227, 264	6:3	257
1:5	164			11:2	234
1:6	164			11:4	247
2:10	267	20:27	164, 227	11:9	234
8:6	227			13:1	247
11:5-7	235	*Ecclesiastes*		13:10	43
13:4	20	2:26	219	13:19-22	247
20:4	272	3:14	219	24:22-23	235
21:3	272	3:17	219	24:23	43, 246
31:1	275	3:19-21	223	26	227
33:12	248	3:19-20	176	26:19-21	226
33:20 LXX	132	3:20	156, 227	26:19	163, 164, 227, 264
34	142	5:6	219		
34:16	142	5:15	264	34:4	43
34:19	132, 263	7:15-16	219	35:1	233
34:20	142, 227	7:15	219	35:4-7	226
42	247	7:18	219	35:10	270, 271
43:3	276	7:20	219	38	246
44	247	7:26	219	40:31	43, 240
49:13	267	8:2	219	43:2	132, 141, 227, 263
49:18	264	8:10	219		
50	247	8:11	219	44:23	234
50:1-6	226	8:12-14	219	49:6	226
69:28	70	8:12	219	49:7	250
71:1	275	8:14	219	49:26	250
73–83	247	9:2	219	52–53	226, 227
76:5	20	9:18	219	52:1-2	226
81:15	267	10:2	219	52:13–53:12	11
87:6	248	11:9–12:14	219	52:13	247
88	247	12:2	43	53:8	247
89	247	12:5	264	54:5	250
89:7	249	12:7	153, 155, 156, 176, 223, 227, 264	54:8-10	226
95:1	273			54:8	250
95:11	248			56:1	226
110	234			58:8	274
110:1	241	12:13-14	219	60:1	164, 227
116:7	178	12:13	219, 227	60:20	245
151	8			63:15	240
152	8			63:16	237

Isaiah (cont.)		3:6	263	*Hosea*	
64:4-11	226	3:18	140	5:1-2	94
64:8	237	4	227	6:2	163, 164, 226, 227
65:17	87, 226, 227	4:1-21	94		
65:22	143	5:7-13	236	14:5-7	233
66:1	250	6	129, 132		
66:22-24	226	6:1-28	140, 227	*Joel*	
66:22	87, 227	7	227	2–3	43
		7:9-14	223	8:1-2	94
Jeremiah		7:9-10	227		
2:1-19	94	7:10	70	*Amos*	
4:23-25	224	7:13-14	62	5:20	43
8:2	245	7:18	62, 227	7:1-3	94
16:4	264	7:21-22	223	8:9	43
22:19	264	7:22	62, 227		
25:30	240	7:25	62	*Obadiah*	
28:39	20	7:26-27	62, 223	9:1-5	94
31:33	76, 250	7:27	224, 227	18	227
35	102	8:14	223		
		9:2	236	*Jonah*	
Ezekiel		9:24-27	22	10:1-11	94
3:1-19	94	10:13	239		
9:6	245	10:21	239	*Micah*	
13:17-21	178	12	62, 162, 163, 227	1:3-4	43
18:31	76, 250			1:3	240
32:7	43	12:1-13	62	6:1-3	94
34	226	12:1-3	1, 227		
36:26	76, 250	12:1-2	227	*Nahum*	
37	220	12:1	26, 70, 239	11:1-4	94
37:1-14	95, 96, 220, 226, 227, 255	12:2-3	44, 227		
		12:2	20, 25-27, 64, 86, 87, 150, 162–4, 169, 227, 234-36, 248, 264, 267	*Habakkuk*	
				3	43
				12:1-13	94
37:1-10	175				
37:1-6	176, 274			*Zephaniah*	
37:2-3	132			1	43
37:2	264			13:1-3	94
37:8-10	176	12:3	43, 44, 89, 130, 151, 227, 240, 263		
37:11-14	145			*Haggai*	
				14:1-2	94
Daniel					
2	227	12:4	44		
2:34-35	62	12:7	62	*Zechariah*	
2:44-45	62	12:12	62, 68, 227, 246	3:2	237
3	129, 132, 261			14:5	63
		12:13	44, 227	14:15	68
3:1-30	140, 227			15:1-6	94

Index of References

Malachi
1:6	237
1:11	273
2:10	237
3:2-3	115, 137, 227, 261
3:24 MT	253
4:1-6	226
4:6	253
16:1-4	94

NEW TESTAMENT

Matthew
1:24	20
3	207
5:3	284
5:10-12	284
5:16	249
5:20	284
6:19-31	248
6:19-20	156, 284
7:13-14	284
7:21-23	284
8:11-12	284
8:11	235
8:24	20
9:18-25	284
9:24	20
10:8	284
10:28	137, 211, 262, 284
11:5	284
12:18	246
12:38-42	284
13:25	20
13:39	237
13:43	284
14:13-23	189
14:24	189, 190
14:25-27	189
16:1-4	284
16:14	255
16:18	275
16:21-28	284
16:27	63
17:1	207
17:2-4	284
17:3-4	34, 87
17:22-23	284
19:16-28	285
19:21	157
19:28-30	236
19:28	247
20:17-19	285
22:23	285
22:28	285
22:30	285
22:31-32	108
22:32	173, 271
24:22	253
24:29-31	63, 285
24:37-39	223
25:5	20
25:31-46	285
25:31	63
25:46	248
26:40	20
26:43	20
26:45	20
26:63-64	285
26:64	223, 237
27:52-53	285
27:52	20, 86
27:62-66	285
28:1-15	285
28:13	20

Mark
1:9-11	234
1:11	246
2:15	249
3:27	235
4:27	20
4:38	20
5:22	285
5:35-43	285
5:39	20
6:14	285
6:16	285
6:31-46	189
6:47-48	189
6:48-50	189
6:48	190
8:31	285
8:35	285
8:38	63
9:3	207
9:4-5	87, 285
9:5	207
9:7	246
10:17-31	248, 285
10:21	157
10:33-34	285
12:18-27	286
12:26-27	108
12:26	261, 262
13:20	253
13:24-27	63, 286
13:36	20
14:37	20
14:40	20
14:41	20
14:62	286
16:6	286
16:9	286
16:12	286
16:14	286
16:19	237

Luke
2:29-32	286
3:4-6	286
6:22-23	286
7:11-17	286
7:18-23	286
8:40-56	286
8:52	20
9:7-9	286
9:19	286
9:22	286
9:23-27	286
9:26	63
9:29	207
9:30-33	87, 287
9:30	207
9:32	20
10:8	70
10:19	235

Luke (cont.)		3:5	248	20:11-18	207
10:20	248, 287	3:14-18	288	20:26-29	207
11:14-22	235	3:16	272	21:1-13	207
11:29-32	287	4:14	273, 288	21:14	288
12:5-6	137	4:36	288	22:32	271
12:19	249	5:21-29	288		
12:20	153, 154	5:24	248	Acts	
12:33	157	5:26	271	1:22	289
12:37	246	5:28-29	223	2:22-27	175, 188
13:28-29	287	5:29	223	2:31-32	289
14:12-14	287	5:40	271	2:33	237
14:15	287	6:33-40	288	3:15	289
15:23	249	6:33-37	277	4:2	289
15:24	248	6:44	288	4:10	289
15:32	248	6:47	288	4:33	289
16:19-31	191, 210	6:51	288	5:30	289
16:23	270	6:54	288	7:60	20, 86
16:29-31	287	8:56	235	9:37	289
16:30	191	10:7-10	278	9:40-41	289
17:28-30	223	10:10	271	10:40	289
17:33	287	10:17-18	288	10:42-43	289
18:18-29	287	10:28	271	12:6	20
18:31-33	287	10:33-36	241	13:30	289
20:27-40	287	11:1-45	207	13:34	289
20:36	223	11:11	20, 86	13:36	20, 86
20:37-38	108	11:12	20	13:37	289
20:38	173, 271	11:13	20	13:46	289
21:19	287	11:24-26	288	16:34	249
21:36	287	11:25	271	17:3	289
22:30	247, 287	11:43-44	288	17:18	289
22:45	20	12:1	288	17:31	289
22:46	20	12:9-10	288	17:32	289
22:69	237	12:23-26	208	20:7-11	289
23:42-43	287	12:23-25	288	20:9	20
24:6-7	287	14:1-4	288	23:6-8	289
24:13-21	207	14:2	249	24:15	289
24:23	287	14:6	271	24:21	289
24:34	287	14:17	271	26:6-8	289
24:36-51	207	14:19	271	26:18	289
24:36-43	190, 191	14:26	271	26:23	289
24:46-47	287	15	274		
		15:8	276	Romans	
John		15:26	271	1:4	290
1:1	271, 277	17:1-9	276	1:16-17	290
1:4	271	17:22	235	2:5-16	290
1:9	257	18:36	34	2:14	171, 270
2:18-22	288	20:9	288	4:24-25	290

5:7	150	15:21	290	*Philippians*	
5:10	290	15:35	207	1:15	150
5:18-19	290	15:36-42	208	2:6-11	291
5:21	248	15:42-45	223	2:6-9	277
6:3-6	3	15:42-44	207	2:16	31
6:4-5	290	15:42	208, 290	3:10-11	291
6:8	290	15:43	208	3:14	291
6:9-10	290	15:44	208	3:20-21	291
6:9	109	15:45-48	208	3:21	223, 246
6:10-11	109	15:49	208	4:3	70
6:10	261	15:50-53	246		
6:11	109	15:50	208	*Colossians*	
7:4	290	15:51-54	207	1:9-14	291
8:11	290	15:51	20, 86, 236	1:15-20	274
8:34	290	15:52-56	208	2:12-13	291
8:38-39	290	15:54	273	2:20	291
10:5-9	290			3:1-4	291
11:26	237	*2 Corinthians*			
12:4	274	1:9	290	*1 Thessalonians*	
13:11	20	4:14	290	1:10	291
14:8	109, 261	4:18	248	3:13	63, 246
14:9	109, 290	5:1-10	290	4:13-18	291
14:10-12	290	5:1-4	246, 247	4:13-15	86
15:6	257	12:2	251	4:13	20
				4:14	20, 246
1 Corinthians		*Galatians*		4:15-17	223
2:3	248	1:1	291	4:15	20
4:9	137, 248, 263	2:2	31	5:6	20
		2:19	109, 261	5:7	20
6:2-3	224	5:7	31	5:10	20
6:14	290			5:23	156
6:17	271	*Ephesians*			
7:31	237	1:4	248	*2 Thessalonians*	
7:39	20, 86	1:6	246	1:5-10	291
9:24-27	137, 290	1:15-23	291	1:7	63, 246
9:24-26	31	1:17	237	1:8	247
9:25	247	1:20	237	2:8	247
11:30	20, 86	2:1-10	291		
13:12	237	2:5	248	*1 Timothy*	
15	3, 207, 208	2:19-22	291	1:1	172, 269
15:4	290	3:6	248, 291	6:12	291
15:6	20, 86	4:4	235	6:18-19	157, 291
15:12-57	290	4:7-13	291		
15:12-28	290	5:14	20	*2 Timothy*	
15:18	20, 86	6:12	246	1:10-12	291
15:20-28	48			2:5	31
15:20	20, 86			2:8-13	291

2 Timothy (cont.)		1 Peter		2:10	247
2:18-19	291	1:3-9	292	2:11	223
3:16	224	1:3-4	3	2:13	65
4:7-8	291	1:4	248	2:26	224
4:7	31, 247	1:11	292	3:4	247
		1:21	292	3:5	70
Titus		2:12	249	3:7	278
1:2	271	3:18-22	48, 175	3:21	65, 247, 293
2:11-14	291	3:18	292	4:4	247
3:7	291	3:19-20	188	6:9-11	191
		3:21	292	6:11	247
Hebrews		3:22	246	7:9	247
1:3	237	4:5-6	292	7:13	247
2:14-15	292	4:13	292	11:3	62
3:7–4:13	248, 273	4:16-18	292	12	65
4:12	156	5:1	292	12:6	62
6:2	292	5:4	247, 292	12:11	235
7:3	237			12:14	62
8:1	237	2 Peter		13:2	65
9:15	292	1:10-11	292	13:5	62
9:23-28	219	2:4-22	292	13:8	70
9:26	237	2:4	224	15:2	65
9:27-28	219, 292	3:4-13	292	17:8	70
10:1	237	3:4	20, 86	19:14	63, 65
10:12	237			19:18-21	223
10:14	237	1 John		19:20	246
10:34	248	2:17	237, 292	20	65
10:35-39	292	2:25	292	20:1-3	64, 65
11:4	292	3:14	248	20:2-3	224
11:5	34	4:17	292	20:2	235
11:6	292	5:10-13	292	20:4-6	65, 223, 293
11:10	292			20:4	65, 66, 224, 235, 246
11:13	292	Jude			
11:16	292	1:9	87, 207	20:5	65
11:19	292	1:14	63	20:6	65, 66, 223
11:35	292	6	224, 293	20:7-15	65, 224
11:39-40	292	9	293	20:9-10	65
12:1	31	14–15	293	20:11-15	247
		14	246	20:12-15	70, 293
James		21	293	20:12	248
1:12	247			20:13	277
1:17	248	Revelation		20:14-15	223
1:23	237	1:7	223	20:14	235
4:10	292	1:18	273, 293	20:15	248
5:11	31	2:7	143, 274, 293	21–22	66, 224
				21:1	66

21:2	66	7:6	133, 226	61:1-5	194
21:8	65	7:7-9	110	62:13-16	194
22:2	143, 235	7:9	134, 136, 193	62:15-16	194
22:4	235			62:15	226
22:14	143	7:10-12	110	81:4	70
22:19	143, 235	7:11	134, 136, 193	83–90	195
				89:36-38	195

APOCRYPHA
2 Esdras

3–14	6	7:13-14	110	89:61-77	70
		7:14	134, 136	89:75	195
		7:15-17	110	90:17-20	70
		7:17	134	90:20-37	195

Wisdom of Solomon

		7:18-19	110	90:26-27	195
2:21-22	193	7:19	134	90:26	63
3:1-4	180	7:20-23	110	90:33	226
3:5-6	226, 227	7:22	136	90:34-38	195
3:7-13	193	7:23	134, 226	91-105	181, 211
3:7-8	227	7:24-26	110	98:76	70
3:18	193	7:27-29	110	102:4–104:8	227
4:16	193	7:28-29	226	102:4–103:4	181
4:20–5:14	193	7:29	134	103:5-8	181
7:9	227	7:30-40	110	104:1	70
13:6	150	7:31	134	104:2-6	151
14:19	150	7:35	134	104:7	70
15:8	153, 154	7:36	134, 193	106–108	181, 195
		7:41-42	110	108	195

Sirach

		7:41	106	108:11	195
1:26	143	12:44-45	193	108:12	195
7:17	226	14:46	193	108:3	70
19:20	143			108:6-7	181
24:23	143	PSEUDEPIGRAPHA			
44:1–49:16	2	*1 Enoch*		*2 Baruch*	
44:7-15	2	1–36	194, 211	14:12	183
44:10	2	1:7	194	21:23-24	183
48:1-11	226	1:9	194	21:23	183
		5:7-10	194	24:1	70, 183
2 Maccabees		5:7	194	30:1-5	199
2:1-8	95	10:11-15	22	30:1-2	183
2:4-8	95	22:2-3	180	30:2	183
6	106	22:3-4	194	42:8	183, 199
6:20-21	111	22:9-13	180	49–52	199
7	42, 110, 111, 133, 136, 147	22:13	194	49–51	227
		24:2–25:6	194	50:2-4	208
		37–71	194, 211	50:2	183
7:1-40	106	47:3	70	51:2	199
7:1-2	110	51:1-5	194, 227	51:3	199
7:3-6	110	51:1	194	51:5	199

2 Baruch (cont.)		3:21	98, 99	8–18	107, 109–11,
51:10	199	5:1-2	99		133
51:12	199	5:4	99	8:1–12:19	106
57:2	199	5:7	99	8:1–9:10	110, 136
59:10	63	5:22	98	9:1-2	107
76:2	183	5:34	98, 101	9:7-9	136, 261
		6:1-10	256	9:7	137
2 Enoch		6:6-10	54, 99, 205,	9:8-9	105, 185,
8:1–9:1	196		244		260
22:8	196, 227	6:6	99	9:8	133, 137,
22:10	196, 227	6:7	97		147, 148
32J	80	6:8-10	99	9:9	133, 147,
32:1J	196, 226	6:13	97		148
33:1-2	48	6:20-21	98	9:11-25	110
39:5	196	6:25	97	9:21-22	261
42:3-14	196	7–8	97	9:22	105, 133,
42:7	196	7	101		137, 260
44	196	7:12-21	256	9:26-32	110
58:6J	181	7:18	54, 99, 100,	9:32	134, 148
65:6J	196		244	10:1-11	110
66:7	196, 227	8:1-2	98	10:1-4	261
		8:12–9:32	97, 100	10:2-4	105, 260
3 Enoch		9	101	10:4	134
2:1	187	9:1-14	257	10:11	134
6:2	34	9:5	100	10:12-21	110
15:1	181, 187,	9:7	100	10:15	134, 147,
	188	9:8	100		148, 185
24:11	187	9:12-14	54, 99, 100,	11:1-12	110
26:3	187		205, 244	11:3	134, 148
27:7-10	181	9:12	100	11:13-27	110
28:7-10	226	9:14	100, 101	11:23	134
28:10	187			12:1-19	110
32:2	187	4 Ezra		12:12	134, 147,
43:2	181, 188	7:32-33	227		148
44:3	187	7:36	63	12:18	134
44:5-6	181	7:75-101	180	13:1–18:19	110
44:5	187, 188	7:97	226	13:1–14:10	110
44:6	187, 188	7:129	226	13:8-18	261
				13:9-18	105, 260
4 Baruch		4 Maccabees		13:14	137
1–4	97, 98	3:19–4:26	106	13:15	135, 147
1–3	99	5:1–6:30	106	13:17	107, 135
3–6	101	7:16-23	107, 261	14:2-6	262
3:8-20	95	7:18-19	105, 107–9,	14:4-6	105, 260
3:12	99		226, 260	14:5	135, 137,
3:13	99	7:18	147		147
3:14	98, 99	7:19	109	14:6	137

14:11–17:1	106	18:14	141	22:1-4	73, 78
14:11–15:32	110	18:15	142	23:1-3	73
15:2-4	262	18:16	143, 227	23:4-5	73
15:2	137	18:17	144, 220	23:4	73
15:3-4	105, 260	18:18-19	145, 226	24:1-4	73
15:3	135, 137, 147	18:20-24	110	25:1-4	73
		18:22	136, 148	26:1-4	73
15:24	135	18:23	136, 137	27:1–29:6	73
15:25-28	262			28	250
15:26	137	*Apocalypse of Elijah*		28:4	53, 72, 73, 77, 84, 204, 243
15:27	105, 137, 260	1:8-10	200		
		1:8	200		
16:1–18:5	110	1:9	200	31–43	72
16:12-13	105, 260, 262	1:10	200	37	251
		4:5	200	37:2	77
16:13	135, 137	4:15	200	37:5	53, 72, 73, 77, 78, 84, 185, 204, 243
16:24-25	262	4:25-26	200		
16:25	105, 107, 135, 147, 260	4:25	184		
		4:27-29	200		
		4:27	200	38:3	78
17:4-6	263	5:2-6	200	39	251
17:4-5	105, 260	5:36-39	200	39:1	78, 84
17:4	137			39:2-3	53, 72, 73, 78, 79, 84, 204, 243
17:5	108, 135, 137, 138, 227	*Apocryphon of Ezekiel*			
		Frag. 1	226		
				39:2	72, 84
17:11-12	105, 260, 263	*Apocalypse of Moses*		39:3	79, 84
		1–4	72	41	53, 243, 251
17:12	135, 137	5–14	72	41:1-3	79, 80, 84, 204
17:14	137	10	250		
17:15	135, 147	10:2	53, 72–4, 84, 204, 243	41:1-2	80, 226
17:17-21	138, 226, 260, 263			41:3	72
		13	84, 250	43	72, 251
17:18	138	13:1-2	76	43:1	84
17:21	105, 139	13:2-6	53, 243	43:2-3	53, 81, 185, 204, 243
18:3-5	263	13:2	74		
18:3	105, 135, 137, 260	13:3-5	72–5, 84, 204	43:2	72, 73
		13:3	84	43:3	83, 84
18:5	135	13:4	76, 84		
18:6-19	139	13:5	76	*Apocalypse of Sedrach*	
18:6-9	110	13:6	84, 185	1:21	198
18:10-23	105, 260, 263	15–30	72	2:5	183, 198
		15:1–16:4	73	4:1	183
18:10-19	110	17:1–20:5	73	9:1	183, 198
18:10-13	139	20:4-5	99	10:1-4	183
18:11-13	140	21:1-6	73	11:11	183, 198
18:12	141			14:5	183, 198

Apocalypse of Sedrach
(cont.)
14:9	183
15:5	183, 198
16:3	183
16:5-6	198
16:6	183, 198

Apocalypse of Zephaniah
2:7	187
4:7	182
5:1-6	187
7:1–9:5	182
7:9	187
8:1	187
8:3	187
9:4-5	187
10:4-9	182, 187
10:12-14	182, 187

Ascension of Isaiah
9:20	70

Books of Adam and Eve
Armenian tradition
37(10):2	74
[41](13):2a	74
42(13):3a-4	75
[42](13):4	76
(43):2-3	81
[44](15):1–	
[44](16):4b	73
[44](17):1–	
[44](20):5	73
[44](21):1–	
[44](21):6	73
[44](22):1–	
[44](22):4	73
[44](22):1-4	78
[44](23):1–	
[44](23):5	73
[44](23):4a	73
[44](23):4b–	
[44](23):5	73
[44](24):1–	
[44](24):4	73
[44](25):1–	
[44](25):4	73
[44](26):1–	
[44](26):4	73
[44](27):1–	
[44](29):6	73
[44](28):4	77
[47](39):1	78
[47](39):2-3	79
[47](39):3	79
[48](41):1-3	80
[51](43):2-3	81

Georgian tradition
37(10):2	74
[41](13):2a	74
42(13):3a-4	75
[42](13):4	76
(43):2-3	81
[44](15):1–	
[44](16):4b	73
[44](17):1–	
[44](20):5	73
[44](21):1–	
[44](21):6	73
[44](22):1–	
[44](22):4	73
[44](22):1-4	78
[44](23):1–	
[44](23):5	73
[44](23):4a	73
[44](23):4b–	
[44](23):5	73
[44](24):1–	
[44](24):4	73
[44](25):1–	
[44](25):4	73
[44](26):1–	
[44](26):4	73
[44](27):1–	
[44](29):6	73
[44](28):4	77
[47](37):5	78
[47](39):1	78
[47](39):2-3	79
[47](39):3	79
[48](41):1-3	80
[51](43):2-3	81

Slavonic tradition
11-15.6a	74
18-20.1–	
18-20.6	73
18-20.7–	
21-22.4a	73
21-22.4b–	
21-22.8	73
23-24.1–	
23-24.5	73
23-24.1-4	78
23-24.6–	
23-24.9	73
25-27.1–	
25-27.12	73
45:46.2b	78
49-50.1-3	80
49-50.4	83
49-50.3-4	81

Greek Apocalypse of Ezra
1:23	198
2:26	198
4:6-24	182, 187
4:36-43	198
4:36	198
5:20-28	182
5:22	198
5:23-28	187
6:3	182
6:17	182
6:21	182
7:2-3	182

Hellenistic Synagogal Prayers
3:19-27	170, 268
3:21	168, 174
3:24-27	161, 168, 172, 186, 206, 265
3:24	172, 174

3:25-26	80, 226	14–16	54, 244	27:10	53, 69, 243
3:26	169, 174	14:1–16:8	102	29:8-9	69
3:27	169	14:1	102		
7:9-12	269	14:2-5	102	*Jubilees*	
7:9-11	186	14:2	102	1	56
7:9	169, 174	15:4	102	1:4	55
7:10-11	174	15:7	102	2–4	56
7:10	169	15:8	102	2:24-33	56
7:11	161, 168,	15:9	102	3:5-6	56
	169, 174,	15:10	102	3:9-14	56
	206, 265	16:1	102	3:10-14	56
12:35-52	170, 269	16:4	102	3:13-19	56
12:37	172, 174	19–23	102	3:17-22	56
12:45	172, 174			3:23-38	56
12:46-50	161, 168,	*Joseph and Aseneth*		3:29-31	56
	169, 186,	1–21	69	3:31-32	56
	206, 265	1–17	69	4:24	52, 55, 242
12:47	172, 174	1:1	69	5–10	56
12:49-50	80, 172, 226	8:8	69	5:10	52, 55, 242
12:49	174	8:9	69	10:15	52, 55, 242
12:50	174	8:10-11	53, 243, 247	10:17	52, 55, 242
12:52	172	12:12	53, 69, 243	11:1–23:8	56
14–16	257	12:15	248	13:25-27	56
16	174, 270	15:1	70	14:20	56
16:2-4	173	15:2-6	248	15:25-34	56
16:3	173, 174	15:3-6	53, 243	16:3-4	56
16:4	173	15:4	70	16:9	56
16:7-9	161, 168,	15:5	70	16:28-31	56
	172, 186,	15:7	53, 243, 248	18:18-19	56
	206, 226,	15:12	53, 243, 248	23:1	52, 55, 242
	265	15:13–17:4	70	23:9-32	55, 56
16:7	173, 174	16:8	53, 70, 243,	23:11	52, 55, 242
16:8	173		248	23:16-31	57
16:9	173, 174	16:13-14	70	23:27-31	52, 245
16:10	173	16:14	70	23:29-31	55, 57, 58
16:11	173	16:20-21	70	23:30-31	58
16:12-13	173	16:21-23	53, 243, 249	23:30	57, 58
16:12	173	16:22-23	71	23:31	57, 58
16:14	173	18–21	69	23:32	56
		20:6-8	249	24–45	56
History of the Rechabites		20:7-8	71	24:33	56
1–2	102	20:7	53, 243	28:6-7	56
1:1-3	102	22–29	69	30:8-17	56
3–15	102	22:8-9	249	30:18-23	56
8:1–10:8	102	22:9	53, 69, 243	30:23	52, 55, 242
11–16	102	27:9-10	250	31:31-32	56

Jubilees (cont.)

32:9-15	56	14:1-2	94	4:14-15	68
33:10-20	56	15:1-6	94	4:14	62, 63, 68
36:10-11	52, 55, 242	15:5	94	4:15	63
36:18	52, 55, 242	16:1-4	94	4:16	64, 65, 68, 184, 203
37:19	52, 55, 242	17:1-4	94		
39:6	52, 55, 242	18:1-5	94	4:17	64, 68
41:23-26	56	19:1-2	94	4:18-19	68, 203
45:15	52, 55, 242	20:1-2	94	4:18	63, 64, 67, 68
46–50	56	21:1-15	94		
49:2-17	56	21:3	94	5:1-16	59, 60
49:22-23	56	21:7	94	6–11	59, 60
		22:1-17	94	6:1-17	60
		22:9-10	94	6:1	59

Ladder of Jacob

1:9-11	96	22:17	94	7:1-8	60
7	96	23:1-2	94	7:4	52, 242
7:10-25	256			7:9-12	60
7:21	54, 96, 97, 244	*Martyrdom and Ascension of Isaiah*		7:13-17	60
				7:18-23	60
		1–5	59, 60	7:22	63

Lives of the Prophets

		1:1–3:12	59	7:24-27	60
1:1-13	94	1:1-13	60	7:28-31	60
1:8	94	1:1	59	7:32-37	60
2:1-19	94	1:2-6	59-61	8:1-15	60
2:4	94	1:2	61, 67	8:14-15	68, 184, 203
2:11-19	54, 94, 95, 204, 244, 255	1:3-5	52, 60, 61, 242, 246	8:14	52, 63, 242
				8:16-28	60
		1:3	63	8:23	52, 242
2:15	95	1:5	63	8:26	63
2:19	94	2:1-6	60	8:27	52, 242
3:1-19	94	2:7-16	60	9:1-5	60
3:10-12	54, 94, 204, 244, 255	3:1-12	60	9:2	63
		3:13–4:22	7, 59	9:6-18	60
		3:13-20	60, 62	9:6-11	60, 247
3:12	95, 204, 220, 226	3:15-20	60, 61, 246	9:7-11	52, 242
		3:15	62	9:7-9	63, 66, 68, 184, 203
4:1-21	94	3:16	62		
5:1-2	94	3:17-18	62	9:9	63, 66
6:1-3	94	3:18	52, 242	9:12-16	66
7:1-3	94	3:21-31	60	9:16-18	52, 60, 66, 242, 247
8:1-2	94	3:25	63		
9:1-5	94	4:1-13	60	9:17-18	63, 67
10:1-11	94	4:12	62, 68	9:19-23	60
10:5-6	94	4:13	62	9:24-26	60, 63
11:1-4	94	4:14-22	52, 60, 242, 246	9:27-32	60
12:1-13	94			9:33-36	60
13:1-3	94	4:14-18	62, 65-67, 203, 227	9:37-42	60
13:2	94			10:1-6	61

10:7-16	61	22:8-12	161, 175, 188, 266, 274	*Pseudo-Philo*	
10:8	67			1–8	86
10:17-31	61			3:9-10	85, 86, 93, 204, 252
11:1-16	61	22:8-10	175, 176, 220, 226		
11:17-21	61			3:9	87, 93, 204
11:22-33	61	23–25	175	3:10	55, 85–7, 93, 226, 227, 244
11:34-35	61	25	175		
11:35	52, 242	25:8-9	266, 275		
11:36-43	61	26	175	6:3	244
11:40	63	27	175	9–12	86
		28–29	175	13	86
Odes of Solomon		28	175	14–18	86
1	175	28:6-8	266, 275	16:3	55, 85, 86, 93, 185, 204, 252
3–15	175	29–33	175		
3	175	29	175		
3:7-9	271	29:1-4	275	19	86
3:8-9	266	29:3-4	266	19:2	55, 85, 86, 244
5–11	175	31	175		
5	175	31:4	266, 276	19:6-7	86
7	175	31:6-7	266, 276	19:6	55, 85, 86, 244
9	266, 272	31:13	266, 276		
10:1-2	272	33–34	175	19:7	85
10:2	266	33:8-12	266, 276	19:12-13	55, 85–7, 93, 204, 244, 253
10:5-6	272	35–37	175		
10:6	266	36:1-2	276		
11	175	36:1	266	19:13	85
11:2	266, 273	38	175	19:15	85, 93, 204
11:12	266, 273	38:1-3	276	20–24	86
11:16	266, 273	38:3	266	23:6	85, 86, 93, 185
11:18	266, 273	39	175		
15	175	40	175	23:12-13	253
15:8-10	266, 273	40:4-6	277	23:13	55, 85, 86, 93, 185, 204, 244
17–23	175	40:6	266		
17–18	175	41–42	175		
17	175	41:11-15	277	25–29	86
17:12-16	274	41:11	266	25:7	55, 85, 86, 88, 93, 204, 244, 253
17:12-15	161, 175, 188, 266	42	175		
		42:11-20	161, 175, 176, 186, 188, 206, 266, 277		
17:13-15	175			26:12	85, 93, 204
20–21	175			28:8	48
20:7-9	266, 274			28:10	55, 85, 86, 93, 185, 244
21:1-3	274	42:14	176, 188		
21:2	266	42:15-17	176, 188, 206	29:4	55, 85, 86, 244
22	175				
22:4-12	175, 206	42:18	176, 206	30–33	86
		42:20	176, 188, 206	31:7	86, 93, 185
				32:17	85

Pseudo-Philo (cont.)		70–96	149	2:34	162, 163, 167
33:1-5	88, 227	91-115	105, 260		
33:1-3	253	97–98	149	2:35	162, 163, 167
33:2-5	85, 86, 93	97-115	149, 185, 264		
33:2-3	55, 244			2:36	162, 167
33:2	89	97-102	149	3	164
33:3	89	98	158	3:3-8	163
33:4	89, 93	99-101	150	3:9-10	163
33:5	89	102	150	3:11-16	267
33:6	55, 85, 86, 244	103-104	149, 150, 158, 205	3:11-12	160–3, 167, 206, 227, 265
34–48	86	104	151, 158		
35:3	55, 85, 86, 244	104b	227	3:12	162, 164, 167, 206
		105-108	152		
36:4	86, 93, 185	105	152, 158	4:24-25	161, 167
38:4	86, 93, 185	106	152-54, 158, 159	9:5	161, 167
44:10	85, 86, 93, 185			13:6	161, 167
		107-108	156	13:11	161, 162, 167
48:1	55, 85, 86, 93, 204, 244, 254	107	152		
		108	158	14	164
		109-110	156	14:1-5	164
49–65	86	110	158	14:3	162
51:5	85, 86, 93, 185	111-113	152, 157	14:6-10	267
		111	158	14:6-8	164
62:9	55, 85, 86, 244, 254	112-113	158	14:9-10	160–2, 164, 165, 167, 206, 226, 265
		114-115	157		
63:4	86, 93, 185	115	152, 156		
64:4-9	86	116-121	149		
64:5-8	90, 226	117	158	14:9	164
64:6-9	55, 89, 244, 254	122-131	149	15	165
		125	158	15:1-7	165, 206
64:6	204	132-152	149	15:6	165
64:7	91, 92	153-174	149	15:7-13	268
		175-227	149	15:8-12	165
Pseudo-Phocylides				15:8-11	165
3–8	149	*Psalms of Solomon*		15:8-9	161, 167
8	158	2	162	15:8	165
9–21	149	2:18	161, 167, 267	15:9	165
11	158			15:10-13	160, 162, 165, 206, 265
17	158	2:28-35	267		
22–41	149	2:31-35	160, 265		
29	158	2:31	161–3, 167, 206, 227	15:10	165
42–47	149			15:12-13	162
48–58	149	2:32-35	162	15:12	161, 165, 167
54	158	2:33	162, 167		
59–69	149	2:34-35	161, 167, 206	15:13	165

16:5	161, 167	8.205-212	197, 226	B14:6	39
17:10	161, 167	8.226-228	197	SrB9:8	39
		8.310-311	188		
Questions of Ezra		8.350-358	181	*Testament of Adam*	
A5	198	8.401	181	1:1–2:12	44
A10	183, 198	8.413-416	197	3:1-6	44
A19-21	183, 187	Frag. 1	221	3:1	45, 46
B12-14	198			3:2-4	241
B13	198	*Vision of Ezra*		3:2-3	45
B2	183	1:1-59	183	3:2	14, 45, 48, 203, 232
B3	198	1:8-55	187		
B5-9	183	1:61	187	3:3-5	46, 47, 151, 203
Sibylline Oracles		*Testament of Abraham*		3:3-4	49, 203
1	211	A1:7	37	3:3	45, 48, 203
1.378	188	A9:6	37	3:4	14, 45, 46, 49
2	211, 221	A10:6	37		
2.199-200	181	A10:9	37	3:5	46, 47, 49, 203
2.211-226	226	A10:11	37		
2.217-218	181	A10:13	37	3:6	48
2.221-251	196	A10:14	37	4:1-8	44
2.221-226	197, 220	A10:15	37		
2.221-222	196	A11:1–13:5	37, 39	*Testament of Asher*	
2.226	196	A11:9-12	41	1:1-2	18
2.227-237	181	A11:10	37	1:3–6:5	18
2.238-250	196	A11:11	37, 41	7:1-3	18
2.245-246	196	A13:6	38	7:3-5	16
4	221	A13:7	38, 41	7:3	18
4.43-44	197	A13:8	37, 38, 41	7:4-7	18
4.45-46	197	A14:4	39, 41	8:1-2	18
4.179-92	197	A14:6	39, 41	8:1	13, 19, 27, 43, 231, 233
4.181-182	197, 220, 226	A18:9-11	39		
		A20:9	39	*Testament of Benjamin*	
4.181	197	A20:10	39	1:1-6	18
4.184-186	197	A20:11	39	1:3-6	17
4.186	63	A18:3	39	2:1-5	18
4.187	197	B7:8	37	3:1–8:3	18
7	211, 216, 221	B7:15-16	39, 41	3:8	16, 18, 25
		B7:16	14	9	25
7.126-128	197	B12:1-12	37	9:1-3	18
7.144-151	197	B12:3	37	9:1-2	25, 26
7.144-145	197	B12:7	37	9:1	21, 25
8	211, 216, 221	B12:10	37	9:2-3	16
		B12:12	37	9:2	25
8.82-83	197	B12:13	37	9:3-5	16, 18
8.96-99	80, 169, 226	B14:5	39		

Testament of Benjamin		7:1	13, 19, 27, 43, 231, 233	5:1-3	29–31
9:3	25			6:1–27:7	28, 29
10:1–11:5	18, 25			6:1–8:3	29
10:2-11	236	*Testament of Gad*		6:1-13	29
10:4-11	201	1:1-2	18	8:1-3	29
10:4-10	13, 21, 25, 27, 231	1:3–2:5	18	9:1–15:9	29
		1:3-9	17	9:1-8	29
10:5-10	21, 25	3:1–7:7	18	9:3	28
10:5	25	8:1-2	18	10:1-6	29
10:6-10	16, 17	8:1	13, 19, 27, 43, 231, 233	11:1–12:3	29
10:6-8	21			13:1-7	29
10:6	21, 25	8:2	16, 18	13:1-6	29
10:7	18	8:3-4	18	14:1–15:9	29
10:8-10	26	8:3	18	16:1–26:6	29
10:8	18, 26, 201, 227			17:1–19:2	29
		Testament of Issachar		21:1–26:6	29
10:9	18, 26	1:1	18	21:1–22:2	29
10:10-11	27	1:2–3:8	18	21:1	31
10:10	25, 27, 201	1:2–2:5	17	22:3–23:11	29
10:11	21	3:5	20	24:1-10	28, 29
11:2-5	16, 25	4:1–5:8	18	25:1-8	29
11:2	25	6:1-4	18	25:9-10	28, 29
12:1-4	18	7:1-7	18	26:1-6	29
		7:7	16, 18	27:1-7	29
Testament of Dan		7:8-9	18	28:1–45:4	29
1:1-2	18	7:9	13, 19, 27, 43, 231, 233	28:1–30:3	29
1:3-9	18			31	31
1:4-9	17			31:1–34:5	29
2:1–5:5	18	*Testament of Job*		31:1-6	29
3:4	21	1:1-7	29	31:7–32:12	29, 33
5:5-9	24	1:1	29	33	14, 28, 232, 237
5:6-13	18	1:2-7	29		
5:7-13	13, 17, 21, 24, 27, 201, 231, 236	2:1–50:3	29	33:1-9	29, 33
		2:1–5:3	29	33:2-3	202
		2:1–3:7	29	33:2	33
5:10	16, 18, 24	4:1-11	29-31	33:3	33
5:11	21, 24, 27, 184	4:3-11	237	33:5-9	34
		4:4-11	32, 33, 227	34:1-5	29
5:12-13	16	4:4-5	31	34:1	34
5:12	24	4:4	30	35:1–38:5	29, 30
5:13	18, 24	4:6-9	31	36:3	34
6:1-11	18	4:7-8	31	37:5-7	30
6:6-7	16	4:9	14, 28, 33, 232	38:6-8	29
6:7	18			39:1–40:14	29
6:9	16, 18	4:10	31	39:4-11	34, 202
7:1-3	18	4:11	31	39:8-12	238

39:11	34, 35, 202	53	14, 232	*Testament of Levi*	
39:12	14, 28, 232	53:5	35	1:1-2	18
40:1-6	202	53:7	35, 43, 239	2:1–12:5	18
40:1	34, 202			2:1-2	18
40:4	35	*Testament of Joseph*		2:2	17
40:6	35	1:1	18	2:3–5:7	18
41:1–45:4	29	1:2–16:5	18	2:5	20
41:1-6	29	10–16	17	2:11	16, 18
41:4	14, 28, 34, 232, 237	17:1–18:4	18	3:1-2	21, 23, 27, 184
		19:1-10	18		
41:5	34	19:3-6	16	4:1	16, 18
42:1-8	29	19:7	16	4:4	16, 18
42:1-2	34	19:8	16, 18	4:5	16
43	14, 28, 232, 238	19:11-12	18	5:2	16
		19:11	16, 18	5:7	21
43:1-17	29, 35	20:1-6	18	6:1–7:4	18
43:4-13	34	20:4-5	233	6:3–7:4	17
43:5	35	20:4	13, 19, 27, 43, 231	8:1-19	18
43:7	35			8:5	16
43:10	35			8:12-15	16
43:11	35	*Testament of Judah*		8:18	21
43:13	35	1:1-6	18	9:1-14	18
43:16	35	2:1–12:12	18	10:1-5	18
43:17	35	8–12	17	10:2	16
44:1-5	29	13:1–20:5	18	10:3	16
45:1-4	28, 29	18:1	21, 23	10:5	21
46–53	28	18:4	20	10:14	21
46:1–53:8	35, 202	21–25	23	11:1–12:5	18
46:1–50:3	30	21:1–25:5	18	12:2-3	18
46:1–47:11	30	21:2-5	23	13:1-9	18
47:2	35	22:2	16, 23	14:1–18:14	18
47:11	14, 28, 35, 184, 232, 239	23:5	23	14:1	16, 18, 22
		24:1-2	23	14:2	16, 18
		24:2	16	16:3	16, 18
48:1–50:3	30	24:4	16, 18	16:5	16
48:2	35	24:6	23	17:1	22
49:1	35	25	13, 21, 23, 27, 201, 231, 235	17:2	16, 18
50:2	35			18:1-14	234
51:1–53:8	30			18:1	23
51:1-4	30	25:1	21, 23, 201	18:3	16
52–53	28, 48	25:3	23	18:4	23
52	14, 232, 239	25:4	17, 20, 23	18:5	23
52:1–53:8	30	25:5	24	18:7	16, 18
52:6	35, 184	26:1	18	18:8	23
52:10	35, 184	26:2-4	18	18:9-12	16
52:11	35	26:4	13, 19, 27, 43, 231, 233	18:9	18, 23

Testament of Benjamin		2:9–3:5	18	*Testament of Zebulun*	
(cont.)		4:1–8:1	18	1:1-2	18
18:10	23	4:5	16	1:3–4:13	18
18:12	23	8:2-10	18	1:5–4:13	17
18:13-14	21	8:2	16, 18	3:4	21
18:14	13, 16, 17, 21–3, 27, 201, 231	8:3	16, 18	5:1–8:1	18
		9:1-2	18	8:2–10:3	18, 24
				9:5-6	24
19:1-4	18	*Testament of Reuben*		9:7	24
19:4-6	18	1:1-5	18	9:8-9	16
		1:6–3:15	18	9:8	18, 24, 226
Testament of Moses		3:1	20	9:9	24
1:15	14, 43, 232	3:11-15	16	10:1-7	13, 21, 231, 235
2:1-9	42	3:12	19, 20		
3:1-4	42	3:13	19	10:1-3	17, 21, 24, 27, 201
3:5–4:4	42	4:1–6:4	18		
4:5-8	42	6:5-7	18	10:2-3	24
5:1-6	42	6:8-12	18	10:2	21, 24
8:1-5	42	6:8	16	10:3	24
9:1-7	42	7:1-2	18	10:4-5	18
9:6-7	42			10:6	18, 19, 27, 43, 233
10	42	*Testament of Simeon*			
10:1-15	42	1:1-2	18		
10:1-10	239	2:1-13	18	*Vita*	
10:1	43	2:5-13	16	1–21	72
10:2	43	3:1–5:3	18	11:1–17:2	73
10:3-7	43	4:1-3	16	12:1–17:2	151
10:8-10	43	4:4	16	13:2–15:3	46
10:8	43	4:6	16	14:3	46
10:9-14	227	4:9	20	16:1	46
10:9	14, 43, 44	5:4–6:7	18, 22	22–24	72
10:10	43, 44	5:4-6	22	25–29	72
10:11	44	5:4	21, 22	30–44	72
10:12	44	6	13, 231, 233	42:1-5	72, 74, 75, 204
10:14	14, 43, 44	6:5	16, 18, 22		
14 B	48	6:6	22	42:2	76
19:7 A	48	6:7	16-18, 21, 22, 27, 201	42:4	76
20 A	48			42:5	76
32–33	42	6:8	23	45–51	72
32:43	42	7:1-3	18	47	252
		7:1	16	47:2-3	53, 243
Testament of Naphtali		7:2	16	47:3	72, 78, 204
1:1-4	18	7:4–9:2	18	49–51	72
1:3	21	8:1-2	19, 27, 43, 233	51	252
1:5–2:8	18			51:2	53, 72, 81, 185, 204, 243
1:6-12	17	8:1	13, 19, 231		

Index of References

QUMRAN/DEAD SEA SCROLLS

CD
16.2-4   57

1Q28a
2.11-21   12

1QH
XI 19-23   282
XII 5-XIII 4   282
XIV 34-35   282
XV 22-31   282
XIX 10-14   282

1QS
3.13–4.26   271
IV 6-8   282
IV 11-14   282
9.9b-11   12

1QapGen
21.23   234

4Q245
Frag. 2   282

4Q385
Frag. 1-3   282
Frag. 12   282

4Q386
Frag. 1 col. i   282

4Q388
Frag. 8   282

4Q416
Frag. 2 col. iii   282

4Q418
Frag. 69 ii   282

4Q504
Frags. 1-2 col. vi   282

4Q521
Frag. 1 col. ii   282

4Q521
Frag. 2 col. ii-iii   282
Frags. 7 + 5 col. ii   282

4Q548
Frag. 1   282

4QDa
7.18-21   12
12.23–13.1   12
14.18-19   12
19.9-11   12

PHILO
De opificio mundi
1.135   155
1.137   155
1.139   155

JOSEPHUS
Jewish Antiquities
4.326   34
18.1.3   283
18.1.4   283
18.1.5   283

Jewish War
2.8.10-11   283
2.8.14   283
3.8.5   283

MISHNAH
Avot
4:21-22   295

Berakhot
5:2   295

Sanhedrin
10:1-3   295
10:1   3

Sotah
9:15   295

Tamid
5:1   279

BABYLONIAN TALMUD
Avodah Zarah
18a   297
20b   297

Baba Bathra
16a   297
16b   297

Berakhot
15b   296
18b   296
26b   296
29a   296
33a   279, 296
40a   100
60b   296

Chagigah
12b   297

Chullin
142a   297

Ketubbot
111a   297
111b   207, 297

Megillah
17b   279, 297

Nidah
70b   297

Pesachim
118a   296
68a   296

Kiddushin
39b   297

Index of References

Rosh HaShana	
17a	296
31a	296
32a	296

Sabbath	
152b	296

Sanhedrin	
70b	100
90a	297
90a-92b	225
90b	87, 207, 297
91a	297
91b	297
92a	297
92b	297
98b	11
113a	297

Sotah	
5a	297

Sukkah	
52a	11
52b	11

JERUSALEM TALMUD

Berakhot	
5:2	296

Ketubbot	
12:3	296

Sanhedrin	
10	296

Ta'anith	
1:1	296

TOSEFTA

Berakhot	
3:9	295
3:24	295

Sanhedrin	
13:3-5	295

TARGUMS

Targ. Jer Zechariah	
12:1	11

Targ. Onq. Exodus	
40:9-11	11

Targ. Ps.-Jonathan Genesis	
3:19	81
4:8	47

Midrash	
Pirke De-Rabbi Eliezer	
22	47

Pirkei Avot	
6:7	143

Sepher	
BS 23 A-B	46

Zohar	
1:73a	100

Deuteronomy Rabbah	
2:9-10	300
3:15	300
7:6	300
10:3	300

Ecclesiastes Rabbah	
1:6-7	207, 300
1:19-20	300
3:2	300
3:11	207
3:18	300
5:11	300
5:17	300
7:16	300
12:5	207, 300

Esther Rabbah	
9:2	300

Exodus Rabbah	
1:1	299
15:21	299
32:2	299
40:2	299
48:2	299

Genesis Rabbah	
22:7	46
13:3-6	298
14:5	298
14:8	298
15:7	100
20:10	298
21:1	298
26:2	298
26:6	298
28:3	207, 298
32:1	298
35:3	298
56:1-2	298
63:11	298
63:14	298
73:4	298
74:1	298
77:1	298
78:1	299
84:11	299
94	299
95:1	299
96:5	299
102:2	299

Lamentations Rabbah	
1:45	300
2:6	300
3:8	300

Leviticus Rabbah	
18:1	207, 299
27:4	299

Numbers Rabbah	
11:2	299
14:1	299
15:13	299
19:13	299

Ruth Rabbah		CLASSICAL AND ANCIENT
3:2	300	CHRISTIAN WRITINGS
6:2	300	Eusebius

Ruth Rabbah
3:2   300
6:2   300

Song Rabbah
1:9   300
2:2   300
2:18   300
7:15   300

APOSTOLIC FATHERS
Barnabas
25   83

CLASSICAL AND ANCIENT CHRISTIAN WRITINGS
Eusebius
Historia ecclesiastica
3.10.6   106

Jerome
De viris illustribus
13   106

Adversus Pelagianos dialogi
2.6   106

INSCRIPTIONS
MS D
209r-201v   101

Index of Authors

Ahearne-Kroll, P. 68
Allen, J. S. 28, 31
Anderson, G. A. 71
Anderson, H. 136
Atkinson, K. 41, 164
Attridge, H. W. 27, 28, 33

Bader, G. 280
Badina, J. 65
Bailey, K. E. 212
Böttrich, C. 96
Buchanan, G. W. 10
Burchard, C. 68, 71

Cason, T. S. 27
Charles, R. H. 17, 43, 230
Charlesworth, J. H. 4, 5, 12, 50, 101, 102, 104, 174, 175, 228
Clarke, K. D. 148
Collins, J. J. 27, 28, 30, 37, 148–51, 155, 157
Combs, J. R. 190

De Jonge, M. 15, 26
DeSilva, D. A. 5, 41, 42, 106, 140–2, 144, 146
Doukhan, J. B. 219

Elledge, C. D. 2
Evans, C. A. 5, 15, 28, 71, 85, 96, 97, 229, 279

Fiensy, D. A. 167, 168
Fisk, B. N. 51
Flusser, D. 160
Fox, M. V. 220
Fritsch, C. T. 5

Hodgens, D. 208
Hollander, H. W. 15, 26

Instone-Brewer, D. 279, 280

Jacobs, J. 109
Jacobson, H. 85, 89
Johnson, M. D. 71
Johnston, P. S. 1

Kee, H. C. 17
Klassen, W. 68, 69
Knibb, M. A. 59, 60, 62, 63
Knight, C. H. 102
Knight, J. M. 36, 62, 64
Kraft, R. A. 28
Kugel, J. L. 15, 20, 55, 57
Kugler, R. A. 15, 16

Lattke, M. 161
Levenson, J. D. 4
Levine, A.-J. 212
Levison, J. 71
Liddell, H. G. 150
Lunt, H. G. 96, 97

Milgrom, J. 179
Morris, L. 219

Newman, J. H. 167, 168
Nickelsburg, G. W. E. 5, 37, 38, 41, 42, 51, 57, 58, 94, 228
Novak, M. A. 175

Orlov, A. A. 96

Penner, K. 20, 21, 26, 32, 97, 99
Philonenko, M. 17
Priest, J. 42

Reed, A. Y. 36
Reeves, J. C. 228
Robinson, S. E. 45, 97, 98, 100

Sailhamer, J. H. 12
Suriano, M. J. 1, 2

Van der Horst, P. W. 148–52, 167, 168, 172
VanderKam, J. C. 57, 228

Walton, J. H. 30
Wilson, W. T. 148, 149, 151
Wintermute, O. S. 55, 57
Wright, N. T. 1
Wright, R. B. 161, 166

Young, B. 212

www.ingramcontent.com/pod-product-compliance
Lightning Source LLC
Chambersburg PA
CBHW070011010526
44117CB00011B/1518